# The Complete
# Trailer Sailor

## How to Buy,
## Equip, and Handle
## Small Cruising Sailboats

### Written and Illustrated by Brian Gilbert

**International Marine / McGraw-Hill**

Camden, Maine ▪ New York ▪ Chicago
San Francisco ▪ Lisbon ▪ London
Madrid ▪ Mexico City
Milan ▪ New Delhi ▪ San Juan
Seoul ▪ Singapore
Sydney ▪ Toronto

The McGraw·Hill Companies

1 2 3 4 5 6 7 8 9 DOC DOC 2 1 0 9

© 2009 by International Marine

All rights reserved. The publisher takes no responsibility for the use of any of the materials or methods described in this book, nor for the products thereof. The name "International Marine" and the International Marine logo are trademarks of The McGraw-Hill Companies. Printed in the United States of America.

Library of Congress Cataloging-in-Publication Data
Gilbert, Brian, 1960-
  The complete trailer sailor / Brian Gilbert.
      p. cm.
  Includes bibliographical references and index.
  ISBN 978-0-07-147258-6 (pbk. : alk. paper)  1.  Sailboats—Maintenance and repair. 2.  Sailboats—Purchasing.  I. Title.
  VM351.G54 2008
  623.88'223—dc22

                              2008002125

ISBN 978-0-07-147258-6
MHID 0-07-147258-4

Questions regarding the content of this book should be addressed to
www.internationalmarine.com

Questions regarding the ordering of this book should be addressed to
The McGraw-Hill Companies
Customer Service Department
P.O. Box 547
Blacklick, OH  43004
Retail customers: 1-800-262-4729
Bookstores: 1-800-722-4726

Photographs and illustrations by author unless noted otherwise.

# Contents

## ACKNOWLEDGMENTS

**M**any people have helped with the production of this book in various ways—some tangible, others invisible but no less valuable. At the top of the list is my wife Karen. Her help, advice, and support I will always treasure. Tied for second is my young son Kyle, who has taught me far more through the years than I will ever teach him. I love you both.

I am also indebted to friends who, through the years, helped and taught me things about sailing, often just by being there and sharing experiences. My first real "crew," Mark Kennedy and Suzanne Shurbutt, remain steadfast friends, though we don't get the opportunity to sail much anymore. My slipmate Larry Lee was always ready to lend a hand or share a tool, and Rick and Barbera Barber became close neighbors after Hurricane Hugo destroyed our marina. I learned much about sailing from these wonderful friends, and remembering time spent together always brings a smile.

I am also deeply appreciative of the many people I contacted seeking opinions—people like John Bell at ACR Electronics, Bill Goggins and Kathy Weishampel at Harken, experienced Bahamas sailors Matt and Mindy Bouldoc, author John Rousmaniere and the members of the Crew Overboard Symposium committee, photographer Eric Martin, and sailor Bill Klein.

Finally, of course, I am endlessly grateful to the production team at International Marine—specifically my editors Bob Holtzman, Ben McCanna, and Molly Mulhern. While writing a book is a huge undertaking, turning it from a computer file and stack of drawings into the book you're reading is a difficult task (more so where I'm involved), and this book wouldn't exist without their hard work and support.

# Thinking Smaller

It is difficult to describe sailing in the pages of a book. Just what is it anyway? Sport? Hobby? Pastime? Lifestyle? In fact, it's any and all of these things, and more. For me, sailing can be described as nothing short of a passion. I wanted to sail even before I ever set foot on a boat.

It started with my father. Mom and Dad both worked—a lot—to support a family of four, keeping the bills paid and groceries on the table. But they still managed to rent a cottage at the beach once a year for family vacations. I remember walking on the beach with my dad one year and stumbling upon an old Sunfish pulled up in the dunes. "Oooh, look, Dad—a sailboat!" "Yeah, sailing's great," he'd say. "You just glide along with the wind—no noise, just waves splashing against the hull. Using the sails and your wits to get where you want to go—it's lots of fun."

"Let's BUILD one!" I said with the enthusiasm that comes naturally to a fifteen year old. Dad had a table saw in the garage, and I thought he could work miracles in wood. (His old saw, which still works, now resides in my basement. I need to replace it with something safer, but haven't been able to let it go.) "Maybe someday," he said. Dad was, after all, a realist, and he was thinking ahead to Monday morning at the office.

My father, the realist, died of cancer a few years later, when I was seventeen. I decided that I would do some of the things he never got around to. One of those things was to go sailing.

And so I did. My first adventures were on Hobie Cats and windsurfers; then after a long time and lots of saving, I convinced a bank to loan me the money to buy a Catalina 27, which I would live aboard. The economies of boat ownership at age twenty-eight pretty much kept me in the marina while I worked to pay for the boat. I dreamed of sailing to exotic places in a bigger, stronger craft, while in reality I took weeklong cruises twice a year and sneaked out for the occasional weekend sail.

I loved my boat, but in truth I was lonely. On a boat that size, there's not enough room for even one person to spend much time—and 24/7 is pretty much out of the question. After five years, I sold my boat and used the money to pay for graduate school. I'm sure you've heard the joke about the two happiest days in a sailor's life: when he buys a boat, and when he sells it. It usually has a ring of truth, but not this time. Selling my Catalina was the smart thing to do—the *right* thing—but I can't say it made me happy. I couldn't afford both the boat and graduate school. While I was working toward my degree, I became engaged to a wonderful, brilliant woman, and we were married just after I finished school.

So just like my dad, I had returned to the world of realists. A few years later, we were blessed with a son, and naturally made our child our number one priority. We moved inland to be near cousins, aunts, uncles, and grandparents. Yet even when we were up to our elbows in diaper pails, onesies, and bills from a marginally successful blacksmithing business, I still wanted to sail. But to keep my dream alive, I had to adapt.

I had long ago abandoned the idea of a 42-foot ketch anchored in French Polynesia.

*My first boat was a Catalina 27—hardly trailerable!*

*My second boat was a '72 MacGregor Venture 222, a $500 restoration project. The whole story of this boat is documented in my first book,* Fix It and Sail.

*My current trailerable sailboat—a '79 Montgomery 17, designed by Lyle Hess.*

There *had* to be a way to fit sailing into the realities of family obligations, a naturally limited income, home ownership—the everyday "stuff" that life tosses you. That's when I started looking at smaller, trailerable sailboats.

How small is "small"? I've limited the discussion in this book to fiberglass sailboats of 15 to 22 feet, with some sort of cabin for sleeping. Some larger boats are deemed trailerable by their manufacturers, but they require such large, powerful vehicles to pull them and can be so time-consuming to launch that they test the limits of practicality. Often these big boats are hauled over the road just twice a year—once in the spring and once in the fall. The rest of the time, they are at a mooring somewhere.

Trailerable sailboats have a lot of advantages over the larger boats that seem to appeal to average folks. But if we focus on the strongpoints of trailerables, their shortcomings seem less of a liability. A smaller sailboat can be every bit as fun to sail as a larger boat, and having fun is why we're on the water in the first place. Going places in your own sailboat is one of the greatest travel experiences you can

have. And you don't need to go all the way to French Polynesia to experience the thrill of discovery that sailing offers. Simply exploring secluded coves in an inland lake can be an adventure that you and your family will never forget. Before you can share that experience, though, you need a boat. Part 1 is all about getting a boat that fits your needs, your abilities, and your pocketbook.

## AFFORDABILITY

Since we've broached the subject of your pocketbook, let's talk about one of the big advantages of trailer sailers—affordability. A trailer sailer can be one of the least expensive ways to go sailing in your own boat, in terms of both initial cost and upkeep. As we'll see in this book, there are very few things that big boats can do that trailer sailers can't. And there are more than a few areas where trailer sailers are better than, say, a 32-foot cruiser-racer.

I'll be honest—I still dream about owning a big liveaboard cruiser. But there is no way I can ask my family to make the financial sacrifices that owning such a large boat would require. Rather than becoming an armchair sailer, however, I've adjusted my dreams a little, and now I own a well-found boat that is capable of going just about anywhere I want to go. I'm also being honest when I say that I'm thoroughly satisfied with my little trailer sailer, and plan on keeping her for a while.

I purchased my first trailerable sailboat in 2000 for $500. It was a badly neglected 1972 MacGregor Venture 222 that had been stored in the woods. When we bought the Mac, we had very little money to spare, and attempts to save enough cash for a new (not used) boat had failed—some pressing need always seemed to come along that outweighed the desire for a sailboat. I rebuilt the boat over a three-year period. I replaced all the old parts and worked on the boat $50 or $100 at a time. In the end, I spent about $4,000 and had a boat that was very nearly new inside and out. The point of this story is to demonstrate that you can get a trailer sailer even if money is tight—and it was *really* tight when we rescued that first boat. That experience taught me a lot about trailer sailers, and I'll talk about these lessons in greater detail in the pages of this book.

I sold my rebuilt boat in 2005 for $3,400, which was about as much as you can get for a '72 MacGregor. Yes, I did lose money on the deal—I figure I lost about $700. But I got three years' use from the boat, so in effect it cost me $233 a year to own the boat. This ignores the considerable hours I spent restoring the Mac, but I knew that restoring old boats is a way to go sailing, not a way to make money.

Shortly thereafter I purchased my second trailer sailer, a 1979 Montgomery 17 for—coincidentally—$3,400. While this boat was in vastly better shape than the MacGregor, it was priced a bit below the book value because it had some deferred maintenance issues. I worked on these issues part-time over the winter of 2005–06. A cerain amount of maintenance work will almost certainly be required should you buy a boat of similar vintage. If you buy a new or late-model sailboat, your needs will be different at first. But eventually every boatowner has to do some maintenance. The more maintenance you do, the better you'll protect your investment, and in many cases, the safer your boat will be.

I talk more about these two boats in upcoming pages, but this book is more about *your* boat. Remember that all boats are different. Some elements are common to all, of course, such as masts, rigs, and hulls. But each design has its own peculiar characteristics. Sailing qualities, layout, seakeeping ability, construction details—all these factors vary from design to design. Each is a compromise, an attempt to balance different qualities for a boat's intended use. Part of the purpose of this book is to help you spot the differences among boats, and find one that suits your needs. You'll learn to evaluate a design so that you can select a boat that's best for your needs on balance. There is no "perfect boat," but somewhere out there is a vessel that's more perfect for you than others.

## SIMPLICITY

Other writers have put forth the theory that sailboat satisfaction is inversely proportional to its complexity. In other words, the larger and more complex a sailboat is, the less satisfying it is to own. I believe this is true in a general sense, but this theory eventually breaks down. Otherwise the most satisfactory boat would be an 8-foot sailing dinghy—a thoroughly unsatisfactory craft for a cruise of several days. But I do think sailboats reach a point where bigger does not always mean better, and a boat loaded with gadgets can often mean higher costs, more maintenance hours, and fewer sailing hours.

Trailer sailers can be very simple affairs, yet still be extremely effective and practical boats. There's not a lot of room for gadgets, so we are forced to choose carefully. Often we discover that what seems essential really isn't. Refrigeration comes to mind—it's rarely seen on trailerable boats, so owners don't spend a lot of time fixing refrigerators or the beefed-up electrical systems required to run them. And that's just one example; there are plenty more.

There are, however, a few additional items that can really make time on the water more fun. I talk more about making careful, informed choices in Part 2, "Outfitting and Handling Your Sailboat." You aren't required to sail with any of this stuff—you can go as minimalist as you want. Or you can load up your boat with gadgets and gear. This book will, hopefully, help you understand the total cost in real terms.

## PRACTICALITY

Trailerable sailboats are a practical fit for many people who might otherwise spend their time only dreaming about sailing. And while dreams

### Are They Safe?

Whether trailer sailers are safe is a legitimate concern. After all, they seem so small compared to bigger boats. Actually, there's no reason that a smaller boat should be any less safe than a larger one. In some cases, they can be made even safer than their larger cruising brethren with the addition of positive foam flotation, which isn't practical in large boats because of the huge volume of foam required. Whether or not any boat is safe depends more on who is at the helm than anything else.

Choosing a boat appropriate for your expected sailing territory is a key safety factor. Trailerable sailboats are designed to operate within a very specific range of waters. Some very small and/or lightweight boats are recommended for use in sheltered waters only. Others are OK for inshore cruising and bay sailing, where a safe harbor is usually very close at hand. Coastal cruising involves significantly greater risks, because there's a greater risk of exposure to severe weather. To my knowledge, there are no trailerable sailboats recommended for offshore sailing. Now, that's not to say it can't be done. Trailerables have gone offshore successfully in several cases, and some have made remarkable voyages. (One that I am very familiar with is a 15-foot Montgomery that made the downwind run from California to Hawaii. But the manufacturer doesn't recommend that kind of jaunt as a regular use for that boat.)

The trouble is that sailboats don't come with manufacturer's warning labels. (And if they did, you can bet that corporate lawyers would require such conservative language about a boat's intended use that the guidelines would be useless.) It's up to you to know how strong your boat is and what level of risk you're comfortable with.

There are ways to increase the safety of your boat, both by carrying safety equipment and by increasing the strength of the boat itself. But the biggest impact on safety is the way you use your boat. Reducing sail at the first sign of a blow, carrying and using extra anchors, having contingency and emergency plans in place, and knowing the capability of your vessel and your crew are of paramount importance.

Learning as much as possible about the design of a particular boat and the voyages of similar vessels can help you get a feel for a boat's ability to sail in a given stretch of water. Most sailboats have active user groups on the Internet. Some groups are quite large, and most are good sources of information. Another very informative and sobering source of information is the accident report. BoatU.S. (Boat Owners Association of the U.S.) publishes *Seaworthy*, a quarterly newsletter that includes selected case studies from its claim files, along with recommendations on how a particular accident or loss might have been prevented or minimized. U.S. Coast Guard accident reports are less detailed but more numerous.

I talk more about making your boat as safe as possible throughout this book, but as a skipper and boatowner, remember three things:

1. Arm yourself with knowledge.
2. Don't take chances.
3. Have a plan in case the worst happens.

are heartily encouraged, it's all too easy to be influenced by the exotic locales and gigantic boats that are showcased in the popular sailing and cruising magazines. You rarely see boats under 22 feet in the big publications, and when you do, they're brand-new. Without an alternative viewpoint, one could easily assume that a gigantic boat, or at least a brand-new one, is a prerequisite to the world of sailing and cruising. That assumption would be incorrect.

For example, the trailer sailer I currently own is a good fit for my family. It nudges the upper limit that my little 4-cylinder Nissan pickup can pull, and while I don't go anywhere fast when towing the boat, I do usually get where I'm going. Two people (even three in a pinch) can sleep aboard in relative comfort. Though it's not likely I'll ever undertake an extended cruise, identical boats have transited the Panama Canal, sailed to the Bahamas, and cruised the length of the Baja peninsula. All this in a package that's only 17 feet long and draws less than 2 feet of water. And don't forget, I can hook this boat up to my car and drive to some of the best cruising areas in the country. Since I still have to work for a living, my cruising time is limited. In a given two-week period, I can drive to the Florida Gulf Coast or the South Carolina/Georgia low country in a long day. I can make the Chesapeake Bay, Pamlico Sound, or Florida Keys in two. That leaves ten to twelve days of cruising time in some prime locations. You just can't experience all this variety in a limited time on a big boat—by the time you've sailed to your cruising destination, it's time to start sailing for home. (Score another point for the trailer sailers.)

Maintaining a sailboat is a big part of owning one, and it's another reason a smaller boat is a practical choice. Maintenance is an area where a trailer sailer shines compared to a larger boat. Since many trailerable sailboats can be kept in a garage, they can potentially last far longer than a large boat that's exposed to sunshine, hot summers, freezing winters, and rain and snow. Washing and waxing the hull take less time, as do the annual varnishing and bottom painting. It is true that fiberglass is a very low-maintenance material for boats, but it isn't "no-maintenance," and owners who neglect their boats do so at their peril—in terms of cost as well as safety. More than one boat has gone to the bottom because of poor maintenance. If this happens while you're sailing, it's especially disconcerting.

I actually enjoy most maintenance jobs. (OK, I'll admit, scraping the bottom is no fun.) But since trailerable boats are smaller, nearly every maintenance chore becomes smaller and more manageable. This is especially important if you buy a used boat, which obviously requires more care than a new one. Most maintenance involves keeping the boat clean and keeping the rain out. If you add covers to keep the sun off, then your maintenance requirements are even further reduced. You'll find maintenance tips and routines throughout this book (especially in Part 4), as well as ways to reduce the time required to keep your boat looking good and operating safely.

This book attempts to provide a pragmatic look at the world of trailerable sailboats and cruising in small vessels. Obviously my advice is filtered through my experience. But it's my belief that just about anyone can enjoy the sailing lifestyle, and my experience supports that view. All you need is the desire, some knowledge, and a dose of perseverance, and the sailing world is yours—welcome aboard.

# PART ONE

# FINDING YOUR SAILBOAT

# CHAPTER ONE

## Thinking about Your Boat

There are lots of questions to ask yourself when you start to think about buying a boat. Whether you can afford it is certainly one of the most important, but you must also consider how you would move it, where you would store it, and whether you truly have the time to devote to this pastime. But let's start with a question that may help you answer some of the others: How big a boat do you need?

### HOW BIG?

Trailerable sailboats with cabins range from a minimum of about 15 feet to a maximum of about 25 feet. The natural tendency for most folks is to covet the biggest boat they can get. Not so fast, Popeye—the biggest boat isn't always the best. To see why, let's use an extreme example—the Lancer 28.

The Lancer 28 was introduced in 1977, when trailer sailers were quite popular. This was about the most boat that would fit on a trailer. To haul a boat on the highway without a special permit, the beam must be no wider than 8 feet (though some states have increased this limit to 8 feet 6 inches). But an 8-foot beam is considered narrow for a boat this size; it was a compromise the designer made to fit the boat on the trailer.

Another compromise was a fairly shallow, wide keel. In order to keep the loaded height

The Lancer 28: 28 feet long, 8-foot beam, 2-foot 10-inch draft; it displaces almost 5,000 pounds.

down, the designer used a shallow keel, which doesn't add much stability. And since the keel is so shallow, the ballast is up high, where it doesn't do nearly as much good. Compare this to a conventional 28-footer, where the draft averages around 4 feet. The keels on these conventional boats are commonly solid—not hollow—chunks of lead or iron. With that much weight so deep in the water, the nontrailerable boat has a *lot* of stability compared to the Lancer. The reason for the Lancer's wide keel also has nothing to do with performance—the designer wanted a boat with lots of headroom, so he dropped the cabin sole down into the keel. The result is sort of a fiberglass trench that you stand in, and the keel is wider than it should be for best sailing performance. If you stand in the trench, the boat has 6 feet 2 inches of headroom—an unheard-of space on most trailerables. This feature may enhance sales, but it does little to improve sailing.

But the real drawback to the Lancer 28 is out of the water. Once on the trailer, this boat is a monster. It weighs almost 5,000 pounds. You can forget pulling this rig with anything less than a large vehicle with a dedicated tow package. And a panic stop at 55 miles per hour might turn you into something like a pressed turkey sandwich. I talk more about tow vehicles and road safety in Chapter 6, but this illustrates some of the problems with taking a large object like a boat out of its natural element and hauling it over the road.

It must be said that while a Lancer 28 isn't my particular cup of tea, many other folks are quite happy with it. There's an active owners' website at www.lancerowners.com. If you'll be sailing in relatively sheltered conditions, and if you don't plan on hauling the boat overland very often, the Lancer 28 might be a good choice for you.

As I noted at the outset, the Lancer 28 is an extreme example of the trailerable category.

*A Lancer 28 on a trailer makes a pretty hefty towing package. (Henry Booker)*

At about 26 feet, trailerable boats stop making sense. If you really want a large boat, then you would do well to consider a model that is not trailerable. But be ready for a significantly larger commitment of time and money. Boat design always involves a series of trade-offs and compromises; if you set your sights a little smaller, the trade-offs required to make a boat trailerable become less severe. Nearly all sailboats around 20 feet long can be launched, transported, and stored on a trailer. Some are designed for easy launching and trailering. Others are optimized for sailing ability, and are more difficult to launch and haul. Most are somewhere in between.

You can learn to evaluate a trailerable sailboat design by looking at a few key factors, such as the specifications, the hull outline, and the sail plan. While you can't predict everything from such information, it will allow you to make educated guesses about performance on the water, ease of launching, ease of hauling, and other factors. It's not my intention to make anyone into a naval architect—I'm far from one myself—but we can infer, for example, that a boat with a tiny swing keel is going to make more leeway than a boat with a larger keel. And don't worry if you don't know that leeway means the way that a sailboat gets pushed slightly downwind as she sails; I cover this in detail in upcoming sections.

So if a Lancer 28 is too big, what's the best size for a trailerable sailboat? Of course, there's no single answer that fits everyone. Instead, consider this question: What kind of sailing do you want to do, and where do you want to do it?

## WHAT KIND OF SAILING DO YOU WANT TO DO?

The sport of sailing can be generally divided into racing or cruising. Some boats are specifically designed for racing only—every feature is built for speed, and all other considerations are secondary. Other boats are specifically designed to be cruisers, where strength and load-carrying capacity are paramount. Many are called cruiser-racers, and are marketed to do both well, but in reality that's a difficult balancing act. Because trailerables are limited by length, weight, and beam, you won't find many that are said to be purely cruising boats.

Presumably you live within a reasonable distance to a body of water that's big enough to sail in. Even this isn't an absolute requirement—many sailboat owners live far from their regular sailing grounds. But chances are you live near a lake, large river, or, if you're lucky, the coast. On average, what's the weather like there? Some places, like San Francisco Bay, are known for consistently strong winds. In that region, heavier boats with shorter masts and smaller sail areas are the norm. On the other hand, the winds at many inland lakes (like Chickamauga Lake in Tennessee, where I often sail) are light and variable. Boats with tall masts have the advantage, and large, lightweight sails are almost a necessity.

The prevailing weather where you'll sail has a direct correlation to appropriate boat size—or more accurately, boat displacement. A boat's displacement is, for our purposes, equal to the weight of the boat and all its gear. (Actually, it's the weight of the water the boat displaces while at rest.) In a nutshell, lightweight boats perform best in light winds, while heavy boats are better for stronger winds (and the rougher seas that accompany them). This is, of course, a broad generality and not a hard-and-fast rule. My current boat, a Montgomery 17, is considered a medium-displacement boat, yet its light-air performance is better than the numbers would indicate. I discuss displacement in more detail in Chapter 2.

Another factor to consider is who will be sailing the boat. Let's assume that you will, since you're bothering to read this. But is anyone else planning on coming along on a regular basis?

While most people are familiar with the captain-crew relationship, I like to think of sailing participation in different terms: solo sailing, couples (or partner) sailing, group sailing (a captain with two or more crew), and, finally, family sailing. (See the sidebar "Sailing Relationships.")

## CAN YOU MOVE IT?

The Lancer discussion touches on yet another consideration relating to boat size: can you pull the boat you're thinking of buying with your current automobile?

I've had quite a struggle with this subject myself. Several years ago, before I owned a trailerable sailboat, I bought a used 6-cylinder van, thinking it would be just the ticket for towing a sailboat. Six cylinders and an automatic transmission should provide plenty of power, right? Unfortunately, I didn't check the manual, which said this van shouldn't pull anything over 2,000 pounds. No sweat, I thought—a MacGregor 222 weighs 2,000 pounds. But add the weight of the trailer, motor, and basic gear, and we're looking at something like 2,800 pounds. OK, so I'll talk to a transmission shop about adding a fluid cooler. Well, I did talk to a transmission specialist, and he informed me that my van was particularly unsuited for towing anything. According to the technician I spoke with, burned-out transmissions are a common repair with vans similar to mine.

So, back to the drawing board. The next vehicle I bought was a Nissan Frontier pickup. My truck is a 4-cylinder, manual transmission model for fuel economy. The manual says that this model can tow 3,500 pounds, so my 2,800-pound MacGregor should be no problem, right?

Well—after spending three years of part-time work restoring my Mac (for the whole story, read *Fix It and Sail*), I hauled it to the lake. Even though it was a big load for my little truck, the Nissan towed and launched it OK. The trouble came when I went to haul it home again in the fall—my Frontier could barely pull the loaded boat and trailer up the steep launch ramp. I had to slip the clutch to get it out, and the smell of burning clutch plates reminded me of smoldering hundred-dollar bills. It was clear that the MacGregor and my current tow vehicle were a poor match.

Rather than sell the truck, I decided to sell the boat in favor of a smaller, slightly lighter boat. My Montgomery 17 weighs

## Sailing Relationships

**Solo Sailing.** This means a sailboat with only one person aboard—you. If you've never been sailing alone, this may take some getting used to. It can be a very quiet, contemplative experience. On the other hand, if the weather acts up and things start breaking right and left, it can be downright scary. Solo, or single-handed, sailing is common on small recreational sailboats, but taking out a larger boat—like a trailerable—requires more careful planning. Most important is safety. I talk about this more in later sections of the book, but clearly a solo sailor who falls overboard is in a very dangerous predicament, especially if the water is cold or the boat is any appreciable distance from shore.

Solo sailing gets back to our discussion on boat size. It stands to reason that a boat that is normally handled by one person would be quite small, but as usual, "quite small" is relative. I purchased my current boat from an older individual who thought that the Montgomery 17 was too much for him to handle by himself. But then I regularly sailed my Catalina 27 by myself (in settled conditions), and I usually sailed my MacGregor Venture 222 solo. From my perspective, the Montgomery 17 is an excellent boat for the solo sailor. The limiting factor isn't so much boat length but sail area. If the wind pipes up, can you get that big 155 genoa sail in the bag all by your lonesome? Another consideration—especially for trailer sailors—can you raise and lower the mast by yourself at the ramp? In each of these cases, you can alter the equation with mechanical aids, like roller-furling for the headsail, for example, or special mast-raising aids, but often these solutions mean an added level of complexity that some folks would rather do without.

While many boats can work for the experienced single-handed sailor, as a general rule, 15 to 19 feet is a good size for sailing by yourself.

about 1,550 pounds, and the trailer another 400. The motor is lighter than the Mac's, and the Montgomery, being a good bit smaller, carries less cruising equipment. Even though it's still a sizable towing package, I'm just able to pull this boat up the ramp—it's a much better fit. (I do wish I had gotten the automatic transmission, though.)

Towing is such an important part of owning a trailer sailer that I devote an entire section to the subject (see Chapter 4). But when evaluating a boat, pay close attention to your tow vehicle's rated capacity. It wouldn't hurt to talk to your mechanic about what you're planning to pull, and get some professional advice about the best way to haul your boat.

## CAN YOU STORE IT?

Unless you are fortunate emough to live in an area with year-round sailing weather, you'll need a place to keep your boat when not in use. This is where the smaller sailboat shines,

as it has more affordable storage options than larger boats.

The most obvious place is at home, if you have the space. Winter repairs are just a few steps away, and you are immediately aware of developing problems like leaks or trailer rust and can take quick action, preventing larger and more costly repairs later. Some boats will even fit in a standard garage. But do check with your homeowner's coverage to be certain a trailer-stored boat will be covered in case it is damaged in any way. The best setting is on level ground, preferably on a concrete driveway. Some homeowners' associations won't allow this, so read carefully any agreements you may have signed.

Another storage option is a rental facility, where your boat will fit right in with the rows of camper vans. These can be expensive, though, and it's hard to maneuver a trailered boat through the other parked vehicles.

Marina storage is another possibility, and it's where I keep my boat. Keeping the boat at

**Partners Sailing.** This refers to the two-person boat, and it's a very enjoyable way to spend time with someone, whether a spouse, significant other, or just a good friend. It's really handy to have an extra pair of hands aboard. One person can handle the tiller while the other gathers the headsail or lifts the anchor. Just be sure that these jobs get shared equally. If you think that being the captain means you get to look spiffy in your cap, firmly grasping the tiller and puffing your meerschaum pipe while your wife wrestles a muddy anchor rode on the foredeck all the time, you will probably find yourself a solo sailor before you can say, "Aaarrrrgh!" Again, speaking in broad generalities, 17 to 23 feet is a good size for two-handed sailing.

**Group and Family Sailing.** With three or more adults aboard, the trailer sailer begins to feel like a tight fit pretty quickly. Sailing with a group of adults is often a social affair, with more people aboard meaning less room and perhaps shorter trips. If you have a family that wants to come along, great! Sailing can be a terrific experience for kids, if it is handled the right way. If you plan on sailing with a group most of the time, you might consider a larger boat, say 22 to 25 feet.

*A small boat like a Sunfish is regularly sailed single-handed, but sailing a larger boat is more complicated. The Sunfish is an especially good platform for learning sailing basics. (Vanguard Sailboats)*

a marina dock is usually the most expensive option, but hard to beat in terms of convenience. You'll do a lot more sailing if your boat is easy to use, and there's nothing easier than untying the boat and raising the sails. However, keeping the boat in a slip all year long accelerates wear and increases the chance of osmotic blisters, which form when the hull is subject to constant moisture. Keeping the boat on a trailer in the winter gives the hull a chance to dry out. Perhaps your marina offers the option of storing the boat near a boat ramp. Stored on the trailer, but fully rigged, it can be launched in much less time than it would take to raise and lower the mast. These arrangements are often much cheaper than keeping the boat in a slip.

An important consideration, too, is weatherproofing and protecting your boat during storage. Boats are designed to withstand direct exposure to the elements and can do this admirably, but any boat will look better far longer if it is in some way protected from the sun and rain. Sunlight—specifically UV radiation—is probably the single biggest aging factor for boats. If you keep the sun off the decks, the gelcoat lasts much longer—just look at a gelcoated interior liner for an example.

Rainwater can also cause problems if leaks develop, and all boats develop leaks in time. Keeping your boat covered will prevent rain damage as well, but of course you'll discover leaks when they're least welcome—while you're using your boat. Whenever you see evidence of leaks, make proper repairs as quickly as possible, since damage can quickly elevate from a minor annoyance to a major repair.

A portable canvas carport is a fairly inexpensive way to pamper your boat. Plan on it lasting about three years, unless you buy a budget model. If you keep your boat at home, you can invest in an aluminum version, which is of course more expensive and less portable but can last far longer. Very small boats may even be stored in a garage. Their loaded height on the trailer is often the limiting factor, apart from the availability of garage space.

A tight-fitting off-season cover is often the most practical solution. A good one is expensive, since they are often hand-built and use pricey fabrics. Stock covers are available for powerboats, but sailboats aren't often on the list. Still, it might be possible to modify a stock cover to accommodate an existing mast. Even if all you do is throw a cheap poly tarp over the boat, it's better than leaving your investment to fend for itself all winter.

## CAN YOU AFFORD IT?

I'd love to toss aside this concern with a salesman's catchphrase, like, "There's a sailboat for *every* budget!" It's just not that easy. Sailboats are discretionary items, plain and simple. Owning one requires that you have enough income to pay for it—both the initial purchase price *and* the annual maintenance costs.

How much does it cost? Well, how much have you got to spend? My MacGregor cost $500. And then I spent approximately $3,600 in parts and equipment to restore the boat to better-than-new condition. Oh, and I almost forgot about the three years of part-time work that I spent restoring it. When I sold the boat, I had owned it for approximately five years. The final selling price was $3,400—which, for a 1972 MacGregor Venture 222, is pretty good. My boat was in excellent condition, but still wasn't perfect.

So it cost me roughly $600 for five years of use, not including insurance or taxes. The initial cash outlay was quite small—$500 for a 22-foot boat is about as low as you can get. But I paid more in ongoing costs for replacement equipment and upgrades, and I "paid" a lot in time spent working on the boat.

My second trailer sailer, a 1979 Montgomery 17, cost $3,400. It was in much better condition than my first boat, but it still had plenty of maintenance issues, and I wanted to make some upgrades. So far, I've owned it for about two years and spent around $1,000 in equipment. Montgomery sailboats are high-quality boats, and used ones rarely come onto the market. New M-17s cost around $18,000, and I'm fairly confident that I'll get around $5,000 when it comes time to sell. We'll look more closely at sailboat equipment, as well as the "new versus used" argument, in upcoming sections.

## Book Value

One research method for finding a good boat is to look at the book value of boats that you're considering. Two major companies publish price guides—BUC International and NADA (National Automobile Dealers Association). Their pricing varies in accuracy; of the two, NADA is reported to be a touch higher. Remember that these prices do not include motors or trailers, and the data is gathered from asking prices, not actual selling prices.

When you begin your search for the perfect boat, it helps to look through these books. The BUC book is quite expensive, but you might be able to find a copy through your local library, and some BUC values are available online.

The first thing you'll notice when you examine these books is the price range for trailer sailers. Some will be in your budget, and some won't. If you're interested in a used boat, pick a model year and compare the prices for several boats from that year. You'll note that some boats are at rock-bottom prices. Several factors affect the market price of any used boat—how many are on the market, the number originally built, the original purchase price, and so on, but it's safe to say that the most desirable boats aren't going to be the cheapest. They aren't necessarily the most expensive, either. My point is, unless lack of available cash is your number one concern, think carefully about considering the bottom of the range.

*Nearly any fiberglass boat can theoretically be restored, even one as bad as this. But it will take a serious investment in time, and the finished vessel will likely cost more than one purchased in good, ready-to-sail condition.*

Since you will most likely sell your boat at some point, it makes sense to buy a boat that is in demand. This costs you more initially, but your investment is preserved when it comes time to sell. Improvements to a well-made boat will most likely mean a higher selling price, whereas improvements made to an unpopular boat will bring little additional revenue when it comes time to sell.

You should also look at the rate of depreciation of a particular model over the years. A boat that holds its value can be an indication of quality, whereas a boat that rapidly declines in value could mean that problems are common. This is good to know if you're thinking of buying a new boat as well.

The book value shouldn't be considered as gospel, but you should be aware of the book value for any boat you're thinking of buying. You'll soon discover that the market value of a sailboat is often less than the sum of its parts, so a boat well-equipped with extra gear can represent a good value, while a boat with lots of broken or missing parts can be a fiscally poor choice.

## Financing a Sailboat

Should you want to get a boat loan, your own bank is the best place to start, since your banker knows the most about your current financial situation. Explain that you'd like to buy a boat, and ask what the best way is to go about it. He or she will tell you what the options are, what the costs and interest rates might be, and how much of a down payment you'll need. Since boats are considered luxury items, most banks will require 20 percent of the total price as a down payment. Don't pull every penny out of your account for the down, either—there will be fees and miscellaneous costs.

A bank is usually far more willing to finance a new boat than a used one. Some banks simply refuse to finance used boats at all. This is because two sailboats that look exactly the same on paper can be worth very different amounts of money. This upsets bankers—they like things that are easily quantifiable, like certificates of deposit or the gold standard. Generally, banks consider the age of a sailboat of primary importance, and some refuse to loan money for boats past a certain age. The good news is that trailerable sailboats generally cost less than their marina-bound brethren, so getting a loan is easier. In some cases, you can buy a boat with a signature loan rather than a boat loan. (A signature loan is a loan that is unsecured by any collateral, such as real estate. It usually requires a very good credit rating.)

But getting a loan from a bank isn't simple. They'll take a look at all your liabilities—including your house payment or rent, car payment, and balances on your credit cards—and roll those into one lump sum. Then they'll take a selective look at your assets. For most of us, this usually means your monthly work income and the value of your house. If you have significant income from things like stocks, bonds, and real estate, you're in a different world than I am. You probably know more about financing than I can explain in a few pages, so skip this section. Everybody else, read on.

Many folks have a fairly new car with a big monthly payment, four or five hefty credit card balances that never seem to get any lower, and very little money left over at the end of the month. If this describes you, then may I gently suggest that you forget about getting a loan for a nice, shiny new boat. It's a bad move. You won't be able to enjoy your new boat much anyway, since you'll be working overtime to pay the bills.

But you can still have a boat. Go to the bank with whatever's in the change jar on the top of your dresser and open a savings account solely for a sailboat. Raid the clothes dryer and look under the sofa cushions. Put whatever extra money you can find into the account, but save that overtime for paying down those credit card bills. Minimum payments on credit cards won't cut it; you'll be in debt for sixty years no matter what your balance is. When you get an income tax refund, split it three ways—one third toward your debt, one third for the boat, and one third to do something nice for yourself or someone else. Yes, it takes

a long time to get a boat this way, but if you *really* want a sailboat, the balance will grow. Eventually, you can get a small used boat. While you're saving, you can use that time to gain experience—perhaps sailing with a friend or reading books on sailing. Watch out for sailing magazines, though—many are full of shiny new boats and tantalizing messages: "You can have the Ostentatious 42 right now with our easy financing—you're worth it!" Just as the Sirens tried to send Odysseus on the rocks, avoid those messages, 'cause they can ruin you. Plug your ears with wax if you have to—it worked for Odysseus.

Let's suppose your situation isn't quite so dire. You're fortunate enough to have a good, secure job and a car that you've half paid off. You're a homeowner and you've been in your house long enough to have paid down some of the principal, and you've got a credit card or two with a low balance or, better yet, you pay them off each month. The bank is gonna *love* you! They'll be happy to write you a big loan for whatever kind of boat you want—because they want you to use the equity in your home to secure the loan.

Plug you ears, sailor! They're using the same old song that the credit card companies use; it's just a different tune. If you want to see something funny, ask them about a loan that *doesn't* use your home equity. They won't believe it, because it's a rare thing when anyone turns down a pile of their cash. They'll start stuttering about the tax advantages of using your home to finance a luxury item—they might even question your intelligence. Don't fall for it. I don't believe you should ever use the equity in your home for financing anything except improvements to your home, and even then, resist until it's absolutely necessary to protect your real estate investment. Remember that a sailboat will decline in value over time. Should something terrible happen—your boss turns out to be Ken Lay or Jeffrey Skilling, for example, and you suddenly find yourself unemployed and you fall back on some payments, the same people who were questioning your intelligence will swoop in and repossess the boat *and* the house, sell both at auction, and lose almost nothing other than a few ballpoint pens. You and your family could be out on the street.

OK, I'm painting a greatly oversimplified and melodramatic picture. I admit, when it comes to money, I'm very cautious. Banks and credit card companies aren't the Evil Empire, but they are in business. They exist to make money—not to do people favors or make friends. It helps to keep that in the back of your mind as you search for boat financing.

If you're considering a new boat, you have one more possible option: financing from the factory. Many manufacturers have worked out deals with lending companies to finance their boats, and their rates can be attractive—often only 10 percent down. For example, West Wight Potter currently offers financing for their 15- and 19-foot trailerables through Priority One financial services. Loans from $10,000 to $25,000 can be made for up to twelve years, with down payments ranging from 0 to 25 percent. Rates and terms vary according to credit history and the amount financed. The application process can be easy as well, since the main business for these companies is financing boats. You still need to do the same income versus liabilities balancing act, but the overall experience is generally easier than dealing with a bank.

**Boat Registration.** Once you've bought a sailboat, the first thing you need to do is get it registered. All but the very smallest boats owned in the United States need some form of legal recognition. Most often they are registered with your state of residence. While boat registration procedures vary from state to state, the process is usually straightforward. State registration typically involves filling out a registration form, presenting a bill of sale, and paying the sales taxes and registration fees. A call to your county tax assessor or courthouse will get you started in the right direction. In Tennessee, all we have to do is bring the bill of sale and fill out an application at our courthouse. My total bill was based on the sales tax on the price of my boat plus the annual registration fee. Our state sales tax is high, at nearly 10 percent. That's a one-time tax, though, and the annual boat-licensing fee is only $20. Don't try to pull a fast one and save money by falsifying the bill of sale—if your tax assessor is like ours, additional forms will be required if the bill of sale is less than 80 percent of the book value of the boat. If you've bought a fixer-upper for $200, then expect some extra paperwork. A few recent photographs can be very helpful in explaining why your yacht was so cheap.

Our courthouse then sends the paperwork to the Tennessee Wildlife Resources Agency. The agency issues hull numbers and registration stickers, which must be correctly displayed on the bow of the boat. Keep your certificate of registration on board; you'll need it if the Coast Guard inspects you.

In some cases your boat must be registered in the state where it is primarily used or moored. This is not often an issue with a trailerable sailboat, since most people will keep it at home rather than permanently moored a long distance away. But sometimes keeping the boat at a marina is a handy option, especially if you live nearby, and it might require special registration procedures. If this applies to you, check with the proper registration departments of both states.

The alternative to state registration is federal documentation, where, in a sense, your vessel is registered to the United States rather than your state of residence, and documented as a U.S.-flagged vessel. However, most trailer sailers are too small to be federally documented; documentation is intended for larger vessels. The rule of thumb is that sailboats above 27 feet can be documented (a vessel must measure at least 5 net tons).

Some states also require separate trailer registration—check with your Department of Motor Vehicles to be sure you're legal.

## Boat and Towing Insurance

You'll also need insurance right away, unless the seller is willing to deliver the boat to your home and it needs a few months of work. If this is the case, though, and a tree falls on your partially restored boat, don't expect your homeowner's insurance to help you. If you have to tow the boat with your own vehicle, then you will need insurance immediately.

Before you do anything, make sure you're legal and insured. Auto insurance won't be enough—you'll need special coverage for towing your boat as well. Be sure you understand your insurance policy carefully. If you get your boat insurance from an agent, ask whether the coverage includes towing your boat with your car. You will especially want to ask what sorts of things might void the coverage, like towing your boat with an undersized hitch system.

Not all insurance agents are familiar with the needs of towing sailboats, so you might get better coverage at a lower cost by buying a policy directly. I have insurance with BoatU.S., and have been pleased overall, though thankfully I've never had a claim.

BoatU.S. also offers supplemental towing coverage, which might be a good idea for you. This covers things like over-the-road problems—bearing failures, flats, and similar problems. I haul my boat infrequently, usually only once per season, so I don't carry the supplemental coverage, but your needs may be different. Numerous companies offer insurance for boats, so be sure to do some research.

## DO YOU HAVE TIME FOR A BOAT?

Owning a boat is an investment in time as well as money, and this is especially true of sailboats. When you go sailing, it takes you longer to get to your destination than in a powerboat. Maintaining a sailboat, with its complex hardware, often takes longer than maintaining a powerboat, and most sailboat owners choose to do the maintenance themselves. If you work 55-hour weeks on a regular basis, you may not have time for a boat.

Boat ownership (and especially sailboat ownership) often requires an adjustment in mind-set with regard to time. Here in the United States, we've grown accustomed to the idea that "You can have it *all*" and "You deserve *the best*." All you have to do is whip out your credit card, rack up a mountain of debt, and spend the rest of your life working to pay it off.

While this makes the corporate community happy, it won't make you happy. The first thing you've got to do (if you'll permit me to rant for a bit) is turn off your TV—it lies. Its sole purpose is not to entertain, but to deliver commercial messages into your household. And the sole purpose of those commercials is not to enrich your life or make you feel good about yourself—it's to part you from your income using any means necessary.

So what does this have to do with adjusting your attitude toward time? Time really does equal money—and you have to make a conscious choice about how you spend it. You have a finite number of hours in your life. The exact number will vary, but no one escapes death. Sure, we all have to work. But do you have to own a Hummer? If the answer to that question is yes, then you will spend a lot more hours working to pay for it (and the fuel to push it around).

"But sailboats are expensive," I hear you saying. "Some cost *more* than a Hummer." And you're right. But the key difference is what we do with a sailboat. Everyone's experience is unique, but for me, sailing is like being in a completely different world. It's as if the real world is far, far away and, at that moment, surprisingly unimportant. What is important is the wind in the sails, the trim of the boat, her distance to the next mark, and her proximity to shoal water. I have enough food and water aboard for a few more days, some good books, and the most beautiful scenery that God has ever created. There's still some ice in the cooler, and when that runs out I can find a marina and pick up some more. Perhaps I can take in a little fishing at the next anchorage, or maybe some snorkeling or exploring in the dinghy.

*A small boat gives you a unique perspective on the world. This is a Montgomery 17 with Bill Klein at the helm. (John Butt)*

Now compare that experience to driving your Hummer to the mall and back. I don't own a Hummer myself, but I feel fairly certain that the two experiences are radically different. I'll take the sailboat, thanks.

It's difficult to shift from a fast-paced, high-speed lifestyle to "sailing speed." You may find that it takes some practice. But remember that on a sailboat, getting there isn't half the fun, it's *all* the fun. You've got just you, the wind, your boat, and your wits to get you there. And when you do arrive at your destination, whether it's a harbor for the night or the ramp after a few turns around the buoys, there's a real sense of accomplishment. If you did the same thing in a speedboat, it would be quicker and more efficient—but it just wouldn't be the same.

So slow down and make time for sailing. An entirely new way of looking at the world can be your reward.

# CHAPTER TWO

# Understanding Sailboat Specs

The specifications of any particular boat are important to understand because they give you some idea about how that sailboat might handle. Some specs, like boat length, are pretty simple to grasp. But to get an idea of a boat's performance without actually taking it out on the water, you have to look at several specifications together. These are often expressed as ratios, such as the ballast to displacement ratio. Let's look at some numbers first.

Here are the specifications for my Montgomery 17. I found these on the Montgomery website; they were originally published in the M-17 sales brochure.

| | |
|---|---|
| Length | 17 feet 2 inches |
| L.W.L. | 15 feet 10 inches |
| Beam | 7 feet 4 inches |
| Weight | 1,600 pounds |
| Ballast | 580 pounds |
| Draft | 3 feet 6 inches/ |
| | 1 foot 9 inches |
| | (centerboard down/up) |
| Sail area | (100 percent foretriangle) |
| | 154 square feet |
| Disp./length ratio | 225 |
| Ballast/disp. | 37.4 |

## BOAT LENGTH

The first specification is usually the length of the boat, in this case 17 feet 2 inches. Just to confuse the goose, this specification is sometimes given as LOA (length overall) or LOD (length on deck). The difference is that LOA includes a bowsprit, if the boat has one. LOD is the length of the boat alone, not counting any

rigging appendages. A bowsprit, by the way, is a short, strong pole extending forward from the boat. It gives the boat a longer effective sail plan than boats with "inboard" rigging. You'll find bowsprits on older, traditional designs, but not often on trailerables. The only such models I can think of are the old MacGregor Venture 23—it has a fixed bowsprit—and the Montgomery 23, which has both a bowsprit and a boomkin. A boomkin is an extension at the stern, similar to a bowsprit, that also lengthens the sail plan.

Another expression of boat length is length at waterline, or LWL. The LWL is more important, hydrodynamically speaking, than the length on deck. In fact, older racing classes were commonly described by their waterline length rather than their overall length. The famous New York 32s by Sparkman and

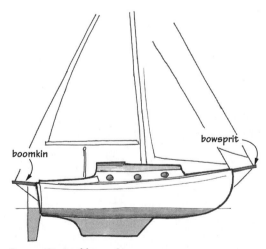

*Bowsprits and boomkins.*

Stephens are actually 45 feet long on dec[...]h-
32 feet at the waterline. Waterline ler[...]nis
important to know for several calculat[...]
you like to crunch boat numbers lik[...]rea-
architects do.

Now, you may have heard that lon[...]lder,
go faster. This is true on paper, but it's[...] they
a good reason to select a larger traile[...]ft, and
a smaller one. Here's why. The maxi[...]rrower
retical speed for displacement hu[...]but as it
nearly all cruising sailboats) can b[...]the boat
using the following formula:

$$SQRT\ (LWL) \times 1.34$$

Plugging in the numbers [...]the wind's
gomery 17 gives the following r[...]'Heeling on

$$SQRT\ (15.833) \times 1.34 = [...]$$

The same calculation for[...]
22 gives a top theoretical sp[...]
That's only four-tenths of a kr[...]
much gain for 5 feet of lengt[...]
use, my M-17 is a bit faster [...]
was—it points higher and i[...]
tender boat heels easily i[...]
estly, I wouldn't worry m[...]
hull speed. The differenc[...]
is small, and is often ou[...]
tors like sail shape, conc[...]
the amount of toys y[...]
you're a racer and ar[...]
race boats, you migh[...]
further, but for norr[...]
wouldn't sweat it. Of[...]
speed calculation is[...]
sailboats only. Mul[...]
(two hulls) and trir[...]
ent beasts altoget[...]
sailboats are desi[...]
ing their broad, [...]
over the surfac[...]
through the wa[...]

## BEAM

The beam is th[...]
widest point. The boat and [...]
can be no wider than 8 feet without requi[...]

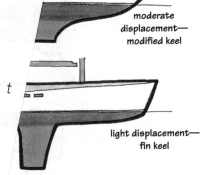

hulls: Heavy-displacement (top, also
[...]l, this one with a wineglass stern);
[...]ement with a modified keel (middle);
[...]ement with a fin keel (bottom).

heavy
displacement—
full keel

moderate
displacement—
modified keel

light displacement—
fin keel

With the coming of fiberglass, though, designers found a way to reduce the ballast needed for stability. On more modern boats, the flatter, beamy hull provides resistance to heeling. The whole boat, being lighter, performs better in light winds. The only downside is that in storm conditions, this type of boat is easier to capsize. And once inverted, it has more of a tendency to stay that way. So if you are out in the middle of the ocean in a really big storm, you want to be in a narrow, heavy, older type of hull rather than a new, beamy, lightweight hull.

You can visualize this somewhat with a couple of glasses and a pitcher of water. Take a wineglass and float it in the water. (Some of these classic, deep-draft hulls were called "wineglass" hull forms, in fact.) You'll notice that it floats in a very stable manner—you can press on the sides or slosh the water around, and the wineglass won't wiggle much—you can sink it only by sloshing water inside the glass.

Now try the same thing with a flat-bottomed tumbler of about the same volume. Pressing on the sides or sloshing the water will cause the tumbler to move quite a bit more. But the tumbler, of course, floats in a lot less water, and that's an advantage of the more modern hulls—they often have shallower draft.

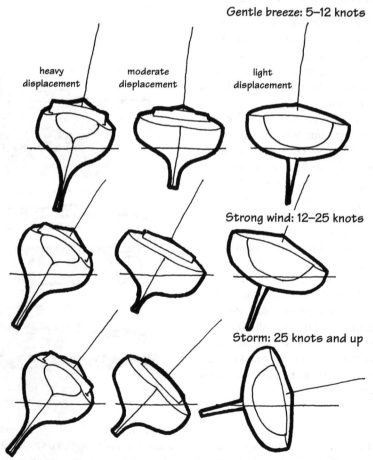

Gentle breeze: 5–12 knots

heavy displacement

moderate displacement

light displacement

Strong wind: 12–25 knots

Storm: 25 knots and up

*Displacement and righting moment—comparing different hull types and heeling.*

## DRAFT AND KEELS

Draft is the measurement from the waterline to the bottom of the boat. Stated another way, it's the minimum depth the boat will float without grounding. Draft includes the keel and the hull combined. A boat's keel (or keelson) is, technically and correctly, the structural backbone of the vessel—in wooden boats, it's the strongest timber running right down the center of the boat to which the ribs are attached. But by this definition, most fiberglass boats don't have keels, or ribs for that matter. So the term *keel* has come to mean the part of the boat below the waterline that primarily resists the leeward (or downwind) force of the wind.

When we talk about a fin-keel sailboat, or a full-keel sloop, we may not be technically correct, but that's the way the term is often used.

Some boats have what is called a swing keel (which technically should be called a centerboard). This is a heavy iron, lead, or fiberglass blade that's attached at the forward end by a bolt. At the after end is a rope or wire pendant (pronounced "pennant") that is used to raise or lower the centerboard, often with the aid of a winch. So in this case, the boat's draft is adjustable—deep when sailing, then raised for trailering or floating through shallow water. Most centerboard boats have a trunk inside the hull that houses the keel when it's retracted. This gives the boat a very shallow draft, and it allows the boat to ride lower on the trailer, making launching and retrieving easier. My MacGregor Venture 222 was built this way. The first time I tried to haul the boat at the ramp, I floated my boat right over the trailer bunks and had a slight collision with the winch post—it required an amazingly thin layer of water to float the boat.

A few trailerable boats, such as the O'Day 22, Cal 20, and J/22, have a fixed keel. A fixed keel doesn't adjust—it's an integral part of the hull. The advantages are strength, simplicity, and reduced cost. The disadvantage is that fixed-keel boats need deeper water for launching and retrieval, and cranking up the centerboard to explore shallow waters isn't an option. It is sometimes said that small fixed-keel sailboats don't point as high to windward, but this isn't universally true. If you're a lake sailer, grounding a fixed-keel boat is a bit more of a problem than in coastal waters, since you don't have the tide to help float you off. In the summertime or in warm waters, it's often possible to go over the side and muscle the boat back into deeper water, since fixed-keel trailerables don't usually draw more than 3 feet or so.

Some boats have a combination of the two systems. Called a keel-centerboarder, a shallow, ballasted keel holds a small centerboard that can be raised or lowered with a keel pendant. This system has a number of advantages, like improved upwind performance over fixed-keel trailerables, and no centerboard trunk taking up cabin space. Since the ballast is fixed in the keel and not the centerboard, the centerboard is lighter. Wear on the pivot bolt and the pendant is reduced. My Montgomery 17 has this type of keel. The disadvantages: greater depth is required to launch, the boat sits higher on the trailer, and occasionally rocks and other debris from a grounding can cause the centerboard to jam in the slot.

Another keel system found on some boats (such as the West Wight Potter) is a daggerboard. This type of keel lifts straight up and down and is housed in a vertical trunk. Like other keels, this system has its advantages and disadvantages. A vertically oriented keel is an efficient foil for upwind work and can enhance performance. It's a simple system requiring little maintenance—you don't have to inspect or replace the pivot bolt, for example. But the downside is that the daggerboard and its trunk can be damaged in a hard grounding, since a lot of stress is concentrated in a small area.

Centerboards and daggerboards are the most common, but not the only, keel systems found on trailerable sailboats. A very few boats use a twin-keel system, where two large fins are fixed at the turn of the bilge. Boats such as the Pegasus Prelude, Signet 20, Westerly Warwick, Pageant, Spirit, Centaur,

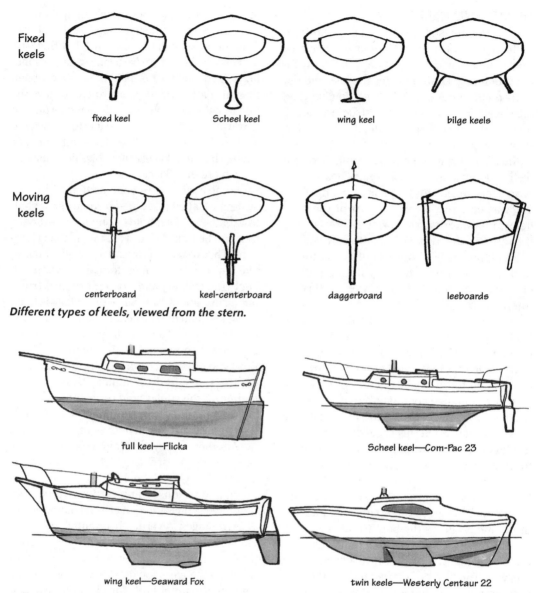

Fixed keels

fixed keel     Scheel keel     wing keel     bilge keels

Moving keels

centerboard     keel-centerboard     daggerboard     leeboards

*Different types of keels, viewed from the stern.*

full keel—Flicka          Scheel keel—Com-Pac 23

wing keel—Seaward Fox          twin keels—Westerly Centaur 22

*Different types of fixed keels, viewed from the beam.*

Hurley 22, Snapdragon 21, Pandora 21, Hunter Duette 23, and the Red Fox 200T were built with twin bilge keels. All of these boats are from British manufacturers—no U.S. boatbuilders manufactured twin-keel yachts in significant numbers. While twin keels are not as effective for upwind work, they have the advantage of shoal draft, easy trailering, and, when the tide goes out, grounding upright rather than falling over to one side. Occasionally you'll find a leeboard or twin centerboards, but not on production sailboats.

Yet another consideration with keels is the loaded height on the trailer. Swing-keel and daggerboard boats can sit lower on the trailer, whereas fixed-keel and keel-centerboard boats must naturally rest higher on the trailer. Some trailerable race boats have keels so deep that

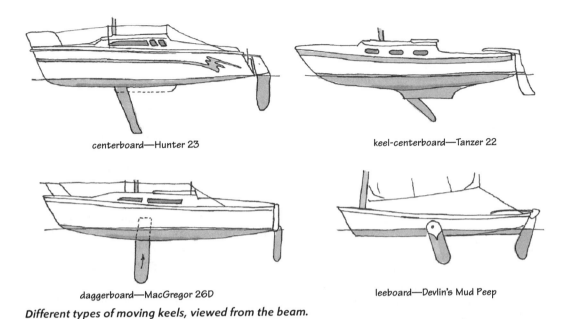

centerboard—Hunter 23

keel-centerboard—Tanzer 22

daggerboard—MacGregor 26D

leeboard—Devlin's Mud Peep

*Different types of moving keels, viewed from the beam.*

swing centerboards can pivot over some shoals with little damage

while daggerboards are more likely to break

*Centerboard versus daggerboard in a grounding.*

*A Cal 20 on a trailer. Consider a boat's loaded height on the trailer. Fixed-keel boats require tall trailers, making storage and launching more problematic. (Bruce Burton)*

the boats can't be launched from a ramp, but must use a crane. Boat manufacturers realize this is a significant liability for a general-purpose sailboat, so nearly all designs allow for ramp launching. But some boats need better ramps than others—they may require trailer tongue extensions to get the trailer deep enough yet not flood the car. The loaded height on the trailer can be a problem if you plan on keeping your boat in a standard garage—it might be too tall to fit.

## DISPLACEMENT

A boat's displacement is a basic measurement. It can be thought of as simply the weight of the boat, but more accurately it's the weight of the water that the boat displaces when floating at its designed waterline. Displacement can be expressed as weight in pounds or tons, or as a volume of water in cubic feet. (Remember that salt water is slightly heavier than fresh water, so the displacement in cubic feet will be different for salt and fresh water. The difference becomes significant only with really, really big boats—like tankers.) Knowing a boat's displacement is useful when comparing boats of a similar or identical length. For instance, if one 17-footer displaces 1,100 pounds and another displaces 1,550 pounds, we can guess that the lighter of the two might have better light wind performance, or that the heavier might do better in a storm. Plenty of other factors play into this equation, like sail area, displacement to ballast ratio, wetted surface areas, and so forth, but displacement is an important factor in evaluating possible performance. At the most basic level, it affects how easily the boat can be pulled with the family car—the lighter it is, the easier it is to haul, launch, and retrieve.

## D/L RATIO

Displacement to length ratio (D/L, or DLR) is a nondimensional expression of how heavy a boat is in relation to its waterline length. The formula looks like this:

$$D/L = (Disp/2240)/(0.01 \times LWL)^3$$

where

Disp = displacement in pounds
LWL = length at waterline

So, using my Montgomery 17 as an example:

$$D/L = (1500/2240)/(0.01 \times 15.83)^3$$
$$D/L = 0.669/3.96^{-03}$$
$$D/L = 169$$

Ths figure is for an empty boat with no one aboard and no gear. If I add 150 pounds for myself and 250 pounds for the motor, gas, water in the tanks, and swim noodles, I get a more realistic figure of about 214. The following chart shows the DLRs calculated for a range of boats.

| | |
|---|---|
| Light racing multihull | 40–50 |
| Ultralight ocean racer | 60–100 |
| Very light ocean racer | 100–150 |
| Light cruiser-racer | 150–200 |
| Light cruiser | 200–250 |
| Average cruiser | 250–300 |
| Heavy cruiser | 300–up |

You won't find any heavy-displacement trailerables these days. In fact, they're pretty rare among larger boats as well. The trend over the last forty years or so has been toward lighter boats. Fiberglass is an inherently lighter construction material, and hull shapes that originally took a lot of wood have been adapted to fiberglass using less material by weight.

Lighter displacement makes more sense for a trailer sailer, but only up to a point. If a boat is too light, the stress of regular use will cause it to wear out much more quickly. Putting a boat on a trailer often increases the point loading on the hull, where the weight of the boat is concentrated at fewer places on the hull—specifically the turn of the bilge, the keel, and the bow. You will occasionally see older lightweight boats with depressions in the hull caused by an ill-fitting trailer or poorly placed chocks.

This is more often a concern when looking at older racing sailboats, though some low-cost boats suffer from inadequate structural strength. It is often said that you buy sailboats by the pound, with heavier boats naturally costing more. High-tech racers are the exception, of course.

## BALLAST

All sailboats have some form of ballast, which is any kind of heavy, dense material placed as low as possible in the hull. It helps provide the boat's righting moment, which is really a fancy term for gravity at work—when the wind heels the boat, the righting moment resists the wind's force, keeping the mast as vertical as possible. Gravity is pulling at the heavy keel, trying its best to bring it to the bottom of the sea. The buoyancy of the hull prevents gravity from accomplishing its mission, provided we can *keep the ocean out of the boat*. This is a major tenet of any form of boating. As the boat heels, and the bottom ballast becomes more horizontal, the weight of the keel counteracts the heeling force of the wind, and the boat reaches a balance point.

Most boats have ballast that is either lead, cast iron, steel or steel punchings, concrete, or, in some newer designs, water. Lead ballast is most desirable—its high density gets the weight as low as possible in the hull, where it is most effective—but it's also expensive. The trouble with steel ballast is that it can corrode, and rust expands with great force. Concrete is cheap and doesn't rust, but its density is comparatively low. If two identical boats were built, one ballasted with lead and the other with concrete, the concrete boat would have a greater tendency to roll.

Cast-iron ballast is often found as a swing keel. While cast-iron keels can and do rust, cast iron is preferred—here's why.

I've owned two trailer sailers with two different types of ballast. The first boat had a swing keel made of three half-inch steel plates welded together. When the boat was originally built, this very heavy assembly was laid in a mold with a few layers of fiberglass and filled with resin. This keel worked fine for a few years, but polyester resin, without much fiberglass to reinforce it, is fairly brittle. Small stress cracks appeared, and water found its way to the steel core. The resulting rust expanded, pushing the brittle resin/glass covering away from the core. This allowed more water in, which finally swelled the keel so much that it jammed tight against the centerboard trunk.

I was able to fix it, but the work took several weeks. I had to strip everything off, sandblast the core, and relaminate the whole thing with several layers of glass and epoxy resin. It wasn't a lot of fun.

My current trailer sailer has a cast-iron centerboard that is housed in an external stub keel. (This is like a shallow keel with a slot in it for the centerboard.) While the centerboard provides some ballast (180 pounds), most of the ballast is in the keel, along the sides of the

centerboard slot. This centerboard also got stuck because of corrosion, but repairing a cast-iron centerboard is a much simpler process. I removed the centerboard, had it sandblasted, and painted it with primer. I took the optional step of filling and smoothing some of the deep pits, then sanded, painted, and reinstalled the board. It was still a pain, it was a lot easier than rebuilding the keel from the core up.

Water ballast for trailerable sailboats isn't a new idea, but it has recently been embraced by contemporary boatbuilders. When the boat is on the trailer, we want the lightest boat possible, but when it's in the water, we need more weight. Water is pretty darned heavy, but this approach does present some design challenges. For water to be effective as ballast, it needs to be above the waterline. Otherwise it's neutrally buoyant, and has little effect other than to lower the boat in the water. Water ballast tanks are usually filled by opening a valve when the boat is launched, allowing the tanks to fill. The same valve drains the tanks when the boat is on the trailer. Some racing boats have more complex arrangements, using pumps to move the water to the windward tank and increase its effect. Popular water-ballasted designs include the Hunter 240, the MacGregor 26, and the Catalina 250. As the boat heels, water ballast is sometimes lifted above the waterline, where it becomes more effective, but this depends on the design of the boat. Water-ballasted boats are sometimes reported to be initially tender, and the plumbing/piping systems can be complex. But they can work well—I once sailed in side by side with a newer water-ballasted MacGregor, which performed admirably. It was quite a bit faster, and pointed almost five degrees higher than my traditionally ballasted boat.

Water ballasting does have a drawback, though. In 2002, the *Burlington Free Press* ran a story of a water-ballasted sailboat that capsized when the operator reportedly overloaded the boat. Seven adults were on deck, but three children were below. They were wearing PFDs, but two of them became entangled in gear and drowned. One reason the boat capsized was that the ballast tanks were never filled. The operator, who had borrowed the boat and didn't know about the necessity of filling the ballast tanks, was charged with BWI (Boating While Intoxicated) and manslaughter. The moral of this story isn't to condemn water ballast, but a warning to know your boat and its systems, and take your responsibility as captain seriously.

## SAIL AREA

Still another predictor of sailboat performance is sail area. Published specifications usually list the sail area of a boat as a combination of mainsail and working jib, but of course the sail area can be adjusted to suit conditions. Many older designs (from the mid-1960s) often had shorter masts and long booms. These are considered low-aspect-ratio mainsails. On newer designs, the booms are shorter and the masts

are taller—known as high-aspect-ratio mainsails. These are most often seen on modern racing boats.

One of the reasons modern boats have higher-aspect rigs is function—some boats that are raced and cruised need high performance upwind. Another reason is style rather than function: boats that *look* fast sell better. But they may also be more expensive, more complicated to rig, and trickier to sail well off the wind.

On a race boat, the high-aspect rig gets more sail higher up, and it's a screamer upwind. But off the wind, the sail doesn't perform as well—it's more likely to stall, which means the wind doesn't flow smoothly across the sail's surface. A tall mast is also more difficult to raise at the ramp, and often requires more stays to give it strength than a shorter mast would. My point is that you shouldn't dismiss an older design as old-fashioned, since a more moderate mainsail might be a better all-around performer. Remember too that taller masts need deeper keels to balance them.

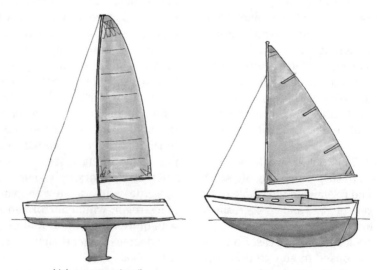

high-aspect mainsail                    low-aspect mainsail

*The boat on the left, a racer with a fin keel, has a high-aspect mainsail. The older, full-keel cruiser on the right has a longer boom and a low-aspect mainsail. (Note that the standing rigging has been eliminated in both illustrations for clarity.)*

# RIGGING

Most trailer sailers are masthead sloops, and it can be said that smaller boats have simpler rigs. With each increase in size, rigging becomes a more complicated, longer task. One popular 16-footer, for example, has no spreaders, a small, light mast, and no backstay. Three wires are all that's required to hold up the mast—a forestay and two shrouds. Setting up a boat like this is pretty fast, and you can often go from highway to dockside in about twenty minutes.

Go a little larger and you'll find sloops rigged with a forestay, a backstay, two lower shrouds, and two upper shrouds. In addition, there will be spreaders, which can sometimes foul halyards and other lines when raising sail. This type of mast is taller and heavier. It's possible to rig a boat like this by yourself, but be prepared for some heavy lifting. If you commonly rig and launch the boat alone, then some kind of mast-raising aid is a good idea. Plan on spending thirty minutes to an hour rigging this boat.

Really big trailerables sometimes have a set of four lower shrouds, two uppers, a forestay, and a backstay. The mast can be so heavy that you cannot raise it alone—two people or mechanical aids are necessary. It can easily take over an hour to launch a boat like this.

These launch times are approximate, of course, and you can shave them down with practice. Just watch someone who is fast and has a lot of experience—it's like watching a strange amateur version of an Indy pit crew in action. Some folks on the sailing e-mail lists have proposed adding a "launching division" to their regular schedule of races.

All sailboats have some form of running rigging. Where the primary job of the standing rigging is to support the mast, the running rigging is normally used to raise and control the sails. The running rigging can range from basic to bewildering, depending on the boat design, the owner, and the type of sailing that is normally done. (See the sidebar "The Difference between Ropes and Lines.") Cruising sailboats

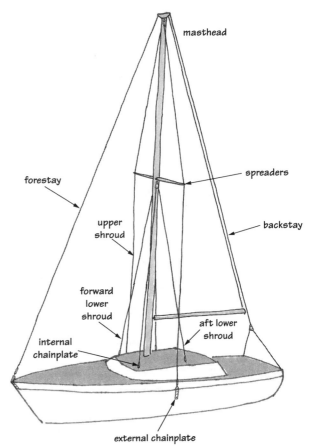

*Standing rigging—the wires and line that are stationary—are shown here on a masthead-rigged boat.*

need simplicity, strength, and ease of repair. Racers need light weight, low friction, and high performance. Being able to fine-tune the sail shape for the conditions can mean the difference between winning and losing, and racing skippers lavish their boats with some amazing "deck jewelry." Even owners of some nonracing boats upgrade their running rigging to improve performance, since in general it's more fun to go fast on a sailboat than slow.

Some running rigging is common to all sailboats. Halyards are the lines that lift the sails. The halyards go from deck level, through a block at or near the top of the mast, and back to a cleat at the mast base. Three halyards are common—one for the mainsail, one for the

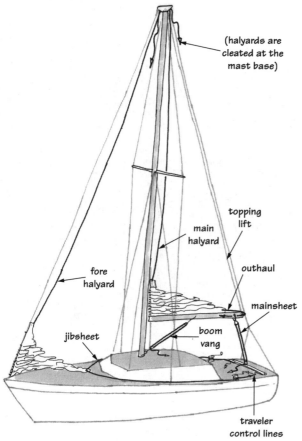

(halyards are cleated at the mast base)

topping lift

main halyard

fore halyard

outhaul

mainsheet

jibsheet

boom vang

traveler control lines

*The primary function of running rigging—the various lines that usually move aboard ship—is to lift and/or adjust the sails.*

number of different forms and pass through several blocks in the process. The headsail sheet (or jibsheet) is usually two lines, one port and one starboard, which often pass through sheet lead blocks on their way back to the cockpit. Jibsheets are commonly tensioned using winches at the cockpit on trailerable sailboats.

Running rigging can go far beyond the basics, however. A sailboat may have the following:

A *traveler*, which is often a rail and car arrangement that spans the cockpit. It adjusts the angle of pull on the mainsheet. Older wooden boats used an iron bar through a ring.

A *boom vang*, which tensions the boom downward to give a flatter sail.

A *reefing system*, such as slab or jiffy reefing, designed to make reducing sail easier.

A *barber hauler*, which adjusts the jibsheet angle without using a track. (See "The Barber Hauler" in Chapter 8.)

A *roller-furling jib*, with corresponding control lines led aft to the cockpit.

This is just a start. There are dozens of tweaks and modifications that can be made to running rigging. Some might be considered essential to one sailer, and expensive frivolity to another. More on running rigging is covered in Chapter 8, but the finer points and multitude of possibilities could take up an entire book alone. (In fact, one of the better books on the subject is *The Optimum Sailboat: Racing the Cruiser and Cruising the Racer* by Ronald Florence. It's out of print but available used on the Internet.)

headsail, and one for either the spinnaker or a spare headsail.

Sheets are lines that pull the sail in. The mainsheet attaches to the boom at one end and the boat at the other. Mainsheets can take a

## The Difference between Ropes and Lines

Believe it or not, you will find very few ropes on a sailboat. If you're new to sailing, I can imagine your disbelief— "Whaddaya, crazy? There's *millions* of 'em!" But on a sailboat, they aren't called *ropes*. Rope is the raw material that comes on a spool in 600-foot lengths. Once the rope is cut off the spool and given a specific job, it's called a *line*. The only two exceptions that I can think of are the bellrope, used to ring the ship's bell, and the boltrope, sewn into the edge of the sail.

Sailboats do have lots of lines, but after a few times out, they won't seem so confusing. Most boats have the same lines for the same job, but the major ones to remember are *halyards* and *sheets*. Halyards lift the sails, and sheets control them. If you can remember those two, then you'll be way ahead. There are a few others, such as a *lift*, which is intuitive—the line that holds the boom up when the mainsail is down is called the *topping lift*.

# CHAPTER THREE

# Evaluating Trailerable Sailboats

Let's say I've convinced you, and you've decided to buy a sailboat. What are your options? You can:

Buy a new sailboat
Buy a used boat in good, ready-to-sail condition
Buy a neglected boat in poor condition and fix her up

You may have other options as well, like partnership or multiple-owner situations, sailing clubs where the members own the boats, charter lease-to-own arrangements, and so on. However, these creative options are most often employed with larger boats, and I have no direct experience with them. One boat, one owner is the most common situation, and that's what we'll confine our discussions to for the purposes of this book.

## WHERE TO LOOK

There are plenty of places to look for a boat. If you're interested in a new boat, a boat show can be a great place to start—as long as it includes sailboats, of course. Check the show's website; most have a published list of exhibitors. If you've got your heart set on a particular design, though, you may have to travel to the factory to see a new one. Fortunately, trailerable sailboats lend themselves to dealer distribution, and many manufacturers have dealer arrangements where you can see and even sail a new boat. (See the Gallery at the back of this book for a sampling of many trailerable boats.)

Used boats may be easier to find or harder, depending on where you live. Newspaper classified ads can be a good source, and it's possible to browse major newspapers for coastal cities at larger libraries. I found my boat by subscribing to an e-mail list for Montgomery sailboats and asking around. BucNet.com is a brokerage website that lists thousands of boats, but only those being sold through a brokerage. And of course boats are listed on eBay, but this can be risky; there are some very unscrupulous sellers of sailboats out there. It's impossible to properly assess the condition or repairs needed without physically examining the boat yourself, and the boat you'll be interested in will invariably be located a thousand miles away. Hire a surveyor if you are considering an eBay purchase.

Some of the very best deals are still found the old-fashioned way—simple footwork. Poke around in the back lots of marinas or storage yards for a "for sale" sign on the bow. Making a few phone calls ahead of time can put you on the trail of the perfect used boat.

Traditionally, if you were buying a larger sailboat with the help of a broker, you would first look over a few boats in your size/price range, and then perhaps make an offer on one. (Your options may be different for a small, trailerable boat, but it helps to understand the typical boat-buying process.) The first offer is usually lower than the asking price. Your offer is accompanied by some cash, which is held in an escrow account, until the sale is finalized and your offer accepted. Your offer is usually contingent on three important things:

1. Suitable financing
2. Acceptable survey
3. Acceptable sea trial

If any one of these conditions is not satisfied, the deal can be called off and your deposit returned. At least, that was the case with my broker. Check the paperwork carefully to make sure of the terms. It might be reasonable for the broker to keep a percentage of your deposit to discourage tire-kickers, who will drag a broker to a dozen different marinas looking at boats when they have no intention of actually buying one. But remember that the broker's commission comes out of the amount you give to the seller; you don't pay the broker yourself. (In other words, the final accepted offer is the price you pay. You don't settle on a price, and then add a broker's commission on top of that.) As with houses, the broker is working for the seller, not the buyer, although it is obviously in a broker's best interest to sell boats. Brokers work best when they keep both sides happy. My point is, don't expect a broker to pull you aside and say, "Look, pal, don't buy this boat— the exhaust system is all below the waterline and hasn't been maintained in years. She could sink any minute." It's up to you and your surveyor to find the boat's faults and use them to lower the price. Hopefully you'll catch that corroded exhaust *before* you finalize the deal.

When you buy a smaller, trailerable sailboat, you may not go through all these steps. If you're paying cash, you don't need a financing contingency. You may or may not want to hire a surveyor, and the boat may or may not be available for sea trials. But this traditional boat-buying model can still be very useful. If you are buying your boat from an individual rather than a broker, then it might help you to structure the deal following the traditional model—make a small deposit, agree on a price, then arrange financing, survey, and sea trial. If any of those steps turns up major shortcomings, you either renegotiate the price or cancel the deal.

## NEW BOATS

Buying a new boat is the easiest way to get on the water in a nice sailboat. It's also the most expensive.

Buying the boat is only part of the story— you've still got to equip it for sailing. New boats are usually pretty bare sailing platforms, and the price doesn't include much of the necessary equipment: anchors, life jackets, fire extinguishers, a VHF radio, a depth sounder, and other basic safety equipment (see Chapter 5 for lists of required and optional safety equipment). Plus there's loads of gear that doesn't count as safety equipment but is nice to have—a stove for the galley, eating utensils, a cooler. The list of things that can be handy to have aboard is almost endless. And don't forget that a trailer and motor are usually options—that is, they're priced separately—though these can usually be financed as part of the purchase price. Taxes will be higher on a new boat, and you'll lose more to depreciation. The plus side? Your maintenance costs will be fairly low for the first few years. And, of course, a brand-new boat can be a joy to own. Just make sure you can handle those monthly payments.

## USED BOATS

Another option is to find a used, late-model boat that has been well maintained and is ready to sail. At first glance, this can seem like an expensive way to buy a sailboat. After all, it's not impossible to find two identical boats— one in great shape, the other a fixer-upper— where the well-maintained sailboat is selling at double the price. Many times (but not always) the more expensive boat is the better buy. Here's why.

Let's suppose the better boat has a fairly new motor in good running condition, a few extra headsails, a working VHF and depth sounder, all the required safety gear, and a couple of anchors. Everything works on this boat; nothing is broken or worn out to the point of needing immediate replacement. Not only can you immediately start enjoying your sailboat, you'll find you have to spend *much* less on equipment at the outset. What you do buy will be more personal in nature, like foul-weather gear rather than equipment for the boat, like a fire extinguisher.

A boat that is better maintained costs less to own in other areas as well. The simple act of keeping the hull and topsides waxed (and covered in the off-season) will keep the fiberglass looking new, and a conscientious owner is much more likely to take this step. This will save you the labor and expense of a paint job in later years.

The downside of this approach is economic, as you'll need more bucks to take this path. Financing is sometimes difficult, as it can be hard to convince a bank that this boat is worth more. You may need to come up with the difference between asking price and the book value in cash. And if you're talking about an older boat in great shape, the bank may refuse the loan on the basis of the boat's age.

## FIXER-UPPERS

Your third option is to buy cheap and fix it up. I've done it, and it *can* be done, but it's not my preferred way to buy a boat. There are advantages—you need only a small amount of cash at the start, a fraction of what's required for a new boat—but the work and ongoing expenses can seem endless. You need skills, time, and a willingness to enjoy boatwork should you take this route. With some folks, because of money, this is the only option available. That was certainly the case with my first trailer sailer, a 1972 MacGregor Venture 222. If this describes your situation, then go for it, but arm yourself with knowledge before making your purchase. Read as many books as you can on the subject of sailboat restoration. (My mother says the best book to get is *Fix It and Sail*, written by Brian Gilbert and published by International Marine, but there are a number of other helpful books.) Read all you can, and talk with other boat restorers out there. (See the Bibliography for a list of resources on sailboat restoration.)

It's smart to fix up a boat that has a higher resale value or a proven track record of sailing ability over an older, relatively unknown design. For example, a Catalina 22 is a very common boat with an active owners' association. This would be a better restoration choice than, say, a Luger, which was sold as a kit to be completed by the owner. My own Montgomery 17 would be a better choice than my previous MacGregor 22, even though my Monty cost almost seven times what I paid for the MacGregor. (It was in *much* better shape, though.)

It can be more economical to restore a smaller boat rather than a larger one. A Seaward 17 can be brought back in less time and at lower cost than a Buccaneer 25, if both are in relatively the same starting condition. You may discover a hidden talent for boatwork and find that you can't wait to start on a larger boat. Or you may discover that it's much harder than it looks, and swear that your next boat will be in better shape to start with.

There is one undeniable advantage to restoring a trailerable sailboat, and that's the education it provides. Sure, it's a school of hard knocks, and the tuition can be pretty steep. But once you've completed a restoration and brought a junker back to grade-A seaworthy standard, you'll know your boat inside and out. If you're out sailing and something goes wrong, you'll be much more able to assess the situation quickly and implement repairs, often without calling for help—which may or may not be available. This ability is a safety issue and is thus an important part of your responsibility as captain and owner of your vessel.

## SURVEYING A USED BOAT

My three sailboat buying choices—new, good-condition used, and fixer-upper—are arbitrary conditions. There are a million shades of gray when it comes to boat condition, and it's up to you as the buyer to determine the seaworthiness of the used craft you're thinking of purchasing.

Depending on the boat and the price, it might be wise to hire a professional surveyor. It is customary with larger boats to hire a surveyor to look over a boat and issue a professional written opinion, much like a house inspection. Some banks require a professional survey before issuing a used-boat loan. Surveys are not cheap—they often start at $300 and can go much higher. Some surveyors require a haulout and unstepping the mast, but this isn't nearly so difficult with trailerable sailboats unless the boat is being sold without a trailer.

For older boats with a lower book value and selling price, though, the cost of a surveyor becomes harder to justify. With a fixer-upper, a surveyor is likely to take one look and say, "She's shot, Captain. Find yourself another." You might be able to find a surveyor who is sympathetic to your needs and will help you find a restorable fixer-upper versus a boat that, for all practical purposes, cannot be fixed. It doesn't hurt to make a few phone calls. But remember, the surveyor is supposed to work for you. I wouldn't rely on a survey provided by a seller, especially if the survey is a few years old. There have been cases where an unscrupulous broker kicks back part of the commission to a "surveyor" who issues a favorable report. This is rare (it's also illegal), but it has happened. So find your own surveyor; don't rely on a recommendation from a broker or a seller. Also, remember that a surveyor's word is not gospel. A recent letter in *Practical Sailor* tells of two surveyors hired by an owner who was selling his boat. The first surveyor gave the boat a fair market value of $33,000, saying the boat was "a moderately built production model using poor-quality marine materials." The second surveyor valued the same boat at $45,000 to $50,000, and called it "an excellent coastal or inland water cruiser/racer." Surveyors are people, too, and not without their biases. It's a good idea to ask any surveyor whom you are considering hiring to provide a sample report or two for you to look over. It is possible for you to do your own survey on a low-priced sailboat. It's very hard to be objective, and a pro will probably do a better job, but it can be done. First, do your homework. Read at least one of the books on surveying in the Bibliography. If you're new to sailing, bone up on basic boat terminology. (See the sidebar "Parts of a Trailer Sailer.") While I was writing about boat surveying in *Fix It and Sail*, I came up with a list of deal killers that can make restoring a boat unfeasible at any price. Here's my list:

- Structural cracks or holes in the hull
- Missing major equipment, like a mast, boom, standing rigging, or sails
- Extensive wood rot
- A "partially restored" boat

A boat with these problems earns an automatic "no, thanks," even if the boat is nearly free. It often costs more than the boat is worth to put these problems right. In addition, any of the following items should rate big discounts:

- Any trailerable sailboat without some kind of motor or trailer
- Any sailboat without a fiberglass interior liner
- A heavily modified sailboat
- Any sailboat with a spongy deck
- A filthy boat, especially one with standing water in the interior
- A boat with missing or hopelessly rotten cushions

A boat with any of these problems, while not automatically rejected, must be heavily discounted by the seller in order to be considered. Correcting these problems can require a serious commitment, and sometimes they can't be fixed at all. Do not be fooled by the seller's claims that "all she needs is a good cleaning" or "needs a little TLC." Such phrases should be illegal when describing boats for sale. These terms are sellerspeak for "needs more dollars in repairs than I could ever hope to get for her if she were fixed." Think about it—if all she really needed was a good cleaning, then the seller would give her one and ask more for the boat.

*Never look at a boat without knowing the book value first!* (See "Book Value" in Chapter 1.) If the seller wants a great deal more than the book value, you should mention that fact to him or her. They'll feign ignorance, but it's a fairly safe bet that the seller has looked up the book value, too. And remember, the bank won't loan any more than the book value. This works to the buyer's advantage with boats in good condition, and to the seller's advantage with boats in poor condition. Well-maintained boats generally sell quickly, while boats that are dirty or unmaintained can take forever to sell.

So let's take an imaginary look at a hypothetical trailer sailer. Say you've got your eye on a 1978 O'Day 22 that's down at the local marina. The asking price is $2,250, not too bad. She comes with an old Evinrude outboard and a trailer. The BUC value for this boat is $2,500 to $2,900, so the asking price is pretty good. And we're lucky—a profile of this particular boat appears in *Practical Sailor's Practical Boat Buying*, where we learn that this boat has a shallow fixed keel and a fairly basic interior. As an option, some boats were built with centerboards, and some with deep-draft fin keels, each giving better sailing performance and pointing ability than the standard shoal-draft fixed-keel model. If this boat has one of those two options, that's a plus, as she'll sail better than the standard model.

Armed with this knowledge beforehand, you're ready to take a look. Bring along a few tools when you look at a boat—a clipboard and a pen to take notes, a pocketknife or fine ice pick to check for rot, and a small digital

## Parts of a Trailer Sailer

If you're new to sailing, it will seem like every little bit of your boat has an arcane and obscure name. Don't panic. You'll find most of these terms will come naturally with use.

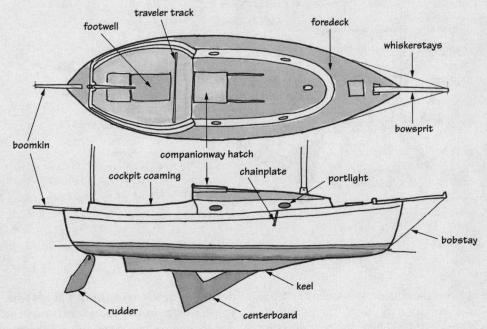

On deck.

*(Continued)*

This is one of those situations where pictures truly are worth a thousand words, so study the drawings labeled here. The parts of your boat may not look exactly the same as what you see here, but they will be similar. Many trailerable sailboat manufacturers use the same handful of hardware suppliers, so you might see the exact same mast step used on a 1976 O'Day 22 and a 2004 Precision 18.

As your nautical vocabulary expands, don't get too hung up on terms, insisting that your crew always use the correct nautical terms. Or worse, don't start slinging marine jargon all over the office, either. You're talking about a trailerable sailboat, for heaven's sake, not the *Dorade* (Olin Stephen's winner of the 1931 Transatlantic and Fastnet races). It's more important to be understood than correct—it's better to stop the boat with a rope than to confuse your crew with commands about breast lines, spring lines, and after cleats.

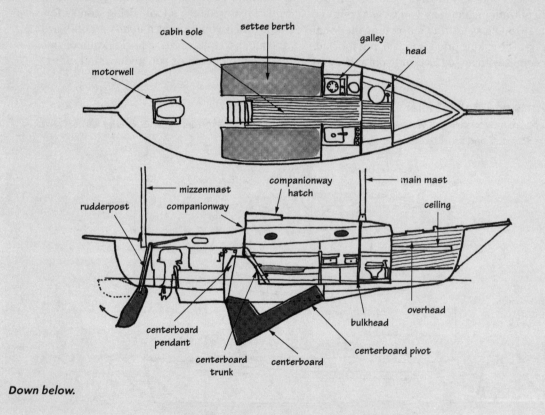

**Down below.**

camera. From the outside, she doesn't look too bad—she's reasonably clean. The portlights show a number of weblike cracks, indicating the plastic has weakened somewhat with age. They'll need replacing, but not immediately. There's a little wood on deck that definitely needs varnishing, but it's teak, so you don't see any rot. The gelcoat looks chalky, and there are some dings and a little crazing, but this has to be expected in a boat of this age. Some rubbing compound and wax can do wonders on hulls like this.

# Interior

While it may seem logical to start on the outside when examining a boat, one of the first things I do is take a quick look inside. This is because it's common to find a used boat that looks pretty good from the outside but whose interior is a nightmare. It takes but a quick glance (and a sniff) to know whether any big discounter problems lurk belowdeck. If the seller expects to sell a boat for a hundred bucks off the book value when the boat is a shredded-cotton mildew farm on the inside, then I know that to go much further is a waste of time.

If you don't see the cushions, ask about them. Some conscientious owners take them off the boat and store them at home during the off-season, which helps to significantly extend their life. But if the seller says, "They kept getting wet so we threw them away," alarms should go off in your head. One, there's an uncorrected leak somewhere in the deck that has probably rotted the deck core as well as ruined the cushions. Two, here's an owner who doesn't care about problems on his boat. Three, replacing a full set of boat cushions will cost at least $400 if you do all the work yourself, and $1,500 or more to have it done by a pro. Hopefully the cushions will be there.

A disgustingly filthy, mildewed interior usually earns at least a 50 percent reduction in boat value, possibly more. All that muck usually hides a multitude of problems that you won't discover until after two weeks of cleaning and repair work. Think like a drop of water—it'll usually, but not always, find the lowest point in the boat. Start low and work your way up, looking for any standing water or evidence of standing water.

## Bilge

All boats of course get a little water in them now and again—after all, they live in a pretty wet environment. Some trailerable sailboats, especially older, deep-draft boats such as the Cape Dory Typhoon or Halman 20, have a bilge, which is a space underneath the floorboards that collects water. This bilgewater gets pretty

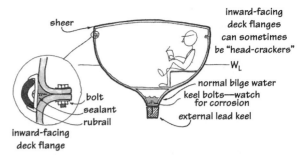

*A heavy-displacement keelboat showing bilge area. A small amount of water in the bilge is no cause for alarm. Water that has leaked down the hull—either from deck hardware leaks (for instance, around the base of stanchions or cleats) or from the hull-to-deck joint—can collect there.*

nasty, with drippings from the engine, dust, and so on. It's best to keep the bilge pumped dry, but usually it doesn't hurt much to have a little water in the bilge. (It is now illegal to put anything in the water that causes an oily sheen to appear, and this includes oily bilgewater. Most inboards now have a separate engine pan underneath them to catch oily drips.)

A little water in the boat for a short period of time usually doesn't hurt anything, but large amounts of water left for any length of time can lead to problems. How much water is too much? Well, if you step below and hear a splash, that's too much. Water shouldn't be allowed to come above the floorboards or saturate any of the interior woodwork. It's the cycling of wet and dry that really accelerates rot in wood.

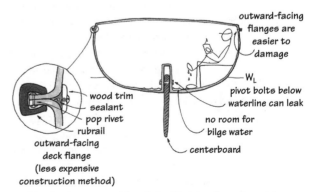

*A light-displacement (shoal-draft) centerboarder without a bilge space. If there are leaks from the deck hardware or the hull-to-deck joint, water will accumulate on the cabin floor.*

If the boat has a hatch in the center of the floor, lift it up to look in the bilge. Clean and dry is best, but a small puddle shouldn't hurt. Look for evidence of flooding and rot in any of the low wood on the boat by poking your ice pick or pocketknife into inconspicuous areas. You'll quickly learn what rotten wood feels like—the ice pick will penetrate the wood with little resistance.

Some boats, on the other hand, don't have a bilge. Instead, the cabin floor is the lowest part of the boat. Underneath the fiberglass is nothing but the deep briny blue. The centerboard trunk protrudes into the cabin space. My MacGregor was designed this way.

Boats without a traditional bilge space are more sensitive to standing water and will be much less tolerant of neglect. If there is a wood bulkhead that runs all the way to the floor, then examine the bottom of the bulkhead carefully for rot. A little water can do a lot of damage here,

and replacing a bulkhead is a big repair job. Ideally the fiberglass liner will extend up from the floor about a foot or so, and the bulkhead will be attached to that, but this isn't always the case. (See the sidebar "Fiberglass Boatbuilding for the Sealorn" for a crash course in boat construction.) If you don't see any standing water in the boat, that's good, but now you should look for a mud line. This is a discolored area where standing water has been—like a ring around the bathtub. You'll often see mud lines in concealed areas rather than obvious places.

When I look at the interior of a boat, I open up all the lockers and hatches. Sometimes you'll find a pocket of standing water that can't drain to the bilge. Clean and dry is best, dirty is normal, but puddles you can step in are a problem.

If you do find standing water, that means there's a leak somewhere. You've got to track it down and look for damage. Most of the

## Fiberglass Boatbuilding for the Sealorn

Naturally, building a sailboat is a complex process, but most boats have three major parts—the hull, the deck, and the liner.

The hull is usually created first. Most are solid fiberglass, though some have a core material of balsa or dense foam between two thinner layers of fiberglass. Cored hulls are lighter and stiffer but can delaminate as the hull ages.

Next comes the interior, often called a liner or hull sock. A complex molding containing most of the cabinets, bunk surfaces, and countertops is glassed inside the hull. Such a boat can be much cheaper to build, since it cuts the amount of time and skilled labor necessary to complete the boat. Better boats have liners glassed to the hull in many places, not just a tab or two here and there. Everything attached to the inside of the hull makes it stiffer and stronger. Wiring and plumbing are often run before the liner is bonded to the hull—easier to construct initially, but harder to repair later. Wooden trim and accent pieces are fitted after the liner is in place, which can greatly enhance the interior appearance.

The advantages of using a liner are obvious for the builder, but for the owner there are pluses and minuses. On the plus side, the boat costs less, and routine maintenance is much easier. The fiberglass liner doesn't rot, and since it's protected from the sun, the gelcoat lasts practically forever. One disadvantage is reduced hull strength, because every piece of furniture bonded to the hull can act as a stiffening member, and these stiffeners are greatly reduced with a liner. The other big drawback is lack of access to all parts of the hull. If you get a leak in your boat in an area that's hidden behind an inaccessible area of the liner, your boat can sink and you'll never know where the water is coming from. On most boats, access and storage can be improved at the same time by adding hatches, drawers, and doors to the liner.

The deck is attached to the boat only after the interior is complete. Decks are usually cored with plywood, balsa, or foam, since uncored fiberglass decks flex and bounce underfoot. But if water is allowed to leak into the deck core, it rots and begins to flex. Repairs are difficult and expensive, so it pays to keep deck hardware well sealed wherever it attaches to the deck. Really thoughtful designers and builders design deck moldings so that fittings pass through solid fiberglass wherever possible.

time, puddles come from rainwater, so look up. Any screw or bolt on the deck—used to hold various deck hardware, including stanchions and cleats—is a potential leak, so look carefully for water tracks or dampness. If you find any, then there's a good chance that the deck core is wet, too, and possibly rotten. Depending on the extent of the damage, repairs can be relatively simple or involve major work, so look carefully.

Sometimes a leak can result from a problem below the waterline. Any hole in the hull is a potential leak, and bedding compounds (the stuff used to further seal deck hardware and various other parts to the boat) do fail over time. One place particularly prone to leaks is the centerboard pivot bolt, and if the centerboard case is inside the boat rather than under it, a leak here becomes a particular nuisance. My MacGregor had this problem. Despite extensive reinforcement and upgrades, the heavy centerboard bent the pivot bolt a little and resulted in a slow, weeping leak after three seasons in the water. The only fix was to continue increasing the bolt size, which is a big job—I had already increased the pivot bolt from $1/2$ inch to a $5/8$-inch grade 8 bolt. So if you can see the centerboard pivot bolt from the cabin, examine it carefully.

If, during your search for rot, you find any rusty fittings, note them, because they'll have to be replaced. All fittings on the boat should ideally be stainless steel or bronze, and sometimes you'll see some mild steel fittings that have been added by the current owner. Occasionally these can work well—I had a hardware-store-variety spring bracket on my Catalina 27 that saw five years of constant liveaboard use, and it worked fine—but if a fitting looks rusty, you should probably plan on replacing it with something more durable, like bronze or stainless. You should also be aware that certain grades of inexpensive stainless steel will rust if conditions are right. Be warned that rusty stainless can fail very suddenly, without further warning, so be especially concerned if you see rusty stainless bolts or chainplates.

## Mildew

Mildew is a problem common to most boats. (See "Preventing Water and Mildew Belowdeck" in Chapter 13.) In the boats I've owned, mildew takes the form of small black spots on fiberglass or cloth, or a grayish powder that forms on wood surfaces. On hard surfaces, it's pretty easy to wipe off using a damp rag with a little Pine-Sol. However, once mildew gets into fabric, like sails or light-colored cushions, it's really difficult, sometimes impossible, to remove. This brings out my pet peeve with many manufacturers of trailerable sailboats, and that's fabric that is permanently bonded to the hull. A popular interior finishing method with many manufacturers is to glue something resembling indoor-outdoor carpet to the hull sides and overhead (the overhead is the interior surface of the boat), which looks great for four years or so. It insulates the hull and topsides (*topsides* is another term for on deck, meaning outside the boat), preventing condensation and reducing noise belowdeck. But after the warranty expires and a good healthy crop of mold sets in, it's nearly impossible to clean. Some builders provide a method for removing and cleaning these covers, but this is seldom the case with less expensive boats. A boat like this has to be kept dry. A week in the summer with a foot of water on the floorboards would be disastrous, so if the boat you're looking at has an interior that resembles a sheik's tent, understand that it'll require diligence to keep the insides nice.

## Electrical System

Chances are your prospective boat has some kind of electrical system. In its simplest form, an electrical system means a battery, a few switches, and some lights, but things are rarely this simple in the real world. Multiple batteries, distribution panels, chargers, radios, and other electronic navigation equipment are commonplace on trailerable sailboats these days. But is all this stuff necessary?

In a word, no. You aren't required to have any electrical equipment on board whatsoever, and a few souls still safely sail without it. Kerosene can be used for lighting, even for navigation lights, and battery-operated equipment is getting more efficient every day. But most of us want some kind of electrical capability on board.

Most people don't think much about their electrical system until something goes wrong. When it does, even the simplest system can seem maddeningly complicated as you try to trace the source of a problem. When surveying a used boat, try to ascertain whether all the electrical components are functioning properly. The worst kind of electrical problem to correct is one that works only part of the time. The question then becomes whether to fix just that single

problem or replace the entire system. There are often sound reasons for replacing rather than repairing electrical systems, especially on older boats. Electrical systems were often optional, and many boats were sold without electrical systems to lower the purchase price. The electrical system may have been added later by a less-than-knowledgeable owner. Some factory-installed systems were very marginal indeed—the wiring on my old MacGregor was just plain terrible. I don't know if the lamp cord was installed by the factory or a previous owner, but it was a tangled mess of bad splices and substandard practice. Lamp cord is cheap wire that you can get at a hardware store, and it should never be used aboard a boat. In fact, all components of the electrical system should be rated for marine use or they will corrode in the damp environment. Corroded electrical components can easily overheat and cause a fire. Marine-rated components aren't cheap, and the differences aren't readily apparent at a glance, but you should never skimp in this area—you'll likely regret it later.

No battery should ever be installed aboard a boat without a good, sealed, marine-grade battery switch. If you ever do have an electrical problem, it's imperative that you be able to disconnect the power source or your day will only get worse. Good switches are sealed and spark-proof, and they're rated for continuous high-amperage operation without overheating.

*The electrical "system" I found on my MacGregor 222.*

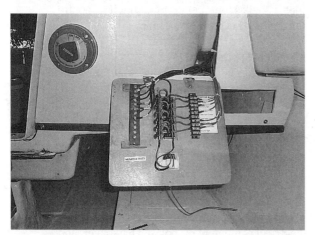

*The rewired MacGregor electrical system. Labeling and bundling every wire makes tracing problems far easier.*

*A heavy-duty battery switch for a single battery. This one does not include an alternator field disconnect, and could damage your alternator if switched while running your motor, if so equipped.*

If the boat doesn't have a battery switch or needs a new one, consider getting a two-battery switch rather than a simple one-battery, on-off switch. A two-battery switch costs only a little more, and allows you to easily increase your total battery power later by adding a second battery. You don't have to connect battery #2 for the switch to work. Be careful of less expensive battery switches, because some—like the one on my old Catalina—don't have an alternator field disconnect. When you change the position of the switch from battery #1 to battery #2, there is a split second when the switch is open, with no load on it at all. If your engine has a charging alternator connected to the switch, and it goes into a no-load condition, the diodes in the alternator will blow. An alternator field disconnect has a line that effectively turns off the alternator when you switch batteries, saving your diodes from damage. If it sounds like I learned this the hard way, you're right—I had to replace my alternator after I switched batteries while charging.

### Plumbing/Seacocks

How many holes does a sailboat have through its hull? Most reasonable people would say none, 'cause if it had a hole, it wouldn't float. While this is technically true, nearly all sailboats come with several holes already drilled through the hull, and any one of them has the potential to sink the boat if these holes are located below the waterline. That's how I like to think about the boat's plumbing.

All the holes in your potential purchase, if located near or below the waterline, should have proper seacocks attached. Some builders save money by connecting hoses directly to through-hulls, which are bronze or plastic flanges that screw tightly against the hull. No shutoff valves of any kind. These installations should be upgraded immediately to include seacocks, and while you're at it, you might as well replace the plastic through-hulls with bronze. Even worse are hardware-store gate valves, with wheels that you turn to screw the valve closed. These are especially dangerous

*Seacocks should be double-clamped with all-stainless hose clamps. This installation shows a marine-related ball valve attached to a through-hull—not the best arrangement. True seacocks have a flange on the base that is bolted to the surface of the hull.*

and should be replaced. Bronze and stainless ball valves on a bronze through-hull, with a proper plywood backing pad against the inside surface of the hull, aren't as good as seacocks, but they are far better than gate valves.

All hoses should be thick, very strong, fiber reinforced, and resistant to chemicals and heat. Clear hose should never be used below the waterline, and garden hose should be used only for washing down the boat. If you see any bulges or cracking in the hose, it should be replaced.

Also take a close look at the hose clamps, because the best hose in the world is useless if

## Straight Threads or Tapered?

One of the problems with using gate valves or ball valves on your boat is the threads. The plumbing in your house uses a special thread called NPT (National Pipe Tapered). Tapered threads are designed to screw together for a few turns and jam tightly, making a watertight seal. But the through-hull fittings you buy at the chandlery use NPS (National Pipe Straight) thread. These threads will screw their entire length without jamming.

If you mix threads, the result is a joint that screws in only partially, engaging just a few threads and making a weak connection that's more likely to leak.

You want to have all the threads match on any below-the-waterline fittings. Look for the letters NPS or NPT stamped somewhere on any fittings you plan to use. Using all NPS threads is preferable, but if you must, a tapered thread can be used as long as both male and female surfaces use the same type of thread. Special sea-cock bases are available with straight threads on the outboard end and tapered threads on the inboard, making a pseudo-seacock using a standard ball valve.

it slips off the seacock. All hoses should be double clamped, and any rusting means replacement. Some hose clamps are made with cheaper grades of stainless and are more likely to rust, especially the screws. Check with a magnet if you have any doubts: in general, as the grade of stainless gets higher, the magnetic attraction gets lower.

So, we've pretty much gone over the entire inside. Note any leaks, rot, water damage, and broken equipment in your notebook. If you're not scared off at this point, turn your attention to the deck and the rig.

## Exterior

### Deck

The first thing I do is use my not-unsubstantial weight to check the deck core. I take off my shoes and walk carefully around all the surfaces of the deck, taking small, closely spaced steps, making a note of anyplace the deck feels spongy. If the boat is an older, less-expensive

model, then more likely than not you'll find at least some deck rot. Pay particular attention to areas around the mast, stanchions, fittings, and deck blocks—anywhere hardware is bolted through the deck is a potential source for leaks and core rot. Small areas can often be fixed fairly easily, but large areas—let's say larger than about a square foot—can mean a big repair job. How big? See "Repairing Deck Rot" in Chapter 13. If deck rot is the only problem on an otherwise great boat, then I might be inclined to buy it with a significant discount, but this is rarely the case. This problem is easily prevented by proper sealing and bedding of fittings on the deck, but it's unfortunately far too common a problem on older sailboats.

*Look carefully at this stemhead fitting (the fitting on the bow where the headstay attaches to the deck). The hardware is lifting off the deck, no doubt causing a leak down into the interior. If the deck is cored in this area, then the core is rotting. (All boats have some sort of core in the deck area, either of plywood, balsa, or foam. The best boats have solid fiberglass where fittings are mounted, but that level of quality is pretty rare in the trailer-sailer market.)*

Note any water stains or puddles on the deck. A properly designed boat won't have any areas that can trap water, but it can and does happen. These can be corrected by installing drains, but hopefully you won't see any water stains or puddles.

## Hull

Next, turn your attention to the hull itself. Look for bad repairs, big cracks, or dings. Since gelcoat is harder than the fiberglass underneath, small accidents and places where the hull flexes under stress show up as gelcoat cracks. Some small cracks are inevitable, but extensive large cracking could indicate underlying laminate that needs to be strengthened. This can be done by reinforcing the boat using epoxy and glass—if you can get to the part of the hull that needs attention.

But getting the gelcoat cracks filled, with a perfect color match, is a bit more problematic. Gelcoat repair kits are probably the best bet for colored hulls, but if your hull is white like mine is, you might try Marine Tex. That's what I've used for a few small spots, and so far it seems to be working fine. But then again, the gelcoat on my hull is 26 years old, and a perfect glossy

*Small gelcoat cracks like this are mainly cosmetic. They can be filled, but may reappear again.*

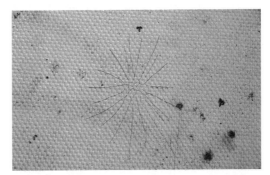

*Larger gelcoat cracks such as these were probably the result of flexing caused by an impact. If any large flakes have popped off, the gelcoat should be repaired.*

*A boat this bad needs more than just a little TLC. This will take major work to clean up.*

color match isn't the same priority as it would be on a newer boat. Epoxy compounds often yellow (or even fail to bond completely in the case of clear epoxies) in the sunlight, since epoxy is sensitive to both heat and UV rays.

### Blisters

An older boat that has been sitting in the water for a long time could be blistered on the bottom. Blisters were a mystery when they began appearing on fiberglass boats because everyone thought fiberglass was completely waterproof. It isn't. Explaining blisters is complex, but here's a simplified version of why they occur.

When a hull sits in the water for years, tiny amounts of water seep into the fiberglass itself where it finds chemicals to bond with. Once the water has bonded with these chemicals, the molecules become larger, the resulting fluid (acetic acid) is trapped, and blisters form. Certain types of fiberglass—specifically, vinylester resin—are more blister-resistant than others, such as polyester resin. Boats with an outer layer of vinylester resin are significantly less likely to form blisters than boats using plain polyester resin.

Most, but not all, blisters form at the junction between the gelcoat and the hull laminate. Thicker gelcoat slows blister formation but doesn't stop it entirely.

A blister or two isn't much cause for concern, but a maze of blisters covering the entire bottom—called boat pox—is more serious. Repair involves peeling off the outer layer and relaminating the hull, usually with epoxy. It requires a big commitment of time and money, even if you plan to do the work yourself, and deserves a hefty discount.

### Keel and Keel Bolts

If the boat you're looking at has a fixed keel, you'll need to check the ballast attachment. Some keels have internal ballast, where the keel cavity is filled with something heavy. Lead is best, but you're more likely to find cast-iron weights, concrete, or steel scrap (such as boiler punchings). As long as the ballast stays

dry, it's fine, but if water gets in and the steel starts to rust, it swells up and you've got big problems. Some owners have gone so far as to cut the keel sides, chip out the rusting mess, and replace it with lead shot. A job like this isn't for the faint of heart. Look for rust stains weeping from cracks in the keel exterior as a sign of possible problems.

The other major way to install ballast is with an external keel. Here, a carefully shaped and smoothed keel casting is bolted to the hull. This system works well, but the keel bolts live in a tough environment—the bilge. The keel bolts need to stay well-sealed. Again, look for rust stains weeping from cracks or persistent leaks. If neglected long enough, the keel bolts can corrode completely away. Repairing or replacing keel bolts usually requires help from the pros.

### Rigging (Standing and Running)

Next, look over the standing rigging and the mast. The rigging should be all stainless steel, with no rust stains or darkening of the metal. Also, run a rag over all of the shrouds and stays. You are looking for fishhooks, which are single strands of broken wire. They'll catch on

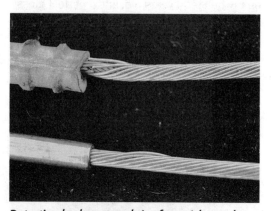

*Detecting broken strands is often tricky, and breaks usually occur near areas of highest stress. In the top example, the broken strands are easy to see at the swaged joint. In the example below, a strand hasn't actually broken but has slipped out of the roller-swaged joint. It's easier to detect by touch, and the result is a compromised cable that should be replaced.*

a rag, immediately notifying you of a problem. Really tough wharf-rat sailors use their bare hands, in which case broken strands are called "meathooks." No matter what you call them, they're a particular problem with $1 \times 19$ stainless steel rigging wire. (It's called $1 \times 19$ because it's made of nineteen strands, one wire each.) If one breaks, it's most likely because the whole bundle is fatigued, and now the other eighteen strands are under a higher load. You'll get no further warning that a shroud is about to break. Rust-stained shrouds or shrouds with fishhooks require immediate replacement, or you risk losing your rig overboard.

The mast should be fairly straight, with no pronounced kinks or bends. Some racing boats are set up to bend the mast aft to flatten the sail, and a gentle curve dead aft is OK, but the mast shouldn't bend to either side at rest, and certainly not forward. Hopefully the mast or boom isn't perforated with holes from old fittings. A kinked or dented mast is especially bad—I wouldn't buy a boat with this problem without consulting a professional rigger for a repair estimate.

Now check out the running rigging. Problems here usually take the form of worn-out blocks, dirty lines, or ineffective or cheap sail controls. These kinds of problems are usually fun to fix. New blocks and lines are expensive, but they are usually pretty easy to install. New boats rarely come with a traveler, but it's a common upgrade, and you'll often see them on boats that have been around awhile. Replacing a complete traveler is expensive, but it can be rebuilt. Winches are expensive, and a boat with high-quality, well-functioning winches is a plus. If the winches are in poor shape, plan on replacement costs of around $100 to $200 each for single-speed standard winches, $400 to $500 for single-speed self-tailing winches, and $700 to $1,300 each for two-speed self-tailers.

## Corrosion

I touched on the subject of corrosion with regard to the mast and rig, but this subject deserves more attention because all sailboats have some metal aboard, and all metals corrode

in certain conditions. Several types of metal are commonly used on sailboats. Some, like stainless steel, are used because they resist corrosion well. Some are used because they are strong and light, like aluminum for masts and spars. Some metals for small fittings are used because they are cheap. (You'll see the term Zamak in marine catalogs—it's mostly zinc, and only slightly better than pot metal.) All of the metal fittings on your boat should be either stainless steel, aluminum, or bronze.

The types of corrosion you're most apt to see are rust, crevice corrosion (both of which affect steel), and aluminum corrosion. Some corrosion is inevitable; see "Dealing with Corrosion" in Chapter 13 for tips on treatment and prevention. But when is corrosion a significant problem? Here's what to look for.

Stainless steel comes in myriad varieties, but in boats you'll most likely find 304, 308, 316, 408, or 416. The numbers refer to the amounts of different metals (chromium, molybdenum, and nickel) in each alloy, but, in general, higher numbers indicate more expensive steels with greater corrosion resistance. You can check stainless with a magnet—lower grades are magnetic and more likely to rust.

Stainless needs good air circulation to prevent rusting. You will often see a rust streak coming from the drain hole of a stanchion. That's because air doesn't circulate inside the tube. Usually this is just a cosmetic problem, but some owners are tempted to "fix" it by plugging the drain hole, which is the worst thing to do. The stanchion should be replaced with a higher grade of tubing.

Any deep crack in stainless steel can trap moisture and prevent air circulation, causing crevice corrosion. This is a serious problem when it occurs in rigging parts. Any rust stains there call for immediate replacement.

When aluminum corrodes, it often takes the form of pitting over the surface with a white deposit of aluminum oxide. Treatment involves removing the oxide and sealing with a polish or wax. Painted aluminum will sometimes corrode underneath the paint; it then needs to be sanded clean, primed with a special aluminum primer, and repainted.

Plain steel on boats is usually found in only a few places—the trailer, which I discuss in a moment—and, in some older boats, in the swing keel or centerboard, where its weight forms part of the ballast. As long as it's kept perfectly sealed from water and air, plain steel is OK, but lead is a better choice. It's heavier and more expensive, but it doesn't rust. Some swing centerboards are made from cast iron. These need to be repainted and faired every five to ten years or so, depending on the quality of the previous job.

### Bent Turnbuckles

A very common problem among trailerable sailboats is bent turnbuckles. The shrouds foul something while the mast is going up, and the turnbuckles are easily damaged. While this doesn't seem like a big deal, very close inspection reveals a problem.

Stainless steel is much stronger than plain steel but more likely to crack if bent. My Montgomery had a bent turnbuckle when I bought it, and I didn't think too much about it at first. Then I looked at the threads under a microscope. I found cracks at the bottom of the threads. This turnbuckle was compromised, and if it had broken, the mast could have gone over the side. An event like that can ruin your whole day. I replaced all the turnbuckles with new ones, just to be safe.

This problem can be lessened somewhat by adding rigging toggles to the turnbuckles,

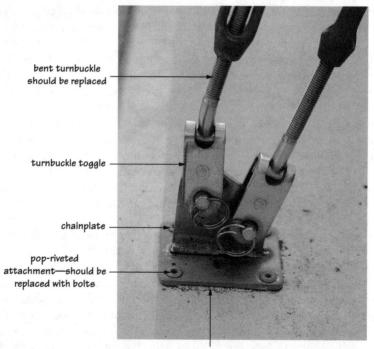

bent turnbuckle should be replaced

turnbuckle toggle

chainplate

pop-riveted attachment—should be replaced with bolts

note failed bedding compound—probably leaking, possibly rotten underneath

*This chainplate and turnbuckle don't look too bad at first, but close inspection reveals a number of problems. The bent T-bolt on the turnbuckle should be replaced, the cheap "pop rivets" drilled out and replaced with stainless machine screws, and the old, dried-out bedding compound cleaned off and renewed. Since this chainplate looks like it's been neglected for some time, you can expect to find at least some rot underneath that should be addressed as well.*

but the main thing to remember is to raise the mast slowly, and have a crewmember on hand to free up fouled shrouds.

## Trailer

If you've gotten this far, you've crossed over the line of casual looker to serious contender. The subject of motor (see the next section) and trailer and their effect on the final price of a used boat can be tricky, as these items are not usually included in the BUC value. But these are both big-ticket items to replace. And besides, what's a trailer sailer with no trailer?

The most important feature of a boat trailer is that it exists. If the trailer is missing, it can be difficult to find a replacement with the right measurements. Often sellers of old boats will scrap an old, rusty trailer rather than try to preserve it, and the trailer will rust away to nothing if neglected—especially near salt water. This creates a problem for you, the buyer, because you'll often need to transport the boat to a new location. Many boat transport companies will be happy to move the boat for you, but this is rather expensive, especially when you consider that boats with usable trailers are readily available. If you have to buy a brand-new trailer, plan on spending at least $1,500, which doesn't make a lot of sense for a boat with a book value of $2,000.

Hopefully, though, the trailer will be there, and in reasonable condition. Don't be bothered by some rust, but if parts of the trailer have rusted clear through, I strongly recommend pulling the trailer to a shop to have it looked over. (Camper and RV dealers often have trailer shops; check the Yellow Pages.) I'd even go so far as to make this a condition of the sale. You don't want to be responsible for an accident caused by trailer failure, and since you don't know much about this trailer's history, you shouldn't take chances.

Fortunately, most trailers can be repaired. New parts are readily available, and even a rusted frame can be rewelded. You can get a completely new axle assembly, with custom grease fittings that let you lube the bearings without disassembling the hubs, for about $175. If you have access to a welder, then you can make some pretty quick upgrades in the form of extra safety chains, lifting handles, and attachment points. (See the sidebar "Making Your Trailer Safer" in Chapter 4.)

## Outboard

When buying a boat, a functioning outboard in good condition is a big plus. Replacing an old, poorly functioning outboard with a new motor is an expensive proposition—prices start at about $1,400—so don't turn up your nose if the power plant on your prospective purchase looks old. If it runs well, it's worth keeping. Quiz the current owner in detail about his outboard—how does he like it, what kind of oil does he use, does he have the manual, has the motor ever fallen off the transom, has it ever left him stranded? Start it up and look at the exhaust—a little smoke is expected, but clouds from the muffler can indicate needed repairs.

If you've never touched a wrench in your life, don't hesitate to get help from a good mechanic. That's the beauty of outboards versus inboards—you can take just the motor to the mechanic rather than hauling the entire boat. Call a few shops, tell them that you're thinking of buying a boat, and ask what they'd charge to look at a small outboard. Rates will vary but shouldn't be too high. (Tips on maintaining outboards can be found in Chapter 13.)

Almost all new outboards these days use four-stroke powerheads, while most used motors for sale will be two-stroke models. The two-stroke models are being phased out because of pollution concerns. What's the difference between the two? To find out, we have to talk about engine design on a basic level. It may be more than you want to know, but trust me, this info will come in handy when your motor conks out in the middle of the ocean, and *all* motors conk out eventually.

### Four-Stroke Motors

The type of engine that you're probably most familiar with is a four-stroke design. This is what you've got in your car. Speaking on a highly simplistic level, each cylinder has an intake valve, an exhaust valve, a piston, and a spark plug. Fuel—gasoline—is mixed with air by the carburetor and travels to the cylinder via the intake valve. This is stroke number one, the intake stroke. The piston travels downward during this stroke, creating the suction that pulls the fuel and air into the cylinder.

Next, the intake valve closes and the piston travels upward, squeezing the fuel/air mix. This is stroke number two, the compression stroke. Both valves are closed during this step.

Now, at just the right time, the spark plug fires. The resulting explosion drives the piston downward. This is the ignition stroke, sometimes called the power or drive stroke.

The last of the four strokes is the exhaust stroke. The piston travels upward while the exhaust valve opens, pushing the smoke out of the cylinder.

It's important to note that the piston is producing power only during the ignition stroke. The rotational force for the other three strokes comes from a flywheel, or, more accurately, the mass of the driveshaft, which acts as a flywheel.

### Two-Stroke Motors

For many years, most outboard motors were the two-stroke variety, mainly because of their lighter weight and greater power. Older two-stroke outboards are fairly simple machines and will last a long time if properly cared for. However, two-strokes have several downsides. First, let's learn how they operate.

The two-stroke design, along with the ported cylinder design, was invented by Joseph Day in 1889. The ports, which are simply holes in the cylinder wall, are covered and uncovered by the piston. The ports replace the valves that the four-stroke requires, greatly simplifying the engine. Although most modern two-strokes use a reed or rotary valve instead of piston ports, the design is equally simple. Reed valve engines deliver power over a greater range of rpm, making them more useful.

The thing to remember about two-strokes is that where a four-stroke needs four motions of the piston for each power cycle (up, down, up, down), a two-stroke does the same thing in two motions (up, down). Explaining this is a little tricky, but bear with me.

Let's start as the cylinder is starting to travel upward. While fuel is being compressed at the top of the piston, a partial vacuum is created at the underside of the piston. The fuel and air mix is drawn in by the vacuum, filling

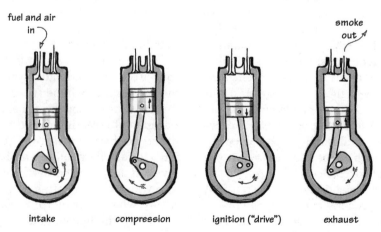

intake          compression          ignition ("drive")          exhaust

*Four-stroke operation.*

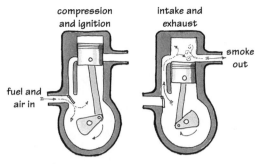

compression and ignition

intake and exhaust

smoke out

fuel and air in

*Two-stroke operation.*

the back side of the cylinder chamber. As the piston reaches the top of its stroke, the spark plug fires, driving the cylinder downward. At roughly the same time, the reed valve closes. Now, as the cylinder travels downward, compression is created at the underside of the cylinder, where the unburned fuel/air mix is. As the piston nears the bottom of its stroke, the exhaust port is first uncovered, allowing some of the smoke to escape. Then the intake port is uncovered. This allows the pressurized fuel/air mix into the upper part of the cylinder, forcing out the rest of the smoke, and the cylinder begins its upward journey again. So we've taken the processes of a four-stroke and accomplished them in two—pretty clever, eh?

### Two-Stoke versus Four-Stroke Trade-offs

Now we can examine the specific trade-offs for each type of engine. Since fuel is swirling around both sides of the piston in the two-stroke, lubrication will be a problem. In a four-stroke, the bottom side of the piston isn't used, so we can give it a luxurious bath of nice, warm oil—just the sort of thing an engine likes. We can't do this with a two-stroke, though, so we have to mix some lubricating oil into the fuel. Some of this oil lubricates the engine, but some is necessarily burned along with the gas. In general, this makes two-stroke enginess more polluting than their four-stroke cousins, and this is why they are being phased out. Many inland lakes have banned two-stroke outboards already, and eventually they will be a thing of

the past. As a rule, two-stroke motors are lighter, simpler, and more powerful, though four-strokes have more low-end torque. Two-strokes are very sensitive to fuel, and if you use this type of motor, the single most effective thing you can do to make sure that your engine runs well is to always, *always* mix your oil and fuel in exactly the correct ratio stated in your manual. Too much will foul your spark plugs, clog your engine with burned oil deposits, and smoke like a chimney. Too little oil will starve your engine of proper lubrication.

### Motor Mounts

Most outboards these days are mounted on the transom rather than in a motorwell, a watertight case that was popular on early fiberglass boats. Transom motor mounts can be fixed or adjustable. Adjustable mounts are preferred, as you can raise the motor farther out of the water, protecting the motor head from following seas. The advantages are not great enough to warrant removing a properly installed fixed mount, though. You've got a little more latitude when installing an adjustable motor mount.

An important thing to check on any motor mount is the pad that the motor itself clamps to. These are commonly made of plywood, and they can rot. I know of one case where an outboard tore away from a rotten pad after it was shifted into reverse. The owner naturally grabbed his expensive motor to keep it from sinking to a watery grave, to the great mirth of everyone watching at the crowded launch dock. A running motor that is not attached to a boat might make a great Hollywood comic routine, but in real life it's extremely dangerous. The laughing bystanders quickly changed their tune when the wildly spinning propeller cleared the water and started swinging their way. Fortunately, no one was hurt, the motor was subdued, and the experience damaged little more than pride—the owner managed to shut the motor off before water entered the air intake.

New motor mounts are built with rot-proof plastic pads, and an old one could easily be

*Two views of an adjustable motor mount for an outboard. With this type of mounting bracket it is possible to tilt the motor up, to further reduce the time the propeller sits in the water when not in use.*

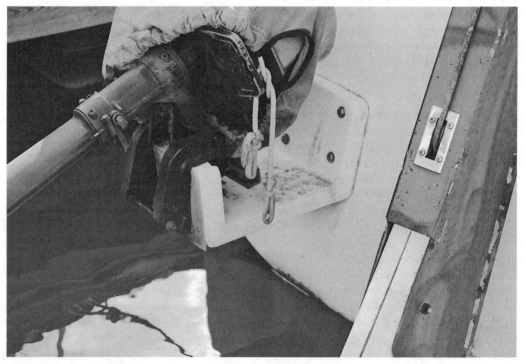

*A fixed transom motor mount.*

upgraded with StarBoard or a similar plastic building material. Knowledgeable owners check the motor mount screws before starting an outboard, and attach a safety leash to the motor and a strong eye somewhere on the transom.

Outboard motors come in short- and long-shaft varieties. For a sailboat, you want the long shaft. Typical lengths are 15 and 20 inches. Short-shaft outboards are designed for dinghies and sportfishing boats, which have smaller transoms than sailboats. Even with a long shaft, it is sometimes a challenge to get the propeller deep enough. Occasionally you will see an extra-long-shaft outboard offered, and the venerable British Seagull outboards, which were designed for sailboats, came with 28-inch shafts.

## Dinghy

Dinghies are less common among trailerable sailboats than larger boats—after all, some of the boats we're cruising in aren't a whole lot larger than many dinghies. Storage is a problem, and with rigid dinghies, towing is often the only option. Inflatable dinghies, even when rolled up, still take up a lot of space.

But dinghies can be a lot of fun, especially for the sailing family. Piloting a dinghy is a great way for a young sailor to develop skills and learn responsibility. Also, a dinghy may be

the only way to get close to shore, and it's great for exploring inshore areas, checking the depth of unknown channels, or hauling out a kedge anchor to pull yourself off a sandbar.

If your prospective purchase includes a dinghy, look it over for obvious damage. Inflatables can last a long time, though the sun eventually rots the fabric. Replacing an inflatable is expensive, starting at around $1,000, so I'd try several patches before giving up on the whole thing.

Any dinghy you buy should probably be the smallest one you can get your hands on. A Walker Bay 8 is a good commercially available model, and West Marine has a 7-foot 10-inch inflatable made by Zodiac. Both are good choices, though if your goal is serious long-term cruising, a larger model might be better.

Rigid dinghies can be rowed or sailed, whereas most inflatable dinghies can be rowed only for a short distance in calm conditions. All dinghies should include basic safety equipment, such as oars, life jackets, daytime distress signals, flares, and an anchor. More than one sailor has died when a dinghy motor malfunctioned late at night and he was swept out to sea. A nice safety improvement is a line of small fenders attached to the gunwale—this makes most dinghies unsinkable and more stable, and they won't bump the boat in the middle of the night.

# CHAPTER FOUR

# Trailers

**B**oat trailers come in a few different types, with plenty of minor variations. These are the four basic models:

Skid-type trailers
Roller-supporting trailers
Float-on trailers
Screw-pad trailers

The skid type of trailer is probably the most familiar. These have long, carpet-covered "bunks" running the length of the trailer that support the bottom of the boat. This is the type of trailer you'll find under most 15-foot motorboats. They're designed for boats with a relatively flat bottom; the boat slides along the skids until it's in place.

The second type of trailer has supporting rollers instead of carpet-covered bunks. The rollers make it easier to position the boat while launching or retrieving. A variation is the tilt trailer, which has a hinge mechanism somewhere along the trailer tongue. In some cases the tilting mechanism does make things go more smoothly, but this depends on the boat. Many owners of tilt trailers report that while the tilting mechanism itself doesn't help much, the rollers have less friction than carpet-covered bunks and thus make launching and retrieval easier. However, the boat can also shift during transport. Extra support straps, tie-downs, and safety chains are important with this type of trailer.

The third type of trailer is similar to the skid type, with long, carpet-covered bunks, but is designed to be completely immersed in the water while the boat is floated on or off the

trailer. You'll find float-on trailers under larger boats (about 20 feet or more) or sailboats with curvy displacement hulls.

A fourth type of trailer specifically used with sailboats is the screw-pad design. The hull is supported not by long bunks but by individual pads adjusted by screws. Depending on the type of boat and depth of the keel, these trailers can be used at the ramp as a float-on trailer, but some require a crane to lift the boat on and off the trailer.

## MATCHING VEHICLE TO TRAILER AND BOAT

An important part of the trailerable sailboat package is the vehicle used to pull the boat. Lots of cars and trucks can pull at least some kind of sailboat safely, but don't make the mistake I did of assuming that vehicle size or number of cylinders equals towing ability. It doesn't. Get the straight story directly from your owner's manual. Another place to research tow ratings is on the Internet, at www.trailerboats.com/towrating/. (For an interesting comparison of towing capacity and gas mileage, see the sidebar "Tow Ratings versus Gas Mileage.")

Lots of variables affect a car's towing ability, like engine size, transmission type, vehicle weight, and so on. In general, bigger, heavier cars make better tow vehicles, but it takes more gas to move them around. You'll want an automatic transmission, and you'll want the factory-installed towing package, which usually consists of a transmission fluid cooler and maybe a larger engine oil reservoir. (A manual

## Tow Ratings Versus Gas Mileage

An interesting comparison that is not readily available is towing capacity versus fuel economy. As a vehicle's ability to pull a heavy load goes up, the mileage naturally goes down, but it's important to note that we pull a boat for a very small percentage of the time we use a car or truck. Still, there are some big diffs in the fuel economy of various cars and trucks.

Here is a look at a few selected models.

### 3,500-pound towing range

| Brand | Model | Towing Range | EPA Mileage (HWY/CTY) |
|---|---|---|---|
| Volvo S60 | 5-cyl sedan | 3,300 | 20/27 |
| Saab 9-5 | 4-cyl sedan | 3,500 | 19/28 |
| Nissan Quest | 6-cyl minivan | 3,500 | 19/26 |
| Toyota Sienna | 6-cyl minivan | 3,500 | 19/26 |
| Chevrolet Equinox | 6-cyl SUV | 3,500 | 19/25 |
| Saturn Vue | 6-cyl SUV | 3,500 | 19/25 |
| Dodge Caravan/GC | 4/6-cyl minivan | 3,800 | 18/25 |
| Audi A8 | 8-cyl sedan | 3,500 | 18/24 |
| Chevrolet Uplander | 6-cyl SUV | 3,500 | 18/24 |
| Lexus RX330 | 6-cyl SUV | 3,500 | 18/24 |
| Mercury Mariner | 4/6-cyl SUV | 3,500 | 18/23 |
| Ford Escape | 6-cyl SUV | 3,500 | 18/22 |
| Mazda Tribute | 6-cyl SUV | 3,500 | 18/22 |
| Accura MDX | 6-cyl SUV | 3,500 | 17/23 |
| Honda Pilot | 6-cyl SUV | 3,500 | 17/22 |
| Infiniti FX | 6/8-cyl SUV | 3,500 | 16/22 |
| Kia Sedona | 6-cyl minivan | 3,500 | 16/22 |
| Ford Explorer | 6/8-cyl SUV | 3,500 | 14/20 |

### 5,000-pound towing range

| Brand | Model | Towing Range | EPA Mileage (HWY/CTY) |
|---|---|---|---|
| BMW X5 | 8-cyl SUV | 5,000 | 16/21 |
| Honda Ridgeline | 6-cyl pickup | 5,000 | 16/21 |
| Isuzu Ascender | 6/8-cyl SUV | 5,500 | 16/21 |
| Nissan Xterra | 6-cyl SUV | 5,000 | 16/21 |
| Chevrolet Trailblazer | 6/8-cyl SUV | 5,300 | 15/21 |
| Volvo XC90 | 5/6/8-cyl SUV | 5,000 | 15/20 |
| Mercedes-Benz M-Class | 6/8-cyl SUV | 5,000 | 15/18 |

### 7,500-pound-plus towing range

| Brand | Model | Towing Range | EPA Mileage (HWY/CTY) |
|---|---|---|---|
| Volkswagen Touareg | 6/8-cyl SUV | 7,700 | 16/21 |
| Chev Silverado/GMC Sierra | 6/8-cyl pickup | 7,500 | 15/18 |
| Chevrolet Avalanche | 8-cyl pickup | 8,100 | 14/18 |
| Chev Suburban/GMC Yukon XL | 8-cyl SUV | 8,500 | 14/18 |

*(Continued)*

### 7,500-pound plus towing range *(continued)*

| Brand | Model | Towing Range | EPA Mileage (HWY/CTY) |
|---|---|---|---|
| Ford F150 | 6/8-cyl pickup | 8,200 | 14/18 |
| Land Rover LR3 | 8-cyl SUV | 7,700 | 14/18 |
| Nissan Titan | 8-cyl pickup | 9,400 | 14/18 |
| Dodge Durango | 6/8-cyl SUV | 8,700 | 13/18 |
| Infiniti QX56 | 8-cyl SUV | 8,900 | 13/18 |
| Nissan Armada | 8-cyl SUV | 9,100 | 13/18 |
| Cadallac Escalade | 8-cyl SUV | 7,800 | 13/17 |
| Ford Expedition | 8-cyl SUV | 8,700 | 13/17 |
| Lincoln Navigator | 8-cyl SUV | 8,700 | 11/16 |

Data from *Consumer Reports 2006*, www.fueleconomy.gov. Actual results will vary; data is for comparison purposes only.

transmission can work—it's what I have in my Frontier—but pulling a boat up a steep ramp with a manual transmission can be a real clutch-burner.) The fluid cooler and oil reservoir help keep the engine and transmission from overheating under the extra load of pulling a boat, and they can save you the cost of replacing your transmission. Many auto manufacturers do not recommend towing anything without their factory-installed towing package. If you don't have it installed and then damage your engine or transmission, you'll probably find the damage is not covered under warranty or insurance. Often a tow vehicle will require heavier brakes or a heavier suspension to properly handle the additional load of a trailer. Follow the factory recommendations for your particular car or truck.

If you've never done a lot of towing, hauling a sailboat can be a bit daunting. In fact, I can never really relax when I'm towing my boat—it always makes me a little nervous, as I'm constantly on the lookout for what *might* happen. While this attitude might be unnecessary, I have been lucky enough not to have experienced any accidents when towing my boat (knock on lots of wood), and I like to think this is partly the result of diligence and conservative driving practices. Of course, part of the equation is just plain luck, but by being careful, you can stack the cards in your favor. I have heard that the top four causes of trailering

accidents are driver error, failure to match speed with weather and road conditions, trailer sway caused by incorrect loading, and failure to perform routine maintenance. An accident can happen to anyone at anytime, but being careful rarely makes them worse.

## PARTS OF YOUR TRAILER

You've figured out what sort of trailer is appropriate for your vehicle, so you're ready to go, right? Not quite—your trailer is a system with several components, and a number of variables should be considered in order to tow your investment safely.

### Trailer Hitches

Before you hook up your trailer, there are a few things you need to take care of beyond having the factory towing package installed on your car or truck. The first priority is having a hitch installed if it isn't included in the factory towing package.

There are several hitch systems available these days, but in order to select the right one, you need to know the total weight of the load you're going to pull. The weight of the boat, trailer, fuel and water, and all your personal gear makes up the gross trailer weight, and this number is used to select the hitch system for your car. The weight of your gear adds up quickly. For instance, I installed a big, brand-new, deep-cycle battery so I have an extra reserve of electrical power aboard my boat. It weighs close to 70 pounds, and the weight of the batteries isn't usually included in the boat manufacturer's displacement figure. Electrical systems are often optional (even though the Coast Guard may require navigation lights on board—see "USCG-Required Equipment" in Chapter 5).

Hitch systems are divided into specific classes:

Class 1—Maximum capacity 2,000 pounds gross trailer weight and 200 pounds tongue weight.

Class 2—Maximum capacity 3,500 pounds gross trailer weight and 300–350 pounds tongue weight.

Class 3—Maximum capacity 5,000 pounds gross trailer weight and 500 pounds tongue weight. Sometimes used to refer to a hitch with any 2-inch receiver, regardless of rating.

Class 4—Maximum capacity 10,000 pounds gross trailer weight and 1,000–1,200 pounds tongue weight. Often any hitch with a capacity greater than 5,000 pounds gross weight is referred to as a Class 4.

hitch receiver

receiver tube

safety chain mounting point

safety chain attachment point

receiver tube

*A Class 2 3,500-pound hitch receiver, adequate for many trailer sailers.*

Each of the hitch systems in these classes is made up of several parts. The receiver is a specially fitted part that bolts directly to the frame of the tow vehicle. The drawbar slides into the receiver and is where the hitch ball is mounted. Some trucks, like my Frontier, have a tow bumper, which is designed to have a hitch ball mounted directly to the bumper. These are usually for fairly small loads—mine is rated up to 2,000 pounds. This was too small for my MacGregor, which displaces 1,950 pounds for the boat alone, not including the weight of the trailer or gear. My Monty comes a little closer, as it displaces only 1,600 pounds, but with the trailer weight and gear probably exceeds the capacity of my bumper hitch, so I have a receiver mounted to my truck as well. The coupler is a part of the trailer that fits and locks over the hitch ball.

It goes without saying that all these parts must be matched. You should never try to put a Class 2 drawbar into a Class 4 receiver and expect to pull a 6,000-pound boat. While matching a drawbar and receiver is fairly straightforward, properly fitting the hitch ball and coupler is harder. It's imperative that the hitch ball and coupler match.

It's also crucial that your safety chains be in good condition. They should never drag on the ground, which will quickly grind the links away, nor should they be so tight that they bind when turning. They should be securely attached to the frame of the car, and they should cross under the tongue in order to catch it if it should separate from the tow vehicle. This is required by law in some states. Safety chains commonly come with specialized S-hooks to attach the chains to the vehicle frame, but I prefer to use quick links, which are threaded to close. Quick links are weaker than S-hooks, so you should use a larger size. The big advantage to quick links is that the safety chain length can be more easily adjusted than with S-hooks. If you have S-hooks on your trailer, know that there is a correct way to connect the safety chains to your car frame—the opening of the S-hook should face forward. A quick wrap with duct tape or wire can secure S-hooks so they can't bounce off the car frame.

There are other types of specialized hitch systems for high loads, like load-equalizer hitches, which use spring bars to distribute the weight of the trailer tongue over all of the tow vehicle's wheels. This sort of system can increase the load capacity of the tow vehicle and offers improved braking and sway control, though it's more complex and expensive than a regular receiver. Note that some of these systems are incompatible with each other—a load-equalizer hitch can interfere with surge brake operation, for example. Check with your equipment manufacturer before towing.

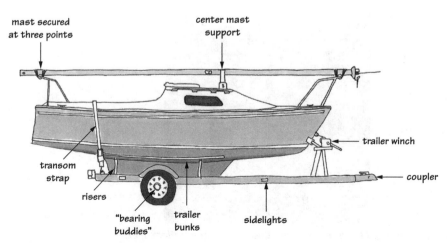

*A standard "float-on" sailboat trailer.*

I'm a firm believer in redundant safety systems for trailers. (See the sidebar "Making Your Trailer Safer.") Take transom straps, for example. These are wide straps that go across the back of the boat near the transom and keep the back end of the boat from shifting as she bounces down the highway. Transom straps are especially important if your trailer is equipped with roller bunks; with no transom strap, if the tiny trailer winch pawl fails, you may launch your boat right in the middle of the interstate. Neither of my trailerable sailboats

## Making Your Trailer Safer

There are several simple things you can do to make your trailer safer. First, if you don't have a transom strap, add one. These can be bought at most hardware stores as "ratcheting tie-down straps" for about twelve bucks. They are prone to rusting, so give them a squirt of WD-40 every now and again. The tie-down points need to be strongly welded to the frame, but this is a quick job for a welding shop. (Welding eyes to the trailer frame is far better than drilling a hole and bolting something in, which can weaken the frame.) If you do all the preparation, such as sanding away the paint in the area of the weld and bending a $^3/_8$-inch piece of round stock into a U-shape, the cost for the welding should be minimal.

These small U-shaped bits of steel can be useful in other areas as well. Welded to the upright, near the winch, they make the perfect anchor for a safety cable for the bow eye. Should the pawl in the trailer winch fail, the safety cable keeps the boat and the trailer together.

*A safety cable on the bow eye.*

Second, upgrade your safety chains; it's easy. You'll often see trailers with safety chains that are either undersized or so long they drag on the pavement. If a safety chain is too long and a loop is allowed to drag, is will quickly get ground away. The strength of a dragged chain will be a fraction of what it should be—the safety chains on my MacGregor were little more than wire slivers in some places.

You'll need a bolt cutter to cut off the old chain. New chains can be installed using threaded links. I like to use threaded links at both ends of the chain rather than the standard S-hooks, which can theoretically be rattled off. These are weaker than S-hooks, so you should use the largest size that will fit your chain. The threads should be lubricated with grease or they'll quickly seize up tight from corrosion.

Third, always carry a spare tire for your trailer. Even a used tire, if it holds air, is better than nothing and might get you to a service station. Most trailer suppliers sell large U-bolts that you can use to mount a spare to your trailer.

Finally, it isn't a bad idea to put together a dedicated tool kit for your trailer. Things to include might be a properly sized lug wrench, a can of spray lubricant, a pair of spare bearing sets, extra chain and links, extra bulbs, and maybe a can of touch-up paint. I once thought it would be clever to mount a tool box to the trailer, but then remembered my trailer would be mostly underwater during launching and haulout, so I decided it's better to keep these tools in the trunk of my car.

*My Montgomery 17 on the day I purchased it. This trailer is a small float-on type, with PVC guide poles along the sides to help position the boat correctly when retrieving. Note that there's no transom strap in place, so I tied on a length of stout line for the trip and added attachment points later.*

had transom straps when I bought them, and it appears that the trailers never had them from day one—I've had to add the straps and weld on the attachment points to both of my trailers. Now, it may be argued that you don't really need transom straps, as both boats went for nearly thirty years without them. But why take the chance? They're cheap and take but a moment to set up. Accidents do happen, but I like to think I've done everything possible to prevent them.

### Trailer Winches

Trailer winches come in two basic types—manual and electric. Unless your trailer has rollers, the winch won't be used to drag the boat up onto the trailer; rather, it will guide the boat into the proper position. Most trailerable sailboats are too big and bulky to respond to brute force, so electric winches aren't often seen on sailboat trailers. Trailer winches are simple affairs, consisting of a gear-operated drum with a pawl to prevent the drum from unwinding. Two-speed trailer winches are available, and

these can be handy. The winch should be solidly mounted on a strong pillar, and should use either a heavy belt or galvanized steel cable. An extra safety chain for the bow eye is a good idea, since winch pawls aren't tremendously strong—even tying the bow eye off with a short length of stout line would help.

Maintaining the trailer winch is a simple matter of keeping it clean and lubricated. If it looks suspect, don't trust it; replace it with a new one.

### Trailer Lights and Wiring

Federal regulations require that all trailers be equipped with tail lights, brake lights, side marker lights, turn signals, and side and rear reflectors. Since your trailer is regularly dunked in water, its wiring is particularly vulnerable, and failures are common. One recent development is LED lights for trailers, which, since they are sealed systems, are less susceptible to water-induced failures. You can extend the reliability of more common incandescent systems by giving all electrical contacts a dab

## What's Dielectric Grease?

Dielectric grease is useful in a lot of applications, but just what is the stuff, anyway? It turns out there's nothing special about dielectric grease. It isn't conductive, as you might assume—in fact, "dielectric" means a nonconductor of electricity. Its job is mainly to seal electrical contacts from oxygen, which prevents corrosion. It lubricates as well. Commercial dielectric grease compounds are usually silicone based. Just about any grease can work in a pinch, like wheel bearing grease or petroleum jelly, but petroleum jelly doesn't hold up when it gets hot, and wheel bearing grease is a little messier.

Now, in my area of the country at least, dielectric grease isn't that easy to find, and it seems that word dielectric on the packaging is worth several dollars. A cheaper alternative is faucet and valve grease, available in the plumbing department. This often silicone-based grease is waterproof, withstands higher temperatures, and is a whole lot cheaper. I paid $1.29 for a 1-ounce tube, whereas dielectric grease was $8 at an auto parts store.

Whichever you use, this type of grease is good to have in your toolbox, and regular use on electrical contacts can prevent all sorts of problems.

of dielectric grease, a squirt of silicone lubricant, WD-40, or wire dryer, available at most auto parts stores.

Mounting trailer lights on a removable board that can be securely mounted to the boat's transom is a good idea for two reasons—it elevates the lights to other drivers' eye level, and it keeps the lights out of the water when launching. Even trailer lights that are supposedly waterproof will fail if repeatedly dunked in water.

A frequent point of failure with trailer systems is the ground wire. It's common practice to ground the trailer wiring to the frame, and trailer electrical problems can often be traced to bad grounds. When you rewire a trailer—a pretty easy job, and new trailer tail lights usually include new wiring as well—consider taking the extra step of adding a dedicated ground wire for each of the lights. I use a green THWN stranded wire (*not* solid), available at hardware stores. Then solder all electrical connections, dab them with a little polyurethane caulk, and cover them with heat-shrink tubing. Secure all of the wiring to the frame every 18 inches, just as you should with the wiring on the boat. Never use wire nuts on trailer wires, even if they are supplied with new lights—save them for your house. I don't like using electrical tape, either.

Although it can be unwrapped for inspection, the glue gets all over the wires in short order, leaving a sticky mess. Heat-shrink tubing is cleaner, stronger, and more permanent.

The trailer wiring connector takes a lot of abuse because it's usually located under the car, where it's commonly splashed with dirt, rocks, and road mud. Don't let it drag along the road, as I did once, or the road will grind most of it away after a few miles. This is a good place for some dielectric grease—keeping both connectors lubricated will protect them from corrosion and extend the life of the sometimes-submerged connector.

### Trailer Tires and Bearings

Take a close look at your trailer's tires. If they look old or cracked or are bulging in strange places, you may want to replace them before you go flying down the highway. It would be a good thing to have a spare already mounted on a rim, but this isn't always possible. You should be aware that trailer tires are different from regular automobile tires. Car tires are designed for maximum traction, and they accomplish this with flexible sidewalls. On a trailer, however, flexible sidewall tires tend to sway, which is just what we *don't* want. Instead, trailer tires are made with thicker, stiffer sidewalls to resist sway. They are also designed for higher pressure to increase the load-carrying capacity. Trailer tires aren't available at every small-town service station, and it seems that tire dealers are always out of the one size or type of tire you need when you have a blowout. "Oh, we can order a tire for you, we'll have it in next week" might mean the end of your cruise that could be salvaged if you bring a spare. Your trailer may have an unusual rim size or smaller lug nuts. Check these details before you tow your boat anywhere, especially if you have a long road trip to your sailing destination.

You'll have to rely on the seller to tell you when the bearings were last serviced. A new bearing set isn't too expensive, usually $12 to $25 per hub. If you want a trailer shop to do the work, however, plan on spending a good bit more. It's worth learning how to replace trailer bearings. Your first bearing job might take an hour or two, but you'll learn how to shave that time down with a little practice. Bearing failures caused by neglect are far too common, and the effects resulting from a failed bearing can include a tire parting company with the axle at interstate speeds, which is not something you want to see in your rearview mirror.

So, check your bearings carefully. In fact, you should double- and triple-check them, because you don't want them to fail. Each time you set out with your trailer, drive a half mile or so and then pull over, get out of the car, and feel the bearings with your hand. Warm is OK, but hot is not good. If they are hot, you need to either do a roadside bearing replacement or call for help. This repair is doable if you have the tools and parts with you, but first move your boat—very slowly—to someplace safe (not the side of the highway unless your bearings have already burned out and your wheel is falling off).

There are different kinds of bearing caps. First is a plain steel bearing cap, indicating a standard bearing set that needs to be disassembled for lubrication. Second is a diaphragm cap. This cap is a little larger and has a

grease fitting in the middle. The idea is to fill the spring-loaded cap with grease, which keeps the grease in the bearing under a little bit of pressure. This pressure prevents water from entering the bearing when the trailer is immersed. A common brand is Bearing Buddy, but generic brands are also available. These work fairly well and do a good job of keeping the bearings lubricated, but reliance on them usually means bearings get less attention. Wheel bearings with either system should be taken apart, cleaned, and visually inspected at least once a year.

A third type of bearing cap—a bearing system, actually—looks like an ordinary cap, but when it's removed, you'll find a grease fitting under the cap, in the center of the axle. This is a spindle-lube system, and it's far superior to the first two. The axle has been drilled with small holes down the center and out to the back side of the inner bearing. When you pump grease into the grease fitting (you'll need a grease gun, of course), old grease gets forced out under pressure and new grease gets forced in, starting with the back bearing and working its way to the front. This kind of axle is available as a retrofit upgrade for many sailboat trailers, and will cost you around $150.

Yet another type of bearing system has become available for recreational trailers—the oil bath bearing. These use a liquid oil rather than grease for lubrication. The advantage is that the oil flows through and around the bearing surfaces, increasing lubrication and dissipating heat. The disadvantage is that they need careful installation and regular care to maintain the seals. If the seals fail and the oil flows out—well, imagine smoke, flames, and/or wheels flying off at highway speeds.

## Brakes

Many states require a separate braking system for trailers with a loaded weight over 1,500 pounds. These are either electrically controlled brakes, which can be automatically or manually activated, or surge brakes, which are activated by a master cylinder at the coupler.

Electrical systems are vulnerable to water intrusion, so hydraulic surge brakes are more popular. The hydraulic system of the tow vehicle should never be directly connected to the hydraulic system on the trailer—they should always be independent. Trailer brakes often suffer from corrosion, since they get hot in use and are then dipped in water when the boat is launched. Trailer brakes are usually best installed and maintained with the help of a professional mechanic, though he or she can certainly give you advice about maintaining them. One thing your mechanic will tell you is to wait a few minutes at the ramp before you launch your boat so the brakes can cool off. Some trailers include flush kits that allow you to rinse the brake assemblies with fresh water. If your trailer has one, use it regularly. Otherwise, rinse the wheels and brakes with fresh water using a garden hose, especially after every launching in salt water. But be advised—wet brakes don't stop very well and should be allowed to dry out before you hit the highway.

## Optional Equipment

Some optional equipment for sailboat trailers is extremely useful. One item is a coupling extension. This can be built into the trailer, using a sliding tube, or may be a separate assembly that connects to the trailer's coupling. There's also a bolt-on hitch extension that will fit a standard trailer. Either way, the result is the same—the trailer will be farther away from the launch vehicle. With some deep-draft boats and shallow ramps, it's the only way to get a boat off the trailer.

Another handy add-on is a keel guide. These are often nothing more than extra carpet-covered boards that channel the keel into position on the center of the trailer. Some owners say that keel guides are essential features and they wouldn't have a trailer without them.

A good trailer will come with a trailer tongue jack. This can be used to raise or lower the trailer tongue, and is essential for hitching or unhitching the trailer by yourself. If the boat is loaded with the proper tongue weight, it's the

*A pivoting trailer tongue jack. Trailer jacks can be fixed or pivoting, with or without wheels. This one pivots out of the way when not needed.*

only way to safely raise the tongue. Some jacks have wheels, and they may be fixed or pivoting. The pivoting types are handy, as they won't decouple the trailer if they hit a rise in the ramp, but the fixed types are generally stronger.

Side-view mirrors are a handy safety feature that is often overlooked. A sailboat on a trailer is so wide and high that it's pretty much impossible to see what's behind you using the factory mirrors on your car. Some side-view types clip onto your existing side-view mirrors and cost less than $20. You can see a great deal better with extended-view mirrors, and they may be required by some states.

## TRAILER TONGUE WEIGHT AND CONTROLLING SWAY

One of the most basic trailering problems is insufficient trailer tongue weight. Measured at the coupler, the trailer tongue should weigh about 10 percent of the total trailer weight. When I bought my MacGregor, the seller proudly told me how the boat and trailer were balanced so that you could easily lift the tongue with one hand. I didn't realize then that this was an extremely dangerous, underloaded condition. I'm sure glad he was the one doing the towing! Lack of tongue weight causes a significant increase in sway, which is a rhythmic side-to-side motion of the trailer behind the tow vehicle. It also increases the chance that the trailer will bounce off the hitch ball. One easy way to increase tongue weight is to remove the motor from the stern bracket and stow it inside the boat, as far forward as possible. (WARNING: Drain all gas from the motor's fuel lines and carburetor first.) The motor mount and transom aren't designed for trailering with the motor attached, and you can easily damage both. You'll also make your expensive motor less accessible to rest-stop thieves, but be sure to wedge the motor in securely. You don't want the heavy motor to shift while driving. A better solution is to build a simple motor mount on the trailer's winch post, and to secure it with a lock.

Having said this, it's important to note that increasing tongue weight isn't a cure-all. Too much tongue weight can lead to a dangerous condition called trailer dive. During a panic stop, inertia causes the trailer to press down heavily on the hitch. Heavy downward pressure at the rear of the vehicle causes the towing vehicle's front wheels to lift, and if the weight is sufficient, you lose much of your braking power as well as your steering—hardly what you want in a panic stop. Heavy loads that are carried high—for instance, a fixed-keel sailboat—increase trailer dive. The only remedy is a lighter load or a weight-distributing hitch.

Controlling trailer sway is extremely important. A trailer that sways back and forth is very dangerous, the third most common cause of trailering accidents. If your trailer sways, reduce the speed gradually. Don't slam on the brakes. Avoid sudden steering changes—you can't steer out of a sway situation. Incorrect weight distribution is a primary cause of sway, though there are other causes, like incorrect tires or tire pressures. Your tongue weight

## A Simple Forward Motor Mount

An easy trailer modification is to add a forward motor mount. This is nothing more than a sizable piece of angle steel (an L-shaped steel commonly sold by steel suppliers; it comes in 20-foot lengths but can be cut by the supplier for a small fee) bolted or welded to the trailer's winch post with some plywood clamping pads. You might want to include a chain or cable to lock your motor while trailering. I wouldn't store the motor here permanently, however. Move it to the garage or basement once you get home from your cruise.

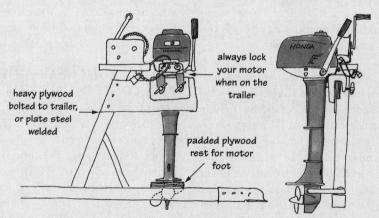

heavy plywood bolted to trailer, or plate steel welded

always lock your motor when on the trailer

padded plywood rest for motor foot

*A simple forward motor mount.*

*Trailer dive is caused by too much weight on the trailer's tongue.*

should be 10 to 15 percent of the total gross trailer weight; with nearly all trailerable sailboats, that means it's too heavy to pick up the tongue and move the boat around by hand. If this is the way you normally move your boat around the driveway, then either you're an incredibly strong person with back problems in your future, or your trailer is incorrectly loaded. Seek advice from a trailer repair shop. They should have scales to determine the exact weight of your trailer and what your tongue weight should be, and they can be an invaluable source of advice. Some axles can be adjusted slightly, and the shop folks will know the correct procedure. They'll also tell you if critical parts look weak and need to be replaced. Even brandnew trailers need adjusting sometimes, and you can benefit by having a shop look over your rig.

# OUTFITTING AND HANDLING YOUR SAILBOAT

# CHAPTER FIVE

## Equipment

Just what equipment should be aboard a trailer sailer? Like so many things in life, that's a simple question with a complex answer. You can be as minimalist or as gadget-oriented as you like; most people fall somewhere in between. One sailor may find a particular accessory an essential part of sailing and can't imagine leaving the dock without it. Another sailor may find the same gadget an expensive waste of very limited space. Still another may find it useful but feel that its weight slows his boat speed. All these points of view are valid. My purpose, for this discussion, is to give you a framework for making your own decisions.

Of course, I've got my own biases and opinions, and I'll mention if I've found a particular thing useful in my travels. But there's lots of equipment I haven't tried yet, especially the costlier items. I've never sailed on a boat with an electric windlass, for example, and the ground tackle on most trailer sailers is light enough that this piece of equipment is unnecessary. But if you are cruising a larger trailer sailer—in the 25-foot range, for example—in

an area with lots of coral heads, and you use an all-chain anchor rode, then an electric windlass might not be such a superfluous expense.

I lean toward the minimalist/traditional side of things, within reason. My boat has a house electrical system and a motor, though some sailors go without these things and are quite happy. I admire these people, and I love sailing with them. I often learn alternative ways to do things from the way they keep their boats. But I like the extra security of having a motor and a depth sounder. Yes, this equipment can and does break down and requires maintenance, which takes time away from sailing. But having these things aboard has made sailing more enjoyable for me, and that's usually the best test of whether a piece of optional equipment stays or goes.

### USCG-REQUIRED EQUIPMENT

We start with the U.S. Coast Guard–required equipment, which must be aboard your vessel for it to be legal. (The equipment that is legally required aboard recreational boats is subject to change. I have relied on the publication

"Federal Requirements and Safety Tips for Recreational Boaters" for the information in this section. An electronic version of this publication can be found online at www.uscgboating.org/safety/fedreqs/landing.htm.) This is a basic, bare-bones list of safety equipment, and most boatowners are encouraged to go beyond this minimum.

The U.S. Coast Guard sets standards for this equipment; to be fully within the law, the equipment must be marked "Coast Guard–Approved Equipment." Ski belts are a good example—some people think that these are personal flotation devices, or PFDs, since they do help people stay afloat, but they are not Coast Guard–approved PFDs. If this is all you have aboard, expect to be fined if inspected by the Coast Guard, or (heaven forbid) sued if a passenger on your vessel drowns.

## Personal Flotation Devices (PFDs)

PFDs—also known as life jackets—are the most basic, commonsense items to have aboard any boat. The Coast Guard lists five approved types of PFDs: four wearable types (Type I, II, III, or V) and one throwable type (Type IV). There must be at least one wearable PFD for each person on board. PFDs must be Coast Guard approved, in good, serviceable condition, and appropriately sized for the intended user. This is especially important if you have young children aboard—adult-sized PFDs won't work for them. In addition, you must have at least one throwable PFD on board.

PFDs must be readily accessible. They're of little help if you have to dig through a pile of inflatable toys and fishing gear to get to them. You must be able to put them on quickly in an emergency. They should not be stowed in plastic bags or in locked or closed compartments. Throwable devices must be available for immediate use in order for them to be accepted as legal equipment.

Though not specifically required in all cases, it's best if a PFD is worn at all times when the vessel is under way. A PFD can save your life, but only if you wear it. Try several

## Coast Guard Life Jacket Classifications

Exactly what are the different types of PFDs? Here are the Coast Guard classifications:

*Type I* is an "Off-Shore Life Preserver," designed to turn an unconscious wearer to a face-up position. An adult Type I PFD has at least 22 pounds of buoyancy.

*Type II* is a "Near-Shore Buoyancy Aid." This type will also turn an unconscious person face-up, but its turning force isn't as great. It's designed for calm inland waters where there's a good chance of a rapid rescue. Adult Type II PFDs have 15.5 pounds of buoyancy.

*Type III* is a "Flotation Aid." These can be the most comfortable, and are often tailored to the wearer's activity, like fishing, kayaking, or waterskiing. The downside of this comfort is that there is often no turning ability, and the device may not keep the wearer's face clear in rough water. It has 15.5 pounds of buoyancy and is designed for inland water use.

*Type IV* is a "Throwable," designed to be held by the user until rescued. Typically, it's what you toss to a person who has fallen overboard. Floating seat cushions are very common throwables, but horseshoe buoys or the Lifesling would be a good choice to have on board in addition to floating cushions.

Type I PFD          Type II PFD

*Type I (left) and II (right) PFDs. Type I offshore vests are bulkier but have much more buoyancy.*

(Continued)

*Type V* is a "Special Use Device." This category can include manually inflatable paddlesports vests or "float jackets," where a PFD is integrated with a rain jacket. You need to check the label carefully with Type Vs, though—in some cases, a Type V must be worn by the user to satisfy the PFD regulation.

*A Type III PFD is easily upgraded by adding reflective patches and a whistle.*

*A Type III special-purpose PFD, a ski vest.*

*A Type IV throwable PFD cushion.*

different types and buy a properly fitting PFD for each crewmember.

While the Coast Guard requirements for PFDs can be satisfied easily and cheaply, your requirements might be quite different, especially if you've just fallen overboard in a storm and your boat and crew are sailing away at a blistering pace. A dark head bobbing in the water is a mighty small target to see. Some simple and inexpensive additions include patches of reflective tape sewn to the PFD, along with a few Velcro pockets. These could hold a flare or two, a whistle or mini air horn, a plastic distress flag, and a flashlight or personal strobe. More expensive items include a personal EPIRB (see the sidebar "What's an EPIRB?"), now available for about $250. A little expensive, maybe, but what's a life worth these days? At the very least, all your PFDs should have reflective patches and whistles.

## Visual Distress Signals

Visual distress signals (VDS) are required for most boats, with a few exceptions. If you operate your vessel in U.S. coastal waters (that is, within 12 nautical miles of the U.S. coastline), the Great Lakes, or the U.S. territorial seas, visual distress signals must be on board. If you sail only in small lakes and rivers, then you might be able to get away with not carrying day signals—check the Coast Guard regulations. Some exceptions to the day signal

## What's an EPIRB?

EPIRB stands for emergency position-indicating radio beacon. An EPIRB is a sailor's last best chance for rescue, only to be activated if you're in the water and the boat is sailing away under autopilot, or the boat has gone down or is about to do so—all extremely unpleasant thoughts. Activating an EPIRB starts an international chain of events using satellites, monitoring stations, a mission control center, and local search and rescue agencies or the Coast Guard. The system allows rescue operators to locate you quickly, without having to conduct a wide area search that can easily be futile. A person in a life raft or in the water is often invisible from a helicopter.

The EPIRB system has been in place since the 1970s, but the older Class A and Class B VHF units will not be monitored after February 2009, so be sure to look for the newer, more accurate 406 MHz EPIRBs. These units are able to locate within a 2-nautical-mile radius. The 406 EPIRBs broadcast a unique identification code that allows the mission control center to determine your name, phone number, vessel type, and emergency contact information, which enables them to verify your itinerary before scrambling the troops. This greatly reduces the number of very expensive false alarms. EPIRBs can be combined with a built-in GPS to transmit your exact position along with the locator radio signal.

A new class of EPIRB is called a personal locator beacon, or PLB. These smaller, less expensive EPIRBs work nearly as well as the larger units. While the large 406 EPIRBs are marine only, PLBs can be used anywhere. Weighing under a pound, they are small enough to be worn with a life jacket. Electronically, PLBs are very similar to the large 406 EPIRBs, but the battery lasts half as long, they don't have a strobe, and they aren't required to float (though most sold for the boating market do).

Both 406 EPIRBs and PLBs must be registered with NOAA/SARSAT, but this is easy. Register online at http://www.beaconregistration.noaa.gov/. Prices currently run from about $500 for a PLB with GPS to about $1,200 for a fully automatic auto-release 406 EPIRB.

Do you need an EPIRB on a trailer sailer? Like everything else, it depends on where you're going. Daysailing within sight of land? Probably not. Heading offshore for a long trip? Can't hurt, especially one of the smaller PLB types. If you take only one long trip per year and daysail the rest of the time, check out the BoatU.S. EPIRB rental program.

requirement include small boats (under 16 feet), boats participating in organized events like regattas, and open sailboats without motors. All vessels are required to carry night signals when operating at night.

Several different types of visual distress signals will keep you USCG compliant. In a nutshell, they are divided into day signals and night signals, pyrotechnic and nonpyrotechnic. Pyrotechnic means flares and smoke signals. Three red meteor flares that have not expired (flares are dated just like a gallon of milk—they are usually good for about three years) and are rated for day and night use will make you legal, though you might want more ways to call for help if your engine conks out and you're being swept out to sea by the current.

Nonpyrotechnic options include a distress flag, which is a large (at least 3 feet square) orange flag with a black circle and a square. Naturally, this is only a daytime signal. A nonpyrotechnic nighttime signal would be an electric distress light, but in order to fulfill the VDS requirement, this light must automatically flash the international SOS distress signal (. . . — . . .) and must be marked "Night Visual Distress Signal for Boats. Complies with U.S. Coast Guard Requirements in 46 CFR 161.013. For Emergency Use Only." (Note that under the inland rules, a rapidly flashing light, such as a strobe, can be used to indicate a vessel in distress, but curiously these types of strobes are *not* considered distress signals under the VDS requirement.)

## Why Aren't Strobe Lights Legal?

Strobe lights have a lot going for them as distress signals. They are very bright, effective attention-getters, and they last a long time under low battery power. Small waterproof strobes are available for use on life jackets and can greatly increase the chances of finding a crew lost overboard, even in daylight. A permanently mounted masthead strobe has prevented more than one collision between sailboats and large commercial ships at sea.

So why aren't strobe lights accepted as legal visual distress signals by the Coast Guard? The reason probably has to do with COLREGS, the International Regulations for Avoiding Collisions at Sea. These are sometimes called the International Rules of the Road. Under COLREGS rule 36, "Any light to attract the attention of another vessel shall be such that it cannot be mistaken for any aid to navigation. For the purpose of this Rule the use of high-intensity intermittent or revolving lights, such as strobe lights, shall be avoided."

The U.S. Inland Rules are different. In Annex IV, Distress Signals, subpart 87.1, Need of Assistance, "The following signals indicate distress and need of assistance: A high-intensity white light flashing at regular intervals from 50 to 70 times per minute." So while strobe lights aren't specifically legal for use in international waters, I personally wouldn't hesitate to use one if my vessel were in any sort of danger, and I have one on board my trailer sailer. I keep flares to meet the nighttime VDS requirement.

## Fire Extinguishers

Hopefully you'll never need to use one of these, but any fire aboard a boat is serious. The Coast Guard requirements are very specific and contain provisions for inboard-powered boats and larger boats, but for the size we're talking about here—under 26 feet—the rules can be summarized by saying you must have at least one Type B-I (5-BC or higher rating) portable fire extinguisher. A typical Type B-I fire extinguisher contains 2 pounds of dry chemical, such as sodium bicarbonate (baking soda), and can be purchased for less than $20. It's not a bad idea to carry more than one fire extinguisher—one for the cockpit, near the engine and gasoline, and one near the galley.

Type B-II fire extinguishers hold twice as much dry chemical and aren't much more expensive than B-I. Of course, you can spend more on a fire extinguisher if you want—Kiddie Halotron 1 Portables are USCG approved and leave no residue whatsoever, whereas dry chemical fire extinguishers are messy (though not as messy as a hull that's burned to the waterline). Expect to pay around $185 for a 5-BC type Halotron 1 extinguisher. Remember that grease fires can sometimes be extinguished by the quick application of a lid, and some fires are made worse by adding water.

Replace your fire extinguisher(s) once every few years, but don't throw the old ones away—use them to practice. In a safe area onshore, start a small fire and put it out with your old fire extinguisher. What you learn may surprise you.

## Ventilation

On a trailerable sailboat, a forced-air ventilation system or a bilge blower is required for gasoline inboard engines with electrical starters. Outboard motors get plenty of ventilation when mounted on a bracket. The big concern is fuel storage—where do you keep your fuel tanks? If you keep them stored in a locker, then that locker must be ventilated with a natural, or passive, system with at least two ventilator ducts fitted with cowls. This usually means both a forward-facing and an aft-facing cowl. (A cowl is a device designed to direct airflow into or out of a duct.)

## Sound-Producing Devices

On a trailerable sailboat, this means a horn. Usually a small compressed-air horn is best. We used to call them Freon horns, but now they use an ozone-safe gas. Unless they're stainless steel, you'll want to renew these every few years—exposure to sunlight can make the plastic weak and brittle, and the cans get rusty. Some horns are quite small and would be really nice to have attached to a life jacket if you were to fall overboard while your off-watch crew was sleeping below. I don't mean to make light of this situation—I once

## Keep Your Horn Ready

I once had the unfortunate experience of being aboard my boat during a hurricane. Hugo didn't change course as the navy's internal weather reports expected it to, and I was anchored 20 miles upriver along with several other boats. During the night, one of the anchor lines on a large powerboat upwind of me parted. The captain was attempting to hold his position by powering into the storm. After six hours of this, he was getting tired and not keeping a good lookout astern—where I was. Late that night, I noticed him getting closer and closer. When he didn't gun his engines and power away as usual, I started thinking, "Maybe I should use my horn about now." In a panic, I threw open my seat locker and started digging through lines, winch handles, and sailing gloves trying to get to my horn. When I finally got it in my hands and blew a long blast, he was about 25 feet away. When he gunned his engines and pulled away, I could smell his exhaust—not that remarkable, except the wind was blowing in excess of 140 knots.

Ever since then, I've kept my horn in a little dedicated pocket on deck, mounted on the side of the cockpit. When you need your horn, you're going to need it *fast*, so keep it in a place where you can find it in seconds.

read a nightmare tale of a woman who was cruising offshore with her husband. She woke up from a nap and came on deck. The boat was sailing nicely along under autopilot. Her husband was gone, presumably fallen overboard, and was never found.

### Navigation Lights

If you operate your boat after sunset, you are required to display navigation lights. The requirements for sailboats can be tricky, since they are considered powerboats when the engine is running and must display one set of lights, but if they are under sail alone, they must display a different set of lights. For most trailerable sailboats, we can summarize the navigation light requirements by saying you need red and green bow lights, a white stern light, and a white all-around masthead anchor light. You'll need a separate switch for the stern light and the anchor light, because sailboats under 39.4 feet may display:

A bicolor bow light and white all-around masthead light (anchor light) when under power (*no stern light*)

A bicolor bow light and white 135-degree stern light when under sail (*no masthead light*)

While you're anchored, you need to display a 360-degree white light "where it can best be

seen." Usually, the best place for this is at the masthead, but you can suspend an anchor light from the rigging. This is possibly a better location than the masthead, because if you are anchored and another vessel approaches on a dark night, your boat is more noticeable when its anchor light is closer to the hull.

If your boat is under 23 feet, the rules state that you *should* display lights as above, but as an option you can carry only a flashlight to show in sufficient time to prevent a collision. I certainly wouldn't want to depend on a flashlight to keep me from being run over, however. The rule is intended for a smaller boat—a Sunfish, say, or a ship's tender—that gets caught out after dark. A flashlight may satisfy the rules, but this isn't the safest situation.

For small boats like dinghies, you can now get really neat self-contained LED navigation lights. They use significantly less energy than incandescent bulbs and look similar to a flashlight. There are several different mounting styles, including suction cup, clamp-on, and inflatable mounts.

### Pollution Regulations

New laws aimed at controlling water pollution have affected recreational sailors, but the regulations affect only boats that are 26 feet and larger. While you are not legally required to display Discharge of Oil Prohibited or Discharge of Garbage Prohibited placards if you sail a vessel under 26 feet, you are still required to know and abide by these laws. If you've got the space, it doesn't hurt to screw these placards to a bulkhead. The Discharge of Oil Prohibited placard reads:

### DISCHARGE OF OIL PROHIBITED

*The Federal Water Pollution Control Act prohibits the discharge of oil or oily waste upon or into any navigable waters of the U.S. The prohibition includes any discharge which causes a film or discoloration of the surface of the water or causes a sludge or emulsion beneath the surface of the water. Violators are subject to substantial civil and/or criminal sanctions including fines and imprisonment.*

Although the placard is optional on most trailerables, spill cleanup materials are required if your boat has a motor that uses gas or oil. The USCG Federal Regulations website says:

On recreational vessels, a bucket, oil absorbent pads and heavy duty plastic bag, bailer or portable pump are some suitable means that meet the requirement for retention on board until transferring the oily mixture to a reception facility. No person may intentionally drain oil or oily waste from any source into the bilge of any vessel. You must immediately notify the U.S. Coast Guard if your vessel discharges oil or hazardous substances in the water. Call toll-free 800-424-8802 (in Washington, D.C. (202) 267-3675).

You can put these materials together yourself for minimal cost. Sealed in a plastic bag, they should last indefinitely if kept dry. A company called Dawg sells an economy spill kit for $33. Most kits contain bilge socks and special oil-only pads that will absorb oil, not water. Bilge socks are made of a similar oil-absorbent material and are shaped like a tube. These materials are also readily available at most boat chandleries.

One thing you don't want to do is disperse a spill by adding detergent. This breaks the surface tension of the water, allowing the pollutant to sink, where it's more difficult to clean. It continues to damage the ecosystem on the bottom, and it will bring you a hefty fine. You can learn more about ecologically sound boating with the "Help Stop the Drops" program from BoatU.S.; for more information, go to www.boatus.com/foundation/cleanwater/drops.

Garbage discharge laws require a similar placard on boats over 26 feet. Again, though most trailer sailers are legally exempt from displaying the placard (but not exempt from the rules), posting the notice is a good idea. The placard reads:

The Act to Prevent Pollution from Ships (MARPOL ANNEX V) places limitations on the discharge of garbage from vessels. It is illegal to dump plastic trash anywhere in the ocean or navigable waters of the United States. It is also illegal to discharge garbage in the navigable waters of the United States, including inland waters as well as anywhere in the Great Lakes. The discharge of other types of garbage is permitted outside of specific distances offshore as determined by the nature of that garbage.

**Garbage Type**
Plastics, including synthetic ropes, fishing nets, and plastic bags—**Prohibited in all areas.**
Floating dunnage, lining and packing materials—**Prohibited less than 25 miles from nearest land.**
Food waste, paper, rags, glass, metal, bottles, crockery and similar refuse—**Prohibited less than 12 miles from nearest land.**
Comminuted or ground food waste, paper, rags, glass, etc.—**Prohibited less than 3 miles from nearest land.**
United States vessels of 26 feet or longer must display in a prominent location, a durable placard at least 4 by 9 inches notifying the crew and passengers of the discharge restrictions.

When I lived on board my first boat back in 1992, this law hadn't been passed. But we (meaning the liveaboard community at the marina) knew how deadly plastic was to marine life. I can clearly remember my good friend and slipmate Larry Lee cutting the rings of plastic bottle carriers before throwing them in the trash, just in case they found their way to a garbage barge that was dumped offshore. (I still cut these up before I throw them away.) We would, however, sink empty glass bottles, thinking that these were fairly inert and wouldn't harm the environment. But the MARPOL regulation brings a "pack it in, pack it out" requirement to coastal sailing and cruising, and that's a good thing. You can't sink a bottle anymore unless you're 12 miles offshore. This may seem like an environmental regulation that goes a little too far, but it's important. If these rules are enforced and followed, our impact on the sea that we all love will be reduced to almost nil, and our children will be able to enjoy the same beauty that we do. Now, if we could just solve the problem of global warming and rising sea temperatures with a placard . . .

You'll notice that I haven't addressed another "trash" issue that no one likes to talk about but everyone has to deal with, and that's the problem of human waste. There are several options, and I discuss those in depth in Chapter 15, but for now it's important to know that there's one place this stuff *can't* go, and that's overboard. The days of cedar buckets as an effective solution are gone forever.

## MSDs

The Coast Guard regulations regarding human waste appear in a section on marine sanitation devices, or MSDs, and apply only to permanently installed heads. Most trailer sailers have some kind of portable toilet (see Chapter 15). However, some larger trailer sailers have a permanently installed head. Basically the regulations simply require that the head be connected to a holding tank that can be emptied at a pumpout station. (It was common

practice on older boats to pipe the head outlet directly overboard, an installation that is now illegal.) Pumpouts are usually located at marinas and some state-run facilities and are much more common than they once were.

MSD regulations can be a thorny subject and are apt to change. There are certain cruising areas where any provision to pump waste overboard—even if it is a locked Y-valve installation (where one hose connects to a deck pumpout fitting and the other to a through-hull for overboard discharge)—has been declared illegal. It's best to check with the Coast Guard before making any changes to your MSD system to make sure the regulations haven't changed.

## OPTIONAL EQUIPMENT

If you are buying a brand-new, empty boat, the list of USCG-required equipment may seem pretty extensive, but it is far from complete. There are several items that aren't specifically required but you'll certainly need for your boat. Other pieces of equipment aren't so much needed as nice to have.

### Anchors

It is almost unbelievable that anchors are not required equipment on boats. In 2005, two teenage boys from Charleston, South Carolina, set out for a little fishing in a small boat—a JY15 with no mast or sails (they were using it as a rowboat). They hadn't heard about the small craft advisory for that day. They were aiming for a sandbar that was perhaps 50 yards out in a protected inlet, but between the shore and the sandbar was a strong rip current. They realized almost immediately that they were in trouble but couldn't row or swim the boat back to shore. Six days later they were found by a fishing boat off Cape Fear, North Carolina, nearly 111 miles from where they started. They were alive—barely.

While an anchor might not have *prevented* this very close call, it probably would have slowed them down enough that they might have been rescued sooner. Over a hundred

Coast Guard personnel were involved in an extensive search, but their drift rate was faster than computer models suggested and they were quickly swept out of the search area. (Then again, their boat had no safety equipment on board whatsoever, and just about anything would have helped. But as all teenagers know, they are immortal and tend to stay out of trouble.)

Of course, every boat should always carry anchors (along with life jackets, distress signals, and other emergency equipment). When the weather begins to sour, sailboats, being naturally slower vessels, cannot run for cover as quickly as a planing powerboat, so good ground tackle becomes very important.

Different types of anchors have their own sets of strengths and weaknesses, and no one type of anchor is best for all bottom conditions. What you carry on board will depend on your local conditions, the space available, and your experience. Some people think I'm nuts for carrying three anchors, but I've seen conditions when all three were needed. Seek the advice of others about anchors, especially those with local knowledge. Here's a very brief summary of anchor types to get you started.

### Danforth Anchors

These popular lightweight anchors have pivoting flukes. They are usually a good all-around choice and are best in hard sand or mud.

Fortress aluminum anchors are Danforth types and are often carried aboard trailerables as a second anchor because of their very light weight.

### Plow, CQR, and Delta Anchors

These anchors look similar to an old-time single turning plow that was pulled by a mule. The shaft can be either pivoting, as in the CQR, or fixed, as in the Delta. Best in sand, weeds, grass, and rocky bottoms.

### Bruce or "Claw" Anchors

A Bruce anchor performs much like a plow but with a lighter weight; reportedly resets quickly if the boat pivots and the anchor breaks out.

A plow anchor.

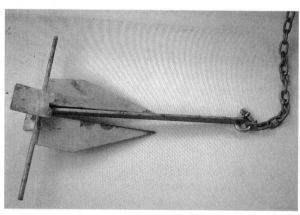

A Danforth anchor.

A Delta and a Spade anchor on a double roller. Some anchor shapes make them difficult to stow.

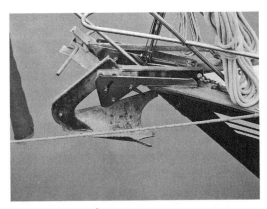

*A SuperMax anchor.*

*A Bruce anchor.*

### Yachtsman or Herreshoff Anchors

This more traditional type of anchor is reminiscent of something you'd see tattooed on Popeye's forearm. It's not normally used among recreational boats but has been reported to hold when nothing else would.

### Mushroom Anchors and "Hookers"

Mushroom "anchors" are usually seen in discount stores as little vinyl-covered things. I'm not quite sure who buys them or what they're used for. They certainly aren't used as anchors, though giant versions work as moorings.

"Hookers"—they really are called that, an unfortunate name if you're trying to research them online—are inexpensive anchors with a long U-shaped rod shaft and a ring. You'll find these at flea markets and used boat places, mainly because, although they make

fine decorations, they don't work that well as anchors. A 1994 anchor test in San Francisco by U.S. Sailing showed this anchor "had no interest in sticking to anything" and had a pull of about 60 pounds as it dragged along the bottom. Even when the flukes were forced in by hand, the anchor popped out at 95 pounds. They'd make good garden decorations or something to drag behind the car of a newly married couple.

Some new types of anchors (such as the Barnacle, Bullwagga, Spade, and SuperMax) have been developed that may prove useful in the future, but they haven't yet seen widespread use. These might work for you if they're offered in small sizes. *Practical Sailor* has done several very good anchor test articles over the years; check their results before spending a lot of money on an unfamiliar type.

I carry three anchors aboard my current boat *Tiny Dancer*—one small Danforth, one large Danforth, and a Delta plow-type. I firmly believe that anchors are not an area for economy. When I was a liveaboard I had two anchors—one was a genuine Danforth, but the larger storm anchor was a low-cost Danforth copy that was rated for a boat three times bigger

*My anchor collection: a small Danforth with 12 feet of chain and 100 feet of nylon rode (left); a Delta plow with 15 feet of chain and 150 feet of nylon rode (center); another older, larger Danforth from a previous boat with about 15 feet of chain and 75 feet of rode (right).*

than my boat. After a particularly bad storm (Hurricane Hugo), my smaller genuine Danforth was undamaged, but the half-inch shaft on the big storm anchor was bent over 45 degrees. Ever since then, I've believed in spending the money to buy good, name-brand anchors.

Size isn't everything when it comes to anchors. Small, lightweight anchors sometimes set better than large anchors, and they are certainly easier to store and handle. I keep the small anchor at the bow, ready to go over at a moment's notice. Its light weight doesn't impact the boat's sailing ability as much as a heavier anchor would. It is generally better to keep heavy stuff off the very ends of the boat, and since trailer sailers are by nature lighter craft, it pays to keep this in mind. My other anchors live in the cockpit locker and are brought out when anchoring for the night.

### How Heavy Should Your Anchors Be?

Actually, this is a pretty tricky question. There is a standard answer—the usual tables published for a 20-foot sailboat show that the "lunch hook" should hold to about 90 pounds, the working anchor needs to hold to 360 pounds, and the storm anchor should be able to hold to 720 pounds before breaking out. If you were using three standard Danforth anchors, this translates to a 3.5-pound lunch hook (with 160 pounds of holding power), a 5-pound working anchor (with 300 pounds of holding power), and a 14-pound storm anchor (with 920 pounds of holding power). Other anchor types list recommended boat sizes rather than holding power. For example, an 11-pound Simpson-Lawrence claw is recommended for 17- to 22-foot boats.

Going with the manufacturer's recommendations is probably your best bet, though a 3.5-pound Danforth is pretty tiny. I think I'd go up to a 5-pounder, because handling either anchor is pretty easy. Some recent work suggests that the long-published and accepted estimates of wind loading don't reflect real-world conditions. A lightweight boat with a fin keel tends to yaw during a high wind or sail around the anchor, first to port, then to starboard. As she does this, the wind loading on the boat increases as she shows more of her broadside to the wind. I've experienced this firsthand: in a very high wind, my Catalina 27 would yaw at anchor until she had the wind on the beam, bringing huge loads on her anchors and rodes.

In a really heavy storm, everything should be increased a size or two—anchor, rode, chain, and shackle. But, conversely, I've come to believe that a light, small anchor has value, too. A smaller anchor will bite in and set with less power, while a larger anchor may not bite very far under power. If it isn't set well, you might not discover this until the wind starts blowing, which isn't a good time to get bad news about your anchor set. And the wind never blows while you're setting the anchor—it seems to always start about 3 a.m. I used to think bigger was always better when it came to anchors, but I've changed my thinking. Most of the time I use a small (but high-quality) Danforth Deepset for anchoring, and it seems to be working quite well. I use my Delta for overnights.

### Anchor Rodes

All of the gear that attaches the anchor to the boat is called the rode. On nearly all trailer sailers, the rode consists of a line and a length of chain.

The most commonly used anchor line is three-strand or braided nylon. It's strong, doesn't rot, and, most important, it's stretchy—it can stretch 15 to 25 percent under a load. This helps absorb shock loads as the boat surges at anchor. (In fact, I keep a length of small nylon three-strand to use as a shock absorber. One end is tied to the anchor line; the other end is led to the sheet winches. In a storm, it acts like a giant bungee cord, stretching and distributing shock loads to several points on the boat.)

Much less desirable but more common is cheap polypropylene rope, which has poor knot strength, rapidly degrades in sunlight, and floats, which tends to foul other boats' props.

Most anchors should have some chain attached to them. The weight of the chain helps hold the anchor shaft parallel to the bottom, and few anchors will set properly without some chain before the rode. Although heavy chain is cumbersome, that weight is essential. Cruising sailors recommend using all-chain rodes, but this isn't practical for most trailer sailers. All-chain rodes usually require a windlass to haul aboard, and the weight of the rode would be tough for a small, light boat to cope with.

Remember that the entire rode is a "chain" in terms of the weakest link. Ten feet of chain before the anchor is good, but longer is better. Anchor shackles are metal clips that connect the chain to the anchor and line (see photo). They are weaker than the chain in the same size and should be rated for a similar breaking strength. Shackles often seize up tight. A common practice is to screw the pin in all the way, then back it out a quarter turn. You can coat the threads with Desitin, Never-Seez, or dielectric grease. It's imperative to secure the shackle pin so that it doesn't work loose. Stainless or Monel wire works, but I've found that electric fence wire costs very little and resists corrosion well. Be sure to dress sharp wire ends so they don't cut your hands. Another noncorroding option is nylon cable ties (often called zip ties). The black ones resist UV radiation better than white. The line should have a thimble—a teardrop-shaped insert—to resist chafe. Special nylon thimbles are good to prevent the thimble from working loose as the eye splice stretches, and seizings around stainless steel thimbles will keep them secure. Other types of connectors are available, though questions have been raised about their strength and the materials used. Swivels should generally be avoided because of strength issues. The big advantage of patented anchor connectors is that they won't foul an anchor windlass. Since most trailer sailors won't need a windlass, you shouldn't need anything more than a standard shackle.

Mark your anchor line so you have some idea how much rode is out. You can buy premade

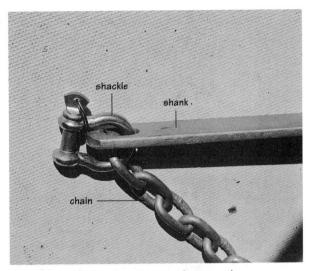

*Anchor shackle and chain properly secured.*

plastic tags, but a few turns of dark thread or tape works just as well. Something that can be identified by feel yet won't snag as it passes through a fairlead is ideal. Wrap a single band of thread at 25 feet, two bands at 50 feet, three bands at 75 feet, and a wrap of tape at 100 feet. Then you continue the sequence: a band of tape plus a single band of thread is 125 feet, and so on. With my rode marked this way, I never have to guess how much of it is in the water.

## Lifelines, Harnesses, Tethers, and Jacklines

We all want to keep ourselves and our crew from falling off the boat. Double lifelines rigged with strong stanchions are a good idea. I know they add windage, tend to snag shrouds as you're raising the mast, and generally complicate things. Nevertheless, I'm extremely nervous working a deck with no lifelines, and I tend to hug the fiberglass like a leech. Anyone who has ever sailed with children aboard will tell you that a boat with lifelines is safer than one without. They can get in the way of deck-sweeping headsails, but they can also help keep sails out of the water as they are being lowered. Netting between the lifelines

*Double lifelines on a small sailboat.*

increases this ability, as well as preventing small children (and bigger sailors) from being swept under the lines.

But lifelines aren't accident-proof. A stanchion with a 150-pound crewmember falling against it is likely to break. Additional measures are sometimes necessary to keep your crew on board, besides the obvious grabrails running the full length of the cabintop. On most boats the grabrails are installed by the builder, though in a few cases they aren't as long as they should be. They should be through-bolted, with large backing plates on the underside.

Jacklines, tethers, and safety harnesses all help ensure that your sailing companions stay safely on board. A jackline is a strong line, cable, or flat webbing that runs fore and aft along the deck, secured to strong pad eyes. A crew clips one end of a tether to the jackline, and the other end to a harness that is connected to the sailor's PFD. The tether should be long enough so the crew can work the deck without hindrance, yet short enough to keep the crew from falling overboard. There is one chilling account of a sailor who was swept overboard. He was wearing a safety harness, but the tether

was too long. His wife, who was not strong enough to haul him back aboard and didn't know how to stop the boat, watched her husband drown in the quarter wave. Some tethers have double ends, a short and a long—that way, you're always connected to something when you're on deck. You should never clip a tether to the lifelines—they aren't strong enough for this. If you don't have a jackline, clip the tether to the windward side of something strong, like a stanchion base or mooring cleat. (This is one reason why larger metal mooring cleats with open bases are better than smaller nylon ones.)

## Docklines and Towlines

You need at least four strong docklines. (See "Docking" in Chapter 8 for tips on technique.) Stretchy nylon is good for preventing shock loads to your mooring cleats, and remember, small-diameter nylon stretches more than large-diameter lines. It's also easier to secure smaller lines to cleats. In addition to docklines, you'll want two longer spring lines. You'll need to inspect docklines for chafe, though—lines smaller than $1/2$ inch tend to wear out quickly. Some books say that all docklines should be at

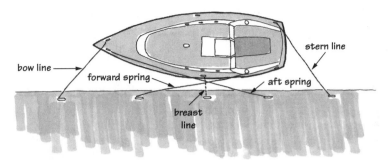

*Five types of docklines.*

least $\frac{1}{2}$ inch, but since trailer sailers are smaller and lighter overall, a smaller line might be easier to handle.

A long towline is good to have aboard to help other vessels. Although it's expensive, the best towline is double-braid nylon. It's still shock absorbing, but not so much as three-strand nylon. A towline should be a little stretchy, but not too much. If a deck fitting rips off under a towing load, it can shoot toward the towing boat with deadly force, potentially causing a serious accident.

## Compass

A compass is not required on a boat, but it should be if only for tradition's sake. My first trailer sailer had no compass aboard and technically didn't need one. The boat never sailed any farther than Lake Chickamauga in Tennessee, where you're never very far from land and nearly all navigation is by eye. But a good marine-grade compass was one of the first things I bought for that boat, and I never sailed it without my hand bearing compass as well. It is a captain's responsibility to know the boat's position and heading at all times, and you can't do that without a compass. No self-respecting captain should put to sea—even if that sea is a lake—without one.

A compass inside the cabin is an even better idea. A long time ago, compass makers developed a special model called a telltale compass. These are designed to be read from the bottom, and are mounted to the overhead above the captain's berth. While you're sleeping at anchor, all you have to do is open one eye to

see if the boat has shifted in the night. If not, fine, you go back to sleep. But if the boat has shifted, and the breeze has gotten up a bit, you had better take a look around the deck, just to make sure the anchor is still set and you're not blowing onto a dangerous lee shore. Or worse, you might find the other boat in the anchorage that was safely downwind has shifted and is now dragging anchor straight toward your boat while the captain is down below sleeping like a baby. I'll bet *he's* never heard of a telltale compass!

You can still buy telltale compasses, but they are expensive. I found one listed at $360.

A hand bearing compass is extremely useful to have in addition to your mounted compass. Davis still makes its old hand bearing model, which is a large ball-type compass mounted on a handle with plastic pointers. It

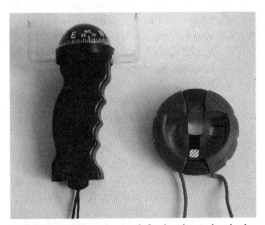

*Hand bearing compasses: left, the classic (and relatively inexpensive) Davis, and right, a hockey-puck type by Plastimo. Either type will get the job done.*

floats. I've also used one of the more expensive hockey-puck types of hand bearing compass, and it was a nice piece of gear. At about $100, it's roughly double the price of the old Davis model, but if my Davis ever gets lost overboard (not likely, since it floats), I'll treat myself to an Plastimo Iris 50.

There are two other types of hand bearing compass to consider—the Plastimo Iris 100 and the Silva 70UN. Both of these include a mounting bracket. This way they can do double-duty as the ship's compass and the hand bearing compass, plus they're easy to take home, reducing the risk of theft.

## Bilge Pumps

Bilge pumps are a good idea, but on certain boats they're apt to be used rarely. If your boat has no bilge, then you won't have a huge amount of use—or room—for a large bilge pump. My first trailerable sailboat had no bilge space, and no place to put a pump that wouldn't be continually tripped over, so I didn't install one. I got plenty of water inside my boat, usually following a large rainstorm or from splashes coming from the keel pendant opening during rowdy sails. (The keel pendant is a line or cable attached to the keel to lift it up; it passes through a small hole in the centerboard trunk. On many boats, water can splash up through this hole when sailing.) However, these were mostly small nuisance puddles that were better addressed with a sponge. Bilge pumps always leave a little water that needs to be sponged out anyway, especially if your bilge is the cabin sole.

If you're sinking, however, a bilge pump may be your only line of defense. You'll want a big, clog-resistant, diaphragm-type pump. A bucket will move more water faster, but you can't operate a bucket and steer the boat at the same time. Plunger-type pumps can be handy, but they're not much help if you're sinking.

Electric bilge pumps are another story. When equipped with a float switch, they can pump out your boat while you're having dinner at a restaurant (try *that* with a bucket). They

*A diaphram-type bilge pump mounted on the side of the cockpit that can be operated from the helm while underway.*

do add a level of complexity to the electrical system, and only large, expensive pumps can handle large amounts of water. Even a small hole below the waterline can admit stunning amounts of water into your vessel—I once had to clean out a speed impeller that was fouled on my just-purchased Catalina 27. It had a screw mount and a cap so that you could do this from inside the boat. All I had to do was unscrew the impeller with one hand and cap the hole with the other—simple. I got everything ready and unscrewed. The impeller shot into my hand with the force from the water, and what seemed to be a giant fountain of seawater sprang up from the impeller's mounting hole. I screwed the cap on quickly—it was all over in three or four seconds—and looked at the water that had come in from a $1\frac{1}{2}$-inch hole. Maybe 4 or 5 gallons! I remember getting a distinctive case of the new-boatowner shakes for a few minutes after that. That experience forever diminished my faith in bilge pumps and their ability to cope with anything but a trickle below the waterline. You'd need a pump almost as big as my Atomic Four inboard motor to cope with the water entering from an unobstructed 1-inch hole.

To summarize, bilge pumps can be useful, important items to have aboard, but only if they're strong, high-quality, high-capacity installations. Don't rely on an undersized, cheap pump to save you if you're taking on water.

## First-Aid Kit

A first-aid kit isn't a USCG-required item, but no prudent mariner should leave the dock without one. Accidents happen, and, depending on your type of sailing, help could be hours or even days away. If your radio doesn't have a lot of coverage or you're out of cell phone range, minor problems can easily escalate into serious situations, so be prepared.

The complexity of your first-aid kit can vary with the type of sailing you'll do. If you're primarily daysailing, you can get by with a relatively small, prepackaged first-aid kit. If you're heading toward more distant horizons, though, you'll want to create a more complete medical kit. However, medical equipment must be accompanied by the knowledge to use it

properly. The first thing to buy for any first-aid kit is a good first-aid manual. A manual written specifically for small-boat mariners is best. One highly recommended guide is *Advanced First Aid Afloat*, by Peter Eastman, but there are others.

Be sure to examine the contents of your first-aid kit annually. The often hot, humid environment of a sailboat seems to accelerate deterioration of medications and adhesives, so check expiration dates carefully and replace supplies as needed. I like to keep my first-aid kit in a fishing tackle box. While this is a little bulky, it helps to keep things organized, and you don't want to waste time hunting for supplies in an emergency.

## Carbon Monoxide Detector

If your boat has any form of heater, you should consider adding a carbon monoxide detector. Some preventable deaths have been caused by the accumulation of carbon monoxide in the confines of a small cabin. In one case, a faulty

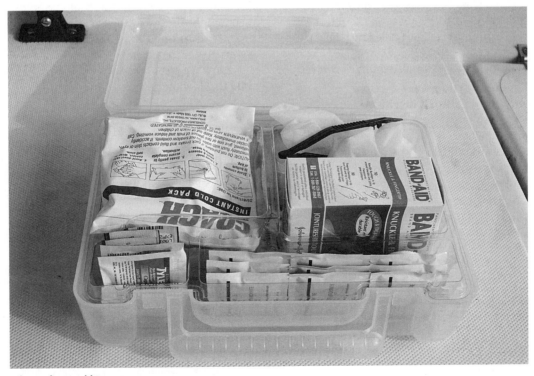

*A basic first-aid kit.*

hot water heater was to blame. Any open flame has the potential to use up available oxygen, of course, but this is less of a problem in warm weather. Adequate ventilation is important for lots of reasons—not the least being the comfort of the crew—but carbon monoxide buildup is an often forgotten factor in sailboat design. If you sail in cold weather, it's especially important.

## A Spares Kit

Putting together a spare parts kit for your boat is a fairly simple matter. Get a small tackle box, and every time you lose a little pin overboard, buy three or four. Put the extras in the spares box. A tackle box is good for another reason—it helps keep things organized. A spare part is useless if you can't find it when you need it. Label the box spaces too, if that's helpful.

While it's impossible to anticipate everything you'll need in a spares kit, here's a list for starters:

RIGGING
- Clevis pins—sized correctly for your boat
- Stainless-steel cotter pins
- Split rings (sometimes called ring-dings)
- Rigging tape
- Bulldog clamps (for *temporary* rigging repairs only)

ELECTRICAL
- Fuses
- Lightbulbs
- Dielectric grease

MOTOR
- Propeller shear pins
- Fuel filter
- Hose clamps
- Spark plugs

TRAILER
- Extra bearing set
- Extra lug nuts or bolts
- Trailer bulbs

MISCELLANEOUS
- 3-In-One Oil
- WD-40
- Matches

## Tools Aboard

In addition to spares, having a small, basic tool kit on board is essential while sailing. It's no use having a spare spark plug for your motor if you don't have a wrench with you to install it. It's impossible to anticipate every eventuality, but there are a few tools that can be adapted to a wide range of jobs.

Tools on board needn't be all stainless steel, but I've learned that inexpensive tools are far more likely to rust than more expensive, professional-grade tools. Good tools generally work better as well. Chinese-made tools seem to be especially prone to rusting, often being made from the cheapest raw materials. Brands like Snap-on, SK, and older Craftsman (which were made in the United States; check the packaging) are often wise investments, as long as you don't drop them overboard. A small lump of charcoal, wrapped in a loose cloth and replaced once per season, is an old-time rust prevention strategy. I give my tools a yearly spray of lubricant like WD-40 or Boeshield T-9. A rag in the toolbox is also essential to wipe away the excess, as slippery tools tend to bang knuckles and find their watery resting place more frequently.

Below is a basic list to get you started. You'll want to add more tools as the need arises.

Knife—a small, locking folder. A Wegner/ Victorinox Swiss Army type, or even an inexpensive stainless kitchen paring blade, can be useful.
Vise-Grips pliers, with wire cutters.
Needle-nose pliers.
Screwdrivers, slotted and Phillips, one large and one small of each.
Cable cutters—capable of cutting your largest rigging cable in an emergency.
Sewing needles, sailmaker's palm, and strong polyester thread.
Spark plug wrench.
Quality multi-tool by Leatherman, Gerber, or Kershaw.
Duct tape—can be used for all sorts of emergency repairs, but watch out: the adhesive on duct

tape can become a sticky, gooey mess after it warms up in the sun. And after it bakes for a few weeks, it's nearly impossible to remove.

## Charts

It's hard to believe, but you are not required to carry nautical charts aboard. I never sail anywhere but the smallest of lakes on the smallest of boats without some kind of paper chart. Even if I had the money for a full electronic chartplotting system, I'd still want paper charts too—electronics can get wet, and they don't like to work that way. A chart can tell you a great deal about where you are and how to get where you're going safely. They need to be kept current and updated through the Notice to Mariners bulletin (www.navcen.uscg.gov). See "Nautical Charts" in Chapter 11 for more information about acquiring and using charts.

## Electronics

Electronics constitutes a huge category of optional equipment that you can add to your boat. Some items can significantly increase the safety of your vessel, while others are just nice to have. Some electronic gadgets are serious overkill for most trailerable boats—radar comes to mind. Mariners have been sailing for eons with nothing more than lead, log, and lookout. Then again, mariners have also spent a lot of time lost in the fog or unable to call for help.

Remember that size and power requirements will limit what you can put on board. Do not go crazy with gadgets. Flipping through the marine catalogs will present you with a bewildering selection of high-tech solutions to problems you never knew you had. Resist the temptation to turn your cockpit into a nautical version of the Starship *Enterprise*, especially before you've had several cruises under your belt. Here is a rundown of the most common additions to an electronic arsenal.

### Depth Sounder/Lead Line

I used to think that a depth sounder wasn't needed aboard smaller boats like trailer sailers—after all, good sailors have been navigating for millennia without them—but experience has changed my thinking.

My Catalina came with a working, high-quality depth sounder. Whenever I sailed, I left it on, and discovered that I was constantly glancing at it. I quickly learned to use it as a navigation tool, and I followed the bottom contours on the chart. It seldom let me down, and knowing I had some water under my keel helped me to relax.

I never got around to installing a depth sounder on my first trailer sailer. Groundings are much less of an issue with a swing keel, right? And you can always jump overboard and push a trailerable boat off a shoal. Well, it didn't always work out that way. The lake where I sail has a lot of gravelly shoals in unexpected places, and I ran aground a few times. I never got stuck, but I did do a little damage to my rudder because I couldn't see the bottom shoaling due to the muddy water. I constantly wanted to know how much water I had, and our lake charts are much less detailed than NOAA charts. (NOAA stands for National Oceanic and Atmospheric Administration, the U.S. agency that produces charts.)

So the first improvement I made to *Tiny Dancer*, my Montgomery 17, was a brand-new digital depth sounder for the cockpit, and I love having that information available again. A new depth sounder costs about a hundred bucks, and for me it's money well spent.

As neat as they are, electronic depth sounders aren't infallible. You should have aboard a lead line, which is nothing more than a light, measured line with a weight on the end. Before the days of electronics, the ship's lead was a large specialized weight with a hollow space in the bottom. A little dab of beef tallow—or Crisco—in the hollow permitted the lead to bring up a small sample of the bottom, which helped select the proper anchor and anchoring technique. The line itself was measured in fathoms, with markers that could be identified by feel, so that a light wasn't necessary to read the depth.

A small-boat version of a lead line can be made with a large fishing sinker and some $1/_8$-inch line. You might want to devise your own system of marking—perhaps mark the first 5 or 10 feet with knots, then larger increments with various materials, like this:

| | |
|---|---|
| 2.5 feet | one knot |
| 5 feet | two knots |
| 7.5 feet | three knots |
| 10 feet | leather strip sewn to the line |
| 15 feet | yarn |
| 20 feet | leather with two corners |
| 25 feet | two pieces of yarn |
| 30 feet | leather with three corners |
| 35 feet | three pieces of yarn |
| 40 feet | leather with four corners |
| 50 feet | cloth |

Or you could come up with your own system. Some have suggested using nylon zip ties, which would be quick and permanent but hard on the hands. Those little printed tags sold at chandleries seem like a waste of money, but some sailors like them.

Lead lines are accurate and never need batteries, but they can be cumbersome and difficult to use in bad weather or higher speeds. You really need a crew to heave the line—it's tricky to take soundings with the lead if you're sailing solo. But they're great for checking the depth around your anchored boat, or to see how accurate your depth sounder is.

### Communications—VHF, FRS, Cell Phones, and Others

It's not a bad idea to have some means of communication aboard your sailboat. Ideally, this should be a way to communicate with shore stations as well as other vessels. The best option for most recreational vessels has traditionally been the VHF radio.

VHF RADIO   VHF—which stands for very high frequency, and is technically called VHF/FM—is primarily a short-range, line-of-sight communications medium. It's the legally preferred medium for radio communication between ships and from ship to shore.

If you've never used one, a VHF radio might take a little getting used to. Early versions had few channels, and the channels were selected with crystals that plugged into the radio. Modern radios use synthesizers for channel selection, and have all channels available for use. But many channels are restricted and should be used only for specific purposes—you can't just flip a switch and start yakking

### Cold-Forging a Sounding Lead

To fashion your own sounding lead, you can use a large (2 to 3 ounces or so—heavier is better) surf-fishing sinker tied to a light calibrated line—I used one for years aboard my boat. But should you have a yearning for the traditional, or want to pull a sample of the bottom, you can cold-forge a small version of a traditional ship's lead rather easily.

All you need is a fishing sinker, a hammer, and a heavy, relatively flat surface to use as an anvil. Lead is one of a few metals that can be shaped to some degree without heating. You'll want to wear gloves, though, as a precaution.

First, flatten the bottom of the sinker a little. You can hold the lead in a vise if you wrap the sinker with a rag, or you can drive the sinker into firm ground upside down, like a tent stake. Once the bottom is flattened, make a slight depression in it. You can do this with a large drill, or you can forge a depression with a blunt piece of steel.

All that remains is to taper the sides a little to form a slight teardrop shape. Hammer the sides square, making a gentle angle between the hammer and anvil surface. Getting the sides even may take a little practice; fortunately, sinkers aren't too expensive.

Once you've shaped the sides, make the surface octagonal by hammering the corners (you always forge a taper square first, then make it octagonal, and then, should you desire, round). After you're done, spray-paint it with a little enamel to seal the lead.

away. Channel 16 is the mandatory distress, safety, and calling channel. If you have a VHF on board, you are required to monitor Channel 16 for distress calls. If Channel 16 is clear and you want to talk to another vessel, ask them to switch to 71, 72, or 78, whichever is not being used. If these channels are busy, you can use 68 or 69, but Channel 70 is reserved for radios equipped with Digital Selective Calling (DSC). Following are the standard reserved channels:

### VHF CHANNEL USE

Channel 16: Distress, urgent messages, safety messages, and calling other stations.

Channel 6: Intership safety. The Coast Guard may ask you to use this channel if you have an emergency.

Channel 9: Boater calling channel, often used by marinas and yacht clubs.

Channel 13: Navigation; the working channel for most locks and drawbridges.

Channel 17: Maritime control, used by state and local governments.

Channels 21A, 22A: Coast Guard working channels.

Channels 24–28, 84–86: Ship-to-shore telephone channels formerly operated by MariTEL, now operated by SeaSmart by subscription only.

Channels 1, 5, 11, 12, 14, 20, 63, 66, 72, 74, 77: Port operations.

Channel 70: Digital Selective Distress and Calling only.

Channel WX1–3: Weather reports.

Channel 87: Automatic Identification System (AIS) Repeater.

Rules and regulations for VHF use aboard boats are very specific. You no longer need an FCC license to operate a VHF radio unless you are cruising in waters controlled by another country. The licensing fee is rather high, around $200, but it's good for ten years (it's not transferable from boat to boat, even if you remove and reinstall the same radio).

Don't use CB language on a VHF—there are no "good buddies" on the water. The Coast Guard does not provide "radio checks" to see if your radio is transmitting. Instead, use a local calling channel on low power. Listen first to make sure a calling channel is not busy, then call for a specific vessel or station and include the phrase "request radio check" in your initial call. "Over and out" is contradictory and used only in the movies. *Over* means "I'm finished transmitting and am waiting for your response"; *out* means "This is the end of my transmission and do not expect a response." Your use of Channel 16 should be kept to the bare minimum.

## What Is DSC?

It is hoped that DSC, short for Digital Selective Calling, will revolutionize the way rescue operations are handled. DSC uses a digital signal to transmit specific information, such as:

The caller's unique ID number (called a MMSI, for Marine Mobile Service Number, it's similar to a telephone number)

The ID number of the unit being called—for example, all Coast Guard stations

The caller's location and the time of day

The requested working frequency

The priority and type of call (distress, emergency, safety, routine, priority, fire, taking on water, etc.)

Ideally, DSC will eliminate much of the human factor in monitoring radio frequencies for distress calls. However, there are still plenty of bugs in the system. For example, the Coast Guard is plagued with large numbers of relayed DSC distress signals, 99 percent of which are accidental transmissions. It remains to be seen whether DSC will mature into a vastly improved communications system as promised.

The BoatU.S. foundation has recently launched a website (www.BoatUS.com/MMSI) devoted to DSC radios, understanding your MMSI, and the Coast Guard's Rescue 21 program.

## What Is AIS?

AIS stands for Automatic Identification System. It's a digital radio-based system that's required by the International Maritime Organization for all vessels over 300 tons, and it's expected that the U.S. Coast Guard will follow suit. With the AIS system, data from large vessels is continually broadcast digitally, and any vessel that can receive AIS data can instantly find out things like the ship's name, position, speed, course, and destination.

While the large transmission systems on the ships are expensive, smaller, receive-only units are less expensive. Currently they are designed to integrate with electronic navigation systems such as chartplotters and onboard navigation computers, but AIS has reportedly "revolutionized marine traffic communications" in the eighteen months since it was first introduced. Just as GPS units have become smaller and more practical for the trailer sailor, look for smaller and more capable AIS receivers in the near future.

Larger vessels typically use a permanently mounted VHF as their main radio, and consider a handheld for dinghy use only. Since VHFs are line-of-sight radios, the masthead is typically the place to mount the separate antenna required. But since masts on trailer sailers are regularly raised and lowered, they need to be kept as uncluttered and snag-free as possible, and a masthead antenna is particularly vulnerable to damage when the mast is lowered. You could use a larger deck-mounted whip antenna—that's what I had on my first trailer sailer. However, it was always in the way, and it didn't have significantly better range than a handheld would.

So when I purchased my second boat, I opted for a handheld instead. It cost roughly $100 and, for me, has been a better solution, even though it has lower power (handhelds typically have a maximum transmit power of about 5 watts, whereas permanently mounted units have 25 watts). It's easier to drop and break or steal, but it is fully submersible. Battery life has been good, and I can run it off the ship's battery with an adapter if need be.

CELL PHONES    In the early days of cell phones, having one aboard was pretty much useless because cell tower coverage was so spotty. While this is still true in remote cruising areas, you may find that your cell phone works in surprising places, especially as you approach major metropolitan areas.

A cell phone is a convenient and economical way to call home, if you can get a signal. Similarly, if there's an emergency at home, your family can try your cell phone number before going to more expensive options. It also allows you to contact a marina to reserve a berth for the night before you're in VHF range.

It's possible to increase the range of a cell phone by using an external antenna mounted at the masthead. Additionally, you can boost your cell phone's output power with an external amplifier. In some areas, you can reach the Coast Guard by dialing *CG. In fact, the Coast Guard sometimes prefers cell phone communications in rescue operations because they are far less susceptible to interference from other stations.

However, relying on a cell phone as your sole means of radio communication aboard a sailboat is folly. They are still one-point, person-to-person communication. If I'm taking on water, I want *everybody* to know about it—not just whoever's in my speed-dial. For everyday ship-to-ship or ship-to-drawbridge communications, a VHF is unsurpassed. That's why, in some countries, VHF is required equipment. Cell phones are certainly convenient and useful, but they shouldn't be your only option.

FRS AND GMRS    FRS stands for Family Radio Service. It's a relatively new, low-power handheld radio system that's better than walkie-talkies but not as good as VHF. FRS doesn't require a license (though some radios also have GMRS—General Mobile Radio Service—channels). Power is limited to 0.5 watt, and the range is usually 2 miles or less. GMRS can be considered an expanded type of FRS. GMRS has higher allowable power at 5 watts. You must have an FCC license to transmit on GMRS channels.

Both these systems are designed for two-way voice communications for family use. They can be useful aboard ship, primarily to keep up with your teenager in the dinghy. They are small, inexpensive, and lightweight, and some models can even survive a minor dunking. But if the budget allows, a pair of handheld VHF radios is probably a better choice, unless you routinely have several family members going in different directions at the same time.

## Ventilation

As noted in the USCG-mandated equipment section, a ventilation system is required on a trailer sailer only if you store fuel in lockers or have an inboard engine. Nevertheless, adequate ventilation is important for cabin comfort, mildew prevention, and safety. It's an especially good idea if you use a heater or cook with propane. (Remember, propane is heavier than air, and explosive fumes from a leaky canister can collect in the bilge.)

So, if ventilation is a good thing, what's the best way to provide it? Ventilators can be broadly classified into two groups: active and passive. Active vents use power and have moving parts; passive vents don't and are usually operated by the wind.

### Active Ventilation Devices

Active ventilation most commonly takes two forms—bilge blowers and powered deck vents. Forced-air bilge blowers use a 12-volt in-line fan to pull air from the bilge to the outside of the boat. They are important safety devices, but they don't do much to increase cabin comfort. For that, you need an active deck vent, and the most popular of these are Solar Vents. These self-contained units include a motor, a solar cell, and, in some models, a battery. When the sun shines, the motor operates, drawing fresh air through the ventilator. The battery-operated units can ventilate the cabin at night as well, which makes sleeping aboard more pleasant. The vents themselves are small, low-profile units that won't foul sheets on deck. They require a pretty big hole through the deck—3 to

4 inches—and they don't like to be stepped on. But they are especially effective at keeping the boat fresh while it is unattended.

Other active ventilation devices include fans to circulate air in the cabin. However, they can put a significant drain on the batteries if left on overnight. Some fans last longer than others—*Practical Sailor* has tested many cabin fans, and Hella is a brand that has consistently performed well.

Another option that may be worth investigating is the use of surplus 12-volt computer "muffin" fans. These are widely available and inexpensive, and often feature a low current draw. Some boatowners have found creative ways to use them, positioning them over berths, in bulkheads and lockers, and inside passive ventilation devices, making them active ventilators.

### Passive Ventilation Devices

Passive ventilators are basically wind-powered devices. If it's dead calm, you don't get much air circulation. But since there's usually some kind of breeze on the water, passive vents can help a great deal.

Clamshell vents are often seen on inboard boats to vent the bilge. As with most ventilators, they are best installed with one vent facing forward and one facing aft. One of their best qualities is their location aft, well out of the way. The best clamshell vents are deep, with a raised edge around the hole to keep out water that runs along the deck.

Mushroom vents are smaller, low-profile, deck-mounted vents that resemble the cap of a mushroom. They don't have a lot of cross-sectional area exposed to the wind, so they don't bring vast quantities of air down below, but they are omnidirectional—performance is the same no matter what direction the wind is coming from. They are available in stainless or plastic, and some look like unpowered versions of Solar Vents. Like Solar Vents, their low profile helps them keep from snagging sheets.

Remember that in good weather, your forward hatch can bring a lot of air below—even more if you rig a wind catcher or other type of fabric cover to help funnel air below. Some designs allow you to keep your forward hatch open in the rain, which can be a great help. Most of these can't be left open while under sail, and those that can would most likely be in the way. There are two basic designs of fabric ventilating sails: directional (or forward facing) and nondirectional. The nondirectional type rises straight above the hatch with a fabric X-shaped divider in the center. Commercial offerings include the original Windscoop, West Marine's Down-the-Hatch, and the self-supporting Breeze Booster. Expect to pay between $40 and $90 for these systems.

On larger boats, there's often room to fit a small opening hatch over the head area; these are great for bringing light and fresh air where it's often most appreciated. High-quality aluminum-framed plexiglass hatches are made by companies like Bomar and Forespar. Expect to pay around $150 for this upgrade.

Most boats these days come equipped with fixed ports or "deadlights." This keeps the price down, as they're quick, easy to attach, and much less likely to leak. Real opening ports are sometimes offered as an option, but the high

cost means few are fitted this way at the factory. And the cost can be staggering—even small, aluminum-framed opening portlights can go for $200 to $400 depending on the size; bronze-framed cost $200 to $650. Plastic portlights are a good bit less, around $130 each, but UV radiation will eventually take its toll. Plastic will deteriorate with age, whereas bronze will not.

Retrofitting a deadlight with an opening port would improve ventilation, but on many boats it's not that simple. Most deadlights are wedge shaped to give the cabin a racy look, and few portlights will bolt directly in their place. During the mid-1980s, some new boats began to appear with an unusual arrangement—an opening port was fitted in the middle of the deadlight. This seemed a pretty odd arrangement at first, but, depending on the style of the boat and the size of the deadlight, it doesn't look too bad. If your boat is a similar type, it might be possible to retrofit new deadlights with an opening port mounted within.

It is possible to fiberglass an opening for a deadlight and install opening ports, but it's very tricky. The work needs to be perfect and the gelcoat match has to be precise; otherwise,

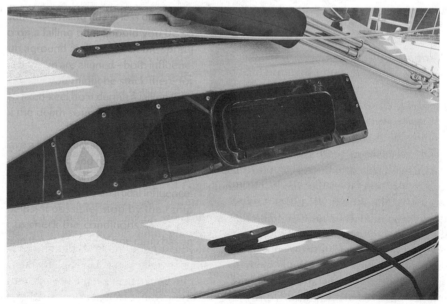

*Opening plastic ports are factory installed in existing deadlights for improved ventilation. This black port in a smoked plexiglass deadlight is on a Precision 21.*

*A plastic portlight used in the side of the footwell for ventilation and light. A clear inspection port works well, too.*

you could easily spoil the looks of your boat and spend a bunch of money in the process.

It's possible to put an opening port in an unusual place, like the inside of the cockpit footwell. This allows light and air to enter the boat in a normally dark and airless place—the foot of the quarter berth or the sail locker. A much less expensive option would be a snap-in or screw-in deck plate with a clear cover. These are only $17 each, and you could add four to the footwell for less than the cost of the cheapest opening port. Although they are made with heavy rubber O-rings for "a watertight fit," they could possibly leak in this sort of application, since they weren't designed for vertical mounting.

Good ventilation usually requires the use of several different types of vents. It's almost impossible to overventilate your boat—no one has ever complained of a boat being too fresh and airy belowdeck.

## Foul-Weather Gear

Since you don't usually have the option of running for cover when rough weather approaches, you'll have to be ready for some less-than-optimal conditions. You might experience rain, waves, spray, or all three while sailing. When this happens, having quality rain gear aboard is a big plus.

Buying foul-weather gear can present you with a bewildering array of choices, but for a trailer sailor we can narrow things down a bit. You aren't likely to need all the features found on a $600 set of offshore bibs and jacket unless you plan on making long passages. On the other hand, a $10 poncho from Sprawl-Mart isn't going to cut it either. A good choice might be a set of house-brand foulies from one of the large chandleries. These are often made by name-brand manufacturers and are a good value with nearly all the features but not the label. A nylon outer shell is better than solid PVC, though I've been using a set of PVC rain gear since Hurricane Hugo and it's still going strong. (PVC is a form of vinyl fabric with a smooth outer covering—the kind you probably had when you were a kid.) An inner liner makes rain gear more comfortable. A hat versus a hood is largely a matter of personal preference. Boots are needed for cooler weather, but deck shoes designed to get wet are an option that many sailors prefer.

# CHAPTER SIX

# Towing and Rigging Your Boat

**H**ere's the scenario—you've saved for months and, finally, she's yours—your first sailboat. All those daydreams and fantasies are becoming a reality. This step is a major accomplishment, something that has taken vision, hard work, and even a little courage, so take a moment to appreciate what you've done. Close your eyes and take a nice, deep breath.

When you open your eyes, you may find yourself thinking, "Man, this thing sure looks *big*."

On a trailer, most sailboats look huge. Even my little Montgomery 17, by comparison a pretty small trailerable, seems to dwarf my pickup truck. How are you going to get this beast in the water?

Don't panic. People tow sailboats safely all the time, and you can, too. Here are some tips.

## TOWING

Towing a sailboat safely does not have to be difficult or overly stressful. It should be a *little* stressful—that's a sign that you're taking things seriously. But if it feels overwhelming at first, don't worry. You can reduce that feeling with the knowledge that you've taken every precaution to be safe. One way to help keep up with the details is to make a towing checklist for your particular boat and tow vehicle. (For example, if your tow vehicle has a manual transmission, you don't need to check the automatic transmission fluid level.) See the sidebar "A Towing Checklist" to give you a start. You might also review Chapter 4, "Trailers."

OK, you've made a list and checked it twice. You're ready to roll. Here are some tips to get you to the water safely. First, *slow down!* Don't be in a hurry when towing a trailer. It's a common sight to see people flying down the interstate, exceeding the speed limit while towing a huge boat behind them. At high speeds, a trailer is much more likely to sway, and air pressure currents from large trucks are more of a problem. If it's raining, slow down *a lot*. You've already got limited maneuvering and stopping ability when towing a trailer. If it's raining, you can add reduced visibility, a much longer stopping distance, and a tendency to slide to your list of worries. You can also double your expected travel time. It's better to take forever to get there than not arrive at all.

Second, back off from the car in front of you, especially in wet weather. You will be amazed at how long it takes to come to a panic stop, especially with a trailer that doesn't have brakes. I know—the minute you leave enough room to stop, some bonehead pulls in front of you with about 6 inches to spare. There isn't much you can do in that event, other than tape a big sign on the back of your boat that reads, "This boat weighs over a ton and takes a hundred yards to come to a stop."

The third tip I can offer is for backing up. Backing up with a trailer for the first time is really tricky, but it becomes much easier with practice. Put your hand on the bottom of the steering wheel. To go left, move your hand to the left, and vice versa. You'll want to use slight movements of the wheel—exaggerated movement will cause the trailer to go all over the

## A Towing Checklist
### In the driveway, BEFORE TOWING

Be certain the ball and coupler are the correct size.

Lubricate the coupler and the latch.

Be sure the coupler is locked and secured with a safety clip or padlock. Test to make sure the coupler is securely fastened to the hitch ball.

Check the safety chains. Make sure they're solidly attached to the frame, facing forward if using open hooks, and crossed under the coupling. Don't let the chains drag on the pavement.

If your trailer has brakes, inspect the trailer brake wiring and harness. Clean if necessary.

Inspect and/or clean the lighting plug and receptacle. Test all exterior lighting, brake lights, and turn signals.

If a trailer license plate is required, make sure it's current and hasn't fallen off.

Inspect all hitch components, leaf springs, clamps, axle components, and so on, for cracking or broken welds.

If your trailer is equipped with brakes, test the breakaway switch.

Check tire pressures and inspect each tire for rot, cracking, or wear.

Check the wheel nut torque.

Make sure the tongue jack is raised as far as possible.

Remove the dolly wheel (if appropriate).

Make sure the boat motor is off the transom and secured in the tow vehicle or on a mounting bar. If necessary, tighten and padlock the mounting screws.

Remove the rudder and store it in the cabin. Do not tow the boat with the boom or the rudder lying in the cockpit.

Make sure the transom strap and bow chain are secure and tight.

Store all loose items on the boat belowdeck. Hatches should have positive latches to prevent them from being blown open, and all should be secured. Items in the cabin, particularly breakables, should be stowed low and securely. Lock the companionway to prevent it from vibrating open.

Make sure the mast is well supported at a minimum of three points and securely tied to the hull.

Check that the hull is correctly positioned on the trailer and supported by the bunks and at the bottom of the keel. If the bunks are causing dents in the hull, reposition the boat until it is correctly supported—the trailer should never cause any deformation of the hull.

### On the road, BEFORE DRIVING AT HIGHWAY SPEEDS

Test the bearings. After driving a few blocks, pull over and feel the bearings with the back of your hand. If they are hot, stop. The bearings must be replaced before you continue. Do nothing until they cool down, then *very slowly* find a place where you can safely work on the hubs, away from traffic. Don't drive more than a few blocks, and don't exceed 15 miles per hour, as your tire has a very real chance of coming off the axle. Call for roadside assistance, if available.

If your trailer sways, stop. Try to determine what is causing the trailer to sway, and correct it. Do not drive at highway speeds if your trailer sways.

### At the launch ramp, BEFORE RAISING THE MAST

Always look up! Make sure there are no power lines of any kind between you and the ramp. Your mast does not have to make contact with a high-power line to conduct a deadly electric surge—very high voltages can jump through the air if your mast gets close enough. Make sure no branches or trees obstruct your launch area.

If possible, point the boat downhill to make raising the mast a little easier.

*(Continued)*

If you have to disconnect the trailer from the car, be sure to block the aft corner of the trailer to prevent it from rolling before you step on the boat.

Make sure all your shrouds and halyards are connected and free of deck obstructions. Check the masthead to be sure the halyards are in their proper sleeves, and tighten the halyards on the mast so they don't foul as you raise the mast.

If you have babystays to limit sideways movement, connect them.

Loosen the headstay turnbuckle. Be sure the correct size clevis pins are ready to secure the forestay.

If you can, get some help lifting the mast.

place. It often helps to have another person out of the car directing you with hand signals. Don't be in a hurry, take your time, and practice. A summer Saturday at a busy boat ramp is not a good time to back your boat for the first time.

You can find other towing tips from the government and in trailer-oriented magazines, like *Trailer Boats*, *Trailer Life* magazine, and *RVLiving*, or on the web at www.nhtsa.dot.gov/cars/problems/Equipment/towing/. If you type "towing a trailer" into a web search engine, you'll get dozens of hits with good information and tips about towing your sailboat.

## RIGGING

Once you get to the ramp, you have to do a little magic. You've got to transform your boat from something that is more like an RV to a small, seaworthy vessel. And you have to do this in a parking lot. Then you have to launch the whole assembly. A fringe benefit to taking a little time for rigging is that it gives the trailer wheel bearings a chance to cool off. (Dipping hot bearings in cool water shocks the steel and pulls water into the bearings, increasing the possibility of failure.)

Some sailboat manufacturers like to tell you how simple rigging is. It's simple only in theory.

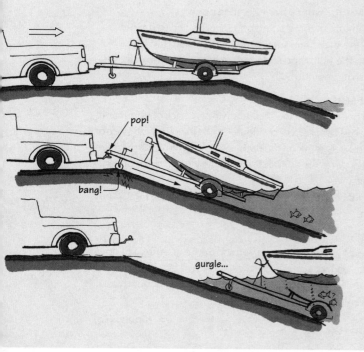

### Safety Tip: Raise Your Tongue Jack All the Way!

Here's an important safety tip. Most boats, especially larger ones, have a crank-down tongue jack to raise the tongue for connecting and disconnecting the trailer. For a 2,000-pound boat, the proper tongue weight is at least 200 pounds—too heavy to lift by hand. Tongue jacks make it easy to lift the tongue. Some jacks pivot to swing out of the way, but some, like mine, are fixed in the vertical position. It's very important, especially with fixed jacks, to raise them up as far as possible before towing a trailer. Otherwise, a sharp rise in the road—most commonly the top of a steep ramp—can hit the jack and force the coupling off the ball.

## Use Wheel Chocks at the Ramp

My good friend Mark Kennedy used to live in a house with a deck that overlooked a public boat ramp. He had great entertainment simply relaxing on the deck and watching people's various hijinks as they attempted to launch and recover their boats. One afternoon we saw one hapless fellow launch his boat *and* his pickup truck. (This scenario is really funny—unless it happens to you. And it's more common than you'd think.) If I remember it correctly, the water nearly made it past his windows as his truck slowly rolled backward while he putzed around on his boat. Just in the nick of time, he raced to the cab and got the truck out of the water before drowning the engine, but I'll bet the saltwater-soaked interior had that special low-tide, dead-fish smell for a long time. I've seen photos on the Internet where car owners weren't quite as speedy, and the tow vehicles were submerged completely.

The lesson: Your parking brakes are often less effective than they should be, and they're quick to wear out. If you depend on your parking brakes at the ramp, you may launch your tow vehicle unintentionally. A simple solution is a pair of wheel chocks. You can buy these at an auto parts store; a short chunk of wood would also work. A small firewood-sized piece of log split in half and drilled with a hole would be ideal. Here's a tip—tie the wheel chocks to your bumper (on a pickup) or the inside of your trunk (on a car) with a short piece of light line. When you are on the ramp, set your brakes, then put the chocks in place behind the rear wheels first thing. They are especially helpful when recovering your boat, because when you release the brakes, the car doesn't roll backward. This was helpful when I pulled the boat with my standard-transmission Frontier—it gave me a second to let the clutch out a little and rev the engine. When you go up the ramp, the line drags the chocks along with you—no need to run back and pick them up before the next person uses the ramp.

In real life, rigging a boat at the ramp is a big job. But with practice, it gets much easier. I have seen some truly amazing, virtuoso performances by sailboat owners who have gotten the setup and rigging of their boat down to a fine science. One sailor I knew had a MacGregor 25 launched within twenty minutes of arrival at the ramp. His wife accompanied him, and it was obvious that these two had launched many times in order to reach such impressive rig times.

In general, larger boats with more complex rigs take longer to rig and launch, but this isn't a universal truth. Each sailboat has its own quirks and characteristics—different hardware and different mast steps. The mast step is where the base of the mast connects with the boat. On trailerables, it's often a stainless bracket with a bolt through it; other times it's a hinged plate mounted firmly to the deck. Most trailerables have deck-stepped masts, though a few might have carbon masts that are keel stepped. The carbon mast passes through a

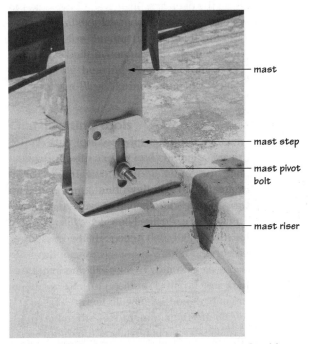

mast

mast step

mast pivot bolt

mast riser

*A common bolt-in mast step seen on many trailerable sailboats.*

mast

mast pivot bolt

mast step

*A hinge-type mast step from a Tanzer 22, a slightly better arrangement.*

hole on the deck and fits in a shallow socket in the keel. Some catboats with unstayed masts work this way.

> Before you do any rigging, **look up**. Do this every time you approach a boat ramp, familiar or not. The most dangerous overhead problem is a power line. Some power lines carry so much current they don't need direct contact to conduct electricity through your mast and boat. Your aluminum mast becomes a very effective lightning rod, and the results can be deadly. Not many launch ramps have these kinds of high-voltage lines strung about, but you can't be too sure. Be careful—people have died because they raised a mast into an overhead power line, and this kind of tragedy is preventable if only you take a moment to **look up!**

Rigging your boat will be somewhat different than described here, as this is an overview of the process. The exact procedure is outlined in your owner's manual. If you don't have a

manual, try to get one. Even if the builder of your boat has been out of business for thirty years, you still have a pretty good chance of finding a manual on the Internet. Most boats have a user's group somewhere online, and those members can be invaluable resources for information about your boat—and not just for old manuals, either. Sources for obsolete parts, procedures, aftermarket suppliers, flotillas, group cruises, races, and crewing opportunities can all be found by being a part of a user's group, so join the community!

Here's how rigging a typical trailerable sailboat might go at a ramp. After checking for overhead power lines and branches, find a spot where you can park your car and boat. Hopefully you can rig the boat away from the ramp. Where I sail, sailboats are pretty rare, so I get some odd looks and questions. Usually these come at difficult moments—like when my mast is halfway up. I try to get as far away from spectators as I can. If you have a choice, park the boat heading downhill or on level ground. Don't disconnect the boat from the car to rig it, as you'll be walking around the deck and you could unbalance the trailer, sending the tongue skyward and possibly moving the trailer! Be careful as you get ready to raise the mast, since you'll be a good distance from the pavement. Falling off the deck could easily ruin your next three months.

First, untie the mast and free the halyards and stays. Most folks use a few bungee cords to hold the halyards, stays, and spreaders securely around the mast for transport. Undo these and stow them where you can find them again when you next haul the boat. Tie the ends of the halyards tightly to the cleats at the base of the mast, but let the shrouds and stays hang loose for a moment. Check the masthead—make sure the forestay is facing up, the backstay is down, and all the halyards are clear, with no twists or kinks.

Next, bolt the mast to the mast step. The mast goes toward the stern, and when it's bolted into the step, you can't reach anything past the spreaders. Make sure the upper shrouds, halyards, forestay, and backstay are clear and don't have any kinks in them. Most boats need something in the area of the cockpit to support the mast before it is raised. My boat has a teak mast crutch that fits into the rudder pintles—it supports the mast while on the highway. Your boat may have something similar. Make sure there's some kind of support in place, ready to receive the mast as you shift it aft. If everything looks OK, shift the mast to the rear and bolt it in the step. The mast is large and ungainly, but usually not too heavy. Sometimes it helps to pad the companionway with an old life jacket to prevent friction from the mast as you raise it, which can crack the gelcoat.

When the mast is bolted in place, attach the after shrouds and backstay. Some boats, like my old MacGregor, use vernier adjusters on the backstay and the shrouds, and a single turnbuckle at the headstay. Vernier adjusters are simple affairs commonly seen on Hobie Cats. They are simply two pieces of metal—one flat, the other U-shaped—with a series of holes drilled in them. The spacing of the holes is slightly different, so you can adjust shroud tension in small increments, depending on where you locate the clevis pin. (A clevis pin is a small stainless-steel pin with a head at one end and a hole in the other—see the sidebar "Clevis Pins" for more detail.)

If your boat uses vernier adjusters, attach the shrouds to the verniers loosely, using the lower holes. This ensures you've got enough slack at the headstay to insert the clevis pin. As you gain some experience rigging your boat, you can mark the verniers where they normally go and save some adjustment time later. If you have turnbuckles, just pin them in—you'll adjust them later. Always secure clevis pins with split rings.

On most boats, you'll have five stays attached to the hull at this point: the starboard upper and lower shrouds, the port upper and lower shrouds, and the backstay. (These terms can get a little confusing. Generally, stays are anything that "stays" the mast, or keeps it in

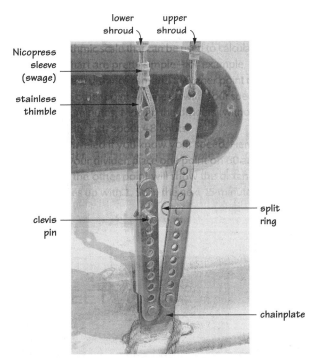

*A vernier adjuster on a MacGregor 22. The adjusters are the two pieces of stainless steel with holes in them. The top half of the adjuster is permanently attached to the shroud with double Nicropress swages. At the bottom, the adjuster is fastened to the chainplate with a clevis pin.*

position. Shrouds are stays that go to the sides of the boat. So you usually have a headstay, a backstay, and a number of shrouds. But please don't call them "sidestays," which is incorrect.) These all seem to have an unnatural ability to hook themselves under something as you raise the mast, and the problem is always worse if you're launching alone. When this happens, there's not much you can do besides lower the mast back down and free the snag. Be especially careful to watch for kinks in the stays and shrouds as you're raising the mast.

If you have any kind of mast-raising system, now is the time to hook it up and use it. (More about mast-raising systems in a moment—see below.) Otherwise, you'll just

*My clevis pin spares kit.*

## Clevis Pins

Clevis pins are tiny, simple things, but they're very important. If you don't believe me, just ask someone who has experienced a clevis pin failure—the results are catastrophic.

Clevis pins are used at various points all over your rigging, and they are a link in your rigging chain. Break a clevis, and you'll likely lose the entire rig. This is why you should use only real stainless steel clevis pins. Never, ever use a bolt in place of a clevis pin. The threads on a bolt make them much weaker in shear strength—meaning forces perpendicular to the axis of the bolt—and that's exactly how a fitting acts on a clevis.

For such little things, clevis pins are horribly expensive. You can sometimes find cheaper galvanized clevis pins at the hardware store. Never use these! They aren't as strong as the stainless ones that you get from a boating chandlery.

Clevis pins are so small and round that they seem to have suicidal tendencies aboard a sailboat. Thousands have leapt from the pitching deck of a sailboat to a watery death, never to be seen again. Whenever you buy clevis pins, buy more than you need in case you get a jumper, and always carry several spares.

Clevis pins can be secured with cotter pins or split rings. Cotter pins can be fine on larger boats with rarely removed standing rigging, but not usually for a trailerable. They can't be reused, and their sharp little legs can cut fingers or sails, so they have to be taped over. A slightly better choice is the split ring, also known by various names such as "ring-ding," "Old Fingernail-Breaker," and "You Little $#@%$!" These tiny things also love to roll off the deck, hiding themselves in some inaccessible little crack or jumping into the water. I think the clevis pins talk them into it. Keep spares aboard.

Clevis pins must be exactly matched to the hole in the fitting. A clevis that's too big obviously can't be used, but one that's a size too small might be tempting. Don't do it! What you get is point-loading of the pin and fitting, where all of the rig's stress is concentrated at a small area. This can either break the clevis or crack the fitting. If the loads are small and nothing breaks, it can wear a little notch at the top of the fitting, which will weaken it greatly. Inspect all your fittings for these little notches and cracks at the top.

Trailer sailer owners are always on the lookout for ways to speed rigging. You may be tempted to use fastpins, which are pins with a split ring on one end and a tiny spring-loaded ball on the other. I wouldn't use these for the rigging or anything critical. If they are solid (not tubular) and properly sized, they'd probably be strong enough. But there's always a possibility that a loose line can snag the ring

a correctly sized clevis pin distributes rigging loads over a large surface

an undersized pin concentrates rigging loads onto a very msall area. . . . either the pin will break, or the chainplate will wear a stress-raising notch

right

very wrong!

*Clevis sizing problems.*

and jerk it out of the fitting, and the mast goes over the side.

There is one possible alternative to traditional clevis pins, and that's a ball-lock quick-release pin. These pins are expensive little buggers at about $20 each. They have a little ball on the end, just like fastpins, but the ball isn't spring-loaded. You have to push a button on the end to get the pin out. Quick-release pins are quite secure, but they can come out accidentally. A very experienced racer I know was racing a small boat rigged with quick-pins, and noticed the downwind shroud dangling—the quick-pin had fallen out of the chainplate! He recommends taping them if you use them. Several trailer sailers use them for their headstay fitting, where speed in securing that pin is an advantage. However, quick-release pins are tubular, not solid, though the tube does have a solid pin passing through the center. They aren't as strong as plain clevis pins. Other sailors do use them and like them very much, but I don't recommend them because of concerns regarding strength and the possibility of their working loose.

*A ball-lock quick-pin—not to be used with standing rigging, but they can work well on a headsail track.*

have to muscle the mast up. Having a second person around is a big help when launching in general, but especially when raising the mast. On my boat, I have to hoist the mast from the cabintop. I can't start lifting in the cockpit and step onto the cabintop—the mast is too heavy and the cockpit too deep. I have to muscle it up while standing next to the mast step, and the leverage point is very short. When I raise the mast by myself, it's very difficult to lift. A second person, standing in the cockpit and lifting as high as possible, is a big help.

A better choice might be to lift the mast from the bow end and work toward the stern, but this technique is problematic on most boats. The port and starboard shrouds attach to the hull just slightly aft, so you can't attach both to the hull if you raise the mast from the bow. You'll be able to attach only one shroud, either the port or the starboard one. Once you get the mast up, you have to get the other

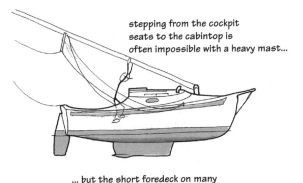

stepping from the cockpit seats to the cabintop is often impossible with a heavy mast...

... but the short foredeck on many trailer sailers doesn't allow enough leverage to lift the mast

*Raising the mast from the stern (top) versus from the bow.*

shroud attached somehow. And until you do, the mast will be quite unstable—a moment's loss of pressure on the mast could result in it crashing down, which we'd *really* like to avoid. Doing this by yourself is very risky, and it's chancy even with help, so I can't recommend this method for a typically rigged trailer sailer with single, aft-swept lowers. (A few boats have double lowers, and these can be raised from the bow in relative safety.)

For now, let's say that you've got a second person to help, and you're going to raise the mast from the stern. Before lifting, loosen the headstay turnbuckle by several turns. This gives you enough slack in the rig to position the headstay clevis pin. Find the clevis pin and split ring that goes in the stemhead fitting, and have them ready. If everything still looks OK at the masthead and all the shrouds look fair, start lifting. Yes, it's heavy. Be careful—don't let the mast get sideways! The most risky part is when the mast is about 45 degrees from vertical. Once you get that far, keep going up—if you stop at 45 degrees, then the mast will probably start drifting around. If the mast starts to make a circular motion to the side, it'll be hard to stop and you can lose control of it. Don't hesitate; get it up quickly—the shrouds and backstay will hold it upright. Once it's up, hold it there—*do not take your hands off the mast for a second!*

When you get the mast up, take another look aloft. Make sure none of the stays are twisted or kinked, and you didn't hoist aloft a stray line. Bending turnbuckles is a common problem when raising a mast, so be careful—I had to replace my turnbuckles after I discovered microscopic cracking along the threads. As the shrouds tighten on the way up, the spreaders will go from their folded position to their normal sailing position. (The spreaders are the short tubes that hold the upper shrouds away from the mast. You'll find them on all but the smallest boats.) Sometimes the spreader brackets jam and don't unfold properly. When this happens, the mast usually stops short of vertical. There's nothing much you can do

except utter a few of those salty sailing expletives, bring the mast back down, get the spreaders in the proper position, and try again. Make sure you haven't kinked or bent your shrouds when the spreaders jam. (When the mast is down, I usually put a shot of lubricant in the spreader brackets once per season to encourage them to operate properly.)

Now you have to install the headstay. Don't relax until you get that stemhead clevis pin in. If the bow is pointing downhill, gravity will help hold the mast upright, but I certainly wouldn't count on it—a good breeze could blow the mast down. Have a crewmate push the mast forward until you get a clevis pin in and secure it with a split ring. Only until you do that can you take a break and breathe freely.

Raising the mast is the biggest job when you launch. The rest is small potatoes, comparatively. Once the mast is up, tighten the standing rigging. Usually you start by getting the forestay and the backstay approximately tensioned, then work on the shrouds. (See the sidebar "Determining the Correct Shroud Tension.")

If your boat uses vernier adjusters, get them as tight as possible by hand, then complete the tightening while under way. If you have turnbuckles, screw them down by hand until the rig is evenly tensioned. To check if the rig is even, lay your head along the mast and look up. If there's a curve to one side, tighten the shroud on the convex side to bring the mast straight. Check the mast for straightness again when launched, as some sailboats flex a little when they are in the water compared to on the trailer. Don't use tools to get more leverage on your turnbuckles just yet, and never use Channellock pliers or Vise-Grips on turnbuckles—you'll chew them to bits. You can do your final tuning once you're under way.

If you want to do a quick, basic setup of your rig tension and you can't find a manual, try this. Tighten everything evenly, make sure the mast is straight, and give each stay a pluck with your thumb, as if you were playing a giant guitar. If the stay can sound a note, then your

## Determining the Correct Shroud Tension

Correct shroud adjustment is something that perplexes many sailors, new and experienced alike. Some manuals seem vague about the subject, with ambiguous phrases like "moderate tension." Your moderate and my moderate might be very different! Other manuals have very specific instructions for setting the tension, which should be followed exactly. Too little or too much tension could potentially damage your rig.

Most nonracing sailboats require a straight mast. Racers often flatten the mainsail by bending the mast slightly while under way. This is done with an adjustable backstay. Tension can be increased or decreased with blocks or even hydraulics. Overuse can result in a mast with a permanent bend aft. (If you have to sail with a bent mast, a slight aft bend is what you want. Side-to-side bends are bad, but a mast that curves forward is worse.)

There is a wire tension gauge on the market called a Loos gauge. It is specifically designed for testing the tension on sailboat sides and stays by measuring the amount of deflection with a spring. It is quite accurate, and costs around $65. The old Model A Loos gauge had a leaf spring that can stretch out with age, so if you're looking for a used Loos on eBay, get the more recent PT-1 model. Also note that once you're under way, a Loos gauge doesn't work—the stresses and strains of a boat in a seaway make the readings go all over the place.

Some racers use a "gaugeless" method to adjust their shroud tension. (This was described in an article by Greg Fisher, "Thoughts on J/22 Tuning: Lose that Tension Gauge," www.northsailsod.com/articles.) First, tighten your rig as tight as you can get it by hand at the dock, and make sure the mast is straight. Then, go out and sail upwind. The leeward upper shroud will probably have a lot of "slop" in it. If it does, tighten the shroud a half turn. Tack the boat and tighten the other shroud the exact same amount.

Now put the boat back on the original heading and check the shroud again. If it's still flopping around (on its own; you don't have to touch the shroud), repeat the process. Continue this routine until the shroud shows a slight movement on its own, perhaps a deflection of about $1/2$ inch. A large deflection of, say, 4 inches is a "floppy" shroud and should be tightened. While Greg didn't mention the subject of lower shroud tension, I believe that you can use similar parameters to adjust them as well. The lower shrouds are shorter and will stretch less in normal use, so if the leeward shrouds are flopping around, they need to be tightened as well. When checked with a gauge, it is common for lower shrouds to be adjusted with less tension than the upper shrouds.

An indicator of a rig that's too loose is a "pumping" motion of the mast in waves or chop. You may need to increase the overall rig tension to dampen the effects of rough water.

Just as important, this can tell you if your shrouds are too tight. If the leeward upper shroud is rock-steady when sailing upwind, then it is too tight and should be loosened. When you complete the adjustment, sight up the mast and check for bends. A small amount of bend to leeward at the spreaders, say a $1/2$ inch or so, is normal, but if you see any significant bending of the mast, then something is wrong and should be corrected. Of course, this procedure assumes your rig is undamaged and in good shape—no broken strands of wire on any of the shrouds or stays, no cracks anywhere, no bent turnbuckles, no loose chainplates, and so forth.

You'll notice that, when using this method, your shrouds will be adjusted tighter when you have higher winds. This is just as it should be—higher winds call for a tighter overall rig tension.

Unfortunately, this doesn't help you much when setting your forestay and backstay. Racers use their adjustable backstays to tighten the headstay as well, tweaking the sag in the jib luff for various conditions. If you're just out for a pleasant afternoon sail, you can hand-tighten the headstay and backstay, then tighten the shrouds, and then give the mast *a little bit* of bend aft by tightening the backstay a little more.

tension should be OK. Don't overdo it, though—the note you want is just above a thud, not an F sharp. More rigs get damaged through overtightening than undertightening.

Once the turnbuckles are tensioned, make sure they're seized with wire, a cotter pin, or small line so they can't adjust themselves. If they're seized with wire, be sure the ends are carefully trimmed and turned in so they cannot tear your sails.

The boom often attaches to the mast at the gooseneck fitting, usually with some kind of clevis pin. Some goosenecks are fixed, others are adjustable. Adjustable goosenecks are often better than fixed, since they make tensioning the mainsail easier. Attach the topping lift at the aft end of the boom. On most trailer sailers, the topping lift is a just a short piece of line tied to the backstay with a clip.

Rig the mainsheet according to your manual or the previous owner's instructions. There are lots of different ways to rig a mainsheet on a sailboat. On most trailerable sailboats, the mainsheet is a compound system—meaning two or more blocks. The mainsheet on my boat has a block that attaches to a bail on the boom via a clip. The lower end of the mainsheet attaches to the traveler in the middle of the cockpit.

A traveler is a rail mounted across the cockpit from port to starboard that has a traveler car—a ball bearing slider that attaches to the mainsheet—that travels back and forth, controlled by—you guessed it—traveler control lines. Not all boats have travelers. Travelers allow fine adjustments to the mainsail shape by altering the position of the mainsheet. In light winds when a full sail with a good bit of curve is optimal, pull the traveler all the way to windward. This allows the boom to lift a little, adding curve to the sail. In heavy winds when a flatter mainsail is desirable, sheet the traveler all the way to leeward. This pulls the boom in a downward direction, flattening the sail. Travelers are usually more of interest to racers. They are fun to play with, but in all honesty, half the time I sheet mine in the cockpit and leave it there. You can easily

spend $300 adding a traveler to your boat, and on most trailer sailers, it's in the way.

A less fancy way to rig the mainsheet on a trailer sailer is to use boom-end sheeting. This method uses two swivel blocks at the aft corner of the cockpit and a block at the end of the boom. While this lacks the fine-tuning capability of a traveler, it's much less expensive and simpler, and has the advantage of keeping the mainsheet above the tiller. The cockpit is much less crowded this way, and you can still get a lot of adjustment in the sail.

But rerigging the mainsheet is something you can do after you've had a few sails. For now, we've still got a hypothetical boat to launch, and we're nearly ready.

Get the rudder and put it in place in the pintles. (The rudder pintles look like pins, and they fit in the gudgeons, which are usually strongly bolted to the transom. The gudgeons have the holes.) Make sure your rudder kick-up mechanism (if your rudder is so equipped) is in good working order. Many kick-up rudders rely on a bungee cord to provide tension. This cord should be renewed at the beginning of every season. While you're at the stern, put the motor onto its mount and clamp it down tightly. (You *do* have some kind of backup line for the outboard, just in case the motor mount fails, right? The easiest solution is a short length of line with a clip snapped onto the motor, attached to the boat at the other end at a ring bolt. Or just tie a short length of line from the motor to someplace strong on the transom, like the backstay chainplate.) Then connect the fuel line and tank, and make sure the kill switch is in the correct position. Open the tank vent and valve on the motor and prime the fuel line before you get it in the water, so you won't have a fuel spill. If the system leaks, take corrective action—it's much easier to fix now than when your boat is drifting out to sea with the tide.

Bend on the sails. (For some reason, we "bend" the sails onto the mast and boom. It's an archaic term meaning to fasten or attach, as in a sheet bend.) You'll most often start at the

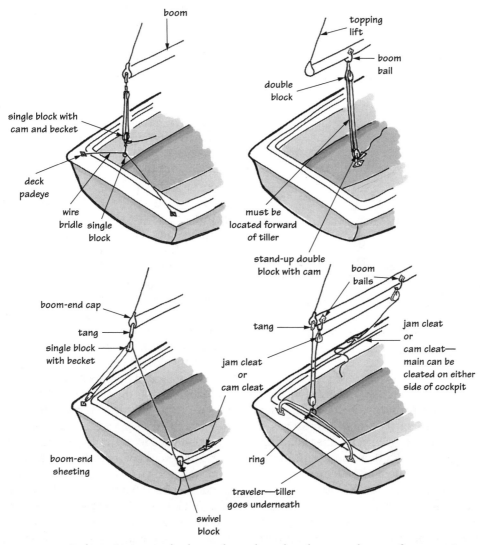

boom

topping lift

boom bail

double block

single block with cam and becket

deck padeye

wire bridle    single block

must be located forward of tiller

stand-up double block with cam

boom bails

boom-end cap

tang

single block with becket

tang

jam cleat or cam cleat

jam cleat or cam cleat— main can be cleated on either side of cockpit

boom-end sheeting

ring

traveler—tiller goes underneath

swivel block

*Four common mainsheet rigging methods are shown here, but there are dozens of ways to rig a mainsheet, using winches, traveler systems, double-ended or cabintop sheeting, and so on. Look at racing boats for some clever (but often expensive) ideas. (Tillers and rudders not shown for clarity.)*

mainsail's tack, which is the lower forward corner of the sail. Feed the boom first, which means sliding the sail's boltrope into the groove that runs along the top of the boom. (A boltrope is a length of rope that's sewn into the edge of a sail. This is one of the few "ropes" found on board. Everything else is called a line.) Tie off the other end of the sail (called the clew) to the aft end of the boom with a

short length of line, stretching the foot of the sail just enough to get the wrinkles out. Next, attach the forward edge of the sail (called the luff). Oftentimes the luff attaches by feeding sail slides into a track that runs up the mast. Feed in these slides, and tie the headsail to the main halyard. Don't get the halyards mixed up. As soon as you hoist the main, it will be immediately obvious if you get it wrong.

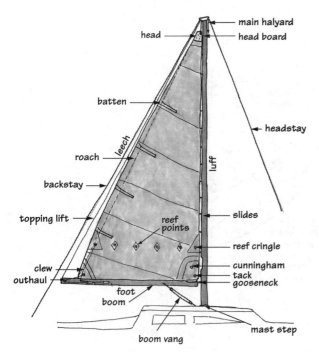

main halyard
head
head board
batten
headstay
roach
leech
luff
backstay
topping lift
slides
reef
points
reef cringle
clew
cunningham
outhaul
tack
gooseneck
foot
boom
mast step
boom vang

*Parts of the mainsail.*

If you have plain rope halyards, the best knot to use for attaching them is by far a bowline, because it's easy to untie after being tensioned. Try to make this knot as short and compact as possible. For many years, larger boats used wire halyards with screw pin shackles or snap shackles, because these have lower stretch. The wire halyards had rope tails so they could be cleated off at the mast base. Newer high-tech fiber lines, such as Sta-Set X or Vectran V-12, have very low stretch, approaching that of wire. These must be carefully spliced or their strength suffers, so they're normally fitted with shackles and eye splices made by a professional rigger.

Usually I wait to bend on the headsail until we're under way rather than put it on at the ramp. This way the foredeck stays clear—often you need that space to maneuver the boat once you get it in the water. More than once, having the mainsail ready to hoist has allowed me to sail out of a tight spot when my engine

sputtered and died. Engines seem to do that when you need them most.

## LAUNCHING YOUR BOAT

The remaining jobs are to put out fenders along the side of the boat and to tie docking lines onto their cleats. There's often (though not always) some kind of dock at a launch ramp, so determine the side you'll approach from and position your fenders accordingly. The same thing goes for the docking lines. Make sure they're long enough to maneuver the boat on the trailer. When I launch the boat by myself, I use two long lines, one at the bow and one somewhere near the middle of the boat. If a line can be secured amidships, then the boat can be brought slowly to the dock using the line alone. I'll try this only when the weather's calm, though. Usually, I'll have someone along to help, and I'll use a single long bow line. Before you launch, take a moment to clear things up on the boat. Make sure all the docking lines are coiled neatly and ready to toss, and be certain that no stray lines are dangling over the side. Now is a good time to load those last few items onto the boat. Remove the transom strap, but keep the bow eye connected to the trailer winch.

Now you've got to back the boat down the ramp. (You have been practicing in an empty parking lot, right?) If this is your first launch, try to avoid Memorial Day weekend. In our area, any Saturday in the summer is like a bass boat mosh pit. Sometimes it calms down around lunchtime, but I avoid launching on a Saturday. If it is crowded, just wait your turn. When it comes, don't let people pressure you into hurrying. The ski boat folks can get a boat on and off a trailer in a flash—those 110-horsepower engines can get a boat onto a trailer while it's sitting in the parking lot, it seems. They hardly take their SUVs out of gear when they launch, so the ten minutes you'll be taking on the ramp will seem like years to them. Don't worry about it. Most people can see that a sailboat is a different animal altogether, and they understand that launching will take a little more time.

At the launch ramp, you won't need to back the boat fast, but it's helpful to make it go where you want without having to make too many corrections. Backing a trailer straight takes practice, so if you start to wander off to one side and you can't correct, stop and pull forward a few feet to straighten things out, and try again. It'll get easier each time you do it. You want the trailer straight when you enter the water. It's tougher to make corrections when you can't see the wheels in your mirrors, and you don't want to roll off the side of the ramp.

You need to get your trailer to a certain depth before your boat will float off. The goal is to have it deep enough that you can push the boat off, but not so deep that the boat floats away on its own. Some ramps are very shallow, and you'll have to practically launch your tow vehicle as well as the boat in order to get the boat to float off. It may be impossible to launch your boat from a shallow ramp, especially if there's a drop-off at the end—you don't want your tires to go over a drop-off, because then you'll need a tow truck to get the trailer out. (This is more likely when trying to launch a deep fixed-keel boat that sits high on a trailer.) You can estimate how much water you'll need at the ramp by measuring the height of the waterline near the wheels (while the boat is on the trailer, of course). Some trailers, especially those with fixed-keel sailboats, have an extension that allows you to get the trailer deeper, but watch out for that drop-off. It's a good idea to ask for advice at a new ramp; if no one is around, put on a bathing suit and walk out to check the length, depth, and condition of the ramp. Wear something on your feet—most ramps are slippery.

If the stern starts to float, then you're getting close to the correct depth. When the angle of the boat changes in your rearview mirror, stop the car. If you have an automatic transmission, put it in park; a manual transmission, leave it in reverse gear and turn it off. You don't want to launch your car, just the boat. Your emergency brake will engage only the rear wheels on most cars, so you'll want to chock the wheels with something. Real wheel chocks from the auto store are best,

though I must admit I usually use a short chunk of wood. (See the sidebar "Use Wheel Chocks at the Ramp" on page 89.) Unhook the bow eye and shove. Hopefully the boat will float off, though sometimes it needs a little more shoving and grunting. If you need to get the trailer deeper, don't forget to pull the wheel chock. Once you figure out your boat and trailer's perfect launching depth, notice how deep the trailer wheels are so that you can repeat this positioning next time you launch the boat.

Once the boat floats free, hand the bow line to your crewmate and park the car and trailer. Either walk the boat to the dock or have your crew toss the line to you, and tie up at the dock while you get the boat ready.

That's sailboat launching in a nutshell. It's obviously a fictional account, since nothing went wrong. It never seems to go that way when I launch—something always seems to goof up, and it's usually my own fault. When it happens to you, don't sweat it. Just take your time, be safe, and fix problems as they come up. Hopefully they'll be minor irritations and nothing that'll cancel your trip.

## MAST-RAISING SYSTEMS

There are some alternatives to muscling the mast up (or down) with brute force and swearing like a sailor. Mast-raising systems can range from very helpful back-savers to fiddly time-wasters. It depends on the system, the boat, and the owner. I haven't used mast-raising systems on my boats because the masts have been fairly manageable, the boats small, and my strength adequate to the task. Your situation may be different.

I know of three basic kinds of mast-raising systems that seem like they'd work. They all use angles to reduce the effort required to raise the mast. Like most everything sailboat related, they all have advantages and disadvantages.

### Single Gin Pole and Babystays

The ideal mast-raising system would consist of parts normally found on the boat already, like the boom and the mainsheet. There's a way to use the boom as a short mast of sorts, holding up a cable that is used to lift the mast. A boom used this way is called a gin pole. A spinnaker pole might work if it were strong, though I wouldn't want to use my expensive spinnaker pole for this kind of job. A push-button or twist-lock whisker pole would not work, because there is a lot of compression on the pole when raising the mast this way.

The downside of using a single gin pole is that it needs a bunch of additional hardware to prevent it, or the mast, from flopping over to the side. This is accomplished with babystays, short pieces of low-stretch rope or wire mounted to a solid point on the deck. But the babystays must be anchored along the same axis as the pivot point of the mast. Otherwise, the babystays will either loosen or

tighten as the mast goes up. The chainplates would be perfect, except that they are almost never in the correct spot. Some sailboat designs can be improved by adding a permanently attached stainless U-bolt to the deck, as shown in the drawing, but make it strong and caulk it well. If your boat has a double set of lower shrouds (as on a Catalina 20), you can use a short bridle connected to the chainplates to create a pivot point at the correct spot. Flush-deck designs like the Cal 20 often have the perfect platform for attaching babystay hardware. Unfortunately, very few trailer sailers have flush decks. The venerable Catalina 22, as well as a few others, has double lowers, but single lowers and uppers, located a few feet aft of the mast step, seems to be a more common method of rigging a trailerable sailboat. You may also need a longer mainsheet or second block and tackle to lower the mast.

Most trailerable sailboats have a raised cabin with a single set of lower shrouds that are swept aft. This is a light, strong, easily rigged, and cost-effective configuration, and that's why it's most often used. In order to use

## What's the Difference between Spinnaker Poles and Whisker Poles?

These two pieces of gear have similar jobs, though the job requirements differ. Spinnaker poles are long poles, usually made of aluminum, with special locking hooks at each end. Spinnaker poles are solid—not adjustable—and they are used only with spinnakers (though they could be used to "pole out" other headsails when sailing downwind). Rigging a spinnaker requires a host of special gear: a topping lift, a downhaul, a mast ring on a track, and three lines for each corner of the spinnaker itself—a spinnaker halyard, a spinnaker sheet, and a spinnaker guy. Racing sailboats usually have plenty of experienced hands aboard. They set spinnakers all the time, no problem. Cruisers don't usually set spinnaker gear unless they've got a long downwind distance to cover in settled weather. The exception is asymmetrical "cruising spinnakers," which are easier to control and require less hardware.

Cruisers routinely use whisker poles rather than spinnakers for downwind sailing. Whisker poles look much like spinnaker poles, but they're usually smaller and lighter. They're often adjustable, using a push-button or twist-lock mechanism. Whisker poles are used to hold the clew of the genoa out when you are running downwind. They reduce the tendency of the headsail to repeatedly fill and collapse, which is hard on the boat. The length of the whisker pole should be the same as the foot of your largest headsail.

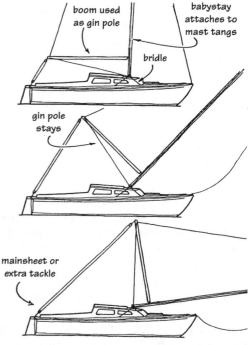

*Lowering the mast with a gin pole and babystays.*

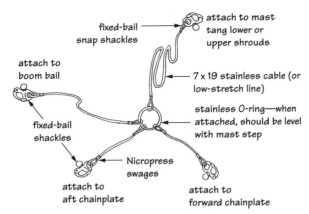

fixed-bail
snap shackles

attach to mast
tang lower or
upper shrouds

attach to
boom bail

7 x 19 stainless cable (or
low-stretch line)

fixed-bail
shackles

stainless O-ring—when
attached, should be level
with mast step

Nicropress
swages

attach to
aft chainplate

attach to
forward chainplate

*A mast-raising "system" you can make yourself. Fixed-bail snap shackles are strong yet reasonably priced, but make sure your chainplate and tang holes are large enough to fit them. If not, regular shackles with quick-pins can be used. A stainless-steel O-ring forms the center pivot point. For boats with single lower shrouds, you would need to add forward and aft attachment points for the lower bridle.*

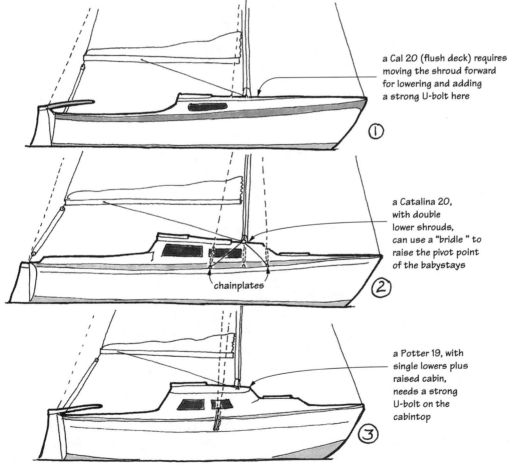

a Cal 20 (flush deck) requires
moving the shroud forward
for lowering and adding
a strong U-bolt here

①

a Catalina 20,
with double
lower shrouds,
can use a "bridle" to
raise the pivot point
of the babystays

chainplates

②

a Potter 19, with
single lowers plus
raised cabin,
needs a strong
U-bolt on the
cabintop

③

*Different rigs adapted for easier lowering.*

a babystay and gin pole system on this type of boat, you need to add a strong attachment point—like a second chainplate or U-bolt—forward at the outside rail or at the cabintop, if the cabin is wide and doesn't have too much crown. Either way, the anchor point for the babystays should be strongly attached to the deck or hull side, with a large backing plate and plenty of bedding compound.

## Sheerlegs

The gin pole/babystay method works, but it means adding a lot of hardware to the boat. There is another alternative that is somewhat

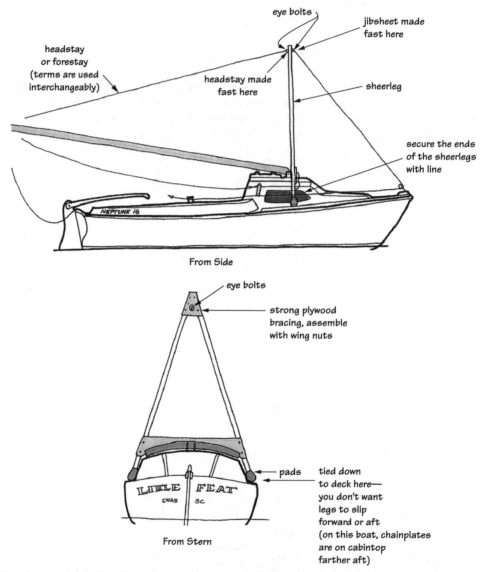

*Raising the mast with sheerlegs. They must be stoutly built of at least 2 x 2 wood or metal. Do not use electrical conduit tube or PVC; they are not strong enough. Pad the feet well, or you risk scratches or gelcoat cracks. If the sheerlegs are assembled with large wing nuts, they can be disassembled and left with the trailer.*

simpler, but it requires some long poles that aren't normally found aboard the typical boat. Suppose that, instead of a single gin pole, we used two poles, fastened together at the top and spread out at the bottom, like a giant A-frame. This method is used by steel boatbuilders to move heavy plates without a crane. They're called sheerlegs, and the principle is pretty simple. Two long, reasonably strong poles are through-bolted near the top. The bottoms of the poles are well padded, and they include a short length of line for securing the sheerlegs to the chainplates, and another line to prevent the legs from spreading too far. The forestay attaches to the top of the sheerlegs, and the sheerlegs are pulled to the deck with the mainsheet. This system requires a pair of babystays for the mast, but the sheerlegs are self-supporting. If you have a second person to help with the mast raising, he or she can take the place of the babystays, following along beside (never under) the mast to make sure it doesn't fall off to one side. Never attempt to raise the mast alone without babystays. As the mast rises higher, the shrouds exert more and more control until the mast is fully raised and the shrouds are tight. Once the mast is up and secured, you've got to find a place to store the sheerlegs, which can be a bit of a disadvantage. In practice, sheerlegs are usually left with the trailer on a rack. They must be well secured for highway travel and locked to prevent theft.

## Trailer Winch Extension

Another intriguing method for raising the mast is to use a trailer winch extension. This method uses a long $2 \times 6$ board or metal pole that extends about 5 feet or more above the deck. The board has a roller on the top, similar to the bow roller. The trailer strap is unhooked from the bow eye, passes over the roller, and is connected to the forestay. Tightening the trailer winch lifts the mast up while a second crewmember guides the mast to prevent it from falling sideways. If you don't have a second crewmember, you'll have to use babystays.

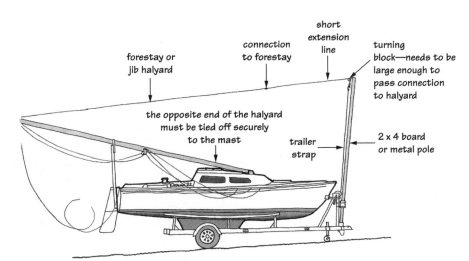

*A trailer winch extension. A large, strong pole is used as a crane to haul the mast upright. You need at least two lines to the mast for this to work. The jib halyard could be used to lift the mast and hold it in place while the forestay is connected, or you could raise the mast with the forestay, secure the mast with a jib or spinnaker halyard, then disconnect the forestay from the trailer strap and attach it to the stemhead fitting. Either way, the other end of the halyard must be tied securely to the mast with a bowline. If it were cleated and it slipped off, the results could be disastrous.*

# CHAPTER SEVEN

# Knots and Lines

ou can use dozens of different knots on your boat, and there are books full of detailed instructions for various bends, hitches, and macramé. If you like the subject of knots and ropework, I encourage you to get one of those excellent volumes and start tying away. The ability to correctly tie the right knot for a particular job is very seamanlike.

However, you don't *have* to know all that stuff in order to safely sail your boat. You *do* need to learn one essential knot, and that's the bowline. No way around it, no substitutions allowed; you *must* learn to tie this knot properly.

The other thing you must know is how to properly cleat a line and secure a coil. Even though you can get by with piling a huge knot of rope on a cleat (many people do; just look at any popular dock and you'll see plenty of cleats with big blobs of line that are holding OK), it looks very lubberly. Besides, cleating a line is very simple to learn; you have to learn it because I said so. Same thing with coiling a line—it keeps the boat neater and the line from tangling, which is safer overall. Simple to learn.

## BOWLINE

The bowline is the knot you'll use 80 percent of the time. What makes this knot so useful is that it can be untied after being put under great strain. This is true for many proper knots. The bowline can be used all over the boat—tying on sheets and halyards, or anytime you need to put a loop in the end of a line. (The sheet bend is similar to the bowline, only it's used to attach two lines together.) There are two methods for

*Tying a bowline with the Killer Rabbit of Caerbannog. First, we make a cave for the rabbit next to a tree.*

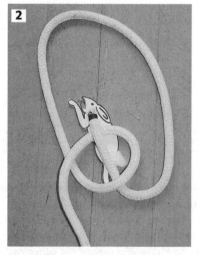

*The rabbit comes out of the cave—*

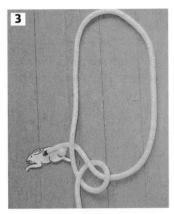

—*goes around the tree, taking out a few knights in the process*—

—*and goes back into the cave.*

*Tighten everything down, and don't leave a tail that's too short or the knot may come undone.*

*An incorrect setup for tying a bowline, also known as a bad cave. Notice the way the loop is formed. If it's incorrect, the knot falls apart. The "tree" should come from* underneath *the loop, and when the rabbit comes out of the cave, he should go* behind *the tree. Try again, making sure the loop is formed correctly, as in the previous photos.*

tying a bowline; I'm going to show you only one. The other methods confuse me, and they'll confuse you, too. I'll show you the simple, non-Cub-Scout-approved, killer-rabbit-in-the-hole method.

That's all there is to the bowline. (But don't get too cocky—some folks can tie this knot one-handed, though that's mostly for cocktail parties.) The only disadvantage to this knot is that it can occasionally be shaken out if tied in a stiff line. Initially you might have difficulty tying this knot because the loop that we are calling a "cave" has to be formed in a particular way. Compare the photos.

## CLEATING A LINE

Properly cleating a line is important because sometimes you need to get a line off a cleat in a hurry. If you've improperly cleated a pile of line on a cleat and the line comes under a lot of tension, the only way to quickly remove it is with a sharp knife.

Although this is the method shown in many books, I have come across one writer who argues that the loop is unnecessary, and could be impossible to remove if the line is brought under strain. He claimed that a turn

*Cleating a line.*

*First, take a turn around the base—*

*—take one turn over the top—*

*—then make a loop, with the tail passing under.*

*Slip the loop over the horn and tighten.*

around the base of the cleat, followed by two or three unsecured turns over the top, is just as secure yet always removable. He makes a good argument, but I still cleat my lines as shown in the photos. Not securing the end with a loop might be OK for a few minutes at the fuel dock, but I wouldn't leave my boat unattended without securing the turns with a final loop.

## COILING AND SECURING A LINE

There's more to coiling a line than you might expect. One thing you shouldn't do is just wrap the line over your thumb and elbow. More often than not, that creates a tight, kinky coil that is very prone to tangle. A line often has a twist in it, and it will be far easier to create a neat coil if you find out which way the twist goes.

To see what I mean, grab a piece of three-strand rope and, with your hands about 2 feet apart, hold it firmly in both hands. Then, without letting it slip, bring your hands closer together. More often than not, the rope will begin to form a spiral. That's the direction in which you want to coil it.

Checking a line for twist. Hold the line firmly—

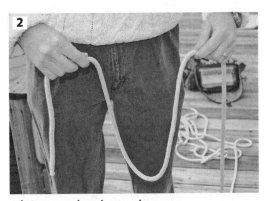

—bring your hands together—

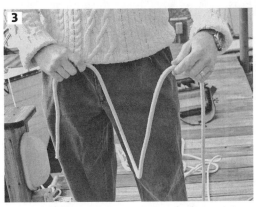

—then follow that twist for the rest of the coil.

To coil the line, reach out and grab about an arm's length of line with one hand and bring it to your other hand, which is busy gathering the line.

Sometimes there won't be an obvious twist to the line, so to help the line coil neatly you can add a little twist of your own. You'll often need to do this when coiling double-braided line. All you have to do is rotate your wrist a little, and the line will twist into a more natural coil.

Don't let go of the coil in your right hand just yet—you need to secure this nice coil of line you've just created. There are several methods for securing a line. The accompanying photo sequence describes one such method.

Coiling a line. Hold the line fixed in your right hand. Reach back a comfortable distance with your left hand—

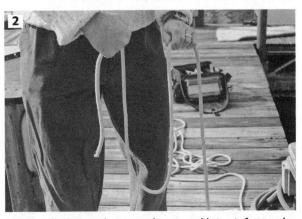

—grasp the line with your palm up and bring it forward—

(Continued)

*—and then rotate your wrist a little, so that your palm is now up.*

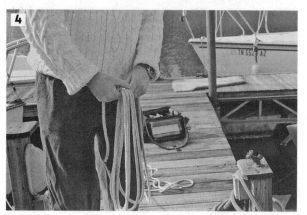

*Grasp the loop with your right hand, reach back the same distance, and repeat the motion. If you're left-handed, of course, you may want to reverse these directions.*

*Securing a coil. Leave a few extra feet loose when coiling.*

*Take three or four turns around the entire bundle.*

*Pass the loose end through the bottom loop—*

*—and then pass the middle of the remaining end through the top loop.*

*Drop the small loop over the bundled loop and pull it snug.*

A coil of line secured this way is ready to stow, and will stay in place until needed.

Securing a coiled halyard is similar, but you don't take three or four turns around the entire bundle. Simply coil the line, then, with the loose end, take a turn or two around the coil and loop the end over the cleat.

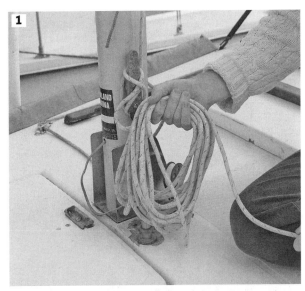

*Securing a halyard on a cleat. Leave the coil open; don't take any turns around the entire bundle. Grab the middle of the loose end—*

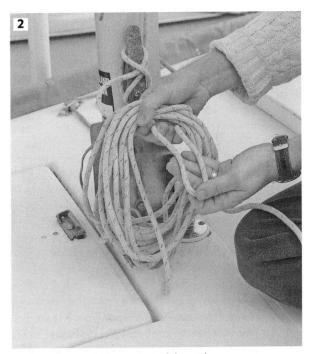

*—pass it through the center of the coil—*

*(Continued)*

*—then twist and drop the loop over the top of the cleat.*

If this seems like too much trouble, there is another option. I saw this in Lin and Larry Pardey's *The Cost Conscious Cruiser* (the Pardeys are among my favorite authors), who in turn learned it from Hal Roth, aboard

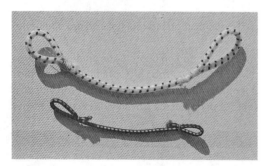

*A pair of halyard leashes made from a short length of bungee cord, though regular line works fine, too. The large example was made by seizing the ends with thread; the smaller one was made in about two minutes using bulldog clips, which are normally used in commercial bungee hooks.*

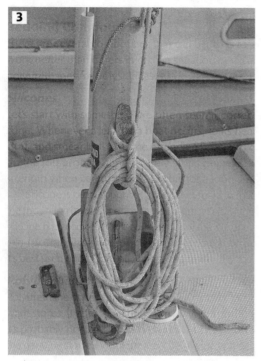

*Securing the halyard leash to an open-base cleat. These work with closed-base cleats, too, if you can size one of the loops to fit the base of the cleat. Stretch it over the base, and you're ready to go.*

*Whisper*. It's nothing more than a short length of light line tied to the hollow base of a halyard cleat. When the halyard is coiled up, use the light line to secure the coil—no knots required. Each coil of line needs its own little leash, though, or you'll get a tangle.

## OTHER KNOTS

There are a few other important knots, though I use only one on a regular basis. This is the figure-eight, or stopper knot, shaped like a figure eight. It's easily untied. What you don't want on your boat is an overhand knot, which

A halyard leash in use. The second loop fits over the upper horn of the cleat, and gravity does the rest.

A stopper, or figure-eight, knot (left) and an overhand knot (right). Leave the overhand knots ashore.

A sheet bend (left) and a double sheet bend (right).

is difficult to untie after coming under a strain. If the line is wet, forget it—you'll never get an overhand knot untied. Stopper knots are used in the ends of the headsail sheets after you've rigged them through the sheet lead blocks; they prevent the sheets from being pulled overboard when they dip in the water.

The sheet bend is handy when you need to tie two lines together. It is tied like the bowline. One line is the cave and the tree, the other line is the rabbit. This knot can be made more secure by letting the rabbit go twice around the tree, making a double sheet bend.

If you need to tie your boat to a piling, you'll need to know how to tie a clove hitch. It's a very simple knot: make one turn around the piling, angle the end of the line down, make a second turn, and tuck the end under the middle.

The last knot that's handy to know is the square knot or reef knot, used when reefing sails. The most important thing to know about

*Another way of tying the clove hitch. Start with two loops, just as you would coil a line.*

*Bring the two loops together, one on top of the other, but notice a small detail—the bottom loop (on the left side of the photo) gets pulled above the top loop (on the right).*

*Continue bringing the loops together—*

*—and throw both loops over the top of a piling. Snug the ends tight, and you've tied a clove hitch.*

*An undesirable granny knot on the left, and a proper reef knot on the right. Leave Granny ashore!*

square knots is that a subtle mistake turns them into granny knots. Often your hands seem to naturally tie granny knots because they use a repeated hand motion, but granny knots are not secure—they either slip or jam. Check your square knots carefully after you tie them. When tied correctly, they look like two loops locked together. The ends of the loop stay together. In a granny knot, the ends are apart.

# CHAPTER EIGHT

# Getting Underway and Sailing

Enough already, let's go sailing! Gather up all your stuff and climb aboard. Before you shove off, stow all your gear in its proper place down below. Remember, your boat will be heeling (leaning over) from the force of the wind, so use lockers or netting to keep things secure. Small bungee cords are handy if you've got some attachment points where they can be fastened. (Small stainless or bronze eye straps for attaching bungees are easy to add, but go sailing a time or two before you install them. You'll often discover the perfect location after a little on-the-water experience.)

Something that's easy to forget is lowering the centerboard. You'll be reminded as soon as you cast off. Most trailerable boats handle very differently with the centerboard up, and some shallow-draft boats seem to like going sideways better than forward with the board up. Another helpful detail—on many trailerable boats, the keel cable and winch are located inside the cabin. The exit point for the cable is a small hole or tube where the cable enters the boat and leads to the winch. A little water often sloshes up through this tube while motoring or sailing. Not much water, but enough to get your shoes wet if you're not expecting it. I wrap a small rag around the cable and stuff a little down in the hole. It saves time sponging up the cabin later. Remember to hang the damp rag outside to dry at the end of your sailing day, or it'll get pretty stinky.

## SETTING UP THE HEADSAIL

If you followed the procedures in Chapter 6, you've already raised the mast and rigged the mainsail. Now it's time to bend on the headsail. Find your headsail and attach it to the forestay. If you have more than one headsail, use the standard jib for your first sail. (See the sidebar "Headsail Sizes" for more about the different sizes and names of headsails.) Initially, you may be a little confused about which corner is the head, which corner is the tack, and which corner is the clew. The head is the sharpest point of the sail. You can leave a sheet tied to the clew. All that's left is the tack, which gets attached to the deck at the stemhead fitting. Or you can take a pencil and write the names on the corners, which will help you remember the proper terms. By the time the graphite fades, you should have the names down pat.

The luff hanks are usually little plastic or bronze clips that snap onto the forestay. Remember, the hanks always face the same direction when you're putting them on the forestay. Of course, if you have roller furling, you won't have to worry about any of this stuff. (See the sidebar "Roller Furling for the Trailer Sailer.") But you'll pay for the convenience at launch time, since roller-furling headsails are often more complicated and time-consuming to set up initially.

Start at the bow and attach the tack of the jib to the stemhead fitting on the foredeck. My boat uses a pin for this; yours may use a shackle. Then, starting at the bottom, clip the jib hanks onto the forestay, starting with the lowest one and working your way up. Then attach the halyard to the head of the sail. Usually a shackle attached to the jib halyard is used here.

## Headsail Sizes

Most trailerable sailboats are rigged as sloops (sloops are single-masted rigs featuring a triangular mainsail and headsail). These usually have a single mainsail that can be reduced in size by reefing. But the headsail, being much easier to put on and take off, is changed to suit conditions. Large sails of lightweight cloth are rigged for light winds, while heavier, smaller sails are used when the wind pipes up. These sails can have different names, depending on their size and intended use. Cruising boats can have anywhere from one headsail to several, depending on the desires of the owner. Most racing boats will have many headsails in order to stay competitive.

There is no standard size for headsails—it varies from boat to boat. Half of the key to a particular sailboat's headsail size is the sail's LP measurement, which stands for luff perpendicular. To find the LP, measure the distance from the clew of the sail to the luff while holding the tape at a 90-degree angle to the luff. The other half of the key is the J measurement. The J is the distance between the forestay and the mast, measured at the deck.

Headsails are often referred to by number rather than by name. A 100 percent jib is a sail where the LP is equal to the J. You can correctly call this sail a 100 percent jib or, more simply, a "100." This is the easiest way to refer to sails. It's a lot simpler to say, "Let's put on the 120" rather than "Let's put on the #2 genoa." Both refer to the same sail, more or less, but the percentage number is more intuitive. Larger percentage numbers equal bigger sails, but the #2 genoa is smaller than the #1 genoa.

Here are the more common headsails found in the average cruisers' inventory:

The jib is the most basic headsail. If sails are included with the boat (not all are), most manufacturers supply a main and a jib. A working jib is usually around 100 percent. You won't see many jibs smaller than 80 percent.

Probably the first sail you'll add to your boat's inventory is a genoa, for use in lighter air. These are commonly around 150 percent. Technically, genoas overlap the main, so anything over 100 percent could be called a genoa. (Just to confuse the goose, anything that overlaps the mast is also called a lapper.) But there's very little difference between a 100 and a 110, and not all books agree on the names.

A really small, tough jib is called a storm jib. If you're a long-distance voyager, you might want one, but trailer

drifter

170 genoa

135 genoa

working jib

storm jib

*Headsails can range in size from the very small and heavily built storm jib to a thin drifter used only in the lightest of conditions.*

sailers aren't exactly open-ocean greyhounds. My boat came with a storm jib. As near as I can tell, it's never been used.

For really light air, there's the drifter or reacher. These sails are big, at about 170 percent or larger, and normally are for downwind work. Several fancy terms are also used for very large downwind sails, like big boy, blooper, ghoster, or, my personal favorite, the gollywobbler. While there are subtle differences in these sails, they are rarely seen aboard trailerables, since storage space for specialized sails is limited. (I'd like to get a small one, though, just so I can say "gollywobbler" all the time.)

Spinnakers are a different beast altogether. They are made of very light, stretchy nylon and are designed to trap air, while other sails are designed to change the way air flows. Spinnakers are tricky to fly, requiring a spinnaker pole to hold them out so they can properly fill, along with a lift and a downhaul for the pole. Spinnakers are symmetrical—they have a head and two identical clews. When you jibe a spinnaker (jibing is turning the boat so the wind crosses the stern; see page 126), you swap the lower corners. Since both sides of the sail are identical, you switch the inboard end for the outboard end, and vice versa. You can't do this with any other sail.

The cruising spinnaker is primarily for use when the wind is on the beam or behind. Cruising spinnakers are asymmetrical, whereas true spinnakers are symmetrical. There are no luff hanks, and the luff isn't attached to the forestay, as it is with a conventional jib. Instead, the sail flies from its three corners only. You can use a pole on a cruising spinnaker, but you don't have to. A particular type of cruising spinnaker is called a code zero. While it sounds like something from a James Bond movie, it's just a cruising spinnaker cut so it can be flown closer to the wind, at angles of 45 degrees to 100 degrees, in winds of 3 to 6 knots. It's a little smaller than a regular asymmetrical spinnaker and it's a free-flying sail—it isn't attached to the headstay. A code zero could be a useful sail for a trailer sailer, but it isn't a common part of the average trailer sailer's inventory. In fact, many race rules impose a penalty for using a code zero sail in the smaller-class boats.

## Roller Furling for the Trailer Sailer

If you've spent any time on the water, then you've probably seen roller-furling headsails in action. There's a small drum at the base of the forestay with a line around it. To get the headsail down, all one has to do is pull a line and the sail wraps itself neatly around the swiveling forestay. It's a very handy and efficient system that makes taming a large foresail relatively easy.

But roller-furlers do have their drawbacks. They are primarily designed for larger boats and are usually permanent installations—most roller-furlers require modifications to the headstay and the sails. They aren't particularly well suited for boats whose masts are raised and lowered all the time, like trailer sailers, and the drums complicate the forestay connection.

With roller-furlers, the headsail isn't changed frequently, since the luff of the sail slides into a slotted foil around the stay. Feeding the sail into the foil is more difficult than simply hanking it to the forestay, and you may wish for a bigger sail on those light-winded days.

*Harken's small-boat furlers.*

*(Continued)*

This isn't universally true, though. I had an older freestanding roller-furling unit on my Catalina 27. The furler was permanently attached to the 170 headsail, and the whole assembly—rolled-up sail and furling drum—was stored in a sailbag. The sail's head had a swivel attached, and it had its own luff cable. You raised the rolled-up sail with the halyard and deployed the sail by pulling on the clew. As the sail unrolled, the furling line coiled up the drum (you had to keep a little tension on the furling line or the line would foul).

Once deployed, the big sail could be easily controlled with the furler, though it was impossible to get a very straight luff. The halyard tension was a mere fraction of the normal headstay tension, no matter how tightly the halyard was winched. The luff sagging off to leeward hurt the boat's pointing ability. Even so, it was great off the wind. These types of furlers are still available from Harken and Schaefer as small-boat furling kits, and they're specifically made for trailerable sailboats. Other small-boat furlers are available from Colligo and Fachor.

Two furling systems that reportedly work well with trailerables are the CDI Flexible Furler and the Schaefer Snapfurl 500s. These are "around-the-stay" systems, using a headstay foil that is more

*A Colligo furling unit.*

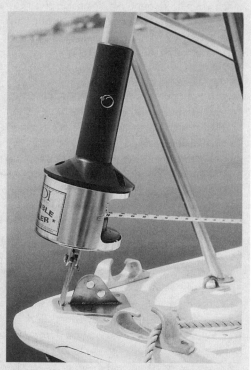

*Typical roller-furling units small enough for use on a trailer sailer; left is a Schaefer unit; above is from CDI.*

flexible than an aluminum foil. The CDI requires some rigging modification, which increases your cost a bit, while the Schaefer unit attaches to your existing rig without the need to change anything. (Remember, with either type, you'll still need your sail modified for roller furling.)

## A Roller-Furling Alternative

There is an alternative to roller furling—a jib downhaul. This is a much lower-tech way to control the sail from the cockpit. You'll need cockpit-led halyards for this to work, though.

A jib downhaul is simply a light line that's attached to the head of the jib. The other end of the line runs through a block at the bow and back to the cockpit. To use it, all you do is release the halyard and pull on the downhaul, and the jib is pulled down to the deck. You'll still need to go forward to unhank and stow the jib, but a downhaul can be put to good use when approaching a dock or an anchorage under sail if you need to depower the boat quickly. California boatbuilder Jerry Montgomery, builder of the Lyle Hess–designed Montgomery 17, told me that he considered a jib downhaul an essential piece of gear—so much so that he considered raising the price of his boats to make it standard equipment.

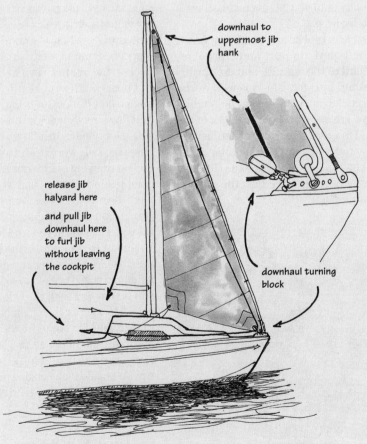

downhaul to uppermost jib hank

release jib halyard here

and pull jib downhaul here to furl jib without leaving the cockpit

downhaul turning block

*A jib downhaul, a simpler and less expensive alternative to roller-furling headsails.*

## ATTACHING THE HEADSAIL SHEETS

Two sheets attach to your headsail. Remember— *halyards lift sails, sheets pull sails in.* Most headsails are rigged with two sheets, one on port and one on starboard. These can form one continous line (see the sidebar "Alternative Ways to Attach Headsail Sheets"), passing through sheet lead blocks and then aft to the cockpit. Only one sheet is used at a time, the downwind or the leeward sheet. The other sheet will be slacked off, and then it's called the lazy sheet. If it gets too slack, it may dip in the water and trail alongside. (Use the stopper knot you just learned to prevent the sheets from coming out of their blocks. Always check for trailing sheets before you start a motor. They'll wrap around the prop shaft in the blink of an eye, and you'll be without maneuverability until you get the mainsail up— if the wind is blowing.)

The sheet lead blocks are usually mounted on tracks outboard, on port and starboard, about one third of the way aft, and are spring-loaded to stand upright. The position of the sheet lead blocks can be adjusted depending on the sail you're using and the strength of the wind. Since I'm more of a cruiser, I adjust the sheet lead blocks forward for smaller sails, and slide them back for larger sails. I determine the exact position once I get the sails up and the boat moving.

*Two separate headsail sheets attached with a pair of bowlines.*

Used boats sometimes have a shackle for connecting the sheet to the clew of the sail. This allows for nice, quick changes of the headsail without rerigging another sheet. It also allows you to get your teeth knocked out when the wind gets up and the sail luffs madly as you try to get the headsail down. If your boat has any sort of shackle or metal clip attached to the headsail sheet, remove it. If the clip can't be untied, cut it off and buy yourself some nice new headsail sheets. Tie the sheets to the headsail clew using bowlines.

Run the sheet through the sheet lead blocks, toss the line in the cockpit, and tie a figure-eight knot in the very end. I always rig both sails— headsail and mainsail—and have them ready to go before I cast off from a dock or mooring. My sails are my backup plan. If something happens to my motor, then at least I have an option. This happened once when my good friends and crew Mark and Suzanne were with me. We were almost back to the marina, right in the middle of Elliot Cut near Charleston, South Carolina, when the engine quit. Elliot Cut is narrow—the tidal current flows really quickly through it—and it often gets a lot of barge traffic and large powerboats. Since the sails were ready to go, we got the main up and drawing before our forward momentum completely died away, and we had enough movement through the water for the rudder to work. (If your sailboat ever becomes dead still relative to the water around it, your rudder no longer works. Water has to flow across the blade for it to steer the boat. You've lost steerageway, which is the minimum speed needed to steer the boat. You can still be moving with the tide, as we were—at a good 3 to 4 knots, if I remember correctly—heading straight for some tricky bends in the cut.) Mark got the mainsail up, Suz got the anchor ready, and we were able to find a spot out of the way so I could make engine repairs.

Once your sails are rigged and ready to hoist, you can cast off.

## LEAVING THE DOCK

Most of the time, leaving the dock is pretty simple. You start the outboard motor and check that it's operating normally. This means making sure there's a stream of cooling water coming from the motor head. Check this every time you can; don't just start the motor, check it once, then forget it. Hopefully your cooling water intake will never get clogged. While

## Alternative Ways to Attach Headsail Sheets

There are a few alternative methods for attaching headsail sheets that you can try if you want to experiment, and if the idea of learning another knot or two doesn't make you want to pull your hair out.

For example, some folks—myself included—like to use a single length of line for both sheets, tied in the middle. One advantage is that the knot at the clew can be smaller. (A pair of bowlines, although unlikely to knock you out cold if they whack you when the sail is flogging, will still hurt like hell.) If you don't mind threading a new sheet every time you bend on a new headsail, you can leave it tied to the sail and stored in the bag. A handy knot for this is a bowline on a bight. A bight in a line is any part between the two ends, but especially a line bent back on itself to form a loop.

But being able to change the headsail without rerigging the sheets would be handy. Aren't there any ways to do this without using something metal?

Yes, there are. I learned a couple of neat tricks from an article by Geoffrey Toye in *Good Old Boat* magazine. A method called a Dutch shackle uses a short length of spliced line attached to a loop spliced into the headsheet. To use a Dutch shackle, you pull the loop through the clew, pass the short line through the loop, and secure it with a stopper knot at the end of the short line. Modifications are certainly allowed, so feel free to experiment.

Geoffrey's preferred method is a short tail of line spliced to the headsail. This is tied to the middle of the sheet (or the bight, if you prefer) using a double sheet bend.

*A bowline on a bight tied to a headsail.*

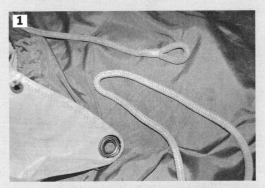

*The Dutch shackle is really nothing more than a short length of line with an eye splice at one end. Here's how it's used to attach to attach headsail sheets.*

*First, pass the middle of the sheet through the eye splice. It helps if the eye splice is sized for a snug fit.*

*(Continued)*

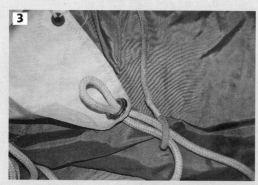

Next, pass the sheet through the clew of the headsail.

Another method of attaching sheets uses a tail of line permanently attached to the sail clew with an eye splice.

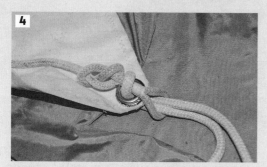

To finish, pass the tail of the eye splice through the loop formed by the middle of the jibsheet, and tie a stopper knot on the other side. To release the shackle, simply push enough of the sheet through the clew until there's room to pull the stopper knot through.

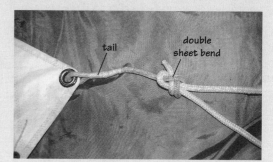

This method is more time-consuming to untie and is less likely to shake out. It's also lighter in weight—one line is at the clew instead of two—so the sails will set better in very light winds. And the knot that will whack you if the sail is flogging is smaller and farther away from the clew.

you're still securely tied up and the motor is at idle speed, put the motor in gear and run up the rpms a little bit. More than one motor has died the moment it was put into gear.

If everything checks out OK, untie the spring lines and stow them, then untie the bow line and toss it aboard. Next I untie the stern line, but I'll hold the stern against the dock for a moment. This is a good time to glance down at the water to be certain that no lines that might foul the propeller have strayed overboard. Usually, the bow will slowly start to drift away from the dock. When the boat is

pointing in the direction I want to go, I release the line and hop aboard with one little shove off the dock. Only after the stern dockline is safely aboard do I put the motor in gear.

This simple little routine can be dangerous if your dockline handlers are careless or inexperienced. You should never allow any part of your body to come between the dock and the boat. Videos of people falling in the water with one leg on a boat and one on the dock are hysterical, but if the boat is at all large and it starts to drift back toward the swimmer—well, just watch what your boat does to a single fender

## Safe Procedures for Gasoline Outboard Motors

On larger cruising sailboats, diesel motors are greatly preferred because they are inherently safer. Diesel fumes won't ignite unless compressed, though they will make you seasick. You don't get the chance to be seasick from gasoline vapors, because you'd likely blow up long before you'd hurl. Gasoline vapors explode, and a nearly empty fuel container can explode like a bomb. If your bilge collects enough gasoline vapors, all you need is a spark from a less-than-perfect electrical connection to put an end to your on-the-water career.

This is why the Coast Guard has formulated very specific rules for fueling boats, carrying gasoline on board, storing gasoline, and venting compartments. These rules should be followed to the letter—even exceeded if possible. The guidelines given here are not a complete or up-to-date representation of all USCG requirements. For a complete look at the USCG rules, go to http://www.uscgboating.org/. If you want to go straight to the source, look up the Code of Federal Regulations, the final word on U.S. maritime law. Go to www.gpoaccess.gov/cfr/index.html and search for "recreational vessels." You'll get more information than you want. A more readable version of the rules can be found in a general seamanship manual, such as *Chapman's Piloting, Seamanship, and Small-Boat Handling.*

In a nutshell, be very careful when handling gasoline aboard your boat; don't become cavalier as you become experienced. Here are some basic guidelines.

Secure on-deck tanks so they can't move about, and of course store fuel in approved containers only. I keep extra fuel for my two-stroke outboard premixed in a 1-gallon fuel tank. The tank is small enough that it doesn't get in the way, and I can keep it on deck so that fumes don't collect inside the boat. Not only does this reduce the risk of fire, it also keeps the inside of the boat from smelling like a gas station. Unless you're motoring down the Mississippi, it's usually better to carry smaller amounts of fuel rather than huge tanks.

When fueling your boat, close all hatches and ports to prevent fumes from entering below. After fueling, open up the hatches and give the boat a chance to air out before starting the engine. If you have portable tanks of 5 gallons or less, it's often safer and less expensive to fill them off the boat, at a gas station rather than the marina.

Do not let any fuel get into the water. (Oil spills of any type are illegal, in fact.) Place something around your fuel intake and your vent to catch drips. Fuel-absorbent pads that won't absorb water are very handy and readily available. Remember, spill-control equipment such as paper towels, rags, and oil-absorbent pads or bilge socks are now required on recreational vessels. (If you do cause any type of fuel spill, you must report it to the National Response Center at 1-800-424-8802 or the U.S. Coast Guard on VHF Channel 16.)

Keep a fire extinguisher close to your outboard and fuel tank. If you ever need one, you'll need it *really* quickly. Buried in the bottom of a locker won't help. You can now buy fire extinguishers that are not much bigger than a can of spray paint. Although some of these are not USCG approved (so you should also have a primary fire extinguisher), they are perfect for a seat locker. See "USCG-Required Equipment" in Chapter 5.

on a windy day and you can see what might happen to a human body.

Pull in your fenders as soon as you leave the dock unless you're headed directly for another dock. Don't leave the fenders lying on deck. Never hang dirty or limp, half-deflated fenders. Stow your docking lines, but keep them in a place that's accessible—you may need to get to them quickly.

Sometimes, if the conditions are right, you can leave the dock under sail, without starting the motor. Check the current and wind direction before you try this, and make sure you've got plenty of room. Sailboats do have the right-of-way over powerboats, but not in a restricted channel or in places where the other vessels are constrained by draft (see "Rules of the Road" in Chapter 9). You shouldn't expect other boats to rush out of your way because you want to try a fancy sailing maneuver at a busy boat ramp. However, if things are calm and the way is clear, by all means give it a try. A

## Teach Your Crew about Safety

Do everything you can to instruct your crew about the possibility of injury while sailing a boat. The risks of getting hurt are remote—far fewer people are injured on sailboats than on other types of watercraft. But still, accidents can and do happen, and the captain is in charge.

I mention risks that I know of, but don't count on this book to tell you all the risks involved, as there are certainly ways to hurt yourself that I can't predict. You can learn a great deal about boating safety by reading accident reports. These are kept by the U.S. Coast Guard and are available online.

For example, in 2004, there were 676 deaths involving recreational boats. Of these, only 16 happened in either a sailing auxiliary—meaning a boat with a motor, like a trailerable sailboat—or a small sailboat without a motor. Of these 16 deaths, 13 were drownings, and 3 were from other causes. So we can deduce that the biggest risk on board is falling overboard and drowning, and we can reduce that risk with lifelines, safety harnesses, life jackets, personal strobes, locator beacons, and so on.

Some insurance agencies publish boating accident data that we can learn from. One of the best is BoatU.S., which publishes the quarterly magazine *Seaworthy*. It's filled with stories and reports of damage and accidents from their claim files, and it's very informative.

If those don't make you cautious, read this lovely little quote I found on a lawyer's website: "If you've been hurt on a boat or a ferry, you may be able to file a lawsuit against the boat or ferry operator and collect compensation for your pain and suffering—No Fee Until We Win!"

I don't believe you need to go so far as to have your crew sign a waiver, but you should carefully instruct them about the potential danger of using a foot as a fender. If your boat is large, even getting a finger caught between a cleat and a line can be serious. Be specific about risk when instructing your crew. Have fun, but be safe!

trailer sailer is the perfect boat to practice leaving (and even approaching) a dock under sail. Since it's smaller and lighter than most boats, you'll be less likely to cause damage if you misjudge something. But many small sailboats react as a big boat would, so you can learn a great deal. If you're brand new to sailing, I advise taking the boat out several times in various conditions to get a feel for leeway, drift, and so on, before trying anything fancy.

In some situations the boat will do something unexpected when you untie it from the dock. For example, the wind might be blowing you against the dock and the bow will stay snugly against it even when untied. Just to make things interesting, let's suppose you're also at a busy fuel dock with boats in front of and behind you. In this case, you'll have to motor out. You could probably tie an extra fender at the aft corner of the hull and have your crew push the bow out until you get enough clearance to put the motor in forward

gear and power out. But be careful—if the wind is strong, it's going to push you sideways, and you may scrape the boat ahead of you as you power away. If possible, point the bow directly into the wind before powering out.

## Stern Swing

The first time you take command of a sailboat, you'll notice something that will take a little getting used to. When you turn a boat, it doesn't track the same way a car does. A car pivots around its front wheels—all you have to do is turn the wheel and the rest of the car usually follows. But a boat is completely different. Its pivot point is somewhere just aft of the mast. When you turn the rudder, the boat rotates around this pivot point. The bow swings into the direction of your turn, and the stern swings out. If you are maneuvering slowly and making sharper turns, this effect is more pronounced.

Many new sailors are painfully reminded to allow for stern swing when leaving the dock for

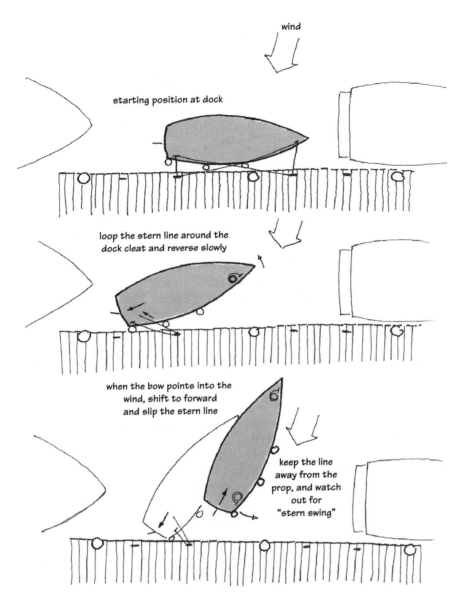

wind

starting position at dock

loop the stern line around the
dock cleat and reverse slowly

when the bow points into the
wind, shift to forward
and slip the stern line

keep the line
away from the
prop, and watch
out for
"stern swing"

*Powering out of a crowded dock in a crosswind.*

the first time, as a sharp turn brings their stern crashing into a piling or, worse, another boat. As luck has it, it's usually a shiny new one owned by a trial lawyer. Be sure to allow plenty of room for stern swing when entering or leaving a dock, and go very slowly until you get a good feel for how your vessel handles under power.

Most trailer sailers have an advantage, and that's their outboard motor. Often there's

enough clearance to turn the motor quite a bit, and you can use this to fight the force of the wind. You may be able to back out of the dock.

Your boat behaves differently in reverse than it does in forward. Inboard boats (boats with engines mounted below) especially want to go sideways in reverse. On a trailer sailer, you counteract this by aiming the outboard where you want to go, but the boat will still do some

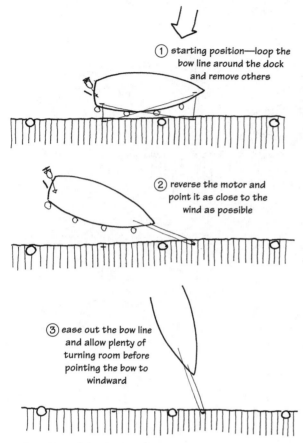

*Backing out of the dock with an outboard.*

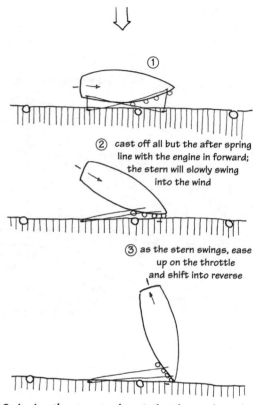

*Swinging the stern to the wind with an inboard.*

odd things. My Montgomery doesn't like to go in reverse at all, even though the motor can spin 360 degrees on its mount. Try powering in reverse when you're out in the bay and can't run into anything, just to see how your boat behaves. It'll help if you have a piling or marker buoy nearby so you can see exactly where you're going and how straight your course is.

Some boats—inboards, especially—cannot back into a beam wind like an outboard can. In that case, you might have to swing the stern into the wind with the engine in forward gear, using a spring line. Be careful, though—this method requires strong cleats and lines, and precision timing once the stern faces the wind.

Sometimes things at the dock can get really tricky, such as when a tide or current flows one way and the breeze blows another. Conditions can get so difficult that you can't power out of the dock without hitting something. I lived at a marina on a tidal river for a number of years. When the tide was outgoing, the current would flow into and across my slip at 4 knots. After several very close calls when docking, I finally learned to wait until the tide turned before bringing the boat into the slip; I'd wait at the end of the dock if there was space, or anchor out for a few hours. If you absolutely have to get out of a slip against the tide and wind, the only choices might be to get a tow from a larger vessel or to row out an anchor with your dinghy (trailing the anchor rode behind you), toss it overboard, and pull yourself out using your winches. Having flexible plans has always been a necessary part of the sailing lifestyle.

## SAILING

You've cleared the dock and are out in the channel. The chart shows plenty of depth around you—you wouldn't sail without a chart, right? There's a nice steady breeze. Time to haul up the sails. I usually hoist the main first. Head into the wind and haul away on the main halyard. Raise the sail as far as it will go. You may have a winch on the mast to increase the tension. If you do, take a few turns around it and see if you can get the sail stretched tight. The halyard should be tensioned just enough to get the wrinkles out of the sail. A halyard that isn't under enough tension usually shows as little wrinkles radiating out from each of the sail slides. If you've hauled the main up as far as possible and you still have wrinkles at the luff, then try lowering the boom a little. (You may have a fixed gooseneck bolted to the mast. If so, you'll have to get the wrinkles out with the halyard alone. If you have a sliding gooseneck, tighten the downhaul until the wrinkles smooth out. The downhaul is a short line at the mast end of the boom that holds the boom down and cleats to the base of the mast.)

Sometimes you can't get the wrinkles to go away, even though the halyard is tight. This could be a sign of a shrunken boltrope (some shrink with age), or it might mean that your sail is ready for retirement. A sailmaker can tell you whether the boltrope can be restitched or the sail should be replaced. Cruising sailors are notorious for using sails far past their expiration date, while racing sailors are notorious for buying a new sail every season. Occasionally, you can find a race class with the same spar dimensions as yours and try a retired racing sail. Sometimes they'll work great, but often they're made with high-tech materials that require special care (such as careful rolling instead of folding), so they don't always stand up well to the demands of cruising.

Raise the jib next. Haul on the jib halyard as far as it can go, again stretching the luff until the wrinkles smooth out. Turn your boat to either side about 45 degrees from the wind. Pull in the sheets and shut off the motor—you're sailing.

## Points of Sail

If you're sailing about 45 degrees to the wind, with the wind blowing over the port (left) side of the boat, you're said to be sailing upwind. To get even more specific, you're sailing close-hauled, on a port tack. (This port tack business will be important later, when we discuss the rules of the road.) For now, just try to remember that port or starboard tack refers to where the wind is coming *from*. If it helps, drop the tack and tell yourself you're sailing on port. Just to confuse you, this is also called beating to windward.

A few maneuvers will help to illustrate the points of sail. Turn the boat a little more to starboard (to the right). When the wind is coming at an angle of about 60 degrees, you're sailing on a close reach. You're still sailing upwind,

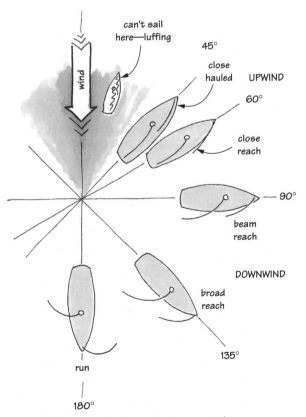

Note: all these examples show a boat on port tack.

*The points of sail.*

and you're still on a port tack. A close reach is one of the fastest points of sail.

If you continue turning to starboard, eventually the wind will come directly on the beam, or at an angle of about 90 degrees. This is a beam reach. You're still on port, but you're sailing neither upwind nor downwind. As you turn away from the wind, let your sails out a little—known as easing the sheets. (I'll talk more about sail trim in a moment.)

Turn a little more and you will start heading downwind. If you turn to starboard until the wind is coming about 45 degrees from the stern, you're heading downwind on a broad reach. As long as the boom is on the starboard side of the

boat, you're on a port tack. Now it is time to start paying attention to the boom, which could swing across the cockpit unexpectedly. Stay low, and keep letting those sheets out.

### Jibing

The last point of sail is a downwind run, where the wind is coming directly from behind, over the stern. When you're going dead downwind, the position of the boom determines what tack you're on. If the boom is on the starboard side of the boat, you're still on a port tack. You can change that by performing a jibe. Before you turn any farther, say to your crew, "Ready to jibe." The crew should stand by the jibsheet. (That's "stand by" in the figurative, not literal, sense, since the boom is about to sweep the cockpit clean of anyone foolish enough to be standing.) The crew replies, "Ready." Tighten the mainsheet all the way, bringing the boom nearly to the center of the boat. As you turn the helm to port, say, "Jibe-ho!" Continue to turn until the wind catches the after edge of the sail (the leech) and the boom switches to the other side of the boat. The crew will cast off the jibsheet and take up the slack on the other side, which is now the downwind sheet. Since your boom has crossed over to the port side of the boat, you're now on a starboard tack. You've just jibed the boat, which means, in effect, making the wind cross the stern of the boat by turning.

### Tacking

You can continue turning to port, going through all the points of sail on the starboard tack, until you're close-hauled again. Now let's tack the boat. Tacking means to make the wind cross the bow of the boat by turning. Tacking won't always work if you don't have enough momentum, so, if necessary, fall off the wind a little (turn a little bit downwind) to get your speed up. Warn the crew by saying, "Ready about." Again the crew stands by the jibsheet and says, "Ready." As you begin your turn, the helmsman always says, "Helm's a-lee," meaning the helm has been put to leeward. As you turn the tiller, make your movement nice and

## Accidental Jibe

Whenever you're sailing downwind, there's a risk of an accidental jibe. This happens when you're going downwind with the boom out, and then either the wind shifts or the boat turns a little and the boom suddenly swings over to the other side of the boat. If someone is unlucky or inattentive enough to be standing up in the cockpit at the time, the results can vary from an embarrassing knot on the head in very light winds to a serious injury in moderate to strong winds. Sailors have been knocked overboard and drowned this way. Here are some safety steps to take when sailing downwind:

1. Keep your crew, and yourself, seated in the cockpit when sailing downwind, especially when running. If someone needs to go forward to tend the jib, they should keep all body parts below the level of the boom. If that isn't possible, sheet the boom in before they go forward, then let it back out once they reach the foredeck.

2. Use a preventer or a boom brake. A preventer is a line that connects the boom to a reinforced point on the rail. Often the boom vang can make a good preventer. A boom brake is a commercial device that uses a drum with a few loose turns of line to slow the speed of the boom down to something a little safer.

3. Watch out for the signs of an accidental jibe. The boom will lift (if it isn't tightened down by a vang or the traveler) and the mainsail leech will start to flutter just before an accidental jibe occurs.

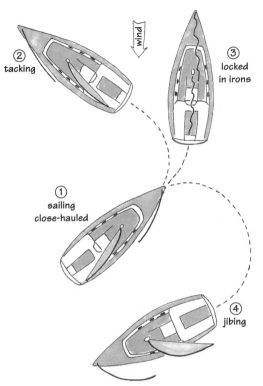

*Tacking, jibing, and locked in irons: (1) sailing close-hauled on a port tack at a nice rate of speed; (2) a nice, even turn to port—the boom has crossed over to the port side, and we're sailing along on a starboard tack; (3) what happens if we try this maneuver without enough speed, or if we slam the rudder over too hard. The boat drifts into the eye of the wind and stays there, like a giant, expensive weather vane. She'll come to a stop and start to drift backward. (4) We should jibe if the wind is really light and we don't have enough speed to tack. By turning the helm to starboard and letting out the sails, we can slowly come around until the boom crosses over—we've jibed onto a starboard tack.*

steady. If you shove the helm all the way to leeward in a quick movement, you'll separate the water flow over the rudder blade, and it'll act like a brake. If everything goes correctly, the boat will turn through the wind and begin to fall off on its new heading.

As the boat passes through the eye of the wind, I uncleat the main and jib and let those

### In Irons

If you don't have enough momentum for tacking, the boat will point directly into the wind and stop. Since no water is flowing across the rudder, trying to turn it has no effect—the boat just sits there, sails fluttering in the breeze. You are locked in irons. Some boats have a bigger problem with this than others. If you're sailing under the mainsail alone, and/or if your mainsail is old, baggy, and worn out, the boat will get in irons much more readily.

This fluttering or flaglike behavior of the sails is called luffing. Try to minimize the amount of time your sails luff. It's hard on the fabric, it shocks the rigging, and it creates an overall feeling of havoc. Some luffing is inevitable, though, and it's certainly no big deal in a light breeze.

Being locked in irons is usually a bigger problem in a light breeze than in a heavy wind, but the first time it happens to you (and it will happen, I promise) can be a little perplexing. The size of trailerables makes it fairly easy to get out of irons. Remember the pushmi-pullyu from the Dr. Doolittle story? That's what you do. First, *push me*, meaning you push the boom and the tiller away from you. The boat will start to drift backward and the stern will swing into the wind. Then, *pull you*, meaning pull your boom and tiller back in, and the boat will be sailing again.

sails luff, or flutter in the wind like a flag. As the boat continues to turn, don't sheet in instantly—let the boat continue to turn a little bit past the close-hauled point, and then sheet in the sails. If you keep the sails sheeted in tightly, there's a possibility that the boat might weathercock, or point directly into the wind and stay there, much as an old-fashioned weather vane would.

### Pointing Ability of Sailboats

When we began our discussion of the points of sail, we started off close-hauled with the wind blowing about 45 degrees from the bow of the boat. Most sailboats can sail at 45 degrees to the wind. Some boats can lie closer to the wind, meaning they can sail at a sharper angle, some as close as 30 to 40 degrees. A boat that can sail closer to the wind is said to have better pointing ability, or it can point higher than other boats.

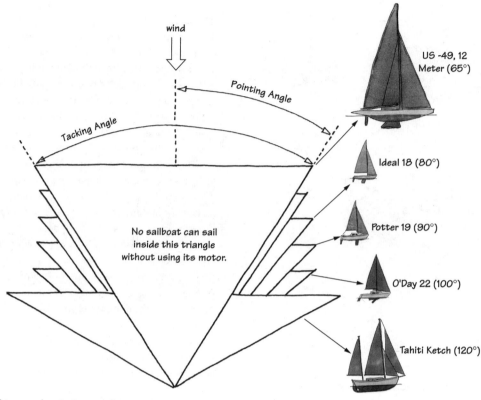

*Tacking and pointing angles.*

Being able to point high is a desirable feature for a sailboat, and some racing designs can outpoint the typical trailerable sailboat. But that ability comes at a price. Often, high pointing ability requires a deep, high-aspect-ratio keel. Like sails, keels can be high aspect or low aspect. A high-aspect keel will be deep, with a leading edge that is more perpendicular to the waterline, with a lot of weight down low—kind of like an underwater airplane wing. A low-aspect keel is long and shallow, often running the entire length of the boat. In general (but not always), boats with more keel area will point higher than boats with less keel area. Hopefully you did your homework when you first went shopping for a boat. A manufacturer will never say, "Sails like a slug to windward, but just look at all that space below!" It's up to you to determine how a boat will point, either by examining

plans, reading the recommendations of other sailors, or test-sailing the boat.

Pointing ability is often described as the boat's tacking angle. You can find your boat's tacking angle with a test. Sheet the sails in hard and sail as close to the wind as possible. Note the heading on the compass, then tack the boat and sail on the opposite tack, again as close to the wind as she'll go. Note the compass heading again. The angle described by the two headings is the boat's tacking angle. It varies depending on the wind—a boat can point higher in a good breeze than in a slight zephyr—and a host of other factors. The pointing angle is half the tacking angle.

Many factors affect your boat's pointing ability. Many are built into the boat and not easily changed, such as your hull shape or the depth of your keel. But the adjustment of your sails and the tension of your rig can also be a factor. A common problem is a blown-out mainsail. As the cloth ages, it becomes softer and baggy, especially in the center, so you can't get a good angle to the wind, even when everything is tightened correctly. In this case, buying a new sail is about all you can do.

## Heaving To

This technique slows the boat without taking down the sails. It's great if you've got to duck below for a quick cup of coffee or even fix a little lunch. (You are legally required to keep a lookout on deck, however.) You still have the steadying pressure of the breeze in the sails, though the boat will make very little headway. Here's how it works, as steps 1 to 3 in the drawing illustrate.

Sail as close to the wind as possible (close-hauled). Sheet the main and jib in tight. Tack without touching either of the sheets. The boat should balance, with the backwinded jib canceling out the forward drive of the mainsail. You'll probably need to trim to get the boat to balance, though, and some boats just plain don't like to lie this way. I never could get my old MacGregor 222 to heave to—it wouldn't balance, but wanted to sail on, backwinded jib and all! I

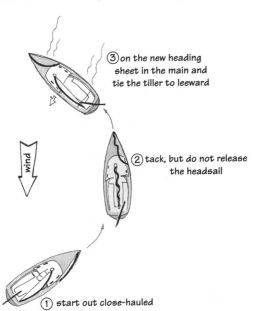

③ on the new heading
sheet in the main and
tie the tiller to leeward

wind

② tack, but do not release
the headsail

① start out close-hauled

*Heaving to is a handy maneuver to slow the boat.*

might have gotten it to work with some experimentation. If your boat has a centerboard, try raising or lowering it a little or lashing the rudder a certain way. If you can get it to work on your boat, this can be a handy maneuver.

## SAIL TRIM

You can use a huge variety of lines and make infinite adjustments to your sails, all of which have various effects on performance. To be honest, on most trailer sailers, these effects are pretty slight. They are all cumulative, and can add up to a noticeable loss of speed—perhaps even as much as 10 to 20 percent. Learning all of the components for optimal sail trim will take many hours of dedicated study as well as time on the water as you apply these techniques to your particular vessel.

Or not.

If you're a new sailor and you just want to make the darned thing go, simply remember this three-step procedure for basic sail trim.

1. When sailing upwind, let the sails out until they luff.
2. Pull them in until they stop luffing.
3. If you're going downwind, make the sails as perpendicular as you can to the breeze.

That's it. I'm assuming that you know enough to raise the sails before you try this, and you aren't trying to point directly into the wind. If your boat is lying at least 45 degrees to the wind, this should work unless you have an anchor out. The only situation I can think of where it won't work is if you're locked in irons, and you can't pull the sails in—they're in all the way and they're still luffing. If that's the case, remember the pushmi-pullyu technique—swing the stern out, let the sails luff, then pull 'em in till they stop.

Now, there are plenty of other things we can talk about if you want to sail faster, but none of them will do you a lick of good until you master the basic steps above. While letting sails luff and pulling them in works on most upwind points of sail, it's actually best when close-hauled to beam reaching. If you're sailing downwind, present as much sail area to the wind as you can. You have to pull the mainsail in a little, until the boom and sail aren't touching the shrouds. The constant rubbing will wear a hole in the sailcloth and chew up the boom. Another potential danger is an accidental jibe. If the boom is resting on the shrouds and you get an accidental jibe, your rig can be severely damaged when the boom crashes into the shrouds.

The "let them out, pull them in" strategy works because nearly all new sailors have a tendency to oversheet their sails, or pull them in too far. This causes all sorts of problems that aren't easily deciphered. The sails will often look nice and full when they're oversheeted, but you won't be going very fast. The reason has to do with flow. Sails don't trap air unless they're going downwind. They work upwind because the air flows over them.

The precise mechanics of why this is so can be demonstrated with a few chapters of theory, including airplane wings, high pressure versus low pressure, the Bernoulli principle, slot velocity, vector diagrams with arrows, dashes, and dots, and so on. You don't have to know all the theory in order to sail a boat, and many folks—myself included—get bogged down by too much of it. If you're interested in sail theory, see the Bibliography for some excellent books on the subject. (And if you really want to learn how to trim sails, here's a simple way: volunteer to be a part of a race crew. There is often an empty spot or two on race day, and if you explain to the captain that you want to learn as much as you can about trim, you'll often get more information than you can digest. You'll need to develop a thick skin, though—there's a reason Captain Bligh always needed people to help run his ship, and things often get intense during a race.)

From a more practical standpoint, just remember that the wind has to flow over the sails in order to generate the lift needed to go upwind. Good sail trim involves keeping that flow moving as smoothly as possible. If you pull the sails in too tightly, the flow is impeded and your speed drops. If you really pull them in, the sail stalls—the flow is completely stopped on the back side of the sail, replaced instead by swirls and eddies

of wind. The sail still looks good, but it's trapping air instead of redirecting it.

You can do a few more things to improve flow. One is when you're setting the sail. A sail without many wrinkles is going to flow air better than one that has wrinkles all over the surface. That's why, when you set the sails, you try to stretch the luff until the wrinkles along the jib hanks and sail slides are pulled out, and the sail sets smoothly. On the boom, the clew of the mainsail is pulled outward by the outhaul. Just like halyards, if you don't have enough outhaul tension on your mainsail, you may see wrinkles along the foot of the sail. If you can, pull the outhaul until you get the foot of the mainsail as smooth as possible.

In fact, this idea of flow is so important that sails have little bits of yarn sewn into them called telltales. These bits of yarn or tape show the airflow over your sails. There's one on each side of the sail—a windward telltale and a leeward telltale. Using your telltales to judge sail trim is much more accurate than the let-them-out, pull-them-in method, but it's a little more complex as well. If you feel like you can't remember all the details, don't worry about it—just let the sails out until they luff, and pull them in until they stop. As you gain sailing experience, reading the telltales becomes easier. If your sails don't have any telltales, install them. You can buy them or make your own. Any strip of lightweight cloth or ribbon will work, though black shows up best; 16 to 20 inches long and a half inch wide will be fine. Even a strip of recording tape from a dead cassette will do, though it won't last as long as fabric. Sew the ribbon into the sail with a sailmaker's needle, and tie a knot on either side of the cloth. (You'll need a real sailmaker's needle—the sailcloth is amazingly tough.) On the jib, the telltales should be about a foot aft of the luff. Sew in three—one near the head, one near the foot, and one in between the two. A few telltales along the leech are also a good idea.

The telltales on the mainsail should be right at the leech—one at each batten pocket—or sew in three, one in the middle of the leech, one

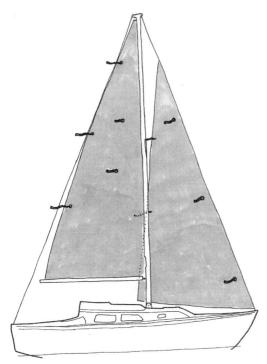

*Telltale locations on the main and jib. Place telltales on both sides of the sail.*

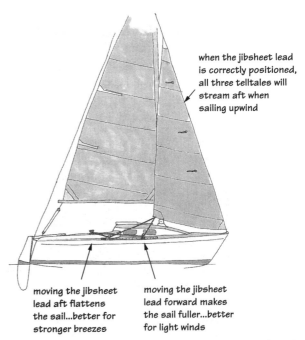

when the jibsheet lead is correctly positioned, all three telltales will stream aft when sailing upwind

moving the jibsheet lead aft flattens the sail...better for stronger breezes

moving the jibsheet lead forward makes the sail fuller...better for light winds

*Adjusting the jibsheet lead blocks. If the lower windward jib telltale breaks (flutters) first (before the upper telltales) as you turn upwind, move the jibsheet block aft. If the upper telltale flutters first, slide the jibsheet block forward on its track. Playing with these adjustments in various winds will help you become a better sailor.*

a quarter of the way up, and one a quarter of the way down. Install another set of two in the middle of the mainsail, about half and three-quarters of the way up.

Interpreting the telltales is a bit tougher than installing them. Ideally, all the telltales should be streaming aft, but you'll often get conflicting signals. Some of the telltales will be streaming aft like they're supposed to, while others will be fluttering in circles or pointing straight up. Different combinations can mean different things.

For example, on the jib, if the lower telltales flutter but the top telltales stream correctly, then the jibsheet lead block is too far forward. Try adjusting it aft on the track. Conversely, if the top telltales flutter while the lower ones stream correctly, the sheet lead is too far aft. If you can't figure out what the heck they're doing and you suspect the jibsheet lead is out of position, you can try another method. Watch the upper telltales on the windward side of the jib

as you slowly turn into the wind. At some point, one of the telltales will "break," meaning it'll stop streaming aft and start to lift and flutter. See which one breaks first—if it's the lower telltale, move the jibsheet lead block aft. If the upper one breaks first, move the sheet lead block forward. If they break at the same time, the sheet lead block is in the correct spot.

When you are sailing upwind, both the windward and leeward jib telltales close to the luff should stream aft. If the leeward telltales are fluttering but the windward telltales are all flowing smoothly, your jib is overtrimmed (trimmed in too tightly). Either let the sail out a little or turn into the wind a little. In the opposite case, all the windward telltales are fluttering but the leeward telltales are streaming; the jibsheet is eased out too far. Sheet in a touch, or fall off, meaning turn downwind a little. Always turn *away* from, or trim *toward*, a fluttering telltale. (See the sidebar "The Barber Hauler" and the drawing for a nifty way to adjust sheeting angle.) If you are sailing downwind, telltales won't help you too much.

### Mainsail Telltales

The telltales on the main are a bit different than those on the jib, but the theory is the same. Again, telltales are most helpful when sailing upwind for maintaining proper airflow across the sail surface.

The telltales on the main can help you adjust for the proper sail shape. Watch the top telltale; if it sneaks around behind the sail, that's an indication that there's not enough twist in the main and you need to ease the mainsheet a little. If you have a boom vang and/or a traveler, those may need adjustment as well. Ease the vang, and if that's not enough, pull the traveler more

to windward to increase the twist and reduce the downward pull on the boom.

The telltales below are there to give you an overall indication of the sail's shape. If the middle telltales are not streaming aft (assuming a wind of about 5 knots and an upwind point of sail), then your mainsail is shaped too full. If your sails are old or have seen a lot of sailing hours, there's a good chance that the fabric has been stretched out of shape. All your telltale readings will be a bit screwy. Try a little tension on the cunningham. Racers will add a little mast bend by increasing their backstay tension, but I prefer to keep the mast straight. My boat's mast has a permanent curve aft from overzealous backstay tension, probably to compensate for a blown-out mainsail. Another possible cause of fluttering lower mainsail telltales is an overtrimmed jib. Try easing the jibsheet to see if that helps.

There are lots of subtleties to telltale readings that vary with different boat types, wind strengths, and points of sail, and even vary with some conflicting advice. (Some captains like telltales near the luff of the main, for example, while others say that leech telltales are the only ones that should be installed.) Again, racing skippers are the experts here, and observing some of their comments online, in books, or in person can be helpful if you want to get the best possible speed from the wind.

Up to now, we've been talking about sail trim mainly as it relates to the position of the sails in relation to the wind. Getting the angle of the sail right is a big part of boat speed. But another factor of sail trim relates to the shape of the sails themselves. When you start adjusting the actual shape of the sails, you're getting into some pretty fancy stuff, because there are lots of variations that can have different effects on how well the boat sails. If the sail shape is wrong, it can result in more heeling force on the boat (see the sidebar "Heeling on a Sailboat").

Sail shape can be summarized as follows:

*High winds need flatter sails*
*Light winds need fuller sails*

## The Barber Hauler

According to Carl Eichenlaub (winner of the Lightning Internationals, Star, and Snipe championships), the best sailors on Mission Bay in the 1960s were the Barber twins, Manning and Merrit. Merrit invented a neat way to adjust the sheeting angle of jibs without a track. It's still commonly used on racing boats. The advantage is that it's a simple system that can be adjusted from the cockpit, and it's easily adapted to boats with a jib track.

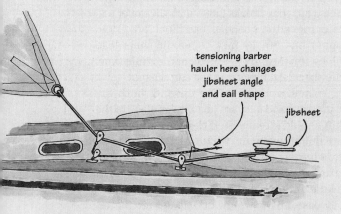

*tensioning barber hauler here changes jibsheet angle and sail shape*

*jibsheet*

*The barber hauler is a way to adjust jibsheet angles if you don't have a track-mounted jibsheet block.*

The jib is flattened primarily by adjusting the jibsheet lead—farther back for high winds, farther forward for light winds. A second way to flatten the jib is by increasing the headstay tension, but this is possible (while underway) only on boats with adjustable backstays. If you don't have them, you might tighten your rigging a little if you're setting the boat up on a windy day, but don't overdo it.

The mainsail can be flattened for high winds in several ways. Increasing the outhaul tension will flatten the lower third of the sail, and bending the mast aft (again, on boats with adjustable backstays) will flatten the upper two-thirds of the sail. Some boats have a boom vang, which is a pair of blocks on a line connecting the mast base with the boom. It's used to pull the boom down, reducing the amount of twist in the mainsail. The boom vang can be used along with the telltales to get just the right amount of twist for your heading and, with the right vang tension, get all your telltales streaming aft.

Another way to flatten the mainsail is by using a cunningham. You may notice an extra grommet near the tack of the mainsail but a little farther from the edge of the sail. That's the cunningham. It's usually adjusted with a line running through it and back down to the deck. It can be thought of as a sail flattener, though it really alters the draft of the sail by moving it forward.

So, what is the draft of a sail? The draft is the curve that the sail forms as the wind blows across the surface. Just as hulls are designed for different sea conditions, so are sails. A sail with more draft—a full sail—gives the boat more power to help it drive through choppy water, but this type of sail loses efficiency as the wind speed increases. A sail with less draft—a flat sail—will point higher and sail faster and is more efficient in higher winds.

The traveler, if your boat has one, can be used to adjust the angle of the sail while keeping its shape. By letting out the traveler car instead of the mainsheet, you can keep the correct tension on the leech of the sail and make

## Heeling on a Sailboat

The term *heeling* describes the way a sailboat leans as a result of the wind on the sails. All sailboats heel, but how much they heel can vary a great deal, depending on the type of boat, draft, ballast, sail shape, and other factors. A catamaran will heel very little at first, because the wide base of her two hulls provides a lot of stability. As the wind gets stronger, a catamaran will lift one of her hulls clear out of the water. At this point, a catamaran will fly like a spooked greyhound—it absolutely smokes across the water since its water resistance has been essentially cut in half. But it's about as stable as a spooked greyhound as well, and the skipper has to be very careful with the mainsheet and tiller or she'll capsize the boat. Catamarans like the famous Hobie are an adrenaline rush to sail, but they're not great for cruising or relaxing.

Let's compare this to a monohull, like our trailer sailer. Initially, when the wind blows, most monohulls lean right over. Some boats do this very easily in a light wind—they're termed "tender." Often, tender boats have a relatively narrow hull with plenty of ballast.

A "stiff" boat will resist heeling at first. Two main factors determine stiffness—hull shape and keel type. A wide, beamy hull with a reasonably flat bottom makes a stiff boat without a lot of additional weight, which is good for a trailer sailer. A deep keel with a lot of lead in it also makes a boat stiff, but heavy.

The trade-off between hull shape and keel weight comes as the wind increases. Many heavy-displacement sailboats are very tender initially but quickly settle into an angle of heel and become rock-solid. The more the wind blows, the greater they resist further heeling.

Newer wide-body lightweight designs are super in light air, but as the wind kicks up, their ability to resist heeling decreases and they are easier to knock down. Add some really big waves and a complete rollover is possible.

Trailerable sailboats are usually more like the latter example—they don't have a huge amount of ballast (so they can be pulled with an average car or truck), and they have a retractable keel that can be lifted into the hull for trailering. This is one reason why most trailerable sailboats don't make good long-distance cruisers. They can be poor choices for storm sailing. There are a few exceptions, of course—a Cal 20 has sailed to Hawaii, and Montgomery 17s to Mexico and through the Panama Canal, but neither of these designs was intended for that kind of sailing.

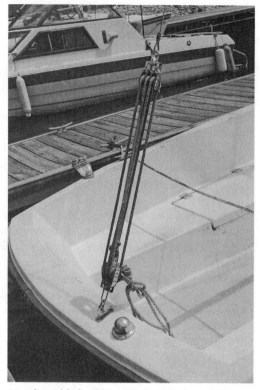

*An adjustable backstay on an older boat. They are powerful blocks that can exert a lot of force on a rig. This particular one is a bad design—the only thing keeping the mast on the boat is that little cam cleat. If it were released accidentally on a run in a breeze, the entire rig could go overboard.*

*The traveler on my boat, while it is a handy and flexible sail adjustment, was expensive and is often tripped over when I'm going down below.*

small corrections for course or changes in wind direction.

### The Leech Line

Most mainsails (and some headsails) have a small line sewn into the fold of the leech that is secured by a small cleat or buttons on the sail. This is the leech line. You use it to tension the leech to prevent the leech from fluttering. If it's too tight, though, the leech will hook to windward and you'll have more heeling force and less forward drive. To adjust the leech, give it just enough tension to stop fluttering but not enough to cause a hook.

## DOCKING

Returning to the dock or a slip after a day of sailing can be a little tense the first few times, but it gets easier with practice. You *can* dock under sail, though it's especially tricky if you're alone, since you'll need to be in several places at once. Most folks approach the dock under power. Here's how it should go.

If at all possible, approach a dock from downwind. If there's room and no other boats are around, a practice run isn't a bad idea. Pull up near the dock, but keep about a boat length or two away. Allow more distance if conditions are tricky. Shift the motor into neutral, noting the speed and the effects of wind and current on your boat. Some boats will glide for a long time before they stop, and it's good to know what to expect. Notice the boat's drift, her response to the helm, and how these combine with the current and the wind. When you've got a good feel for the conditions, place the motor in gear, loop around, and try again.

Place your fenders near the widest point of your hull, tying them to cleats or stanchion bases. Don't let any lines trail in the water. For docking, you'll need a bow line, a stern line, and two spring lines. (See "Docklines and Towlines" in Chapter 5 for a rundown of this equipment.) Station a crewmember on the bow with a long line secured to the bow cleat. This will be the bow line. Remember that it will need to run underneath the lifelines. If you're by yourself, run the line from the bow cleat, outside the lifelines and stanchions, and back to the cockpit so that you can throw the line from the stern.

(Quick tip—if you regularly come alongside pilings that seem to evade your fenders, you might try a long swim noodle. Get the fattest one you can find, run a light line through the center, and hang it horizontally along the widest part of your hull. It won't replace your fenders, but it could add a little extra protection against bumps and scratches.)

*Approach the dock slowly.* Outboard motors commonly die when they're needed most, and if you're depending on yours to deliver a quick burst of reverse, then that's the time it'll run out of fuel or foul a line. Too many people think it's impressive to power into the dock, slam the boat into reverse at the last minute, and stop on a dime. It is impressive when everything works, but it causes impressive amounts of damage, and possibly even injuries, when things don't go as expected.

Remember that a sailboat's turning axis is around the center of the boat. As you turn, the bow swings into the turn and the stern swings out. Ideally, you want to turn just at the right moment, so the bow doesn't crash into the dock but the midsection of the boat gets as close as possible. If you get it right, you'll coast into the dock with a gentle bump of the fenders.

Step off the boat with the bow line and go directly to a cleat. Loop the line over the cleat and let it slip until the boat is where you want it, then stop the boat by pulling upward against the cleat. Don't try to stop the boat by tugging on the line. That works fine for wrangling calves, but try that with a large boat and it'll just pull you in the water. Again, never put any part of yourself between the boat and the dock. (See "Leaving the Dock" earlier in this chapter.)

If the boat is moving forward and the bow line is stopped, the stern will swing out. This is especially a problem when coming into a slip, since you've got to stop and you don't want to crash sideways into the boat next to you. Placing a fender on the opposite side of the boat and on the stern corner can save the day. If the finger pier on the slip is long enough, you can stop the boat with the stern line, or if your crew is experienced they can go ashore with two lines, one for the bow and one for the stern.

## PICKING UP AND DROPPING A MOORING

Picking up a mooring, like docking, is fairly easy with a little practice. Approach slowly and have a crewmember at the bow ready with the boathook. There should be a pickup float attached to the buoy or to a chain beneath it; snag the float with the boathook and bring it aboard. Make the line fast to your bow cleat. Some skippers will toss out a stern anchor to control the swing, or tie off to a second mooring astern.

Probably the biggest hazard to watch out for is fouling a line with the prop. Keep a sharp lookout for stray lines from other moorings or boats as you approach and leave a mooring. If conditions are settled and it's not crowded, try it under sail!

## ANCHORING TECHNIQUES

Anchoring techniques are the same for a small vessel as they are for a large one. You can use smaller anchors, naturally, which are much easier to handle and more affordable. (See "Optional Equipment" in Chapter 5 for a description of the different types of anchors and the conditions for which each is designed.)

First, you've got to pick a good spot to anchor for the night. A good anchorage will have protection from the wind and waves on several sides, be deep enough for your boat, and have a good-holding bottom so the anchor can bite. Your chart is probably your best bet for finding a good spot, though a place that appears ideal on the chart can turn out to be a bit of a dog. After all, the chart doesn't list a factory that's particularly smelly, and there's no chart symbol for mosquitoes. A local cruising guide can be a big help in guiding you—and sometimes lots of other people—to a particular anchorage. If there's a cruising guide for your area, bring it along and add your own notes. You might even wish to try writing your own someday!

Any anchorage needs depth and swinging room. You'll want to remain floating during your stay unless you want to scrub your bottom. Make sure you can get out when the tide goes down, too. How much swinging room you need refers to the amount of anchor rode you have out, which in turn depends on the depth. Your anchor scope is the length of rode out at a given time, usually expressed as a ratio. For a rope and chain rode, a 7:1 scope is generally considered the minimum you should have out, meaning if the water is 10 feet deep at high tide, you should have 70 feet of rode out. In a blow, 12:1 isn't too much, and 15:1 provides about the maximum benefit. For an average trailerable, a $3/8$-inch-diameter rode with 20 feet of $1/4$-inch or larger chain is a pretty good combination. Some say that you should have half the length of the boat in anchor chain; others say the chain should equal the length of the boat.

It's the weight of the chain in front of the anchor that helps the anchor hold. An anchor sentinel or kellet is a heavy weight that slides down the middle of the rode and lowers the angle of the rode closer to the bottom, giving a better grip. The rode must be protected from chafe.

Another idea is an anchor buoy. It holds the bow of the boat up, allowing it to ride over the waves rather than pulling it downward.

A nice plus for an anchorage is two landmarks that are visible in the dark so you can check whether you're dragging during the night.

You've settled on where to anchor; now how do you do it? The basic method is to bring your bow to the precise spot you want your anchor to lie and then stop your forward progress by putting the motor in reverse. As the boat starts to go backward, slowly lower the anchor over the bow until it touches the bottom,

crown first, then slowly pay out the line until you have the proper scope. Oh, by the way—you *did* tie the bitter end of the anchor rode off to something before you tossed it overboard, didn't you? Plenty of anchors have been lost by not doing this. And I *don't* need to warn you to keep your feet clear of the rode as it pays out, do I? It sounds like a funny situation, but the forces on the rode can be pretty strong. When you have enough scope out, quickly take a turn around a mooring cleat and snub it up tight to set the anchor. Hopefully the anchor will bite and stop the boat. The anchor should be able to take full reverse power without moving. Check the set of the anchor by sighting a landmark across some part of the boat. You can also check the rode with your hand to feel for any vibration from the dragging anchor. If the boat shows any indication of moving, haul up the dragging anchor and try resetting it.

Sometimes you'll want to lie at two anchors from the bow. This is called a Bahamian moor, and it works well for anchoring in a tidal stream. The two rodes sometimes twist together and make a monstrous snarl, though. The only way to prevent it is to check the rodes at each change of the tide and re-cleat them if necessary.

In storm conditions, two anchors on a single rode will often hold better than the same two anchors on their own rodes. Perhaps the extra

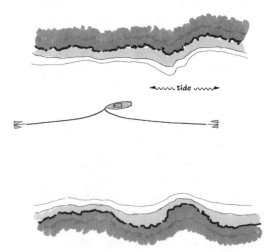

*A Bahamian moor.*

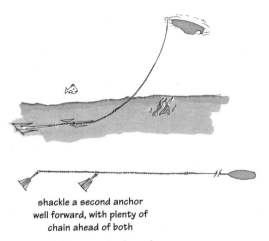

shackle a second anchor
well forward, with plenty of
chain ahead of both

*Two anchors on a single rode.*

weight of the forward anchor acts as a kellet. But it's easy enough to try, and it's a good way to use a smaller anchor in a storm.

Keeping your small lunch hook ready to go at the stern can be a real lifesaver. If you secure the coil of line with rubber bands and keep the bitter end attached to a cleat somewhere, you can toss the whole assembly overboard. The anchor's weight breaks the rubber bands, deploying the line and stopping the boat without having to leave the helm. A stern anchor might be the only way to approach a dock in a strong tailwind.

One nifty trick has worked well for me in a storm: you can buy rubber snubbers for the anchor rode that act as shock absorbers, dampening some of the shock loading caused when the boat pitches in the waves. Or you can use light nylon line, about $1/4$ inch, to do the same job. Tie the line to the rode 20 to 30 feet before the end of the rode, then lead it to the sheet winches. Tie it on using a rolling hitch. Crank on a few turns until the main rode has a little slack in it. The nylon is very stretchy and acts like a giant rubber band. You can make adjustments with the winch as the night goes on, tightening or loosening as necessary. You need to watch carefully for chafe, though, if you lead the line through the bow cleat.

When you anchor for the night in normal conditions, take a few bearings of some prominent landmarks before you go to bed. You'll want to check your position a few times during the night to make sure you're not dragging, especially after a tide change or if the wind picks up. If the anchorage is completely featureless, then a small float tied to the anchor on a separate line can show whether you're dragging.

If you're sailing with friends, you may want to anchor together. It's easy if you take a few precautions—see the sidebar "Rafting Up."

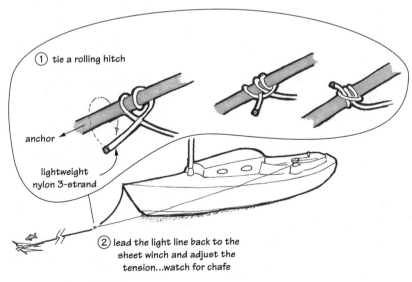

① tie a rolling hitch

anchor

lightweight
nylon 3-strand

② lead the light line back to the
sheet winch and adjust the
tension...watch for chafe

*Snubbing an anchor using a light line.*

## Rafting Up

Rafting up or tying your boat alongside another can be lots of fun. It's best to keep the total number of boats tied together low, say three or four, though people will raft up more. The procedure is fairly easy. One boat—the largest—serves as the host and places its largest anchor off the bow, making certain it's well set. Then the other boats, with plenty of fenders out, slowly come alongside and pass bow and stern lines to the host. The host boat is the only anchored vessel; the others just hang on for the ride. Naturally you need settled weather, plenty of swinging room, and good holding ground. As you tie up to the host boat, look up. You don't want your spreaders to tangle, so use the lines to bring your boat forward or aft as necessary. Make certain that if the wind kicks up, you can get clear quickly and have an alternative anchorage nearby. Keep your ground tackle ready to go while you're rafting. When it's time to turn in for the night, break up the raft and lie at your own anchor.

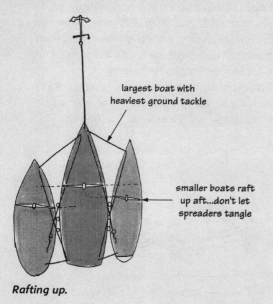

largest boat with heaviest ground tackle

smaller boats raft up aft...don't let spreaders tangle

*Rafting up.*

## BEST PRACTICES FOR THE PRUDENT MARINER

All captains, with time and experience, develop their own boating methods, procedures, and rules to live by. The following guidelines are by nature highly opinionated and personal, but they work. Consider them with an open mind.

A good captain rarely yells unless he or she needs to be heard above the wind. In some cases, like raising or lowering the anchor, the foredeck can communicate with the helm with prearranged hand signals. If, however, your crew is not taking a safety situation seriously, by all means yell to keep them out of harm's way.

"Swearing like a sailor" generally referred to the lower deck. Good captains rarely required crude language for the usual operation of the ship.

Never frighten a child (or anyone) who might become a sailor. Long before I knew her, my wife went sailing as an eighteen year old with a hotshot Hobie sailor. Eager to show off his manly prowess, he insisted on flying one of the hulls. It wasn't long before they capsized, throwing my wife into the rigging and inflicting a long and painful gash in her leg, which still bears the scar. She has never really enjoyed sailing since.

If the work of sailing your boat is segregated into men's jobs and women's jobs, it won't take long before they all become *your* jobs. Sailing a boat should be gender-neutral. Unless you like sailing alone, rotate the jobs of helmsman, sheet trimmer, anchor hauler, cook, galley cleanup, and so on. A good captain involves her crew in decision making whenever she can, yet is always ready to take command instantly if the situation requires it.

Never embarrass any member of your crew in front of others.

When you start out for the day, always sail *upwind* first. If you're sailing in tidal waters, know the times for high and low tide before you set out so you can take advantage of favorable tidal currents.

All of your lines should be whipped, without unraveled ends or fluffy tails. A proper whipping, with thread, is better (and slightly safer) than ends with a turn of masking tape and a big blob of melted line on the end. (See "Ropes and Lines" in Chapter 13 for more on whipping.)

Tension your halyards appropriately. Besides looking sloppy, a sail with a scalloped luff is inefficient.

Learn to dress your halyard tails correctly. This is as much a matter of safety as keeping your decks neat. Sometimes you will need to get your sails down in a hurry. A Gordian knot of a halyard, dangling halfway up the mast, has to be experienced in a blow to be fully appreciated. The consequences can range from comical to downright dangerous.

Don't run a loud generator or crank up the tunes when sharing an anchorage with others. Respect their privacy and do not anchor too closely. If another boat is first at an anchorage and lays out excessive scope, there's little you can do besides anchor in another location.

If you must fly flags or ensigns, learn how to fly them correctly. Flags aren't decorative—they have specific purposes and meanings, even if misunderstood by most people. Don't fly a flag that's dirty or worn out.

Always operate your boat in a safe, conservative manner. Ask yourself, *What if this maneuver doesn't go as planned?* Always look for options and alternative plans of action.

Always be polite and respectful of dockside personnel. Never try to impress anyone with the size of your boat or the size of your purse—there's always going to be a bigger one. How well you treat others is the only impression worth leaving.

Remember the three rules of sailing:

1. Keep the water out of the boat.
2. Keep the people out of the water.
3. Keep the boat on the water.

# MORE SAILING KNOWLEDGE AND SKILLS

# CHAPTER NINE

## Rules of the Road

The first few times out on your boat should be eventful experiences as you learn about your boat and how it behaves. Surely some unexpected things will happen, but hopefully you won't need the Coast Guard.

After you've figured out the basics, you'll want to bone up on the Coast Guard's Navigation Rules (also called the Rules of the Road) that are essential for any captain to know. This section won't make you a licensed captain, but hopefully it will help you handle some of the more common situations that you might encounter.

First, though, an important disclaimer: The rules contained here summarize only a small part of the basic Navigation Rules for which a boat operator is responsible. Think of this section as advice only; *it is by no means everything you need to know!*

Get a copy of the Coast Guard's Navigation Rules and study it. The book is available through the U.S. Government Printing Office or on the Internet at www.uscgboating.org/

regulations/nav_rules.htm. The legalese can be hard to interpret, but fortunately there are lots of resources to help you understand the meaning and intent of the rules, if not the actual rules themselves. The U.S. Coast Guard's Office of Boating Safety website at www.uscgboating.org/ has lots of help in plain English. The U.S. Power Squadron, a nonprofit educational organization dedicated to boating safety, offers classes (both classroom and web-based), vessel safety checks, and other materials at reasonable prices—their computer-based America's Boating Course is $35. BoatSafe.com offers a free course called Basic Boating Safety and their Coastal Navigation course for $78. There are other resources as well, including books, of course, such as *Chapman's Piloting and Seamanship*. (It does help to get a current edition—my new copy of Chapman's includes information on new restrictions involving the Department of Homeland Security, pollution regulations, and updated radio licensing requirements that won't be found in an old copy.)

## BASIC RULES

A busy harbor on a nice, sunny Saturday can look a bit like a free-for-all. There are boats of all shapes and sizes going in all directions at once. There are no roads to stay on and no lanes to follow. How all these boats keep from running into one another is, at first glance, a mystery.

But the more you understand about the Coast Guard Navigation Rules, the more you begin to see that there is a defined system in place, and it does make sense—most of the time anyway. In some instances, there are "lanes" (called Traffic Separation Zones) and even something like "roads" (navigation channels defined by buoys).

Learning all of the rules is a tall order, especially when you consider that there are two different sets of rules, and they don't always agree. The International Rules, sometimes called COLREGS, are generally used in the open ocean. The Inland Rules apply to most areas where you'll be taking a trailerable sailboat, so I'd concentrate on them, but check your chart. If you see a COLREGS Demarcation Line, that's where the rules change. These are the federal rules, and they don't include state laws or local regulations. For example, a no-wake zone or requirement to stay a hundred yards away from a swimming beach would be covered under state law.

You can take comfort in the fact that in many parts of the country, if you learn only a few of the rules, you'll be ahead of the majority of the recreational boaters on the water. Unfortunately, far too many captains learn little more than where the throttle is. The Navigation Rules are federal law, and while you don't have to memorize them unless you're taking the captain's test, a working knowledge is essential.

There are a few important overall rules— rules about the rules, if you will.

First, the Navigation Rules can be overlooked to avoid immediate danger. Do whatever it takes to avoid a collision. If you're about to get run over, don't worry about sounding three short blasts on you horn before you put her in reverse.

Everyone shares the responsibility for good seamanship. If there's an accident, everyone is at fault. Never assume that the operator of the other boat has ever heard of the Navigation Rules. Some haven't.

Another important principle: the closer you get to another vessel, the more important the rules become. If you can sail in an area where you can avoid other vessels, you won't have to worry much about the various rights-of-way. Now, there are very few places in the world that meet this description, and you will be forced to sail close to other vessels at some point. But you can often make a simple course correction as soon as you see a boat approaching in the distance, and avoid a situation where you will need to know the rules. I always do this when a commercial vessel is in the area, especially ships or a fishing vessel with nets out. Both of these vessels have the right-of-way over a recreational sailboat.

The Navigation Rules establish a certain pecking order among vessels, giving some the right-of-way over others. Some people believe that sailboats have the right-of-way over powerboats, regardless of size. This is occasionally true, but not always. Here's a list of the right-of-way for boats, starting with the most privileged (termed the stand-on vessel).

1. A vessel not under command—for example, one with a broken engine or rudder
2. A vessel restricted in ability to maneuver
3. A vessel engaged in fishing
4. Sailing vessels
5. Power-driven vessels

In many cases, a powerboat in a narrow channel is restricted in its ability to maneuver because it is constrained by draft. Likewise, a commercial vessel or vessel engaged in towing is restricted in its ability to maneuver. While the rules don't say anything specifically about ferryboats, the courts have repeatedly ruled that ferries have the right-of-way. In general, give commercial vessels a wide berth whenever possible.

Additionally, the rules have provisions for the meeting of two sailboats:

1. When both boats are on opposite tacks, the boat on a starboard tack (the wind coming from its starboard side) is the stand-on vessel. The vessel on a port tack is the give-way vessel.
2. When both vessels have the wind on the same side, the vessel to windward (or upwind) is the give-way vessel; the vessel to leeward (or downwind) is the stand-on vessel.
3. If a vessel on a port tack sees another to windward, and cannot tell what tack the other boat is on, then it must keep clear of that vessel.

Take a look at these three photos and try to imagine the correct course of action (the answers are on page 143).

Note that if your sailboat's motor is running and in gear, you are considered a power-driven vessel even if your sails are up.

### Keeping a Lookout, Maintaining Safe Speed, and Determining Risk of Collision

The rules require that you keep a lookout on your boat at all times. They define a lookout as a person with no other duties besides watching out for other boats. On a trailer sailer, this usually means the helmsman, but you can't always see too well around a big deck-sweeping genoa. If you have extra people aboard, let them help you watch for other boats, or let them take a turn at the helm while you do the lookout duty. There's nothing in the rules that prohibits single-handed or short-handed sailing, but while you're underway, you have to keep watch for other boats.

Let's suppose you're on lookout duty and you see another boat heading your way. How can you tell if you're on a collision course? The most common method is to take a relative bearing on the vessel and watch for a change. If the angle of a boat in the distance seems to change as it gets closer, then you are most likely not on a collision course. You can use your own boat to help determine this—for

*This Ericson 25 is approaching on a constant bearing (that is, my angle to it stays the same). What would you do in a situation like this?*

*What if things looked like this?*

*Here's another situation—quick, what should you do?*

example, you first notice the boat off your bow. From where you're sitting, she appears right in line with, say, the leeward grabrail. You look two minutes later, and she appears larger but in line with the mast. The other vessel's relative bearing has moved forward, and you probably aren't on a collision course. If

*In photo 1, both boats are on a similar point of sail but different tacks. Since I'm the boat on a port tack, the other boat has the right-of-way. I have to keep clear.*

*In photo 2, we're both on the same tack, but I'm downwind of the other boat. The rules require that I maintain course and speed.*

*In photo 3, I'm sailing on a beam reach while the other boat (on a port tack) is approaching from upwind. I have the right-of-way, and I have to maintain course and speed.*

*But here it looks like the captain doesn't know the fine points of right-of-way and he's getting too close without changing course. The rules say that I should do whatever it takes to avoid collision. In this case, tacking or luffing is the best course of action.*

*Keeping a close lookout is especially important aboard sailboats with headsails, as they can cause a blind spot forward. This sail has a high clew, which helps with visibility. Some sails have small plastic windows sewn into them, which also help. Shift your position frequently to be sure the way is clear, or assign a crewmember to be your forward lookout.*

her bearing changes only slightly, then a potential for collision exists.

Be especially watchful of large vessels and ships. While the Navigation Rules treat all vessels equally, it's only common sense that a conflict between a fiberglass pleasurecraft and a large steel ship will leave the smaller boat with all the damage. Avoid getting close to any large ship that you see, and be wary of its speed. A tanker might be traveling four to six times as fast as the average trailerable sailboat, so the speck on the horizon can become very large in a surprisingly short time.

Usually, sailboats easily comply with rules for safe speed because they go pretty slowly—relatively speaking. The rules state specific factors that determine safe speed, including visibility, traffic density, sea state, and your draft and maneuverability. Usually a sailboat's displacement hull is self-limiting, but there are times when even 5 knots is too fast. Beam-reaching through a crowded anchorage on a windy day could easily be considered operating a boat at an unsafe speed.

## The Danger Zone for Powerboats

The Navigation Rules imply (although they don't actually spell out) a concept for powering called the danger zone. It extends from dead ahead to 22.5 degrees aft of the starboard beam. A powerboat approaching from this side has the right-of-way. Coincidentally, this is the same area covered by your green sidelight. At night, the approaching boat sees a green light—and in this case, green means go. Usually, the preferred course of action is to alter your course to starboard, slow down, or stop. The give-way vessel should not turn to port for a vessel forward of the beam, but by turning to starboard you'll "show him your red" or, in other words, alter course to starboard and pass port to port. You can't always do this if you're in a channel or near shoals or if the approaching vessel is far on your starboard side. But if you're meeting nearly head-on and there's still plenty of time, the preferred action is to alter course to starboard and pass port side to port.

The danger zone principle doesn't work in all cases, like in the Great Lakes or Western Rivers, and it wouldn't work for boats under sail (such as a starboard-tack crossing versus a port-tack crossing, for example). But it's a general rule that's good to know.

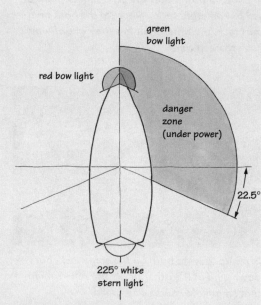

*The danger zone for powering.*

# CHAPTER TEN

# Weather on the Water

Weather is important to all mariners, but especially for sailors. The comparatively slower speed of most sailboats means we are less able to run for cover when the water gets rough. Moreover, because the average trailer sailer is smaller and lighter than most other vessels, we feel the effects of stormy weather more acutely. But although we're more uncomfortable in bad weather than our larger siblings, at least we have the advantage of smaller, easier-to-handle sails and gear.

Your exposure to heavy weather will depend on how far out you go. Generally speaking, you won't have the same concerns as a vessel crossing the open ocean. But you could have to deal with some short-term rough weather if you sail more than an hour or so away from a safe anchorage, and a real duster on the water can be a scary—and even dangerous—experience.

The best way to deal with unpleasant weather is to avoid it if at all possible. An accurate, detailed weather forecast is essential before you head out for anything more ambitious than a quick day sail in the harbor. Weather reports from television news, while valuable, shouldn't be your only source of information. Up-to-date weather summaries are available through the Internet, VHF weather channels, and dedicated weather radios. Most marine VHF radios include a number of channels that receive NOAA weather radio broadcasts. If not, you can buy a dedicated weather radio receiver. These broadcasts are automated brief summaries of local weather conditions, and they are useful to monitor before a day of sailing. Conditions can change fast, especially in the summertime, so check the weather channels frequently.

Of course, a weather forecast can be a far cry from what you actually experience on a given day, so you'll need to develop your own meteorological sense. Local knowledge of summertime weather patterns is gained through experience, observation, and talking with other mariners. Commercial fishermen and professional mariners (tow vessel captains and pilots, for example) spend more time on local waters than anyone, and are vast sources of knowledge—if you can find them and get them to talk. Recreational fishermen and other sailors can also be helpful and are easier to find. (Books about weather written specifically for sailors can greatly increase your knowledge; it will help to read one or two of those as well.)

Some signs that the weather is about to change are obvious: heavier cloud cover on the horizon, a sudden shift in wind direction, or a drop in temperature. Other signs are more subtle: you hear a lot of static on an AM radio, or you suddenly notice you're the only small vessel still out sailing while everyone else has headed for the dock. Sometimes these changes amount to nothing, but other times they warn of a heavy line squall coming your way.

If you notice signs that the weather is about to change, what should you do? Prepare your boat and crew, shorten sail, and consider altering course for home or sheltered waters if possible. What to do first will depend on your situation.

## ALTERING COURSE

If you're just out for a day sail and you notice a line of dark clouds on the horizon, consider turning for home, but only if you can make it. Try to imagine what you will do if a big wind hits you right in the middle of a tricky docking or mooring situation, and have plan B ready just in case. If your marina is tight or your mooring crowded, it may be better to stand off and wait the weather out, but make sure you have plenty of room in all directions. Many boats have come to grief when the wind suddenly shifted and the slackened anchor rode wrapped around the propeller. If you're cruising far from home, check the chart for a safe spot, preferably with a good anchor-grabbing mud bottom and shelter from the wind and waves. It's often difficult to predict which direction the wind will come from, so be ready if it changes.

## PREPARING YOUR BOAT AND CREW

If it looks like you won't be able to outrun a storm, you need to make preparations. Talk things over with your crew, discussing your plan of action and your options. Calmly go over the procedures for "man overboard" and "abandon ship." Don't overdo it—a panicked crew won't be able to help you—but don't be too casual about it either. Put on life jackets and harnesses, and go over the rules for use. For example, no one can be on the foredeck without a harness clipped to a jackline or a solid base. (Never clip a harness to the outer lifelines.) Pump the bilge

### Don't Play Around with Summer Storms

Once I had a boatload of friends on my Catalina, and we were heading for the harbor for an afternoon of daysailing. Several had never been on a sailboat before and couldn't wait to go sailing. The forecast was for a typical Charleston summer day—clear skies and an afternoon sea breeze. With so many friends aboard, finding room to stow everyone's coolers and food got a little crazy, and I forgot to turn on the VHF to get a last-minute weather update. We'd just cleared the dock when I noticed the clouds building on the horizon. I wasn't immediately concerned, but commented that "we needed to keep an eye on those clouds."

Within fifteen minutes, it was obvious that rough weather was heading our way, and fast. I broke the bad news that we'd better head back. Everyone was disappointed; a few even questioned whether it really looked all *that* bad. But no, I said, I'd rather not take the chance. We put the cover back on the main (which we never even raised) and wheeled around to head toward the marina. Just as a precaution, I casually passed out life jackets and said, "You probably won't need these, but I would like anyone on deck or in the cockpit to wear one."

The return trip was faster thanks to a 3-knot tide, but we were clearly being chased. The clouds built with amazing speed, and I was presented with a dilemma—should I stand off and wait the storm out or try to get the boat back into the slip before the storm hit? I decided that since I had two experienced and trusted line handlers with me, we could try to get the boat into the slip. I talked over the docking plan with them. We would try it, but turn and run for open water if conditions deteriorated. Heavy, fat drops of rain were just starting to fall.

We managed to get the boat into the slip and tied up quickly without any mishaps. Everyone was gathering up their things in the cabin and getting ready for a dash to the parking lot when the real storm hit. The wind went instantly from 15 to perhaps 40 knots, and visibility dropped to about 50 yards. The boats in the marina were heeling 20 degrees. I remember feeling the mast shake and shudder from the wind. Everyone's eyes got as big as pancakes. I smiled and said, "I told you so."

You really don't want to play around with storms on the water. Be conservative and don't take unnecessary risks.

dry, so you can see if you're taking on water later. Secure all hatches and stow any loose items below. If you have any young children aboard, make sure someone is in firm charge of them. Allowing them to help with appropriate jobs can help ease fears, and allowing them on deck to watch—if things are under control—can be a great learning experience for them. Double-check your position, and give yourself plenty of sea room if you can.

## SHORTENING SAIL (REEFING)

Headsails are usually reduced by changing to a smaller one; you can also bring in the headsail altogether and sail under the mainsail alone if your boat will do that. Some boats reportedly refuse to sail to windward without some form of headsail. Some boats have a very heavily built jib called a storm jib, though it's debatable whether a trailerable sailboat will see conditions that warrant its use. A storm jib was included when I bought my boat. It has never been used, as far as I can tell, and I honestly hope it stays that way!

On most boats, the mainsail can't be changed to a storm sail. (On some boats, small sails called storm trysails can be hoisted in place of the main, but they are rare aboard trailer sailers.) Rather, the lower portion of the sail is gathered at the boom and secured there, leaving the upper part of the sail standing. This process of reducing the exposed area of the main is called reefing. Although there are other methods, the most common system you will find on trailerable sailboats is called slab or jiffy reefing. Lines led through reinforced eyes (called cringles) sewn into the leech and luff are tensioned, pulling the new tack and clew down to the boom (after you've eased the halyard, of course). The remainder of the sail is gathered using short lines through reef points sewn into the middle of the sail. A mainsail can have any number of reef points. Two or three are common, though it may have more or none at all. You can have a sailmaker add reef points or add them yourself. Sailrite sells a reef-point kit, but you'll need a powerful sewing machine to install it.

When the wind picks up, reefing the mainsail can make a big difference in the way the boat handles, but the key is to reef before the wind gets too strong. If you wait until a storm hits, it's much harder to reef the mainsail. If you're heeling more than 25 degrees, it's time to reef. The usual process goes something like this:

1. Ease the main halyard but don't lower it completely. Marking the halyards with a few turns of contrasting thread at the correct reefing position can help determine how much to lower it.
2. Pull down the luff cringle (a metal ring sewn into the sail close to the mast) and secure it with either a line and cleat or a reefing hook—an upside down hook mounted near the gooseneck at the boom.
3. Pull down the leech cringle and secure it. This is usually done with a line that's secured to the boom at one end, passes up through the leech cringle, then back to a cheek block in the boom where the line is led forward and secured. The cheek block should be a little aft of the leech cringle so the foot of the sail will be properly tensioned.
4. Gather the rest of the sail using short lines through the reef points and secure them along the boom. (Remember how to tie a reef knot?) There should be relatively little stress on the reef points; most of the load is carried by the leech and luff cringles.

There is no reason why a headsail can't be reefed in a similar fashion, with reef points and extra cringles, but this is usually done by cruising sailors who don't have room to carry dozens of bags of sails. It's an option, though, and reef points are usually cheaper than a second headsail.

If you've waited too long to reef and the wind is blowing strong, reefing is more difficult, but it will be somewhat easier if you heave to before you reef. The mainsail will be somewhat blanketed by the jib, and the boat will be a little steadier than if she were underway.

## Sailing with the Tides

If you live near the ocean, you'll quickly become familiar with the tides and the tidal current. In most areas they have a big impact on sailing and how long it takes to get from point to point. In the areas around Charleston, South Carolina, where I used to live, the tidal range was around 6 feet—enough to cause a hefty current to run through the rivers and sounds twice a day. If I neglected to check the tides before planning a sailing trip, and the tidal current was against us (called a foul tide), the result was about an extra hour of motoring against the current to get to the harbor.

General tide predictions can be found in the newspaper, but tides vary locally. Detailed tide tables are available on the Internet at http://www.co-ops.nos.noaa.gov/, and NOAA printed tide tables are still available for around $14. Also, Nobeltec publishes tide-prediction software for U.S. and worldwide regions.

The times of high and low tide are only part of the story. A tidal current chart can tell you the direction and speed of the tidal current. The speed of the current can typically run around 4 to 5 knots, and since the top speed of a trailerable sailboat might be around 6 knots, the importance is obvious. Ignore the tides and you might become the captain of the proverbial slow boat to China.

The tides also affect the charted depth of the water, of course, but most importantly, what happens afterward. Running aground on a rising tide is less dire a situation than doing so on a falling tide. Should you be so unfortunate as to run aground at the peak of the spring tide, when the moon and sun are aligned—both influencing the height of the tide—you might be stuck there for months. When I sail a fixed-keel boat during a falling tide, I'm very watchful of the depth sounder, and I check the chart frequently.

Tides can also have a big impact at the ramp. A strong crosscurrent can make launching and retrieving your boat difficult if not impossible at certain times of the day, though most ramps are located in areas with minimal tidal influence. Local knowledge helps; if possible, stop by the ramp without your boat to check the conditions. (You can sometimes find clues in the parking lot. If one ramp has an empty lot, another only a few powerboat trailers, and yet another is filled with trailers for sailboats and powerboats, that third ramp just might have better conditions. Or there might be a fishing tournament or race going on.)

## LIGHTNING

Being struck by lightning is rare, but it is a real risk to a sailboat. If you are caught in an electrical storm, avoid the shrouds and stays—lightning sometimes runs down them to get to the water.

There is no clear consensus about lightning protection. The American Boat and Yacht Council (ABYC) has updated its lightning protection standards. It's been said that poorly done lightning protection systems can actually increase a boat's chances of being hit. Providing a good, straight-line path from the mast to the water is the basis of most lightning protection systems. You need at least a square foot of metal below the water to ground lightning. If you have an external metal keel, a #4 cable wired to the nearest keel bolt provides a ground path, and extra protection can be provided by adding #6 cables from the chainplate to the metal keel. A pointed copper lightning rod at the masthead is recommended. More information on lightning protection can be found on the Internet and in the books listed in the Bibliography.

## SAILING DOWNWIND IN STRONG WINDS

If you are heading downwind in a storm, be very careful of an accidental jibe. The wind can shift at any moment, and when it's strong, it can bring the boom around in the blink of an eye and with great force. (See the sidebar "Accidental Jibe" in Chapter 8 for safety tips.) Running downwind before large waves can be dangerous because of broaching. In a broach, the stern is lifted by the following seas and the bow goes down. The boat's balance shifts as more of the forward part of the hull is immersed in the water. The boat suddenly wants to turn upwind, and you'll feel a large increase in weather helm. The boat will try to turn sideways, presenting the beam to the waves, which could knock down or even capsize the boat. Anticipate this tendency and head off slightly as the stern lifts; try to slow the boat down by reducing sail or dragging something off the stern. A broach, an accidental jibe, and a knockdown all at once could damage or sink a boat, so be careful.

Two old mariner's sayings I found in John Rousmaniere's *Annapolis Book of Seamanship* bear repeating:

When the wind before the rain, let your topsails draw again *(the blow may be fierce, but short-lived)*

When the rain before the wind, topsail sheets and halyards mind *(the rain is the result of an approaching front, and the blow may last a few days)*

And this one:

The sharper the blast
The sooner it's past.

# CHAPTER ELEVEN

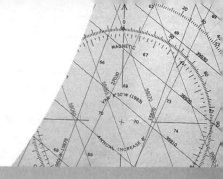

# Navigation and Piloting

People sailed for a very long time using more or less the same techniques to figure out where they were going. Then things went modern, first with the Chinese and their newfangled compass in 1117. When John Harrison developed the H4 chronometer in 1761, and sailors could finally determine their longitude aboard ships, we entered a veritable age of reason in the sailing world.

The idea that you can now switch on a GPS, push a button, and see your position plotted on a chart is almost unbelievable. Not too many years ago, this trick would have gotten you burned as a witch.

GPS is a wonderful tool, but you can still get burned if you rely on it too much. More on that in a moment. First, though, let's consider some of the techniques that have been used for the two millennia or so before push-button fixes.

## NAVIGATION TOOLS

The fact is that the basic old techniques work. Navigating a boat with a compass, chart, your eyes, a watch, the boat's log, and a pencil isn't that difficult or tricky. (The logbook is the official written record of the boat's daily progress, which traditionally contains all the important happenings onboard: weather, navigation data, watch keepers' names, sightings, and other information deemed important to the master.) You can get a pretty good idea of where you are on the water using just your eyes, though this takes practice. And as long as you have a chart (and can read it), you can get a good idea of where you *don't* want to be. There's a saying

that goes something like this: "A superior skipper is best defined as one who uses superior knowledge and judgment to keep out of situations requiring superior skills."

## Nautical Charts

The first navigational tool that all sailors should buy is a chart of the area they'll be sailing. A chart that's printed on paper, that is. Electronic versions of charts are widely available now, but they aren't the same. You can print out your own charts at home for some areas, but they'll be very small, and, if printed on an inkjet printer, the ink will run if they get wet, so it's best to use a laser printer for this job. Most NOAA-approved chart agencies print current charts using a special chart-on-demand service. Charts are printed as required by the customer on water-resistant paper. Plan on paying about $20 each. One big advantage of these new charts is that they can be printed without LORAN (long-range navigation) grids, which are rarely used anymore.

A good deal of the information on a chart is self-explanatory; for the rest, refer to NOAA's Chart No. 1, which defines all the terms, colors, and symbols used. The bound version is about $10, and a CD version (together with all nine *Coast Pilots*) can be purchased for $5.

One of the problems with marine charts is their size. Storing them flat is best, of course, but that works only for something the size of a navy ship—no trailer sailer will have the space to store full-size printed charts flat. Probably the best solution is to fold the charts into quarters, and unfold them as needed. You can do

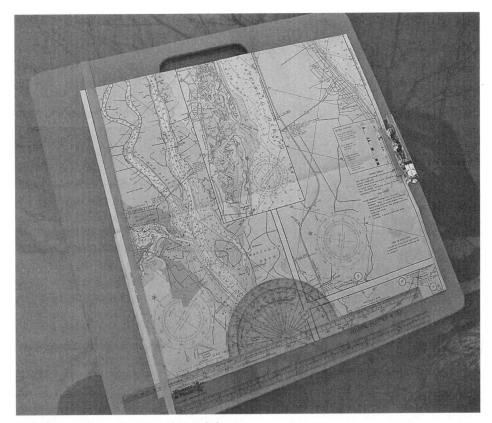

*A sketch board used to hold a navigational chart.*

your navigating at the dinette table, if you have one. My boat is too small even for this, so my solution is an inexpensive, oversized clipboard (available from art stores in several sizes).

Of particular interest on the chart is the compass rose, usually located in the corners of the chart. The outer ring shows true north, and the inner ring shows the variation calculated for magnetic north. The variation changes over the years, so if you're using an old chart (not recommended, but better than nothing), you might check the inner ring of the compass rose to see how close it is. (A magnetic variation calculator is available at www.ngdc.noaa.gov/seg/geomag/declination.shtml.) If the amount of variation calculated versus the amount shown on your chart is slight, you can probably use the printed magnetic compass rose.

It's difficult to take a bearing from the deck of a moving, pitching sailboat without at least a degree or two of error. In fact, it's a good habit to consider all your "fixes" as approximate. Look for danger spots near your fix, like rocks or shoals. There shouldn't be any. Always leave plenty of room for mistakes and misjudgments when navigating and piloting your boat.

## Print Resources

Besides charts, there are other resources published by the U.S. Coast Guard that are essential for safe navigation of your boat. These include the *Coast Pilot*s, Local Notices to Mariners, Light Lists, and tide tables. Government-printed versions were traditionally available for sale through NOAA chart agents like Bluewater

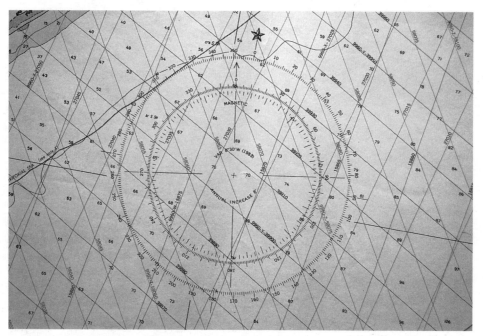

*The compass rose shows true north and the magnetic variation for the chart's printed area.*

Books and Charts and Landfall Navigation, but the U.S. government has ceased printing most of these publications.

For the trailer sailor, it turns out that this is a good thing, as long as you have access to the Internet and a printer. Free versions of the Local Notice to Mariners, Light List, *Coast Pilot*, and other government publications are available for download to your PC. You can then print out only the sections that cover the areas that you sail, saving money, weight, and trees. But what are these publications, and why should you have them on board?

The *Coast Pilot* is a publication containing up-to-date details about navigating the waters in a given area. It contains details that aren't easily gleaned from a chart, such as sailing routes, tide ranges, areas of difficult navigation, harbor entrances (some with photographs), repair facilities, and marina locations. Some of the information is geared toward commercial vessels, so you can skip those pages, but it's all useful to the small-boat mariner.

The national Notice to Mariners and the regional Local Notice to Mariners contain important corrections and changes to the information found on the chart since it was published. This includes chart discrepancies like extinguished lights, missing buoys, and shifting sandbars. Issues of the Local Notice to Mariners were formerly available by subscription in the mail, but now they are published only in digital form and delivered via the Internet.

The Light List is a written description of all aids to navigation—not just lights but buoys, daymarks, radio beacons, and so forth. The list supplements the printed chart and gives remarks about an aid's characteristics, such as visibility, height, and range.

Print resources such as these are useful to the trailer sailor because, when it comes to navigation, forewarned is forearmed. Print resources still work when the batteries go dead or a connection gets damp. And having these resources aboard and using them shows that you are taking your responsibility as captain seriously.

## Binoculars

A compass is useful for determining your vessel's heading, of course, and that's about all you can expect of it if you're out of sight of land or marks. A pair of binoculars can increase your range of vision dramatically, allowing you to identify marks that would otherwise be invisible. A good pair of binoculars is an important navigational tool.

But how good do the binoculars need to be? It depends on your sailing area and the type of sailing you do, as well as your own preference and finances. If you go onto eBay and type in "marine binoculars," you'll find dozens. And marine catalogs show everything from basic compact binoculars to models with a built-in compass, digital image stabilizer, nightscope, and even a laser range finder/speed detector! Prices range from around $75 to $1,300.

Any pair of binoculars is better than nothing. Usually, more expensive pairs work better than cheap ones. For boat use, waterproof, nitrogen-filled binoculars are nice because they won't cloud up from humidity and condensation, though I've had a pair of inexpensive nonwaterproof binoculars on the boat for a

*A pair of binoculars. This is a very low-end pair of 7 x 21s that will cause no heartache if they're dropped overboard, broken, or stolen.*

while now and they haven't clouded up. Beware of buying used binoculars, since you cannot know if they have been dropped—something binoculars do not like. If the prisms get knocked out of alignment, the binoculars must be sent back to the factory for repair. If you want to buy a used pair online, be sure to ask the seller if they've ever been dropped. The lens coating should look intact, the image should focus 100 percent sharp, and the binoculars should show no indication of rough treatment.

With binoculars, higher price doesn't always equal higher performance. Binoculars are rated with two numbers—for example, 8 × 24. The first number means magnification; the second number means lens diameter. Often, the second number is most important when deciding between two similarly priced binoculars. A larger number means more light-gathering ability, which can equal a brighter image, but other factors such as the type of glass and the lens coatings play a big role as well. I recommend trying a cheap discount pair for your first few sails, and then upgrading to a better pair. Hopefully you can find a chandlery with several display models that you can look through before buying them. A pair of binoculars with a built-in compass is extremely handy for sighting bearings, and I've heard good things about West Marine's compass models.

## Chartplotting Tools

A few other low-tech devices are useful when navigating with a chart and compass. A pair of dividers with two points is handy for taking measurements and walking off distances. Dividers are easy to find at office supply stores. (These rarely wear out; I still use a fine pair that my father owned—patent date 1903.) With a set of parallel rules, you can walk a bearing line from the compass rose to your observed mark and draw a line of position (LOP) on your chart. (If the rules are at all wiggly, though, don't use them, since the error can magnify itself with each step that it is walked across the chart.) A new type of parallel rule called a GPS plotter expands and contracts in a perpendicular line.

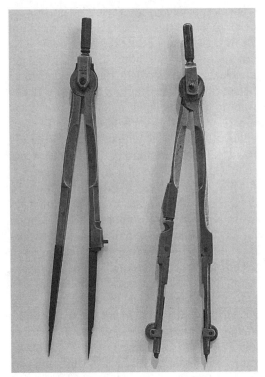

*A pair of dividers, left, and a draftsman's compass, right. Many of the better drafting sets have interchangeable points, so a compass can be used as a divider. The compass in this photo is an inexpensive find that didn't come with extra points. On a boat, you want a dedicated, full-time divider rather than having to switch out the points. A compass is handy, but, if forced to choose, I'd opt for the dividers.*

It's expensive, but some navigators swear by it. You can get other nifty devices, such as rolling plotters and protractors. Some sailors like them; others find them unnecessary. Generally, the farther you sail, the more you'll find them useful. Consider the type of sailing you do before you buy a host of navigation tools.

## MEASURING TIME

Some way of accurately measuring time is important for correct speed and distance calculations. For celestial navigation, accurate time is critical. Until recently, this required a chronometer that could compensate for errors

such as drift, and a shortwave radio to get accurate time broadcasts from radio station WWV. But nowadays most digital watches are inexpensive and quite accurate. My Timex Chronograph is waterproof, includes a stopwatch, and cost $45 on sale. It's fine for basic speed and distance work, though the tiny dials are sometimes hard to read. A digital chronograph would be a fine choice. A stopwatch is nice for measuring time from point to point.

## PLOTTING A FIX

In a nutshell, navigating your boat is a simple process. You note your starting point on the chart, with a starting time, and lightly draw a line noting your compass direction and speed. Some sailors use tracing paper over their chart to avoid marking it. Then at regular intervals you update your position on the chart. If your speed is 2 knots and you're sailing the same course (no tacking), after an hour you measure 2 nautical miles along your course line and note your *estimated* position along that line, along with the time. Then you correct that estimate using whatever data is available.

The best data will probably be fixed landmarks, if you can see any. A radio tower, an island in the distance, or a headland that you can identify are ideal. Take a bearing with your hand bearing compass and draw it on the chart. Two or three bearings are better than one.

When you draw these bearings, the usual result is a triangle. Your "fix" is somewhere within the triangle. If your angles are good and your observations accurate, the triangle will be small. One thing I can almost guarantee is that your course line will not go through the center of your triangle. All sailboats make leeway. Remember, leeway is a sideways motion as the sailboat is pushed by the wind. Current, sea state, and variations in speed will push your boat off your original course line. It is a good idea to take bearings often, especially if you are approaching any sort of shoal water or hazard.

Bearing lines shot from a buoy are always suspect. Buoys are often moved, renumbered, and subject to drift. Some can be pulled nearly

## A Logarithmic Scale for Speed/Distance/Time

At the margin of most large-scale harbor charts, you'll find a logarithmic scale that can be used to calculate speed, distance, and time relationships. The instructions on the chart are pretty simple—for example, to determine your speed, simply place one point of your dividers on the distance run, and the other point on the time it took to run it. Then move the divider point to 60, and the other point will line up with your speed in knots. For example, let's say you've gone 2 nautical miles in 25 minutes. Moving the dividers (without changing the spread, of course) to 60 shows that you're going pretty fast, about 4.8 knots.

You can also work the other way to estimate your distance traveled if you know your speed. Here's an example: suppose you're traveling at a steady 4 knots. To set your divider, place one point on 60 and the other on 4. Now you can move the divider to the time, and the other point will show the distance you'll go. Placing one point on 15, you'll notice the other point lines up with 1. So in the next 15 minutes, you'll cover 1 nautical mile.

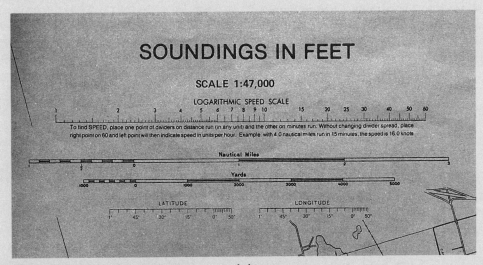

*A logarithmic scale that appears on nautical charts.*

EXPANDED
LOGARITHMIC
SCALE

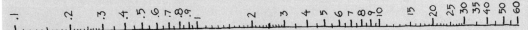

*If you don't have a chart, you can try use this scale to determine your speed using your dividers. You can copy this and place it in your logbook.*

under the surface by a strong current. Changes in buoy position are published in the Local Notice to Mariners, and you should update your chart when you read of a buoy change. (You can read the Local Notice to Mariners on the web at www.navcen.uscg.gov/LNM/default.htm.) Do use buoys, but don't treat their position as gospel.

But what if you are out to sea with no fixed landmarks—nothing to take a compass bearing on? Nothing but lots and lots of water? Well, you do basically the same thing. Note your course, time, and speed. If you know the direction and speed of the current, you can increase your accuracy by correcting your estimated position for current. Current data is published in the *Coast Pilot* for nine different regions. Print versions are for sale at most chart agents; the downloads are free.

What you're doing is making an educated guess about your position. Called dead reckoning, or DR, it's your best guess about where you are on the water. You can never really know where you are until you can make a minimum of two observations of fixed landmarks. If you sail past a buoy, you can note that as a probable fix. Even a navigation mark that's pounded into the bottom of the channel could be moved, though they're moved less frequently than buoys. Oh, by the way, it isn't called "dead" reckoning because most of the navigators who practice it meet a watery end. The *dead* or, more correctly, *ded*, stands for "deduced." It's still a guess, though if you're careful it can be a pretty good guess.

## DANGER BEARINGS
Another useful idea for the navigator is the concept of danger bearings. Very often your sailing

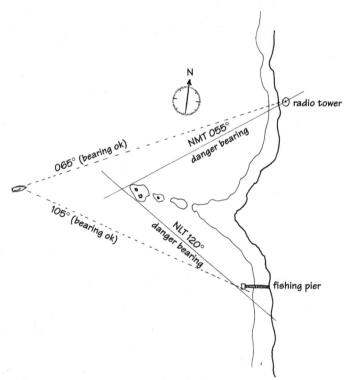

*Danger bearings. Rather than telling you where you are, danger bearings tell you where you don't want to be. In this hypothetical example, we avoid submerged shoals if our bearing between the radio tower and the offshore rocks is no more than 055 degrees, and our bearing between the same rocks and the fishing pier is no less than 120 degrees.*

area will consist of a good-sized body of reasonably deep water, but there are always a few problem spots—a sandbar, for example, or a shoal bank that extends out in the water. Depending on where you sail, the worst offenders might be marked with a buoy or channel marker, but not all hazards can be marked. Naturally, these are spots you want to stay away from. You can use danger bearings to do just that.

First, identify the limit of safe water on the chart. Then find a prominent landmark nearby and draw a line. On one side of this line lies the danger—shoal, rocks, whatever—and on the other side lies safe water. This line is labeled danger bearing—in our example at left, NMT (no more than) 55 degrees M (magnetic) or NLT (no less than) 120 degrees M, depending, of course, on which side the danger lies.

## CAN WE TURN ON THE GPS NOW?

All this discussion about dead reckoning, bearings, and fixes begs the question, why not just turn on the GPS and know where you are. Yes, you should use a GPS, but only after you can navigate the hard way. As mentioned before, don't rely on GPS as your only means of navigating your boat. This should be obvious—the story of the sailor who goes out with his push-button wonder, finds the battery has expired, gets hopelessly lost, and has to call the Coast Guard to rescue him is the stuff of urban legend.

There are many accounts of good, experienced sailors who damaged or lost their boats because of overreliance on GPS. Anything can happen. Batteries can die, and electronics don't like water. A lightning strike can wipe out all of your electronics—remember that big metal mast sticking out of the middle of the boat? It happened to one boat, and they were carrying no paper backups for charts. Many charts have not been verified or corrected with GPS coordinates; electronic charts can be incorrect; hazards can be out of position compared to GPS; some marine television antennas can screw up your reception—a whole host of problems can exist.

Because GPS units are so incredibly accurate *most* of the time, people have come to rely on them *all* of the time, and that's a dangerous mistake. They are just another tool—a really good one, but not so good that you should toss all your other tools overboard. People have tried to enter unfamiliar ports at night (which should never be attempted in the first place) using only GPS coordinates and lost their boats. They ignored the cardinal rule—*never enter an unfamiliar port at night*. Another notable example occurred in the Bahamas, when a large powerboat had programmed a waypoint for the Northwest Channel into a GPS. The skipper turned the boat over to the mate and took a nap. The boat ran directly into the channel light, which crashed onto the deck along with some of the tower. They took the whole thing with them on to Nassau.

Cautionary tales aside, there is no doubt that, on the whole, GPS units have made boat navigation safer. In the 1970s Jimmy Cornell, author of several books for sailors, including *World Cruising Routes*, did a casual survey of cruising sailors about losses and came up with fifty lost boats, which were mostly attributable to errors in navigation. In 2004, he did the same survey and came up with less than a quarter of that number.

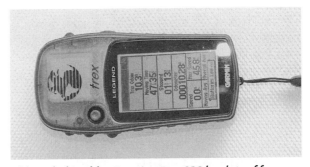

*Although this older Garmin eTrex GPS has lots of functions and abilities, including basic maps, more expensive units can show your position on an electronic marine chart. GPS units seem to get more capable and a little less expensive every year.*

## What Is GPS?

By now, most folks are familiar with GPS, which stands for Global Positioning System. The system consists of twenty-one satellites (with three spares) that transmit radio signals to dedicated receivers. GPS receivers are small handheld computers that calculate the distance to the satellites. By comparing the distances to three satellites, it can derive position information. Usually, five satellites are in range at any given time, so the system works with amazing accuracy. Differential GPS (DGPS) systems include additional radio information from fixed, land-based radio towers. By referencing this extra signal, the system can be even more accurate.

A basic handheld GPS like the Garmin eTrex can be found for as low as $100, and there are several models under $300. If you add fancy features like built-in digital charting, the price goes up quickly, and it's easy to spend $1,000 or more. But while these more expensive systems are certainly powerful navigation tools, they aren't any more accurate at finding a position than the basic units are.

A GPS that includes mapping features, on the other hand, is extremely useful. I purchased a Garmin eTrex for under $100, a black-and-white-display unit that was discontinued (all the new GPS units have color displays). The eTrex can give me a fix with the push of a button, as well as speed over the ground, actual distance traveled, and lots of other data. But the mapping feature is crude. If I were to do any serious cruising, a unit that includes charts would be worth having. Being able to see your location superimposed over an electronic chart would be a big advantage—especially on a trailer sailer, where the room to spread out a chart is hard to find.

It's difficult to fight the allure of simple, push-button navigation, and a working GPS does make your ship safer. But don't forget to use your eyes, ears, and all the information at your disposal. Use the GPS to confirm your position, but don't let flipping a switch be your only navigational skill.

## SAILING AT NIGHT

Nighttime sailing is an entirely different world. More risk is involved than in daytime sailing. Even the most familiar sailing grounds become disorienting at night. Distances are difficult to judge and lights become confusing. Nighttime sailing is best done in the open ocean, clear of hazards and shipping. Your DR plot becomes critical, as fixes are few and far between. Having others on board to relieve the on-deck watch after three to four hours is a great asset.

Nighttime is not the trailer sailer's best element. These boats are generally small and don't have room for a large crew. Most of these boats aren't designed for open-ocean passage-making, though in some situations they could manage. For example, a large, well-found trailerable might want to set out for the Bahamas Bank around midnight in settled weather, making landfall during daylight hours.

If you're going to sail at night, you have to learn the various navigation light combinations and what they mean. There are free programs you can download to learn these, and other study aids like flash cards might help. Weems & Plath makes a nifty little slide rule type of device called a LIGHTrule, which shows light combinations from both sides along with their definitions. It would be *really* useful if it had built-in LED lighting so you could use it in a dark cockpit. If you can't remember anything about the various light combinations, remember this: stay away from anything with a whole bunch of navigation lights. Bigger boats, boats with nets out, barges, and towboats will usually show more lights than a simple red or green at the bow, white at the stern, and a white steaming light. Stay clear of ferry channels and commercial shipping lanes at night.

A few tricks are helpful for night sailing in certain situations. If the night is clear and you're sailing a parallel course along a reasonably straight beach, you can use basic observation to judge your distance offshore. From the deck of a typical small sailboat, the beach will be under your horizon at a distance of about $4\frac{1}{2}$ miles. If you can just make out the beach, then you should be $3\frac{1}{2}$ to 4 miles out. If you can make out the light from individual windows in houses, then you're about 2 miles out. Again, this is assuming good visibility, and you've kept your annual appointment with your optometrist.

Navigation lights can sometimes be tough to pick out amid a confusion of rampant beach-front overdevelopment, but the distance from which you can see a navigation light usually depends on two factors: visibility and height off the water. (And whether or not the light is actually working—that makes three factors.) Lights in the United States are more reliable than in, say, the Bahamas, but they can go out anytime. Problem lights are listed in the Notice to Mariners. In good visibility, you can usually see a lighted buoy 1 to 2 miles out, though if you look on your chart, you'll see a description like this: Hen and Chickens Fl R 2.5sec 35ft 5M 40. (See the accompanying chart.) Fl R means a flashing red light. "Flashing" means the light is on briefly, then goes dark—in this case for 2.5 seconds. The next number means the light's height above the water in feet. If you want to use a range finder to determine how far off you are, don't forget the tide—the light's height is listed at mean high water, which means the average of *all* high tides. The 5M means the light's nominal range is 5 miles in good visibility. The "40" is the number

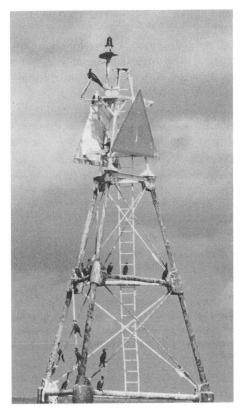

*Hens and Chickens light tower. (Eric S. Martin)*

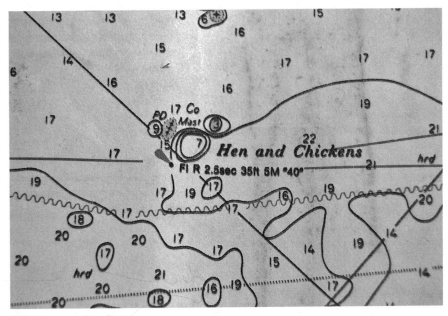

*Hens and Chickens on the chart.*

painted on the mark—often a dayglow orange triangle.

All these definitions can be found in NOAA Chart No. 1, Symbols, Abbreviations, and Terms. If you don't already have a copy, you'll certainly need one before making a nighttime passage.

When sailing at night, a masthead tricolor light will use less current than separate port, starboard, and stern lights, allowing you to go longer without running the engine. You'll need plenty of battery power as well as alternative methods of charging the battery unless you're sailing from marina to marina.

Use every navigational tool you can get your hands on when sailing at night. This includes the GPS, but I repeat—don't treat its readings as gospel. (Don't believe me? Turn it on at the dock. It isn't unusual for a GPS to show your position as somewhere in the parking lot.) Borrow a second GPS if possible. Use depth-sounder data to check your position using bottom contours; if your estimated position lies in 30 feet of water and the depth sounder shows 60 feet, something's wrong. If it shows 12 feet, something is *really* wrong, and it's time to stop the boat and figure it out. Make sure you're using an up-to-date, corrected chart and you've checked the Notice to Mariners, the Light List, and the *Coast Pilot* for your area. Everyone on deck should wear a life jacket and harness at all times and have a personal strobe light and a compressed-air horn. Going overboard is always serious, but going overboard at night can easily be deadly.

Naturally, nighttime sailing isn't for beginners. It's a much bigger deal than a casual afternoon 'round the buoys. Remember the cardinal rule of sailing after dark—*never enter an unfamiliar port at night*. I don't care how tired you are. Heave to and wait until daylight.

# CHAPTER TWELVE

# Emergencies

**S**ailing is a safe activity compared to most other watersports. It's quite possible that you'll never have to deal with an emergency situation aboard. But anything can happen, and aboard a sailboat, help is not often minutes away. It's more commonly hours away. You'll have to either get yourself out of a jam or hold down the fort until help arrives.

An emergency can be anything that poses a risk to the vessel, its crew, and the people nearby, so the short version of this chapter could read, "Be ready for anything." And remember, the captain can be injured—or fall overboard—as easily as the crew. Can the remaining crew get the sails down, the motor cranked up, and then navigate to the nearest source of aid? Do they know the radio procedures to call for help? If anybody answers, can they tell them their position?

In most cases, adrenaline is great stuff. It gave us the quick burst of strength that enabled us to outrun saber-toothed tigers. But an emergency on a sailboat, while just as adrenaline producing, isn't a fight-or-flight situation. Panic might help you outrun a tiger, but it almost never helps in an onboard emergency. *Stay calm!* Do not yell unless people can't hear you or aren't taking you seriously. A head wound produces lots of blood, and it's important to protect the victim from shock. Screaming for the first-aid kit and yelling into the VHF that you've never *seen* so much blood won't help your patient relax. You can throw up later—in this situation, you need to be the essence of calm. The captain should always be in control, and that starts with self-control.

Some situations require fast action. It's possible to be quick without panicking.

The key to staying calm is mental preparation. If you lack knowledge in a certain area, do some reading or Internet research. Continuing education programs often offer good first-aid classes, and sometimes these are specifically targeted to recreational boaters and sailors. Successful completion of one or more of these courses would be invaluable. If you wait for the emergency to come to you, it'll be too late to learn what you should do. The most common emergencies aboard a sailboat include a medical emergency, a risk to the boat, or a person overboard.

## MEDICAL EMERGENCIES

There are many potential medical emergencies that you should be prepared for, and proper preparation must include a good first-aid manual. Written by qualified doctors and experienced sailors, a first-aid manual is invaluable—both for study beforehand and for reference during a medical emergency. It should be an important part of your first-aid kit. Your level of preparedness can be adjusted to reflect the sailing you will do. Most manuals aren't written strictly for daysailing and therefore assume that treatment may be days away, as some cruisers will venture long distances into countries with minimal medical treatment facilities. Since trailer sailers will rarely be so far from medical care, you shouldn't need to stock heavy antibiotics.

So, what are the more common medical emergencies aboard sailboats? Dr. Andrew Nathanson, assistant professor of emergency medicine at Brown University, collects data on sailing injuries. In an article for Lifespan.org titled "Sailing Injuries," Dr. Nathanson and Dr. Glenn Hebel say that some of the most serious accidents are being swept overboard and being hit by the boom. Head injuries caused by the boom are listed as the second leading cause of death aboard sailboats. Other common injuries result from falling down open hatches, tripping over lines and cleats, and catching fingers and hands in winches and cleats.

Warn your crew about these dangers and read the sections in your first-aid manual covering head trauma, lacerations, broken bones, and hypothermia/drowning. The law requires that an accident victim give consent before any first aid is applied. If there is an accident aboard your boat and the victim is conscious, ask if you can proceed. And administer first aid only if you know what you are doing. If not, your only recourse is to call 911 on your cell phone or call the Coast Guard on Channel 16 on your VHF.

Other medical emergencies that are less life threatening can sometimes be treated aboard. Jellyfish stings, for example, can be treated with a sprinkling of meat tenderizer, which neutralizes the neurotoxin. Seasickness is very common and often responds well to Dramamine or Bonine tablets, scopolamine patches, or motion-sickness wristbands. Bonine or Dramamine can make you really sleepy, though. Heat exhaustion can happen while sailing, especially if accompanied by dehydration. Victims should *not* be given alcohol, but moved to the shade and cooled as rapidly as possible.

## Carbon Monoxide Poisoning

Carbon monoxide (CO) poisoning is called the silent killer because it has no odor and no color. You can't see, smell, or taste it. It makes you feel drowsy, and if you go to sleep, you don't wake up. There's even some evidence that CO exposure can lead to delayed heart problems because of muscle tissue damage.

CO poisoning on boats is rare, but it does happen. Early propane water heaters were

found to be a culprit. Anytime you use an oven or a heater in the tight confines of a cabin, you are at risk. If you ever feel oddly dizzy or suddenly sleepy in the cabin, get fresh air immediately. Be sure you have plenty of cabin ventilation. If you sail in winter, a CO monitor for the cabin is a must. (See "Optional Equiment" in Chapter 5 for suggestions regarding CO detectors and ventilation.)

## CREW OVERBOARD

Crew overboard is a serious situation, but it can largely be prevented by good sailing habits and a high level of preparation, including wearing a life jacket. Life jacket users are two to four times more likely to survive a fall overboard. Boats with lifelines and bow pulpits tend to keep their sailors on board, though there are many cases of sailors being swept under the lifelines and overboard. Wearing a harness on the foredeck and in rough weather also reduces crew-overboard cases.

Practicing crew-overboard drills in various conditions also helps. One of the best crew-overboard articles I've read is John Rousmaniere's 2005 Crew Overboard Rescue Symposium Final Report, where four hundred tests were conducted over a four-day period using fifteen boats, forty different pieces of rescue gear, and numerous recovery techniques. (The full text can be downloaded at http://www.boatus.com/foundation/findings/COBfinalreport/).

When a person falls overboard, there are four actions that are critical to his/her survival:

1. Get flotation to the person in the water and maintain visual contact at all times.
2. Change course quickly to get the boat back to the victim.
3. Connect the victim to the boat by tossing a line.
4. Get the victim back on board the boat.

Your crew-overboard plan has to allow for all of these things to happen quickly and with a minimum of confusion, even though the conditions may be chaotic. Let's go through a recovery plan step-by-step.

## Flotation and Visual Contact

You've got to see the person in the water, and a dark, wet head can disappear among the waves quickly, even during the daytime. A strobe light, personal Freon horn, whistle, and signal mirror can all help locate someone in the water if he or she is conscious and able to operate these devices and you've attached him or her to a PFD (see "USCG-Required Equipment" in Chapter 5).

If others are aboard, assign one crewmember to keep the victim in sight. Get flotation to the person immediately, as well as any additional man-overboard gear you have ready, such as a man-overboard (MOB) pole or a Lifesling.

## Altering Course to Return to the Victim

Several methods can be used to return to the location of a person who has fallen overboard. One is called a quickstop. As soon as a person goes over, head the boat straight into the wind and sheet everything in. Get the jib down and sail in a circle around the person in the water, coming to a stop just upwind of him or her. This is the maneuver used when recovering a crew overboard using the Lifesling.

Another method of returning to the location of a person who has fallen overboard is called a fast return. If you're sailing upwind, bear off the wind (see art page 164). After two and a half boat lengths, point the boat into the wind, letting the sails luff. Let the bow of the boat fall back toward the person in the water.

There are other crew-overboard recovery maneuvers, such as the figure eight or the deep beam reach, but the quickstop and fast return are probably more useful aboard smaller trailer sailers. Improvisation is certainly allowed, and different boats will have different success rates depending on the circumstances.

Of all the recovery maneuvers tried at the 2005 Crew Overboard Rescue Symposium, stopping the boat to windward at the end of the recovery maneuver was almost unanimously preferred. A boat will drift faster than a

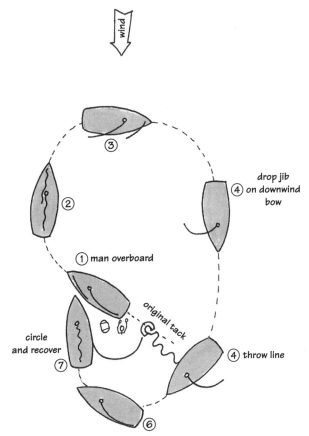

*The quickstop recovery maneuver might be thought of as sailing a circle around the victim. Throw a float to the victim immediately, and then tack. Drop the jib on the downwind leg if you have the crew, then jibe and approach the victim, letting the sails luff as you throw a line. If the water is clear of lines, you can always start the engine and use it to aid your recovery, since stopping a sailboat in any sort of wind or tide is harder than it looks.*

person in the water. In rough weather there is a risk that the boat could drift over the victim. The boat should be sailed as slowly as possible when approaching the victim, but not so slowly that the boat loses steerageway.

## Connecting the Victim to the Boat

Never count on swimming ability during a crew-overboard emergency. When wearing clothes, even expert swimmers cannot swim

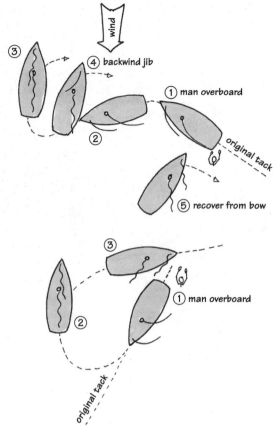

*The fast return recovery maneuver might be thought of as luffing and drifting back to the victim instead of sailing a circle around him or her. Depending on your point of sail, you head immediately into the wind, and then drift, sails luffing, back to the victim. Toss a line as the boat gets close. In both these maneuvers, try to position the boat upwind of the victim as it comes to a stop. The hull will shield the victim somewhat from the wind and sea swells. And since boats drift faster than people, you will more likely drift toward the person in the water rather than away.*

very far without becoming dangerously tired. It's better to bring the boat close to the victim and connect to the person with a line. When to deploy the line depends on the maneuver—a quickstop maneuver deploys the line right away, and then the circular path of the boat brings the line to the person in the water. In the fast return, the boat is brought back to the victim and a line is tossed. Naturally, a floating

line such as polypropylene should be used, but these deteriorate in sunlight and should be renewed annually or stored in a bag.

Five different commercial throwing lines of various prices were tested during the Crew Overboard Rescue Symposium, and all worked well. (A popular example is the Lifesling.)

## Getting the Victim Back On Board

Recovering a person who has fallen overboard can be especially difficult. There are several tragic stories about people who have fallen overboard and, unable to scale the smooth side of the hull, drowned while still connected to the boat. You have to have a plan for lifting the victim that final 5 feet or so up to the deck.

If the victim is conscious, the job is much easier. You can trail a loop of large line into the water, one end tied to a stanchion and the other led to a winch. The victim stands on the looped line and is lifted up to deck level by cranking on the winch. This method requires some upper body strength, though.

In terms of a commercial system, the Lifesling, which includes provisions for lifting the victim into the boat, has a long record of success. If the victim is unconscious, then a second crew, tethered to the boat, must jump into the water to place the Lifesling over the victim. In another method, called a parbuckle, a triangular-shaped piece of cloth is attached to the rail of the boat at two corners, and the third corner is lifted with a tackle. This system also has the potential to help with an unconscious victim.

### Swim Platforms and Boarding Ladders

Most of the time a swim platform is a recreational accessory, but it becomes much more than that when someone has fallen overboard. Newer and often larger boats feature a reverse transom or a "sugar scoop" stern, where the transom itself is inset a little from the sides of the hull. This makes a convenient area, just above the water level, for entering and leaving the water for a swim or, more importantly in this case, recovering an overboard victim.

Unfortunately, these hull configurations aren't very common on smaller boats, where a sugar scoop can complicate a rudder installation and an outboard motor mount.

So, many owners install an aftermarket swim platform onto the stern. These are desirable upgrades, as long as the platform is well built and the installation is strong. Because transoms are often somewhat flexible due to their large, flat surface, you may need to reinforce the transom laminate from the inside. All attachment points for the swim platform should be through-bolted to the transom and have a large backing plate. This can sometimes be a problem because you may not be able to reach all the attachment points from the inside, so installations must be planned carefully. If there is room on your transom, the bigger swim platform you can have, the better. The platform on my boat is small, but very welcome when you are in the water.

Boarding ladders can range from a simple wood-and-rope affair that's tossed over the side when needed to expensive telescoping or folding stainless assemblies that are permanently attached. If you have a swim platform, an attached boarding ladder goes hand in hand. But it's essential to make sure that the ladder is long enough. My boat came with a swim platform and a single-rung ladder that swings over the side. It's just barely possible for an adult to get back aboard. The single rung is too close to the surface to get your feet into, and the swim platform is too small to flop yourself onto like a seal. A new boarding ladder is currently on my upgrades list.

A boarding ladder isn't a good place to save money. Cheap boarding ladders are really flimsy, and I wouldn't want to count on one as being my sole means of getting back aboard. Permanently attached ladders are slightly better than the folding type, since the folders are usually stowed and out of reach when someone goes over the side. And since the ladders are fairly large items, stowage on a small boat is tricky. The ladder is likely to be deep within a quarter berth or locker, with lots of other

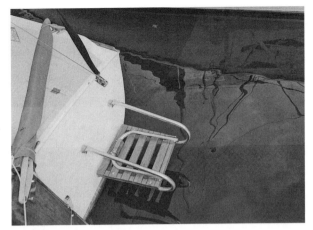

*Could you haul yourself back aboard using this platform? Probably not—the ladder isn't long enough, and the platform is too small. The transom size limits the use of a larger platform, but a telescoping stainless ladder would be a big improvement.*

stuff on top of it. But the folders do have one advantage—they can be deployed midships, where the motion of the boat will be more steady, rather than at the stern, where the motion is more pronounced.

## RISKS TO THE BOAT

### Taking on Water

All sorts of emergencies can pose a risk to the boat. Probably the most frightening is water getting into the boat, as in a serious leak. First, try to locate the source of the leak. Check all keel bolts and seacocks and any hose below the waterline. In one case, badly corroded keel bolts gave way on a large boat being delivered near Hawaii. When the keel fell off the boat, the captain felt the boat "jump up" in the water, and the next minute the interior was flooded. The boat sank in less than two minutes.

Sometimes, a sailboat on a given tack can siphon water into the hull through a sink drain or head intake, so make sure these are secure.

If no obvious collision has occurred to account for a leak, the problem could lie somewhere near a normal opening in the hull, such

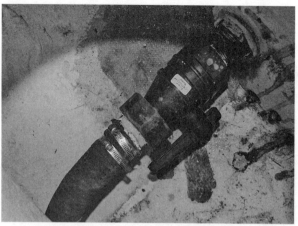

*Seacocks should be double clamped, and a tapered plug (not shown here) should be located nearby.*

as a seacock. A burst hose or a frozen seacock has sunk more than one boat—keep softwood plugs taped to each seacock just in case.

As you locate the leak, have your crew keep the water at bay using the bilge pumps or a bucket, if necessary. A bucket in the hands of a truly motivated sailor can remove impressive amounts of water. If the leak is really bad and getting worse, consider beaching the boat if you're near relatively protected shoal water.

### Collision

A collision on a sailboat can be anything from a hard bump to far worse. Collisions between sailing vessels are more frequent during races. The result is often a simple protest with the race judges, but it can be more serious. Collisions with powerboats operating at high speed can split the average trailer sailer in two. Of course, you've done everything possible to avoid a collision, but let's assume it's happened anyway.

First, make sure your crew is accounted for and there are no injuries. If there are, get on the radio and issue a Mayday or Pan-Pan as required by the situation (see the sidebar

"Mayday and Pan-Pan Radio Procedures" for specific tips).

Second, check for hull integrity. Even if everything looks dry, lift the floorboards and see if water is entering the bilge. You may have a hull crack that is allowing water into the boat, but the crack may be behind the interior liner. If the water is rising, slow the leak somehow—stuff anything into the leak that will slow the water—while your crew contacts the Coast Guard on the VHF.

If everything looks dry down below and there are no injuries, you still need to contact the Coast Guard. (Except for very minor scrapes, you are required to file an accident report with either a state agency or the Coast Guard. If colliding vessels are involved, both of them must file a report, regardless of who is at fault.) Establish contact with the other vessel, if possible, and check for injuries or flooding there. But by far the best way to deal with collisions at sea is to avoid them using any means necessary, as stated in the Navigation Rules. (See Chapter 9, "Rules of the Road.")

### Fire

Fires on board can be very serious, especially fires involving fuel. A propane accident won't be a fire; it will be an explosion. Concentrated gasoline vapors will cause an explosion followed by a fireball. There isn't much you can do to "fight" either of these situations other than prevent them from happening in the first place. (Adequate ventilation is the key to prevention; see the suggestions under "Optional Equipment" in Chapter 5.)

More common are galley fires. Keep a lid handy for the frying pan, as you can quickly smother a grease fire that gets out of hand.

Your first line of defense in a fire is your fire extinguisher. Ideally, you'll have more than one, kept within easy reach. See "USCG-Required Equipment" in Chapter 5 for a description of the basic types.

## Mayday and Pan-Pan Radio Procedures

If your vessel is in immediate danger or there's an immediate risk to life, it's time to issue a Mayday. Here is the correct procedure (your emergency may vary from the one below, but this gives you the idea).

Set VHF to Channel 16, high power, and say:

MAYDAY, MAYDAY, MAYDAY—this is sailing vessel TINY DANCER, TINY DANCER, TINY DANCER. MAYDAY POSITION IS [give your latitude and longitude, or bearing and distance from the best landmark you can shoot from your position].
We are TAKING ON WATER. We request PUMPS and a vessel to stand by. On board are two adults, no injuries. We estimate we can stay afloat for one hour. TINY DANCER is a 17-foot sloop with white hull, white decks. Monitoring Channel 16. TINY DANCER. Over.

Wait a few moments, then repeat.

Please note that being becalmed and out of fuel *is not* a Mayday situation, and you should not issue a Mayday if there is no immediate danger. The Coast Guard used to respond to this type of call, but this is a convenience call that should be directed to a towing service such as TowBoatU.S. If you're on a large body of water, out of fuel, becalmed, and have lost all your anchors and are slowly drifting toward shoal waters, that's the time for a Pan-Pan.

Set the VHF to Channel 16, high power, and say:

PAN-PAN, PAN-PAN, PAN-PAN, ALL STATIONS, this is TINY DANCER, TINY DANCER, TINY DANCER. We are out of fuel and drifting into shoal water. All anchors have been lost. Request a tow to safe water. On board are two adults, no injuries. We estimate we can stay afloat for two to three hours before grounding. POSITION IS [give your latitude and longitude, or bearing and distance from the best landmark you can shoot from your position]. TINY DANCER is a 17-foot sloop with a white hull, white decks. Monitoring Channel 16. TINY DANCER. Over.

If you're in sheltered water and there's no risk of damage to your boat, you shouldn't issue a Pan-Pan. Contact a commercial towing company or ask another station to relay the information to someone who can help. Pan-Pan calls are for very urgent messages regarding the safety of a person on board or the vessel itself. Mayday calls are only when immediate danger threatens a life or the vessel. Rising water in the cabin or an out-of-control fire is a Mayday; a stabilized injury is a Pan-Pan.

Never issue a false Mayday—that can get you a $5,000 fine and possibly a hefty bill for gassing up a helicopter and a Coast Guard cutter.

If possible, use your cell phone to call for help. The Coast Guard sometimes prefers cell phones over VHF because cell phones are always a "clear channel," and personnel don't have to worry about other transmissions interfering with a distress call. For more information about communications, see the communications section under "Optional Equipment" in Chapter 5.

## Accepting Assistance from Other Vessels

If your boat is disabled to the point of needing help from another vessel, you need to be aware of salvage rights. Salvage rights are a very old part of the law that gives a vessel that aids another in distress the right to claim financial compensation. These laws originated long before the days of engines, a time when going to sea for pleasure was unheard of, and being on the water involved great risk and specialized knowledge.

Towing a vessel has a host of legal ramifications. If you become stranded and need a tow, you should never accept a towline without asking the other captain, "Is this tow or salvage?" Assumptions on your part can cost you dearly. A simple tow is a matter of convenience, as when you run out of fuel. But if you're in real trouble—if your vessel is taking on water, or there's a risk to life, to your boat, or to the environment—any assistance could be considered salvage.

Salvage doesn't require a contract to file a claim; a salver has to prove only that salvage was voluntary and successful, and that the salvaged vessel, or the environment, was in danger. Do not sign a Lloyd's Open Form Salvage contract, even if it's "standard procedure for a tow," according to a commercial towing captain. If you do sign one, you can be sure that your vessel will get a salver's lien as soon as she reaches port. Many captains have been shocked to find a bill presented to them for 20 percent of a vessel's value for a few hours' work, but salvage law allows this. (But without those few hours' work, the boat could have been a total loss, and the owner could be presented with a bill for wreck removal and cleanup.)

Inexpensive towing insurance packages are available through organizations like BoatU.S., and buying insurance now might prevent a monumental payment later on.

The Coast Guard will not tow a vessel unless the situation involves a risk to life. While there's nothing to prevent the Coast Guard from claiming salvage, it has a very long history of assisting distressed vessels at sea without claiming salvage rights.

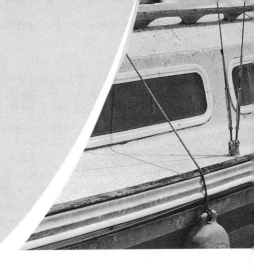

# MAINTAINING AND MODIFYING YOUR SAILBOAT

**CHAPTER THIRTEEN**

## Maintaining Your Sailboat

Today's fiberglass sailboats are remarkably low maintenance. They often require nothing more than a semiannual scrubdown and a once-a-year coat of varnish on the woodwork to look good for perhaps five to seven years. After that, the gelcoat will start to fade and turn chalky, but the boat will still be functional. (A wooden boat under similar treatment would almost fall apart after a few years. The very best wooden boats are built in a way that minimizes maintenance, but rot can still sneak in, and it needs to be addressed immediately or the consequences can be dire.)

If you're fortunate enough to own a new or nearly new boat, your maintenance and repair chores will be minimal. But as the boat ages, things naturally start to wear and require attention. Remember that a little maintenance done when a boat is new pays big dividends later: if you keep your boat clean, dry, lubricated, and protected from the sun, you should have few problems and it will last a very long time. Check everything carefully for signs of fatigue

or stress, and replace problem parts as soon as you notice them. A sailboat is a series of interconnected systems, and one weak link can affect the entire vessel. If you can keep up with all these little links, it can make owning a boat a much smoother experience. Neglect them, and boat ownership becomes a chore.

What follows isn't a complete treatise on sailboat maintenance, just the high points. (A complete treatise would take an entire book, several of which are listed in the Bibliography.)

### FREQUENT WASHDOWNS

If your boat is used in salt water, frequent freshwater washdowns of the hull and deck will be required to keep it looking good. Use a mild, *nonphosphate* detergent, a soft, long-handled scrub brush, and plenty of water to rinse. When I sailed in salt water, my boat got a wash after every trip. Pay particular attention to the trailer, especially the brakes, as salt water left to dry on the mild steel parts is particularly damaging. If you notice stains in the boat's gelcoat that resist the usual scrubdown, try simple solutions first. Sometimes plain lemon juice or vinegar works. Nonabrasive spray cleaners like Fantastik, Simple Green, or 409 sometimes work well. Rust stains and organic stains like blood can respond well to a mild solution of oxalic acid.

When a gelcoated sailboat deck gets more than a few years' exposure to sunlight, it becomes porous. Under a strong magnifying glass, you can see thousands of tiny holes. These holes become perfect little petri dishes for mildew, and down here in the warm, humid South, we get thousands of black mildew specks. They're actually a mixture of mildew and dirt, brought in by rainwater and accelerated by the humidity and the organic material in the dirt. If you park your boat under a tree, it'll get dirty much faster. When a boat is neglected for an entire season, the stains can get really bad. Scrubbing doesn't do a thing for these stains because they're firmly embedded in the pores of the gelcoat.

For really impossible mildew stains on old, porous gelcoat, I've used spray cleaners made for fiberglass tubs and showers—though not while the boat is in the water, and only as a last resort. Check the product label—if it includes sodium hypochlorite or just hypochlorite, it has chlorine in it. This is pretty harsh stuff—bad for you and the environment and corrosive to metals. Keep it away from your stainless

*A bad case of gelcoat mildew. This boat will be tough to clean.*

and aluminum. If you choose to use it, don't rinse it off with a hose—that puts the chlorine in the salt or fresh water. Instead, spray lightly, let it work for a few minutes, and remove the residue with a damp rag and a bucket of water.

The more I read about chlorine and bleach-based cleaners, the less I want to use them. There are alternatives to chlorine, such as borax or hydrogen peroxide. Or, if you can stand your boat smelling like a pickle for a while, try household vinegar for killing mold. Spray it on straight and let it sit until the mold is gone. You can also purchase stronger forms of vinegar, such as pickling vinegar (7 percent acidity) or even photographic stop-bath concentrate. Lemon juice and citric acid work much the same way as vinegar, but they don't smell nearly as bad. Several commercial companies offer "green" bathroom cleaners and mold-removal products. They are rather expensive but might be worth a try.

## PREVENTING WATER AND MILDEW BELOWDECK

One of the most effective ways to maintain your boat's interior is to prevent problems before they occur. One of the most common and preventable problems is damage caused by leaks. Mention "leak" aboard a sailboat and most people imagine sinking from a leak below the waterline. While such leaks do occur, they're fairly rare; most leaks form in the deck, where hundreds of little screw holes have been drilled to mount deck hardware. Although each of these holes should be sealed well with good-quality bedding compound, all compounds fail eventually.

Allowing lots of rainwater to collect in the boat (and, even worse, stagnate) is a surefire way to ruin much of the value of your boat. You might as well light up a few thousand-dollar bills right now. If you see even the slightest leak, find it and repair it right away. (See the sidebar "Repairing Deck Rot.") Some leaks can be particularly difficult to track down because the water runs along a horizontal surface for some distance before appearing in the cabin. If you have a mystery leak and can't find the source, try this rather extreme solution:

1. Borrow a leaf blower.
2. Cut a piece of plywood or stiff cardboard the same size as one of the companionway dropboards. Two or three layers of cardboard glued together should do it, but it needs to be painted so that water doesn't dissolve it. Cut a hole so you can insert the hose of the leaf blower in it.
3. Seal up the cracks in the companionway and hatches with duct tape. Close all opening ports and seal all ventilators.

4. Hose down the deck with soapy water.
5. Turn on the blower so you are blowing a strong jet of air down below; then walk around the deck and look for bubbles. Any fittings that have bubbles coming from underneath have potential leaks that should be rebedded.

Preventing mildew inside the boat can be just as tricky as finding mystery leaks. Fortunately, since the gelcoat on the interior of your boat is protected from exposure to UV rays, it will be in much better condition than the exterior. It won't have the thousands of

## Repairing Deck Rot

Repairing small areas of deck rot can be done fairly easily, but it will take some time. Deck rot is caused by water entering the core of the deck, where (since the deck is sealed top and bottom with fiberglass) it's nearly impossible for it to dry out. First off, identify all sources of water intrusion. If the deck is spongy around one of the fittings, chances are the bedding is failing around other fittings as well. Remove the deck hardware and remove a sample of the core with a pocketknife or an ice pick. If the core sample is dry, good; if it's wet, you'll need to drill into the core and dry out the spongy portion of the deck as much as possible.

First, plug the bottom of the hole(s) where you removed the deck hardware. I've used a small rubber stopper and good-sized square of duct tape with pretty good results. Add acetone to the hole. Some acetone might leak through to the cabin, so be sure to remove any cushions below and have a rag ready underneath the hole. Acetone bonds with water and evaporates readily, so if you can get the wet parts of the core flooded with acetone, you've got a better chance of removing the rot. Acetone is very flammable, though, so be extremely careful. Fill the bolt hole with acetone and let it soak in. Do this several times a day over several days. If the weather is bright, sunny, and dry, the heat from the sunshine will help evaporate the acetone and the water. In damp weather, make sure this area of the deck stays perfectly dry.

The longer you can keep this area warm and dry, the better. Try to wait at least two weeks in summer, longer in winter. I don't advise using heat guns, blow-dryers, or heat lamps to accelerate the drying process because of the danger of fire, but it has been done. The fiberglass should never get too warm to touch, though.

Once you've waited a while, pick out a sample of the core, which should by now be at least somewhat drier. A bent nail chucked into a drill works well to pulverize the core. Vacuum out the chips and mix up some thinned epoxy. A commercial product called Git Rot is just the ticket. Following the manufacturer's directions, mix up a little and pour it into the hole. Hopefully it'll soak into the core. Keep pouring as long as it continues to soak in—the more epoxy you can get into the deck, the better. The idea is to fill up the hole with epoxy, and then redrill the bolt holes. Now you've got a nice little epoxy compression pad under the deck, and you've sealed the hole as well. It's best to give any hole that penetrates the deck core this treatment, whether the area around it is rotted or not.

Large areas of deck rot are another story. One letter I read told of estimates of $2,500 to $8,000 to repair the rotten deck of a Ranger 28, reflecting the seriousness of the job. It's doubtful that the above method will work for areas of rot that are greater than, say, a square foot or so. The deck needs to be cut up, and then the rotten areas removed and replaced with sound core, and then resealed. It's a huge job.

tiny holes that are common on the decks of older sailboats. (Still, it's not a bad idea to wax the interior gelcoat once every few years or so.) It's easy enough to clean mildew from hard, smooth surfaces. A wipe with a damp rag with a little orange Pine-Sol is one of my favorite methods, and it leaves the interior of the boat smelling good. Wood surfaces may require a bit more elbow grease, especially if the wood has been left bare. The best approach is to prevent, or at least minimize, the mildew growth in the first place.

Mildew spores are everywhere, but to grow they need two things—still air and humidity. Still air can be avoided by adding ventilation (see "Optional Equipment" in Chapter 5). Humidity is a little tougher to reduce. If you have a 110-volt power source, a Goldenrod heater can be used to gently warm the air in the cabin, thus reducing mildew. You can also find small dehumidifying heaters

with an aluminum casing and a fan to circulate dry air. They're designed for continuous safe operation, though I would hesitate to leave anything plugged into my boat for a long period of time given the risk of fire. Another unit, the Eva-Dry EDV300, is a small closet dehumidifier that retails for about $20. The interesting feature is that it's rechargeable, though not in the usual sense. It's a chemical dehumidifier with a built-in heating element. When the crystals inside the unit become loaded with moisture, an indicator window changes color and you plug the unit into the wall to warm the crystals and drive off moisture. The unit is small, so don't expect one to turn your cabin into the Sahara. Two or three units might be needed to make a noticeable difference in a cabin, but they're also useful in lockers or any enclosed space.

There are chemical compounds that reduce humidity and don't consume power, making them safer to use. Some silica gel dehumidifiers can be warmed to drive off moisture and reused, while others are designed to be discarded after use. You can even make your own low-tech chemical dehumidifier (see the sidebar "Make Your Own Dehumidifier"). The chemical eventually washes away with the condensate, but it's pretty cheap to refill. In general, though, improving ventilation is a better strategy.

## GELCOAT MAINTENANCE

A new fiberglass sailboat has a very shiny finish. New gelcoat gloss can be practically blinding when it's fresh from the mold, and, if cared for, this finish can last a long time. Far too many owners ignore this aspect of boat care until they start to see a problem, and by then the issue is restoring rather than simply maintaining the boat's former gloss. Restoring is always a lot more work than maintaining.

Aging gelcoat loses gloss and becomes porous and chalky for several reasons, but the

## Make Your Own Dehumidifier

You can make your own small chemical drip-type dehumidifier using a pair of small plastic tubs with lids (I've used inexpensive food-storage containers). Use tubs that are reasonably flat on the bottom, since you'll stack one on top of the other. Using a larger tub on the bottom makes the whole assembly less likely to tip over. Use a 1- or 2-cup container for the top and a 5-cup (or thereabouts) container for the bottom.

Make large holes in the lid of the top container to allow air to contact the chemical; make a few small holes in the top tub and the lid of the bottom container to allow water to drain (but not so large that the chemical will fall through). You can drill the holes or melt them with a hot nail held by vise grips.

Fill the perforated container with calcium chloride ice-melt pellets. These will absorb moisture from the air, which will drip into the lower container.

Secure the top container to the lower one with a few rubber bands. The total cost for the containers and 9 pounds of calcium chloride should be around $15.

biggest culprit is the sun. Ultraviolet rays are a powerful aging force. If you could keep your boat in the shade, the gelcoat would last *much* longer. This is tough to do with the mast sticking out of the middle of the boat, but you can work around that. I have never bought a brand-new boat, but when I do, the very first thing I will buy (or make) for it is a full fitted sun cover, made of a tough fabric like Odyssey or Top Gun.

Keeping your gelcoat waxed also pays off in the long run. It's a big job to properly wax an entire boat, but doing so once or even twice a year will help seal the gelcoat as well as add some degree of UV protection. Waxing is a lot easier when the gelcoat is in good condition.

The decks and cockpit, being more or less horizontal, get the greatest sun exposure and thus benefit from waxing, but the hull should get a coat as well, at least once a year. The best waxes contain UV inhibitors. Be sure to completely remove the excess wax—sun-baked wax buildup is almost impossible to remove once it's been left on the hull for a while. If your boat is new or nearly new, make sure your wax doesn't contain abrasive compounds, which can wear down your gelcoat if applied too often or buffed too vigorously. However, if your gelcoat is heavily oxidized, you may need to take more drastic measures to restore the shine. Rub your finger on the deck. If it leaves a powdery residue on your finger, the fiberglass will need to be "compounded" or buffed with a buffing compound before waxing. Use a compound made specifically for fiberglass. Automotive compounds are too aggressive and could damage the gelcoat.

Start with a squeaky clean hull and apply the wax immediately after cleaning. Let it dry, then buff. The wax helps to seal the gelcoat from the elements and will prevent further oxidation for a while. Depending on the starting condition of the gelcoat and the size of your boat, plan on spending anywhere from a few hours to the better part of an afternoon.

Whether or not to use a power buffer is largely a matter of personal choice and power availability. As always, be careful when using anything attached to an extension cord if your boat is at the dock, and never let any part of the cord sag into the water. A safer alternative is a cordless buffer. I use a Motor Scrubber, a heavy-duty industrial-grade tool that can be bought only from professional cleaning suppliers. It's rechargeable, runs for 4 hours on an overnight charge, and comes with a handle that extends to 80 inches. The power head is completely sealed, and it works underwater. You can get all kinds of additional brushes and pads, like wax applicators and terry-cloth bonnets. The only downside is that it retails for about $350—but it works really well.

Deciding what kind of wax to use on your boat can be difficult because there are literally hundreds of choices. It isn't always necessary to get a specialized boat wax either. *Practical Sailor* thoroughly tested several different kinds of wax in two articles, one published in 2004 and the other in 1988. In 2004, their two longest-lasting top waxes were Collinite #885 paste wax and Meguiar's Mirror Glaze paste. Collinite is marketed for marine use and is available in boat chandleries, but you can find Meguiar's paste wax at an auto parts store. Waxes that are easy to apply and remove are, of course, preferred over those that are more difficult, and many automotive waxes contain buffing compound. These have a slightly gritty feel and shouldn't be used on fiberglass, since the gelcoat is much softer than automotive paint finishes. The 1988 article tested waxes based on ease of application and removal and the presence of abrasive compounds. Simonize II liquid was one of the favorites based on those criteria. I've used it on my boat, but I don't like the greenish color of the wax, which gets in the gelcoat pores and leaves slightly darker swipe marks here and there. The wax does go on and off easily, though, and where the gelcoat is smooth, it works fine.

## Bedding Compounds

There are several compounds that can be used to seal bolts and keep water out of your boat, and some work better than others in certain situations. All can be broken down into one of three types: silicones, polyurethanes, or polysulfides.

### Silicones

Let's start with something I've often seen incorrectly applied to used sailboats, and that's good old silicone. Whenever a leak on a boat occurs, folks head down to the hardware store and grab a tube of this stuff, and smear it all over the offending leak. This only creates a bigger mess to clean up before you can do the job properly, and it rarely stops the leak. This is because silicone caulk has very low adhesive strength when cured. It stays flexible for a long time, though.

Silicone is best thought of as a gasket-making material. Spread a good, thick coat under a fitting and insert the mounting bolts, but don't tighten them. Wait for the silicone to cure first, then compress the "gasket" after the silicone has solidified. Otherwise, most of the silicone squeezes out of the joint, and you get a gasket that's too thin. (Actually, this is true for any type of bedding compound.) Silicone should not be used below the waterline—it's best used under plastic fittings. It also makes a good insulator when you're joining dissimilar metals.

### Polyurethanes

Polyurethane-based sealants were once hard to find; now you can get them from building suppliers and hardware stores. (I've used PL Premium Polyurethane Window and Flashing sealant. Available in white or black, it's probably not as good as genuine 3M 5200 Polyurethane, but it's close. It costs $3 a tube versus $15 for the genuine article. I wouldn't use it below the waterline, though.) The thing to remember about polyurethane is that it's very strong. Once you've bedded a fitting in poly, you've pretty much glued it in place. It'll be tough to remove without special solvents or a heat gun. Polyurethane doesn't stick well to plastics, but it sticks really well to human skin and from there it has a tendency to get all over the boat, so have several rags handy when you use it. While it's wet, you can thin it with regular paint thinner, so that helps cleanup.

### Polysulfides

This compound is my favorite. Polysulfide has been around for a long time—the granddaddy of them all. When I once ripped apart a section of old teak decking salvaged from a long-gone Chris Craft, I found that it had been sealed with polysulfide. There's no way to know how old it was, but I was probably in diapers when the polysufide was applied. It was still as tough and flexible as new, and it took forever to remove.

Polysulfide is most commonly seen as LifeCalk, from Boatlife. It comes in white, black, and brown. Polysulfide can be used for just about any bedding application aboard except for plastics.

One last thing about bedding compounds, and that's what to do with the extra that squeezes out from under the fitting. The correct way is to wait until it cures, then trim it with a razor blade. This is probably how you should do it, though I'll admit to wiping it up with a rag or a dampened finger while it's wet. You certainly have a greater chance of making a mess with the second method, but it works.

## Rebedding Deck Fittings

It's a fact of life that fittings on boats, especially older boats, need to be rebedded every now and again. Sealants have a finite life span, and once you notice the slightest trace of a leak, it's time to remove and rebed the fitting. Please note that smearing additional goo on top of the fitting will not stop the leak—it'll just make more of a mess for you to clean up later, when you properly rebed the fitting.

First, remove the old fitting and every trace of the old compound. If the fitting was bedded with polyurethane, you might need to use a heat gun to *gently warm the fitting* to get it off. You should never let the fiberglass get too hot to touch. (A new product, Anti-Bond 2015, will supposedly debond polyurethanes, but I haven't tried it yet.) Clean the area and the fitting until they are spotless. For the deck, I scrape, then sand, then wipe with acetone. For the bolts and the fitting, I like to use a wire wheel mounted in a bench grinder (don't forget the safety glasses!) followed by a wipe with acetone on the underside. While I'm there, I usually polish the rest of the fitting with a buffing wheel and compound—this leaves stainless parts looking like new.

Before I get out the compound, I like to set the fitting back into position and mask off the area with high-quality masking tape. This is usually easier and cleaner than trying to wipe up the excess later with solvent.

Next, if the fitting is in an area where the deck is cored, I seal the core. Tape off the bottom area and pick out the core as much as you can with a bent nail chucked into a drill. Vacuum up the chips and fill the hole with thinned epoxy like Git Rot. Keep filling the hole until no more soaks in.

Once the epoxy has cured, redrill the hole, compound the fitting, and set the fitting into place. Don't forget to compound the bolts, too—I like to run a little ring of compound under the heads. Position the bolts in place and tighten, but not all the way. Snug them up enough so that sealant begins to squeeze out from under the fittings, and then wait for it to cure—24 hours for polysulfides or polyurethanes. (I don't like to use silicone; it's good only for bedding plastic.) Then fully tighten the bolts. After the compound has fully cured—in about a week—trim off the extra compound with a sharp razor blade.

Yes, this is involved and kind of a pain, but not nearly as big a pain as getting dripped on in the middle of the night, or replacing a rotten deck. This is one of those "do it right, or do it over" choices.

## TEAK MAINTENANCE

Traditionally, topsides wood is teak, because teak contains natural oils and resins that keep it from absorbing water and rotting. There are three alternatives for teak maintenance: oil, varnish, or no treatment. Brightwork generally refers to wood items on the deck of a boat that are finished with clear varnish so that the wood grain shows. Topsides woodwork that isn't varnished is usually called trim.

### Untreated Teak

If left unfinished, the sun quickly bleaches out the rich brown color of the teak from the surface, and the wood turns a silvery gray, which some boatowners prefer. In fact, teak decks have to be left bare, because coating them would destroy the wood's natural nonskid properties. Handrails that are untreated are slightly safer, too, because the bare wood provides a better grip. Untreated teak weathers more rapidly than treated teak, though, and a few years of scrubbing leave the wood deeply grooved as the softer summer growth rings wear away.

### Oiling Your Teak

You can use several different types of oil on teak, including boiled linseed oil, tung oil, or specially formulated teak oils. The advantage of this option is that an oiled teak surface is very easy to renew; you just brush a coat of oil right on top of the old oil, as long as the surface is free of mildew or dirt. The downside is that oiled surfaces have to be renewed regularly in order to keep the trim looking good. In summer, if your teak is unprotected by a cover, you can expect to oil it every two to three months. You have to be very careful about drips and runs, too. Teak oil will stain gelcoat, especially if the gelcoat is a few years old and porous. Teak oil will run if applied in direct sunlight, as

I once discovered. I had carefully applied a coat of oil and masked the deck with tape. When I finished, I removed the tape, since masking tape left in the sun often leaves a sticky residue on the deck. When I returned to the boat a few hours later, I discovered that the sun had warmed the teak oil, causing a few ugly runs on portions of the deck that I had carefully protected with tape. That was seventeen years ago—the stains are probably still there.

## Varnishing Your Trim

Varnishing your brightwork is a third alternative. Varnish is a hard coating that seals the teak from water, while oil is a soft finish that feeds the wood as the natural oils wear away from the surface. The oil resists water, but water and humidity eventually take their toll. Varnish coatings eventually break down because of exposure to UV radiation, though they last much longer than oil treatments. Depending on the varnish, the coating can last anywhere from six months to two years. When the coating begins to break down, the effect is immediately noticeable—the varnish loses its flexibility and bond to the wood, and the natural expansion and contraction of the wood causes small cracks or pinholes. Water enters the cracks, and the result is ugly dark water stains underneath the varnish. When this happens, the only cure is to sand off the old varnish, treat the stains with a teak cleaner, and reapply several new coats of varnish—usually at least three coats, with light sanding between coats.

A varnished finish is initially very labor intensive. Many boatowners dislike varnishing so much that they refuse to have teak trim on their boat, instead replacing all topsides teak with a white plastic product called StarBoard, which never needs varnishing. But when properly done, the effect of a little golden teak with a few coats of varnish is breathtaking.

### Preparing Teak for Varnish

First, you need to remove all the old varnish and get the teak back to smooth, bare wood. I've always used a scraper, sandpaper, and plain old elbow grease for this task. Some people loosen old varnish with the *careful* use of a heat gun and a putty knife or chemical paint removers. However, either can ruin nearby gelcoat. If the teak has been badly water stained, you may need to bleach it. You can use teak lightener, available in marine chandleries, or bleach thinned with about 85 percent water. Add a little more water or bleach if necessary. Another good, inexpensive product can be made with oxalic acid crystals, sometimes available from boatyards or janitorial suppliers. Dissolve as much as you can in some warm water and then paint the solution onto the teak. Let it dry, then remove the resulting crystals with a stiff brush, taking care not to leave the powder on your deck—it might bleach something you don't want bleached. After you bleach teak with oxalic acid, you need to neutralize the wood surface with borax. Bleaching teak weakens the top surface of the wood, so use this method only when absolutely necessary.

### Choosing a Product

Teak coatings, like wax, present another purchasing conundrum. How do you choose the best when there are so many types, all claiming to be superior? Ask an owner of a sailboat with nice varnish what he or she uses, as local conditions can be a big factor in varnish performance. The same varnish might last longer in Massachusetts than in Florida or Arizona.

Word of mouth was how I first learned about Sikkens Cetol. The previous owner of my Montgomery 17 gave me half a can when I bought my boat. This isn't classified as a traditional varnish but rather a pigmented synthetic stain. I think that description is a little misleading—it looks and performs more like a pigmented varnish than a stain, developing a tough film that cures in the presence of air. The pigment does two things: it gives Cetol greater UV resistance than an unpigmented coating, and it gives the wood a distinctive hue that some find objectionable. It's not bad, but it does look a little orange. Once you've tried this product, you'll be able to spot Cetol-treated teak easily.

*Practical Sailor* publishes a test of teak products every few years or so, especially as new products are developed and old ones change their formulas or cease production. Their top performer in terms of traditional varnish is Epifanes. New synthetic formulas are constantly being developed, and some are quite expensive. I haven't had any experience with these synthetics. I prefer a traditional varnish because it is usually compatible with tung and linseed oils. Most traditional varnishes include some oil in them.

### Applying the Varnish

There are many methods of varnishing that are favored by brightwork professionals. (See the Bibliography for several good books on the subject.) When I varnish using a traditional formula, I like to start with a thin primer coat of mostly tung oil with a small amount of varnish and thinner (mineral spirits or turpentine) added in. I want the first coat to penetrate as deeply into the wood as possible. Each successive coat has less oil and thinner, until the top coats are straight varnish with a little thinner added. Not all varnishes are compatible with tung oil, so test your brand on a piece of scrap before applying it to your expensive teak.

Some varnishers build up a base coat consisting of several layers of clear epoxy followed by several layers of clear varnish. Epoxy is very sensitive to UV rays, so the varnish top coat must be well-done and deep. A finish like this will be very difficult to remove, but the epoxy provides a very good, stable base for the varnish to adhere to.

Other varnishers apply a single coat of varnish that's thinned about 50 percent and leave it at that. This gives a matte finish that looks good, protects the teak well, and is easy to apply. It needs to be recoated every two to four months if exposed to the weather.

It's essential to use a high-quality soft brush for varnish work. Badger bristle brushes were once considered the highest quality but are now rarely available. Most natural bristle brushes are called China bristle, since that's where the hairs come from, and some professional finishers who use them (or a natural/synthetic blend) get results equal to those from badger brushes. Good synthetic bristle brushes can now be bought that are equal to natural bristle in terms of quality, and synthetics can last longer than natural bristle, making them more cost-effective. Any brush used for paint cannot then be used for varnish, because the solvents will soften tiny paint bits left in the brush that will then pollute any clear finish. Foam brushes can work in a pinch, and can give surprisingly smooth results.

## DEALING WITH CORROSION

Metal corrosion happens in many different ways and for various reasons, but losing electrons is an easy way to think about it. When this happens, the metal deteriorates, changing from one form to another. Preventing corrosion involves keeping electrons in the metal where they belong. Metal corrosion is a vast subject—simple rusting can actually be a very complex process. The Resources section of this book provides further references. What follows is the Cliff Notes version.

Some of the most useful metals aboard boats—like stainless steel, bronze, and aluminum—develop a uniform surface corrosion when exposed to the air, but this layer of corrosion (called an oxide layer) can be stable and strongly attached to the base metal. The oxide layer seals the metal from the atmosphere, protecting it from further deterioration. This is called passivation, and certain metals can be treated in specific ways to enhance this process.

Maintaining the metals aboard your boat usually means treating corrosion wherever you find it, and preventing it from occurring if you don't find it. Basically, you'll see three types of corrosion on your boat:

Atmospheric corrosion
Galvanic corrosion
Electrolysis

Crevice corrosion is another form that often occurs with stainless steel—more about that later.

## Atmospheric Corrosion

The most common form of atmospheric corrosion is rust on steel or cast iron. It's caused by humidity, but pollution, temperature changes, salt, and other factors accelerate it. Preventing atmospheric corrosion in steel usually involves some kind of barrier to seal the steel from the atmosphere. Most often this means paint, though varnish, oil, waxes, or a thin layer of another metal like zinc can also be used.

Once steel starts to rust, it never stops without your intervention until all of the metal has been changed into iron oxide. If you have a rusty part on your boat, get rid of the rust—it will only get worse with time, and if you ignore it too long the only option will be replacement. Two good things about steel, though, are that it's strong and cheap. Steel parts are often built to withstand a certain amount of rusting and still perform well. If you can clean the rust off completely, the steel can be recoated with paint and put back into service. If the surface is regular and smooth, you might be able to do the job with a rotary wire brush. However, it's impossible to do a complete cleaning with the part bolted in place—it must be removed from the boat, and the screws or bolts also treated, though replacing them is a better option.

The best way to remove rust completely is by sandblasting. Small parts can be cleaned in a blast cabinet, but large pieces—like a cast-iron keel—have to be cleaned by a professional. It takes a huge high-volume air compressor to do the job properly. Forget those little suction sandblasters that you see in the Harbor Freight catalog; they aren't powerful enough to clean anything larger than a cleat. Sandblasting is preferred because it roughs up the surface slightly, leaving a good uniform surface for the paint to grip. But sandblasting has to be done on a dry day, and the part should be coated with a good-quality primer immediately afterward.

Although sandblasting is the best method for getting rid of rust, other options are less dependent on industrial equipment. One is to use a phosphoric acid solution, which chemically converts rust from iron oxide to iron phosphate. Naval Jelly is a classic product. I've never used it, but I have used Ospho, which is mostly phosphoric acid plus some wetting agents. It works well for rusty spots on the trailer, where sandblasting the whole thing would be expensive. You can also remove rust using an electrolytic process, which is a little more complicated but well within the abilities of most people with a garage workshop. (The process is outlined in *Fix It and Sail*.)

## Galvanic Corrosion

Whereas atmospheric corrosion occurs in a single metal exposed to air, galvanic corrosion occurs when two (or more) metals are touching each other or placed close together in a conductive environment, such as damp wood or seawater. Electrons travel from one metal to the other simply because one metal has a stronger electron bond. In galvanic corrosion, no external electric currents are involved—just the molecular bond in the metals. (Galvanic corrosion is often incorrectly termed electrolysis; I discuss the difference next.)

Some metals corrode faster when placed together than they would if they were isolated. These are called anodes or anodic metals. Others corrode slower than if they were alone. These are called cathodes or cathodic metals. Over the years, engineers and scientists studying corrosion have developed the Galvanic Series of Metals (see the list "Galvanic Series in Seawater").

A metal's position in the galvanic series tells us its corrosional relationship to other metals. How fast one metal corrodes depends on the voltage difference between the two metals and their relative size. The anode corrodes more rapidly as the voltage difference increases and as the cathode gets larger compared to the anode.

Remember that the two metals don't have to be underwater for corrosion to occur. Damp wood or an occasional dose of salt water, or even rainwater, is enough to cause quite a bit of damage. Notice the special position of

## Galvanic Series in Seawater

*Alloy*

**(Anodic/Active End)**

Magnesium

Zinc

Aluminum alloys

Cadmium

Cast iron

Steel

Aluminum bronze

Red brass, yellow brass, naval brass

Copper

Lead-tin solder (50/50)

Admiralty brass

Manganese bronze

Silicon bronze

400 sodas stainless steels

90-10 copper-nickel

Lead

70-30 copper-nickel

17-4 PH stainless steel

Silver

Monel

300 series stainless steels

Titanium and titanium alloys

Inconel 625

Hastelloy C-276

Platinum

Graphiite

**(Cathodic or Noble End)**

aluminum, way up at the top of the scale. In a galvanic battle, aluminum always loses except with zinc. But you'll notice that all aluminum spars have stainless fittings on them, right? They're usually attached with stainless screws. How come they don't suffer from galvanic corrosion?

The short answer is they *do*. It's rare to remove a stainless steel screw from an aluminum mast without a fight—they are usually corroded in tightly. On better masts, you'll find small plastic washers under stainless steel mast tangs. On cheaply built masts, you'll often find some pitting and corrosion underneath.

It's a good idea to put Never-Seez or a similar compound on stainless threads that are screwed into aluminum. But don't use grease. I had a masthead come off my boat once because the stainless steel screws were lubricated before they were installed. Three sheet-metal screws backed themselves completely out of their holes because the boat was moored where ski boats went by all summer, setting up a wicked quick, steep chop. I use Never-Seez on all mast fastenings now, and I wire all my turnbuckles to prevent them from unscrewing themselves.

Underwater, we have a different story. Let the same mast hang over the side for a week or two, and you'll likely pull up a corroded mess when you next visit your boat. Aluminum is very high on the galvanic series; only zinc and magnesium are higher. This is why it's unusual to see aluminum used below the waterline. The only common cases I can think of are aluminum-hulled vessels and outboard motor castings. These are protected with a heavy coating of paint and plenty of sacrificial zinc anodes (see below). If aluminum is the only metal used—as in an aluminum rowboat—you don't have as much of a problem with galvanic corrosion. But if that same rowboat is fastened with copper rivets, she'll dissolve in no time.

When metals are mixed below the waterline, they need to be as closely matched on the galvanic series as possible. If you have all bronze props and shafts, avoid replacing them with stainless steel. Bronze isn't as strong as stainless, but it tends to last much longer.

All metals should be protected underwater with zinc anodes, and the condition of the zincs should be checked regularly. If they seem to be wearing away quickly, that indicates a problem somewhere that you need to address. When you replace a zinc, make sure there's good contact with the metal it's attached to. Zincs are most effective when electrically connected to the metal they are to protect or, if not actually attached to the part itself, as close by as practical. Never paint a zinc.

## Electrolysis

Electrolysis is a type of corrosion that is similar to galvanic corrosion, but with a subtle difference. Electrolysis is caused by external electrical currents acting on dissimilar metals in seawater. In the real world, stray electrical currents can come from incorrect installation of individual parts on your boat, an improperly wired boat nearby, a shore power line dangling in the water, or an improperly wired dock.

Electrolysis can cause damage in a surprisingly short time. While normally a zinc anode will last for months, if there are stray electrical currents in your boat or nearby, a zinc can get eaten away within weeks. Many boatowners will just add additional zinc anodes, not realizing the actual cause of the problem. But to be fair, electrolysis problems can be maddening to track down and correct. (See the Bibliography for books on marine electrical systems.)

## Specific Corrosion Problems on Trailer Sailers

While there are lots of different possibilities for corrosion aboard any boat, what you'll probably see most often are three types: rust (which we've already discussed), crevice corrosion on stainless steel, and aluminum corrosion.

### Crevice Corrosion

Stainless steel comes in many varieties. Some are very corrosion-resistant; others are less so. Inexpensive grades of stainless will rust quickly in the marine environment, as some buyers of discount hardware store fasteners have discovered. (An easy test is to take along a magnet when buying stainless hardware from an off-the-shelf source. If the magnet sticks, then the item is made from a low-grade stainless that will probably rust.)

Most alloys used on boats are corrosion-resistant in the marine environment if prepared and used correctly. But occasionally you'll find a stainless part with traces of rust trailing from it—usually coming from a hole or a crack. What's going on here?

What's happening is crevice corrosion. Stainless works because it forms an oxide layer on the surface of the metal. The oxide layer is very thin, but it's an effective block against further corrosion. For the steel to maintain its oxide layer, though, it needs oxygen. If the stainless can't get enough oxygen to maintain the oxide layer, it begins to rust just like conventional steel. Where you'll most often see this is in a crack where water can be trapped and prevent oxygen flow, or sometimes from the drain hole of a stanchion. In some instances, a scratch can be deep enough to hold water and prevent proper oxygen flow. That's why stainless is often buffed to a smooth, polished finish.

What do you do if you notice rust weeping from stainless? First, look for any signs of stress in the part. This is particularly important in chainplates, turnbuckles, or other rigging attachment parts. Any sign of rust here is a loud call for replacement of the part. Rigging wire that has signs of rust deep within the wire shouldn't be trusted. Any part that carries an important load, which means pretty much any part of the standing rigging, should be replaced if you see any sort of rust. The only exception might be when replacing a part that involves major structural work to the boat, like chainplates that have been laminated into the fabric of the hull at the factory. If that's the case, call in the pros for a second opinion. Owners of larger boats will use specialized inspection techniques, such as Magna-fluxing and portable X-ray, to ensure the integrity of inaccessible chainplates, though this might not be practical for smaller boats.

For nonstructural items, such as a stainless hinge, try removing the part and buffing it with a felt bench buffing wheel and fine white buffing compound. Check the part with a magnet before you go to all the trouble, because if it's low-grade stainless, you'll probably experience the same problem again later. Reinstall with plenty of clean bedding compound and see what happens, or replace the part with a higher-grade item.

If you have a weeping drain hole in a lifeline stanchion, *don't* plug the hole, however tempting that may be. The hole is there to drain water that gets inside the tube. Even if the hole is perfectly sealed, condensation will still build up inside. Sealed up, the inside of the tube will get even less oxygen and suffer more corrosion, which you might not discover until you need it most—say, when a lee lurch tosses you against the lifelines and the stanchion is the only thing preventing you from going over the side—at night—in a storm. Instead, try adding a second hole, or *very slightly* enlarging the first hole if it's tiny. Ideally, the drain hole should be in the stanchion base, and the stanchion should be open at the bottom, allowing in plenty of air.

If you have rusty screws or bolts, the best course of action is to replace them. If the bolt is holding a part to the deck, go ahead and take the part off, clean it, and replace with new bedding compound. You probably need to renew the bedding compound anyway. (For a how-to, see the sidebar "Rebedding Deck Fittings" on pages 174–175.)

It's common to see some spotty surface corrosion on stainless parts like stanchions or bow rails. This is more a nuisance than a danger. The best thing to do here is buff them out with stainless polish and a rag. You might see surface rust forming at the sides of a weld bead in stainless steel. Usually a problem with a new part rather than one that's been installed for a while, this is a different form of corrosion in stainless called weld zone corrosion or weld decay. It's caused by the alloys precipitating out of the steel because of the heat of the weld. This is the result of improper welding procedures, and the manufacturer should replace the part.

General stainless care involves washing away salt and dirt, inspecting carefully for stress cracks, and polishing with a little stainless polish or wax once a year. Some light machine oil on the shrouds doesn't hurt. Oil the threads of the turnbuckles while you're at it. Even though oil does attract dirt, metal-to-metal contacts often benefit from an occasional oiling.

## Aluminum Corrosion

Aluminum relies on oxide formation for protecting itself from corrosion, much like stainless steel does, but in the right conditions aluminum can corrode more rapidly than stainless. It is higher in the galvanic series, so galvanic corrosion is more serious and rapid. The oxide films that aluminum forms by itself are very thin, measured in atoms. In order to make the protective oxide layer thicker, aluminum masts are commonly anodized. Anodizing aluminum requires passing a current through the aluminum while the mast is submerged in an acid bath. The oxide layer of an anodized aluminum part grows from a few atoms thick to 0.0002 to 0.001 inch. There are several techniques—a room-temperature (type 2) anodized surface is microscopically porous, and anodized parts can often be easily colored. Hard-coat anodizing (type 3) is done at colder temperatures and higher currents. It's thicker at 0.002 inch but can be dyed only black or dark green. This is usually how a black mast has been treated.

Aluminum is reactive with acid. This characteristic is commonly used when painting aluminum. It's necessary to use a special etching primer before painting this metal, and then a very hard topcoat, like Imron or two-part polyurethane.

Aluminum is so reactive that naval architect Michael Kasten (who designs aluminum sailboats) recommends isolating aluminum from any metal it contacts, even other aluminum parts! Isolation pads, bedding compounds, and/or paint should be used underneath a fitting that will contact the mast. Crevice corrosion and pitting are particular problems with aluminum in a saltwater environment.

All aluminum spars are either anodized or painted. Anodizing is probably the method of choice—and properly done, an anodized coating can last for years. The only downside is it's unrepairable in place. A painted mast looks really nice and can theoretically be spot-repaired if necessary, but paint does not protect the metal nearly as well as anodizing. If your anodized mast is severely corroded in several places, your only options are:

1. Replace the entire spar—time-consuming and very expensive.
2. Strip off all the parts and ship the mast to a company that anodizes masts—time-consuming and very expensive.
3. Strip off all the parts and sandblast and paint the mast yourself—time-consuming, not as expensive, but you'll still spend a bundle.

If you have a painted mast, you're more likely to see corrosion blisters under the paint. Unless they're very small, these should be addressed immediately, as the mast can corrode completely through underneath the paint.

You can attempt a spot repair on a corroded mast as long as the pitting isn't too severe. First, you need to clean out all of the powdery corrosion and get the mast back to sound metal. If you have a painted mast, sand off the paint until you reach bare metal. Then prime it with aluminum etching primer. (An example is Pettit's two-part Aluma-Protect strontium chromate primer. Sounds expensive, doesn't it?) Before you add a top coat, it's a good idea to test the paint on a small area of the mast, like near the base, to make sure the solvents in the new paint don't soften and lift the old paint. Hopefully you'll be able to get a good color match.

Don't sand an anodized mast, since you want to preserve the anodizing as much as possible. Use a stainless wire brush to remove the white aluminum oxide, and be sure to get it all! Don't use plain steel wool for this, as it will leave tiny bits of iron embedded in your aluminum that will later rust. With an anodized mast, there's not much else you can do, except maybe try a coat of wax.

Small holes in an aluminum mast are sometimes a problem. These can be the result of corrosion, but more frequently they occur when a piece of hardware has been relocated. Usually old hardware holes are more cosmetic than anything else, except when the holes are along a perpendicular line, which weakens the mast

considerably. You can try fixing the holes the easy way or the hard way. On my old MacGregor 222, I wanted to fill several large holes, so I mixed up some J-B Weld epoxy, filled each hole with a little blob, and smoothed the blob by covering the wet epoxy with masking tape. After the epoxy cured, I peeled off the tape. It worked, after a fashion. My "repair" was better than nothing, but it didn't make the mast any stronger. The J-B Weld has a gray color, which was somewhat similar to the aluminum color. A better choice would have been an aluminum-filled epoxy—Devcon makes one.

Better yet would have been a welded repair. A professional welder with a portable rig can do this, if he has experience welding sailboat masts. Aluminum requires a very expensive heliarc-welding machine, but there are repair rods available now that can be applied with a propane or MAPP gas torch. Durafix is one brand; HTS-2000 from New Technology Products is another. These special repair rods aren't cheap, but they are far less expensive than a heliarc machine and six months of welding classes. Both repairs require clean and properly prepared surfaces, and it helps if you've done a little soldering before. And both repairs have the potential to damage your mast by burning it or ruining the heat treatment, but if it's corroded through, you don't have a lot to lose.

## MAINTAINING YOUR ELECTRICAL SYSTEM

The electrical system on your boat can be anything from a simple battery and a few lights to a complex installation involving multiple batteries, 120-volt shore power, inverters, chargers, and other gear. If your boat leans toward the complex side, you should invest in a specific manual about marine electrical systems—there are far too many variables to cover here. Be very, very careful around shore power or generators, and don't fool with them unless you know what you're doing. Twelve-volt systems have generally lower amperage so there is less danger, but still, be careful if you do electrical work. If you're uncomfortable with it, call in some professional help. A marine electrician can advise you about maintaining your system.

Since most trailerable sailboats have fairly simple electrical systems, maintainance and repairs are also simple. Here are a few general things you can do to keep the electricity flowing where you want it.

1. Keep your battery charged properly (see the next section). Different batteries have different charging requirements, so know what type of battery you have and charge it with a good marine charger. Your battery must be kept secured with a strong strap, and the terminals should be covered (Coast Guard regulations require a covered, ventilated battery box).
2. Keep the battery connections dry and lubricated. One of the reasons why electrical systems on boats fail is that the connections oxidize in the humid environment and develop shorts. Oxidation can be prevented using silicone dielectric grease, which seals the surfaces from the air and prevents oxidation. Silicone faucet grease makes a good substitute for dielectric grease, but even plain Vaseline is better than nothing. WD-40 or other silicone sprays work as well, though they don't last quite as long as grease. Lightbulb sockets, terminals, fuse holders, and switches should be either greased or sprayed.
3. Secure loose wiring. All wires should be secured to the boat at least every 18 inches. Your boat should have only multistrand and marine-rated wire aboard, though THWN strand is a less expensive alternative. (THWN stands for Thermoplastic Heat and Water resistant insulated wire, Nylon jacketed.) Never use solid copper wire aboard a boat.
4. Replace any wire that looks old or cracked or has worn insulation, broken or corroded terminals, or splices in wet locations.
5. Remember to double-check those spare fuses. When a fuse blows, investigate the cause; it's almost never because the original fuse was too small. Replacing with a larger fuse could cause your wiring to overheat.

## The Battery

Before we discuss charging, let's take a look at the battery itself. Recent advances in battery technology have finally made it down to the retail level, and you can choose from traditional wet-cell batteries, sealed gel-cell, or AGM (absorbed glass mat) types. Some batteries can deliver a large amount of power quickly, as in a starting battery; others are optimized for deep-cycle use. Deep-cycle batteries are able to recover fully after long periods of slow discharge better than starting batteries.

Wet-cell (also known as flooded) batteries are cheapest per amp-hour, but they can be damaged by discharging to a completely flat condition. They will self-discharge at a rate of about 5 to 6 percent per month, so they need to be charged in the off-season.

Sealed gel-cell batteries require no maintenance (wet batteries need to be watered occasionally), can be mounted in any position, and, if the connections are carefully sealed, they can even be operated underwater. Their self-discharge rate is lower, at only about 3 percent per month. But gel-cells are sensitive to overcharging, and charging—which requires expensive chargers with smart voltage regulators—must be closely monitored. Gel-cells cost a little more than double the price of a wet-cell battery of a similar size.

### What's an Amp-Hour?

An amp-hour is a typical measurement of electrical power for a battery. It's the total amount of energy that a battery can deliver for 20 hours before the voltage drops to 10.5 volts, which is the voltage of a dead battery. A fully charged battery measures 14.4 volts, though this number slowly declines throughout the life of the battery. So a typical Group 27 battery ("Group 27" refers to the size of the case; this example measures $12^{1}/_{2} \times 6^{3}/_{4} \times 9^{3}/_{8}$ inches) rated at 90 amp-hours can drive a 4.5-amp load for about 20 hours. If we turn on more lights and increase the load to 9 amps, expect about 10 hours before the battery goes flat.

Absorbed glass mat batteries have a low self-discharge rate of about 3 percent per month and are sealed and maintenance-free. They charge quicker than flooded-cell batteries and cost a little less than double the price of a traditional wet-cell battery. AGM batteries work well as dual-purpose batteries, since they can deliver a large amount of power quickly (required for starting an engine) and still provide deep-cycle capability. Portable "jump-start" power supplies are usually small AGM-type batteries.

When buying batteries, it's usually best to stick with one type. Each has specific charging requirements, and feeding them the wrong voltage will reduce battery performance and life span. You shouldn't mix an old battery with a new one for the same reason. Keep the terminals clean and coated with dielectric grease to prevent oxidation, and clean the terminals as required with baking soda and water and a wire brush. (Don't let any baking soda get into the cell of a flooded-cell battery, though, as it will neutralize the acid in the cell.) Use good-quality, appropriately sized cables on your batteries. If you are not using your battery for starting the motor, then you don't need thick, 170-amp cables.

## Charging the Battery

Obviously, all batteries need to be charged, and there are several ways to do this. What type of charger (or chargers) to use depends on the battery type, its capacity, and the way you use your boat. If you plan to spend a lot of time on a mooring and away from 120-volt power, then you'll need an onboard generator or solar or even wind power. First, let's look at the charging requirements.

To get the best life from a battery, specific charging conditions must be met, and some batteries (like gel-cells) are more finicky than others. A battery charger must deliver a current at a rate that the battery chemistry can accept. If it delivers the current too quickly, it will damage the battery. Furthermore, the charge rate is not linear—it changes over time.

And the battery charger needs to know when to stop as well.

When does a battery need charging? The most accurate method to determine your battery's state-of-charge (for a wet-cell battery) is to measure the specific gravity of the electrolyte using a hydrometer. Check with the manufacturer for specific readings and procedures. Most boatowners use the battery's voltage, measured with a digital voltmeter, to determine the charge. In order to get a correct reading, wait at least 12 hours after charging, and remove the "surface charge" by placing a brief load on the battery. Switching on all the lights for a few minutes should do it. With the battery switched off, voltage across the terminals should be 12.7 volts. AGM (absorbed glass mat) and gel-cell types might read slightly higher, at 12.8 to 12.9 volts. If the voltage falls to 11.9 volts, the battery is dead and needs to be recharged. A reading of 10.5 volts indicates a bad cell, and the battery must be replaced.

## Some Electrical Definitions

Electricity is often tricky to comprehend. Here are some simple definitions, based on a plumbing analogy:

**amp:** Short for ampere, this is the amount of current flowing. Somewhat equivalent to water flowing through a pipe.

**volt:** Pressure or "push" of electricity, roughly equal to the amount of pressure in a water pipe.

**watt:** Measurement of electrical power; 746 watts equals 1 horsepower.

**resistance:** The amount of electrical drag in a circuit. Continuing our plumbing analogy, it would be the size of the pipe—a large pipe can accommodate the flow of lots of water.

amps × volts = watts
watts ÷ volts = amps
watts ÷ amps = volts
amps × hours of use = amp-hours
1/1,000 amp = 1 milliamp (mA)

You can get a better understanding of the different types of charging requirements for different batteries by looking at the following typical charging profiles used by Deltran, a maker of battery chargers. The standard wet-cell and gel-cell batteries are pretty similar, but it's easy to see that AGM batteries are a different beast altogether, with double the charging time.

So, that brings us back to the question of which charger is best for your system. For now, let's consider AC-powered chargers. It's easy to say what type of charger is *not* the best, and that's the small, cheap trickle charger. These are typically unregulated power supplies that are supposed to maintain a fully charged battery, but they can easily overcharge and damage your battery.

A very basic type of charger for wet-cell batteries, called a taper current charger or manual charger, depends on the internal resistance of the battery to control the current. A small manual charger is better than a large one, since it's less capable of delivering too much current to the battery, but these will overcharge if not turned off when the battery is completely charged. They shouldn't be used with gel-cell or AGM batteries, but you might get away with using one with a wet-cell if you monitor it closely.

Ferro-resonant chargers are the next step up in quality. These are inexpensive and commonly available at auto parts stores, and they are better than taper chargers because there's less chance of overcharging or undercharging. Some will even turn themselves back on and recharge the battery when the voltage drops to a predetermined point. Automotive chargers aren't waterproof and shouldn't be left on board, but you can bring them to the dock and

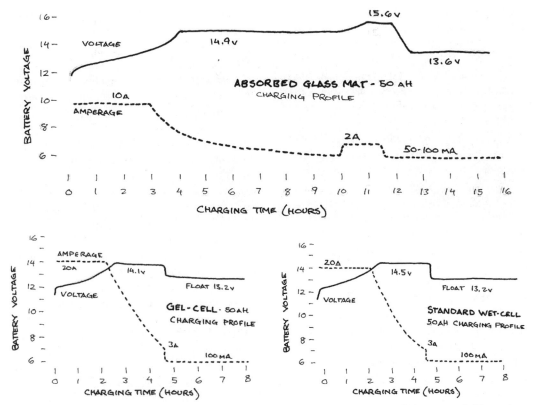

*Charging profiles for absorbed glass mat (top), gel-cell (bottom left), and wet-cell (bottom right) batteries.*

charge the battery as required, or, if your battery is small, you can take the battery home to charge. I used this method on my MacGregor; my electrical loads were small—just the radio and an occasional interior light. I used a small lawn-tractor battery, which was about half the size and cost of a standard battery. The plan was to add a second similar battery to gain capacity, but I never got around to it. Be very careful when using any sort of portable electric equipment near the dock—never place it in a position where it might get knocked overboard, and never let the supply cable droop into the water.

Smart chargers are best for battery life, and are practically required for gel-cell and AGM batteries (they also work for wet-cell batteries). These are commonly three-stage chargers, whereas a ferro-resonant charger is a two-stage charger. Smart chargers start at about $60 for a portable unit and $100 for an onboard bulkhead-mounted model. (Prices can continue upward to about $850, but big, expensive chargers are intended for large boats and liveaboard battery use.) An onboard charger isn't required unless your boat is wired for 120-volt shore power; most trailer sailers can use the less expensive portable units.

## BOTTOM ISSUES—BLISTERS, BARNACLES, AND PAINTING

If you use your boat in salt water, bottom painting becomes a necessity. In some areas, marine growth (often including barnacles) can start to form on your hull in as little as a week. In fresh water, the problem is grass and slime, and occasionally zebra mussels, but these are usually much less severe than barnacles.

Bottom paint can be either hard or ablative. Ablative paints slowly wear away over time; hard paints don't. Ablative paints leave a soft surface that is easily damaged by trailer rollers or bunks, so most trailer sailors choose hard paints unless their boat is kept at a marina year-round.

Painting preparation involves hauling the boat out of the water, pressure-washing to knock off as much of the marine growth as possible, and then scraping and sanding what's left. It is easier, though much more expensive, to do this at a boatyard with a hoist rather than crawling around a trailer. Usually two or three coats of bottom paint are applied by roller. Owners of racing boats must take the extra step of polishing and buffing the bottom, which requires a special paint.

New environmental laws regarding toxins in bottom paints keep the manufacturers busy developing products that are effective against fouling yet still legal to use. California is especially stringent; its VOC (volatile organic compounds) regulations mean that paints common in other parts of the country are illegal there. The most successful development to date is the use of water-based paints that have low

## A Safer Extension Cord for Dockside Use

If you use portable electric equipment at the dock and your boat isn't wired for shore power, there's a safer way to get power to the boat than stringing skinny extension cords together. First, go to the hardware store and buy a single extension cord—a grounded one—that's long enough to reach your boat. (If you connect two short ones together and happen to dip the connection into the water, it's snap, crackle, and pop—a very dangerous situation.) Also pick up a waterproof junction box and a ground fault interrupt (GFI)–protected outlet.

Cut off the female end of the cord and wire in the GFI outlet in its place. Follow the instructions that come with the GFI outlet, and be certain to wire the ground properly. Carefully seal the openings of the junction box with silicone (to protect the GFI from corrosion and help it last longer), and give it an occasional spray of WD-40 or similar lubricant. Even so, replace the GFI if you see any signs of corrosion or if it fails to test properly. You might want to add a length of light line to secure the cord at the plug end, and keep the cord coiled securely when not in use.

The advantage of a GFI-protected extension cord is speed—a GFI will trip far faster than a line protected only by a circuit breaker. That's why GFIs are required near sinks and in bathrooms on shore. A GFI extension cord adds an extra layer of protection to your electrical equipment at the dock—but your drill will still probably fry if you knock it into the water.

VOC plus easy soap-and-water cleanup. (Boatyards have to keep track of all the solvents they use, including thinners for cleaning brushes and sprayers.) Other high-tech coatings, such as Teflon, haven't yet been proven effective at stopping marine growth, but racers like the super-slick surface. The research continues.

Hull blisters are, fortunately, much less of a problem on trailer sailers than on larger boats. Since most trailerables are stored on land, blisters are much less likely to form.

If you have a new or blister-free boat, and you expect to keep your boat at a marina year-round, then you might be interested in blister prevention. Current fiberglass boatbuilding practice is to use vinylester resin as a barrier coat, as this more expensive type of resin has been shown to resist water penetration. You can also add your own barrier coat. All the major paint manufacturers offer epoxy-based barrier coat systems with very specific preparation and application instructions, which must be followed exactly. Some boatowners have suggested using coal-tar epoxy paints as a barrier coat, such as Interlux's VC Tar 2. Coal-tar paints are extremely tough; they are commonly used in industrial applications and for protecting steel hulls from corrosion. But as with any epoxy, total barrier coat thickness is critical for good performance. The hull must be thoroughly dry before applying any type of barrier coat. With a trailer sailer, this is fairly easy: just pull in the boat in the fall and keep it warm and dry until spring. A heated garage or building is best, but you can completely cover the boat with a good tarp and leave it outdoors.

If you already have blisters on your hull, you have a choice—treat them, or just live with them. Pop one to see how deep it is. (Note—wear goggles. The fluid inside a blister is a mild acid, and it's often under pressure. It would be bad to have this stuff squirt in your eyes.) If it seems to be on the surface of the hull, just under the gelcoat, then it's primarily cosmetic. It won't sink your boat. For practice, rinse the blister, let it dry, sand it smooth, fill it with epoxy, and add a touch of bottom paint. Now decide if you want to repeat that process for each blister on your hull.

If the blistering is severe, you should probably plan on storing the boat ashore to let the blisters and the laminate dry out.

If you sail in salt water and keep your boat at a dock or on a mooring, you'll have barnacles and other marine growth to deal with. Scraping and painting the bottom is an annual ritual for boatowners, and doing this job on a trailer is a pain in the tuckus. If you have access to a boatyard, I recommend hiring boatyard personnel to lift the boat off the trailer so you can get a clear shot at the hull. If you've got a bad case of barnacles, you'll definitely want to pressure-wash the hull as soon as the boat clears the water, because barnacles are harder to remove if you wait a day. I've also heard that spraying barnacles with a vinegar solution makes them easier to remove.

## RUNNING RIGGING

The running rigging on your boat deserves special maintenance attention. Since this is the part that you handle when you sail the boat, you want to keep it working as smoothly and efficiently as possible. Fortunately, it's often not too difficult or expensive, and your attention to detail can pay off with smoother, more enjoyable sailing.

### Winches

Winches, especially good-quality ones, can be wonderful bits of engineering. On trailer sailers, the winches are most often small, single-speed affairs, so they are comparatively easy to take apart, lubricate, and put back together. Yet they are often neglected, and some boatowners have never serviced a winch. There's no reason for this—you can probably do the job in an hour or so, and the second winch always goes faster. All you need is a tube of winch grease, some light machine oil, a rag or two, an old coffee can, maybe an old stiff paintbrush, and some solvent, like paint thinner, diesel fuel, or kerosene. (Don't use gasoline; it's pretty dangerous.)

The tools you need to take your winch apart vary with manufacturers. Barlow winches often require hex wrenches, while some Lewmar winches will come apart with a single flat-bladed screwdriver. If you have old, cheap plastic winches and want to upgrade, consider getting good, chrome-plated bronze winches. Check to see how easy they are to take apart and service, as easy-to-lubricate winches are much more likely to receive proper care and thus provide better service.

Follow the instructions that came with your particular winch. If those are long gone, you might be able to find them on the Internet. If you do, print out a copy and keep it in your logbook.

As you disassemble the winch, lay the parts out in a straight line on a rag in the order they were removed. This makes it less likely you'll find a mystery part when you put the winch back together. Clean the parts in solvent one at a time, and preserve their place in the line. Use an old paintbrush to get off all the old grease and dirt—an old toothbrush works, too, but it tends to flick little drops of dirty solvent in your eyes and all over the gelcoat. Wipe each part dry of solvent.

Grease the parts lightly and reassemble in reverse order. Be sure to grease the pawls and the drums where they contact, as well as the roller bearings and cages—in short, anyplace where two metals come together. A bicycle mechanic once told me that you should grease threads on screws in order to get proper readings on a torque wrench, and I still do. (I don't lubricate mast fittings or wheel lug nuts. Usually a specialized compound like Never-Seez is a better choice because it isn't quite so slippery.) Some spots, like the grip of the winch handle, call for a drop of machine oil. Grease the locking mechanism, too, if that's the kind of handle you have.

## Blocks

Servicing your blocks is usually simpler because most don't come apart. (On a sailboat, they're called blocks, never pulleys. Pulleys are cheap, and you buy them at the hardware store. Blocks cost an arm and a leg in comparison, so you should at least call them by their proper name out of deference to your ever-dwindling bank account.) Many Harken ball-bearing blocks are made with self-lubricating bearings and should not be oiled. Oil attracts dirt and gums up the races over time. Instead, use a dry lubricant, like McLube Sailkote, dry Teflon, or dry silicone sprays. Harken recommends frequent freshwater rinses for their blocks, even an occasional cleaning with detergent. Usually the black plastic parts of modern blocks fade over time. The discoloration is cosmetic and doesn't affect the strength of the block, but it can be removed with a very fine abrasive. I've been giving my blocks a wipe with a silicone protectant that includes a UV inhibitor, much like you'd use on car interiors. I use F21 by Turtle Wax because I have heard rumors that other protectants contain detergents that can actually accelerate fading if not used regularly (though I haven't been able to confirm these rumors). The blocks look great when treated with protectant, though the silicone soaks right into faded plastic. It doesn't last too long on deck hardware. Watch out for overspray because it can make your deck *very* slippery.

Caring for other deck hardware, such as travelers, goosenecks, and roller-furlers, usually requires a similar treatment of just flushing with fresh water and adding the occasional dry lubricant. Check with your manufacturer and follow their recommendations. Sail slugs and tracks can be lubricated with dry lubricants, though an old remedy has been to use a dry bar of soap rubbed into the tracks and slugs.

## Ropes and Lines

Maintaining your ropes and lines is fairly straightforward. If you sail in salt water, rinsing them with fresh water every so often cleans away abrasive salt crystals. In time the lines get stiff and dirty, so tossing them into a pillowcase and machine-washing them helps.

Regular fabric softener can restore some of their lost flexibility. If they look really worn and frayed, you should replace them for safety's sake.

The only other maintenance item for most lines is keeping the ends whipped. While there are many ways to whip a line, here's a fairly simple method that holds up well.

1. Using strong thread or tarred marline, make a loop and hold it in place against the line with your thumb. Leave a tail of thread hanging out to pull.

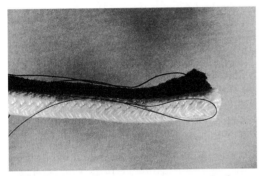

*Hold a length of strong thread against the line about an inch from the end.*

2. Tightly wrap the thread around the line, capturing the loop and working toward the end.

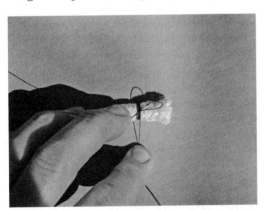

*Wrap the thread neatly around the line, working toward the end.*

3. After you've covered the line with about $^3/_8$ inch of thread, pass the end through the loop, keeping tension on the line. Pull the tail, and the

loop will bury itself under the windings, but don't pull too hard or the loop will pop out the other side.

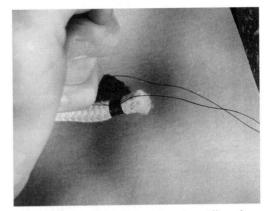

*Bury the loop under the turnings by pulling the thread's tail.*

4. You can really do a first-class job with a few extra steps. Tie the loose ends together with an overhand knot; then, with a needle, run the ends through the line to the other side and repeat. This whipping captures the seizings four times, though I usually do it only twice.

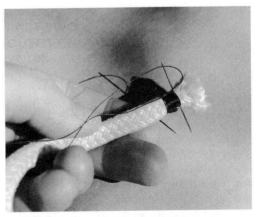

*Twist the loose ends together using an overhand knot, then run the ends through the line to the other side using a needle. This captures the seizings and prevents them from working off the line.*

*The completed whipping.*

## Sails

Maintaining modern sails is simple and straightforward. Most often they need nothing more than a simple rinse with fresh water. Let them dry before storing them—wet sails grow mildew, and the stains are very difficult to remove. Rust stains on a sail can sometimes be cleaned with a salt and lime juice paste—squeeze a lime over a teaspoon of salt, rub the mix into the stain, and leave it in the sunlight. It will take multiple treatments to remove the stain, but this works and is about as easy on the cloth as you can get.

An old, tired sail can be sent off to a company called SailCare to be cleaned and recoated, and I hear that they do impressive work. But it can be expensive—a quote for my MacGregor mainsail was around $200, and a new sail was around $430.

Modern Dacron sailcloth has two enemies—UV radiation and chafe. Unfortunately, there's plenty of both aboard a sailboat. Chafe can be controlled with sacrificial patches sewn to the sail wherever they're needed. Exposure to UV rays is addressed by keeping sails covered whenever they are not being used. This means always using your mainsail cover, and if you have roller-furling, make sure the dark strip sewn to the leech stays intact and in good shape. The dark strips need to be replaced every so often, since they're exposed 24/7.

If you notice a small tear, patch it immediately or you'll soon have a large tear, which is infinitely more work to patch. Adhesive sailcloth patches are good, but a real stitched repair by a sailmaker is better.

## OUTBOARD MAINTENANCE

There are several things you can do to get good service from your outboard. The most important is routine maintenance. Your manual will give the recommended sequence of periodic maintenance steps; follow them. If you don't have a manual, get one—most can be found on the Internet. Here are some of the things that the manual will tell you to do:

### EVERY TIME YOU START THE ENGINE

Check for oil buildup around the prop or foot, which could indicate a bad lower shaft seal. (It's best to store the outboard in a lifted position, tilted forward, with the foot clear of the water.)

Check the fuel lines for gas leaks or cracks.

Check the transom clamps and motor mounts to make sure everything is tight.

While the motor is running, make sure cooling water is flowing from the head.

If you run the motor in salt water, be sure to flush the engine with fresh water after each operation.

### ONCE A MONTH

Check the condition of the zinc anodes and replace if required.

Check under the hood for corrosion or loose parts.

Lubricate the throttle and gear shift linkages.

Check the fuel filter and strainer for dirt or water, and clean or drain as necessary.

### ONCE A SEASON

Grease all points as specified in the manual.

File off any nicks in the propeller.

Replace the oil in the lower unit. If the old oil comes out milky or contains water, have the lower seal replaced.

If you operate your boat in muddy water or you run the motor offshore, replace the impeller annually and clean out the thermostat housing (if the motor has one).

Check the compression. If it's borderline or low, have the engine serviced over the winter.

Remove the spark plug and spray the cylinder with fogging oil.

Apply silicone grease to the inside of the spark plug boot.

### SPECIAL SEASONAL CHECKS FOR FOUR-STROKES

Check and adjust the valve clearances.

Change the engine oil and filter.

Check the timing belt.

There are several very good books on outboard maintenance if you decide to do your own. Depending on your motor and its history, your outboard can be a dependable workhorse or cantankerous problem child. In theory, though, outboards are relatively simple machines that can be owner-maintained and, if necessary, repaired. (See "Outboard" in Chapter 3 for a primer on how they work.) The more you learn, the better off you'll be.

## Fuel Additives

There are two schools of thought about fuel additives. One school says you shouldn't have anything in your fuel except for oil (for a two-stroke, of course). The oil companies invest significant amounts of time creating fuels that are as effective as possible, and if improvements would make their products more competitive, they'd make them. They have whole laboratories and teams of chemists at their disposal.

The opposition camp says that fuel performance can be improved with additives, and I have to admit I'm in this group for my own motor. First off, gasoline is formulated for use in cars. Usually, the gas in a car doesn't have a chance to get old, so long-term stability isn't as important as reducing pollution. If you look at the sticker on the side of the pump, you'll see that it reads "oxygenates added." This extra oxygen, often in the form of ethanol, makes the fuel burn cleaner. When burned, the fuel produces less carbon monoxide and more carbon dioxide. But think about it—when something oxidizes, it changes in the presence of oxygen. In iron, this means rust. In fuel, it means more gum and varnish.

## E10 Troubles

The use of ethanol in fuel has been on the increase in recent years, and a relatively new blend, called E10, has been causing many boaters some trouble. This blend—10 percent ethanol, 90 percent gasoline—was brought about by the replacement of MTBE. MTBE is a fuel additive that is a groundwater polluter and suspected carcinogen, and many states have outlawed its use. E10 is the result, and while it is safer, the different fuel is causing some odd reactions with marine engines.

The large amount of ethanol in E10 acts much like an engine cleaner that works a little too well. It loosens rust and debris inside your fuel system, which clogs fuel filters. The first few tanks of E10 will likely require a few new fuel filters, unless your engine is brand new.

Ethanol absorbs water, which naturally forms inside your tank as condensation caused by temperature changes. This water used to slosh around in the bottom of the fuel tank, below the pickup tube. Now it could become a water-ethanol mix of up to 10 percent of your fuel. Gasoline water absorbers can help, and an additional fuel/water separator filter in your fuel line is a good idea. A fuel line vacuum gauge can tell you at a glance if your filters are clogging.

Moreover, ethanol acts as a solvent for some plastics, including fiberglass, and fiberglass fuel tanks have been common on boats for years, though not so much on trailerable sailboats. If you have a fiberglass tank, watch out. The ethanol can create leaks, and some folks have reported a mysterious goo in their fuel systems. Other plastic parts, rubber O-rings, hoses, and primer bulbs that are not alcohol-resistant need to be replaced.

In a sailboat, it's not uncommon to burn just one tankful of fuel in an entire season, which is a long time for gas to be sitting around. The newer blends of fuel have plenty of time to break down. A fuel stabilizer will prevent this from happening. I use Sta-Bil each time I buy gas, and I always buy the highest octane fuel available.

As an extra measure to fight gummy fuel and burned oil residue, I add a little Sea Foam, a fuel conditioner and stabilizer, to my fuel. At the end of each season I run a stronger dose of

Sea Foam to clean out the engine. This might be a bit of overkill, but so far I've never had to deal with any stuck needle valves, seized float bowls, or badly fouled plugs—knock on wood.

## Outboard Spares and Tools

A few tools are essential, both for onboard use and for working on your motor at home. First, determine whether you have SAE or metric bolts on your motor—they're probably metric unless it's an older outboard. A spark plug socket is essential, as are tools to replace the impeller. Phillips-head and standard screwdrivers, pliers, a feeler gauge, an inexpensive volt-ohm meter, a small grease gun, a freshwater flushing adapter, a socket set, and some combination wrenches make up a pretty good tool set for outboard work. You won't normally need these tools on board—the flushing adapter won't work while you're sailing unless you bring a very long hose—but most of these would be handy if you broke down while underway.

## Electric Propulsion for Sailboats

If all of the preceding seems like just too much bother, there is an alternative that, despite its limitations, is slowly gaining popularity. Electric outboard motors can be used aboard the trailer sailer, and for smaller sailboats especially, it might be worth a look. Several boatowners have clamped large trolling motors to their transom for short periods of motoring. In general, these owners are quite happy with the arrangement. Larger, more powerful electric outboards are now available.

The limitation of electric power usually means slower speeds. It takes a lot of battery powery to exceed 3 knots. An electric trolling motor can completely flatten a fully charged battery in under an hour at full throttle. Increasing your motoring time is as simple as adding more batteries, but remember, they're heavy and need to be located low and near the boat's centerline. Increasing your speed through the water can be done only with a larger motor, which means a correspondingly faster power drain. But even a small trolling motor is easier than rowing. And as long as the battery has a charge, electric motors almost always start with nothing more than a flick of a switch.

For spare parts, you definitely want to have extra propeller shear pins, a new spark plug, an extra fuel filter, and a new impeller. Some extra engine oil wouldn't be a bad idea, especially if you have a four-stroke engine, and I like to keep a small tube of silicone dielectric grease on board. Some spare hose clamps, a little binding wire, and even a bit of extra fuel line might save the day.

## TRAILER MAINTENANCE

Just like your boat, your trailer needs regular maintenance. Since it's less attention-getting and glamorous than a sailboat, it often receives less maintenance than it should. But if you ignore your trailer, it can generate a very large amount of negative attention in the form of an accident, and that's to be avoided at all costs.

Maintaining your trailer becomes more involved as trailer size increases, and different types of trailers may have different maintenance requirements. The following is a general maintenance checklist, but, if possible, check with the trailer manufacturer for specific advice concerning your model.

### BEFORE EACH USE

Check the tires. Be sure that you have adequate pressure and there are no cracks in the rubber or any bulges indicating a possible tire failure. Check the spare as well.

Check bearings and wheel lugs. Look for any looseness or "play" in the trailer tires, or evidence of failed grease seals, such as oil weeping from the hubs. Correct any problems before driving under a load.

Check wiring and trailer lights, especially brake lights. Lubricate all electrical connections with grease or spray lube.

If your trailer is equipped with brakes, make sure they are operating correctly before hauling a load. Flush with fresh water if you launch in salt water.

### ONCE PER YEAR

Visually inspect the trailer for signs of rust. Treat and paint any spots you find, no matter how small. The job only gets bigger if you wait, and, like Neil Young says, rust never sleeps.

Inspect the bearings by jacking up each wheel and spinning it by hand. If you feel or hear any roughness or grinding, replace the bearings. If they are OK, repack the bearings with fresh grease.

Grease lightbulb sockets and wiring connections, and check for corrosion.

There's lots of information about working on trailers and trailer maintenance on the Internet. At http://www.championtrailers.com/techsup.html you'll find nearly thirty short articles on everything from installing new bearings to building a utility trailer from scratch. Champion Trailer Supply also sells a kit that can convert a standard boat trailer into a sailboat trailer, which just might save the day if you want to buy an older sailboat that's deeply discounted because of a missing trailer. There are other trailer supply companies out there as well.

# CHAPTER FOURTEEN

# Modifying Your Sailboat

**B**uying equipment for your new or not-so-new sailboat is only part of the boat ownership story. There are any number of ways to personalize your boat to fit your specific needs and desires. Much more so than a car, a sailboat is somewhat of a blank slate. Even if you've found the perfect used boat, chances are that something on board will need renewing or updating. If you read boating magazines, no doubt many projects will capture your imagination. Those projects are practical and enjoyable ways to learn new skills, such as woodworking, metalwork, and proper tool use—all of which have plenty of useful applications outside of boat ownership.

This chapter will walk you through three projects that are handy improvements on many trailer sailers: building a navigation tool rack, installing a midships cleat, and installing cockpit-led halyards.

## BUILDING A NAVIGATION TOOL RACK

This rack is a small, simple project that's useful for woodworking pros and easy enough for novices. There are lots of good books that will guide you through the beginning stages of woodworking. One that bridges the gap between beginning woodworking skills and boat projects is Fred Bingham's *Boat Joinery and Cabinetmaking Simplified*. (See the Bibliography for this and other resources.) Just start small and go slowly. Another and possibly better option is to take a continuing or adult education class at a technical college. A class often gives you access to some very nice, large,

and expensive stationary tools as well as knowledgeable instructors to show you how to use them. Remember, most of these skills can be mastered by high school adolescents. If they can do it, then mere mortals like you and me should have at least a fighting chance.

Although the rack I built for my boat is for small navigation tools—pencils, pens, dividers, and the like—you could use the same basic method to design racks to hold any number of small items. A nav tool rack is just two small strips of teak—the bottom one is cut with a lip to keep things from sliding out, and the top is cut with perpendicular notches to hold things in place. You can size these notches by using the actual items that are to fit in them. For this job, a table saw or router table is definitely the way to go.

A couple of tips before you start: not just any glue will hold a resinous wood like teak. Resorcinol glue is best, and polyurethane Gorilla Glue also seems to hold well. Wiping the surfaces to be joined with some acetone reduces the oil content a little and helps the glue to bond. Epoxy doesn't hold well on teak by itself, especially when the glued part is used on deck.

Cutting and sanding teak also deserve some mention. While I love the way teak smells, the dust from sanding and sawing is extremely irritating to the lungs. (The dust from ipe, another wood you might use for trim projects, is worse.) Always wear a respirator when working with these woods. You'll definitely want to use carbide-tipped saw blades, as teak will very quickly dull carbon-steel blades.

A rack for navigation tools is a relatively simple and satisfying project. Here the finished rack is shown mounted to a bulkhead.

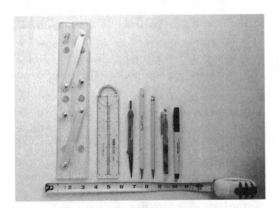

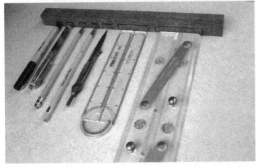

*Step 1. Lay out and mark the stock for the rack.*

*Step 2. The bottom rail is made of two pieces glued together. One piece has notches just like the upper piece, but the bottom has small slots cut in to drain any water. The bottom rail is ripped in two pieces.*

*Step 3. Mill the notches in the rails. The top rail is taped to half of the bottom rail, and the notches are milled with the table saw.*

*Step 4. Here the bottom rail is set in place; the small drain notches have been marked (left). All three pieces are shown (right).*

*Step 5. Glue the bottom rail.*

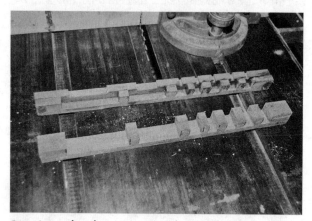

*Step 6. Let the glue cure overnight; visible here are the top and bottom rails of the rack. After carefully drilling mounting holes in the ends, soften all sharp edges with a sharp block plane and sandpaper. Finish the rack with Danish oil or some equivalent.*

*Step 7. Cut plugs to cover the mounting screws from a scrap of the same type of wood. Mount the rack on a bulkhead near your navigation area.*

## INSTALLING A MIDSHIPS CLEAT

One of the minor irritations about docking a sailboat is the location of the cleats, typically one at the bow and one at the stern. This arrangement usually works fine until you try to dock shorthanded in a storm, with a nice 15-knot tailwind. Then, as your boat is heading for the dock, faster than you like and barely under control, you get to make a choice. If you jump from the boat and stop the forward motion with the bow line, the stern will swing wide into the boat next to you. (In this situation, that boat will be brand new,

without a scratch on it. The owner will be aboard, watching your every move.) The other option is to try to stop your boat's forward motion with the stern cleat. If you have a lot of space at the dock, this might work better, though the bow will swing out of control. Trying to wrangle the boat with *both* lines is usually comical at best, as it's difficult to get two lines around a dock cleat fast enough to stop the boat.

The solution is midships cleats (one on each side of the boat). If there's room on deck, a cleat can be installed at the middle of the boat. When a docking line is attached to the midships cleat, neither the bow nor the stern will swing outward as the boat comes up against the dock, and she will be a lot easier to handle at the dock.

You can figure out the correct location of a midships cleat by using your anchor and the tide. What you're looking for is the boat's center of lateral resistance. On a calm day, toss out a small anchor that's tied around the mast. The boat should lie more or less beam to the current, though usually a boat's center of lateral resistance is a bit aft of the mast. Pull the anchor rode back a bit until the boat lies parallel to the current—that's the spot where your midships cleat should go.

The downside to a midships cleat is that it can be tricky to locate so it isn't in the way. If you have really narrow side decks, you may not have room for this cleat, but if you can find a spot near the center of lateral resistance that won't snag your sheets or stump your toes, then mount one.

But make it strong. Forget about nylon mooring cleats—I selected these for my first boat, and they were a mistake. You could see them flex under load. Their two mounting holes were spaced too closely together to hold the cleat firmly to the deck. Although they didn't leak when I owned the boat, it is only a matter of time before they do—and it'll be sooner rather than later because of the movement. A much better solution is a bronze or stainless mooring cleat with four mounting holes. Regrettably, it's a more expensive solution—a 5-inch nylon cleat is less than $3, whereas a bronze four-hole cleat is about $15. And cast aluminum four-hole cleats can cost near $50. But since you're adding just two cleats for a single boat, the extra expense is minor.

The cleat needs to be mounted strongly to the deck. Before you drill, take a look under the deck to be sure you can get to the nuts, and make sure there's clearance for a backing plate. What's a backing plate? Glad you asked. (And if you didn't ask, humor me for a moment.) A backing plate is an essential part of your hardware. It's a sheet of extra material underneath your hardware—in this case a cleat—that's drilled with the same mounting holes as the hardware. Sort of a one-piece washer on steroids.

Backing plates are important because any hole in the deck is a potential leak, and any leak can potentially rot any organic material nearby.

If your deck is solid fiberglass, then there's no risk of rot, but most decks on fiberglass boats are cored with either plywood, balsa, or Airex foam. Consider this scenario—a small leak develops around a fitting because the compound installed twenty years ago has aged, dried out, and lost its bond to the fitting. (This process is accelerated if the fitting is highly loaded.) After ten years or so, the tiny bit of water that finds its way in through that small leak has rotted the plywood core around the fitting, and weakened the whole area. Along comes a nice springtime squall with 45-knot winds. It's not unheard of for the bolts to pull straight through the core, damaging the fiberglass, and if there are tiny washers under the bolts, the fitting could conceivably pull clear through the deck.

A backing plate spreads the load over a much larger area, greatly increasing the strength of the fitting it's attached to. Backing plates can be made of the following materials:

- Stainless steel (best for stainless bolts and fittings).
- Sheet bronze (if you can find it; best if you use bronze fittings or bolts).
- Aluminum (lightweight and easy to work but has to be watched for corrosion).
- HDPE (high-density polyethylene) plastic (somewhat hard to find, but rot-proof).
- Plywood (easy to find and work but needs to be watched for rot; can be coated in epoxy for longevity).

Of these materials, the last two are best used in combination with a metal backing plate or large fender washers on top. Don't try to get away with standard washers; they're too small to be effective. It's not uncommon for some builders to skimp when mounting cleats since it takes time, and few buyers seem to care about this area until it's too late. You'll occasionally see bolts held by little more than a dab of compound and a few washers.

If you want to be really thorough, take this extra step: drill the mounting holes and examine the core. If it's balsa, you can chip out some of the core with a bent finish nail chucked into a drill bit. This won't work so well with a plywood core in good shape, but if it's rotten, it'll chip out easily. Seal the bottom hole with tape, and pour in some Git Rot (a proprietary blend of very thin penetrating epoxy). Pour some into the upper hole, and keep adding more as it soaks into the core. Once the hole is completely filled, let the epoxy cure for 24 hours. When it's fully hard, redrill the hole through the epoxy. Now if a leak does develop, the water won't migrate into the core, and your deck won't develop soft spots, which are a huge pain to repair.

Complete the installation by adding plenty of polysulfide bedding compound (see page 174) under the fitting, in the hole, and around the bolt heads. Attach the fitting using bolts and nylon lock nuts, if there's room. These nuts will poke down into a space where your head often goes when you're sitting down below. Keep this in mind, because bumping into them can really hurt!

So, now that you've got your new midships cleats mounted with polysulfide and nice, big backing plates—do you know the seamanlike way to stop a boat? Just a hint—it isn't by jumping on the dock and pulling on the line. That's how most folks end up in the drink. And you don't want to be the fender between a dock and a heavy boat. First you find the dock cleat and take a loose turn around it. Let the mooring line slip through the cleat until the helmsman tells you to stop the boat. Then, by pulling upward against the cleat, you have ten times the stopping power.

## INSTALLING COCKPIT-LED HALYARDS

Sometime in the mid-1970s, I read a magazine article that said halyards made fast at the mast base weren't preferred for going offshore. That raised the question, "Are the halyards led to the cockpit?" Armchair sailors seemed to take great interest in the location of the halyards, and hundreds of boats were "improved" with triple turning blocks and rows of line stoppers.

Although the cockpit is undoubtedly a safer position for the crew, especially offshore, it isn't

necessary for every sailboat to have aft-led halyards. When halyards are cleated at the mast, your standing position gives you added leverage when tensioning the sail, and since you've got fewer blocks to turn the halyard, there are fewer friction losses as well. My personal preference is having halyards at the mast, but there are some good reasons for cockpit-led halyards on a trailer sailer. Because the deck is usually smaller—and the boat tends to pitch a lot more—than on a larger boat, you'll often find yourself raising the halyards on your knees. You don't get much of a leverage advantage that way. You can pretty easily add a stand-up deck block at the mast and a single turning block, and if you don't like raising the halyards from the cockpit, it's easy to go back to securing them at the mast.

The hardware required for this modification is fairly straightforward. For most boats, you'll need a spring-loaded stand-up block at the base of the mast, a cheek block for the corner

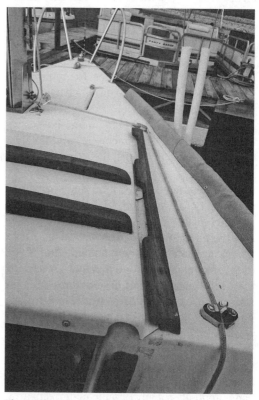

*The cockpit-led halyards on* **Tiny Dancer.**

of the companionway hatch, and a cleat at the cabintop edge where you can secure the halyard—that is, unless you really want to spend money. Then you can get a stopper instead of a cleat. They both do the same thing. Stoppers are probably better for racing because they allow faster headsail changes and are easier to adjust. I use cleats 'cause I'm more of the "up the lazy river" kind of sailor.

Mount the stand-up block a few inches away from the base of the mast. Check underneath first—you'll probably need to go a few inches forward or aft as well, since there's usually a reinforced area or beam running underneath the mast. Generally, you don't want to perforate the mast beam with holes. The stand-up block needs to be through-bolted strongly, just like a docking or mooring cleat, because there are large loads pulling it upward. Seal the mounting holes with epoxy, as discussed for the midships cleat, and bed it well with compound. Use good-quality, roller-bearing blocks.

With nearly all boats, you'll need a second block to lead the line around the companionway. There are special deck organizer blocks for this, or you can use a standard cheek block. This one needs the same high-strength installation. Forget using sheet-metal screws for this; they won't be strong enough.

The third element to install is a cleat or stopper on the cabintop. Remember that you'll still be going on deck all the time, so locate the cleat out of the way. I blasted my knee on my cleat just the other day. As you position these lines, remember that they can't be allowed to rub on any part of the boat. If they do, not only will the sails be difficult to raise, you'll quickly damage the fiberglass as well.

Don't automatically assume that your halyards should be raised and lowered from the cockpit. Think carefully about it before you start drilling holes all over your deck and spending dollars on hardware. The hardware may already be there—it was on two of the three boats I've owned—so your choice may already be made, and you can try it both ways. But do take the time to seal the mounting holes and properly bed the hardware.

## Epoxy

Epoxy resin is available in quarts or gallons from specialty suppliers. Epoxy resin is not the same as standard polyester resin that your boat is made from—it's far stronger, especially in adhesive strength. When properly applied to a cured fiberglass boat hull, epoxy forms a permanent bond that can be considered a structural part of the boat itself. Polyester is fine for new boat construction, but when you need to add something to polyester that has already cured, epoxy is the easiest way to get a good bond.

Epoxy resin is more expensive than polyester, though prices have come down a bit as it has become more widely available. Using small specialty suppliers usually results in better prices than buying from a major catalog dealer. Epoxy is more sensitive than polyester to mixing in the correct ratios, so you must be more careful when you mix it. This problem is greatly simplified by buying calibrated pumps when you purchase your resin.

As good as epoxy is, it has a few weaknesses. One is that it deteriorates rapidly under UV rays. Resist the temptation to coat your woodwork with a layer of epoxy, like my friend Larry Lee did on his anchor platform. It looked good at first, but within a few months the sun had taken its toll, and his carefully applied coating was lifting up in great cloudy sheets. Another weakness is its sensitivity to heat. Some epoxies can lose their bond at fairly low temperatures, even becoming noticeably soft on a hot and sunny day. Not all epoxies exhibit this trait, though, so examine the specifications carefully.

Another property of epoxy that isn't really a weakness, but you should be aware of it, is "blush." As epoxy cures, part of the process is the formation of amine acids. The acids migrate to the surface of the epoxy, and in many resins this can prevent the full bonding of additional layers of epoxy. The amine blush

*(Continued)*

is easily removed with a little soap and water. Recent developments have resulted in low-blush and even no-blush formulations. I've never had a problem with blush with the epoxy I've used.

Epoxy resin, though strong and useful by itself, is only part of the story. When used in combination with other materials, epoxy becomes far easier to handle, easier to sand, stronger, and more penetrating. Epoxy suppliers usually carry these additives as well, so it's easiest to order them when you buy your resin. Additives can save you money by stretching your resin further. Here's what you'll commonly use:

RESIN. Often mixed 2:1 or 3:1 with hardener, though some epoxies can have a 10:1 mix ratio. Resin cures by generating heat—an exothermic reaction—so you don't want to mix too much at one time, as some epoxies can overheat and actually boil. Often available as fast or slow cure, you'd use fast in winter, when ambient temperatures are lower, and slow in summer. The pot life, or working time, varies. Sometimes the resin will begin to set in as little as five minutes. Any epoxy should usually be left to cure overnight, with the full cure coming in about a week.

MICROBALLOONS or MICROSPHERES. These are microscopic glass bubbles that are mixed into the resin, lightening it up and making the cured resin easy to sand. Available in white (glass) or red (phenolic); the main difference is that the red is easier to sand. When mixed 100 percent with epoxy, the resulting compound is somewhat runny and will not stay on vertical surfaces well.

FUMED SILICA. Also known as Cab-O-Sil or Aerosil, fumed silica is a very fine, threadlike silica powder. When mixed with epoxy, it forms a strong, nonsagging compound that is very difficult to sand. Some epoxy suppliers sell this as glue powder. When silica is mixed 100 percent with epoxy, the resulting compound looks and handles much like Vaseline.

WOOD FLOURS. Fine dust from sanding wood, "flours" can be used to create strong, nonsagging glue. They are usually used in combination with silica.

MILLED FIBERGLASS FIBER. Very short lengths of chopped fiberglass. Creates a very strong compound, but it tends to be a little lumpy and difficult to handle. You can create your own in small quantities with a pair of scissors and some regular fiberglass, but prepare yourself for an itchy experience.

GRAPHITE POWDER. Graphite can be added to epoxy to make a smooth, abrasion-resistant compound. It's quite messy, of course, until it's mixed. It's also used to protect epoxy from UV rays, though large areas will certainly get hot in the sunshine.

FIBERGLASS. This is the same fiberglass that was used in making your boat. Combined with epoxy resin, it's extremely strong. It comes in cloth (1.5-ounce plain weave is common), roving, or mat. When you use epoxy, alternating fiberglass roving and mat with cloth isn't as critical as it is when using polyester resin, as the greater adhesive strength allows more leeway when layering material. In all the repairs and construction I've done with epoxy, nearly all have used fiberglass cloth. And as far as I know, all are still stuck down tight. Fiberglass cloth comes in 56-inch-wide sheets, but a handier form for boatowners is fiberglass tape. This comes in various widths, but I've got a roll of 4-inch tape that I use all the time for making small patches, fillets, and structural members.

Mixing a batch of epoxy is easy if you have the pumps. Squirt out one shot each of hardener and resin, and stir thoroughly. Though epoxy vapors are much less noticeable than the styrene vapors from polyester resin, you should still mix epoxy outside. Some people develop a sensitivity to epoxy, and once this happens, it's nearly impossible to be around the stuff. The dust from the additives is bad for your lungs, especially dust from fumed silica. Silica dust can cause silicosis, so protect yourself accordingly. Add the fillers as required. I do nearly all repair work with a combination of resin, silica, and microballoons—usually a squirt of resin, a spoonful of silica, and 2 or 3 spoonfuls of microballoons. If I need a stronger compound, I'll use more silica and cut back on the balloons.

## Relocating Deck Hardware

On anything other than a brand-new sailboat, you'll often find that deck hardware added by a previous owner is located in a less-than-optimal position. Before you change anything, confirm that this is indeed the case with a few test sails. Sometimes hardware may seem to be in a bad place, but after a few sails its location makes more sense. But more often, hardware is installed without careful planning, or someone's great idea turns out to be not so great. Or a part becomes worn out, but new replacements have different bolt patterns. Or better methods leave a particular piece of gear unused. How do you take care of these situations?

Often you'll want to remove a part and fill in the holes. The first rule of thumb is, don't do anything that's temporary. Far too often people remove a part, tape over the holes, and never get around to finishing the job properly. This leads to all sorts of problems, like tape residue baked onto your deck and water intrusion into the deck core. And forget about using any sort of caulk or compound. This is a job for epoxy.

But as always, preparation is the key. Remove the old hardware and scrape away any trace of bedding compound. (A single-edged razor blade scraper has long been the preferred tool for this job, but a new option is ScrapeRite plastic razor blades. These come in three grades: red for general-purpose delicate scraping, a blue polycarbonate blade for fiberglass and gelcoat, and yellow for use on hard, flat surfaces.) Remove any loose chips of gelcoat from the hole, and then lightly sand the area near the hole.

If the hole goes through the deck core, check the core for rot. If you find any, chip away the rot and fill the hole with thinned epoxy, as previously discussed in "Rebedding Deck Fittings" and elsewhere.

Next, wipe the entire area with acetone to clean off dust and dirt. Mask the gelcoat near the hole, leaving about a half-inch border exposed. If possible, mask the back side of the hole as well.

Fill the hole with a thickened epoxy. The easiest way to do this is with a commercial preparation. My favorite is Marine Tex, which is sandable after it's cured, but you can mix up your own by adding some fumed silica and microballoons to a dab of epoxy from a hardware-store squeeze tube. Add enough until the mix doesn't sag on vertical surfaces. Smooth the compound over the hole with a paint scraper. This will minimize the sanding you have to do in the next step.

After the patch cures, sand it smooth. If you're doing it by hand, start with 120 grit and finish off with 220 or 320 grit to get a smooth surface. Pros will do this with a disk of fine sandpaper in a side grinder, but don't try this unless you consider yourself an expert with this tool. It does the job in no time at all, but the slightest hiccup will put a deep gouge in your gelcoat, requiring a much bigger repair.

Marine Tex comes in white, which is ideal if your boat happens to have a white gelcoat like mine. If your deck is tinted gelcoat, the epoxy can be colored using fiberglass tints, but exact colors are difficult to match. You can add a dab of paint over the repair, which might be best for darker colors.

# PART FIVE

# CRUISING IN COMFORT

# CHAPTER FIFTEEN

## Personal Comforts On Board

On a craft that may be as small as 16 feet and occasionally heeling up to 45 degrees, accomplishing the tasks of daily living takes organization, planning, and patience. A sense of balance helps, too. The challenge is part of the fun, however. In this chapter we examine how you can manage meals, a fresh water supply, personal storage, and that all-important but often-neglected topic—the bathroom on board.

### COOKING ON A SMALL BOAT

Meals on any sailboat cruise require careful planning, and this is doubly true for a small sailboat. Even for short cruises with a limited crew, you still need careful meal plans for each day of your trip as well as some backup meals in case you are out longer than expected. Dehydrated backpackers' meals or dry pasta-based one-pot dinners work well for this. Try to limit canned items to single-serving sizes. Once you open a can, you've got to use it all, because cooler space is *very* limited. There are some good galley cookbooks available, and don't overlook backpacking cookbooks.

You can keep ice for a day or so on a boat in a standard cooler, which is long enough for a night or two of fresh food, milk, and a few cold drinks. After that, it's either find a marina or do

without. You can usually find ultra-high-temperature (UHT) milk—sold in aseptic packaging and needing no refrigeration—in single-serving cartons in the United States; other countries have UHT cream as well. Adding an extra layer of insulation to your cooler will make a small improvement in its ice-holding ability, but don't expect miracles. The meltwater, if it's uncontaminated, can be used for rinsing dishes, but I wouldn't drink it.

Several types of stoves can be used to heat food on a sailboat. There's no best type, though certain characteristics may cause you to prefer one type over another. Most trailer sailors use a small, single-burner stove, though some have room for a two-burner stove. Below are some of the stove choices. Note that Coast Guard regulations require cookstoves to be secured against movement in heavy seas.

### Alcohol Stoves

A few years ago, many boats came fitted with alcohol stoves. Alcohol was believed to be the better fuel for onboard use since the vapors are nonexplosive and have no objectionable odor. I used a pressurized alcohol stove for years, and it worked fine. My current stove is an Origo 1500 nonpressurized alcohol type that works quite well. If your boat has an operational alcohol stove, and you can still get parts for it, you don't have to replace it until it starts giving you problems.

Alcohol has its drawbacks—it takes longer to boil a pot of water, and fuel spills can burn with an almost invisible flame. Alcohol is expensive if you buy it through most readily available sources, like hardware or drugstores. But denatured alcohol is handy to have aboard since it has medical uses, it's a good disinfectant, and it thins uncured epoxy.

## Gimbaled Stoves

Gimbaled stoves are designed for marine use; they swing from front to back, matching the boat's movement, and hold up well in damp, salty air. If you have the room, the Optimus Sea-swing is a nice gimbaled stove. Forespar makes one called a Mini-Galley, and Force 10 makes the Seacook. These are all propane models. Gimbaled stoves are about the only cookers you can use when it's rough, although you probably should skip cooking in a storm. To be mounted properly, they do require some vertical space, which you may or may not have on your boat.

## Propane Camping Stoves

Propane camping stoves are readily available, inexpensive, and popular on trailerables as well as larger cruisers. The flame burns hot and clean, with no smoke and little odor. The problem is, other than the gimbaled stoves discussed above, most are not designed for marine use, and may have mild steel parts that can rust out in a few seasons. Some, though, are made of stainless steel. You can extend the life of a camp stove by spraying the entire thing, especially the inside, with silicone wire dryer. It does a fair job of preventing rust but doesn't contain lubricants, like WD-40, so it feels less greasy after the silicone evaporates. There's no oil film that could, in theory, ignite.

Another downside is of course the risk of explosion. It is crucial to keep the stove and propane tank leak-free. Don't unscrew the propane cylinder once you've started using it, since the seals on the cylinder can leak once they've been installed on the stove and then removed. (An explosion is pretty rare, but I wouldn't risk it.) *Do not store propane cylinders down below!* Propane vapor is heavier than air and can settle in the bilge. All you need is a little water and some time—the stove rusts, the tank leaks, the propane settles to the lowest point on the boat, and hopefully you won't be below when she blows to bits. A chemical called mercaptan is added to propane to make it smell bad, so you'll know there's a leak. If you can smell gas, you've got a problem. Shut everything off and take the stove immediately to the cockpit until you can sort it out.

## Lightweight Backpacking Stoves

These tiny little things do a surprising job. If you haven't been to an outdoor-gear store in a few years, go have a look at modern backpacking stoves. Some can burn multiple fuels, like alcohol, kerosene, or white gasoline. (I wouldn't use gasoline in the cabin.) Their tiny size can be their downfall on a boat, though, since they are designed to be used on a very stable surface—the ground. Slippery fiberglass surfaces and the occasional ill-timed boat wake mean that most backpacking stoves need some form of modification to prevent them from slipping. Many also require that the pot stay carefully balanced on the exact center of the stove, which would, of course, be quite difficult on a boat. If you can figure out a way around these requirements, then a backpacking stove might be a workable option.

## FRESH WATER

Fresh water aboard a boat is always important— you'll need it for drinking, cooking, and cleanup (including yourself). Often the stock water tanks that come with a boat are too small for cruising, and you'll want to supplement the boat's capacity. For small boats, the best solution is tanks. Water is, of course, very heavy and needs to be kept well secured in the lowest possible part of the boat. Several smaller tanks of 1 to 2 gallons are better than a single large tank. Collapsible plastic tanks, like those used for camping, are good on a boat, but you must protect them from chafing. A 2-gallon unit with a canvas bag to protect it would work well.

Delivering water to the user is easier with a gravity-fed system than a hand-operated pump. If you have the room, a high shelf near the sink is an ideal place to keep a 2-gallon water jug while you're at anchor; then you can secure it in a lower spot while you're underway.

If a gravity system isn't practical, a foot pump is better than a hand pump. Foot pumps need to be strongly mounted. Hand pumps do have one big advantage—they are such a pain to use, you conserve lots of water. Of course, if you use several small 1-gallon tanks, the water can simply be poured as needed. This low-tech approach saves water but might be tricky if you are bouncing around on a brisk upwind tack. A pressurized water system isn't really practical on a trailerable sailboat because its complexity reduces tank capacity, and you'd likely run out of water long before your cruise was over.

Showering on board is certainly possible, and really isn't a big deal. You shower in the cockpit. If you're in an anchorage with other boats or sailing with a crew, you can shower in a bathing suit. A suit that's a little baggy or stretchy helps.

Hot water can be supplied two ways. A Solar Shower is a dark-colored bag with a shower nozzle and an on/off spigot; you fill it with water and let it warm in the sun. Hang it from the rigging and let gravity do the work. The water never gets really hot, but it's certainly better than a cold shower.

An easier system is the garden pressure sprayer. A 3-gallon size works well, and a dark color will warm the water a little in the sun. Or use 2 gallons of cold water and 1 gallon of hot water from the stove.

To take a shower using the minimum amount of fresh water, use a bucket full of salt water for your initial hose-down, then soap up. Use fresh water only for the final rinse. Only a few soaps will lather in salt water—some options are diluted Dawn or Lemon Joy dishwashing detergent (showering with dishwashing liquid tends to dry out your skin, however), Lever 2000 bar soap, Suave shampoo, and specialty soaps for salt-water washing, like SunShower, Saltwater, or Sailor Soap.

## PERSONAL GEAR

Fortunately, sailing doesn't require a lot of fancy duds, but some clothes are better choices than others. Certain fibers, such as bleached cotton, are nearly transparent to UV rays, unbleached cotton has a higher SPF. Silk and some high-luster polyesters can protect your skin because they're reflective. In general, darker colors absorb more UV radiation than lighter colors. Denim blocks UV rays well—it has an SPF approaching 100—but it isn't very practical if it gets wet. To check a particular garment to see if it offers sun protection, hold it up to the light. The more you can see through the fabric, the less effective it will be against sunburn.

Specialty fabrics are now available that are lightweight, quick-drying, and offer better sun protection, but they're usually expensive.

One thing you will need is a good hat, especially if you have a head like mine. Right on schedule, at about age 42, most of my hair disappeared. From the eyebrows up, I now resemble a naked mole rat, so rather than attempt to disguise my obvious middle age, I regularly shave off my remaining air with clippers. Now sunburn happens in the blink of an eye, so a good hat is a requirement. There are many styles to choose from, but something with a wide brim offers more protection for your neck and ears than the typical baseball hat. Whatever you get, make sure it has a chin strap or a collar clip so it won't blow off, or won't go overboard if it does happen to blow off.

Good deck shoes are important as well, and there have been some improvements in recent years. Once upon a time, deck shoes meant Sperry Topsiders, but I've never liked them—the low-cut uppers make them feel like they're always slipping off my feet. (And wearing socks with topsiders looks so silly that even I know better and Bozo the clown was a snappy dresser compared to me.) Harken makes deck shoes that lace up like sneakers, and newer styles of deck shoes combine appropriate soles with lace-up security and good looks. A deck shoe's sole should be covered with ridges that are cut into the sole; they aren't easily seen unless the sole is bent. Cheap imitation deck shoes have molded-in ridges. Good soles can also be found on sandals and water shoes that are designed to get wet, drain well, and dry quickly.

Where to put your carefully planned wardrobe? Any sailboat that is small enough to be put on a trailer is not going to have a great deal of space down below. Gear nets or gear hammocks are handy for storing clothes along the V-berth. They keep your clothes easily accessible yet out of the way, and they stay put when you're on a good heel. Also, for fewer wrinkles, roll clothes instead of folding them, and keep them in a soft duffel or canvas bag.

## WHAT ABOUT THE BATHROOM?

Some people find it impossible to believe that you, or anyone else, would be crazy enough to sleep on such a tiny vessel as a trailerable sailboat. They look down below and say, "But where's the bathroom?"

A few hundred years ago the bathroom, or head, was at the head of the ship, where the breeze was most likely to carry away the smells. Two hundred years later, and it still smells. Nobody likes to talk about the head, and I can't blame them—it's an unpleasant, stinky, embarrassingly personal subject—but everyone has to deal with it one way or another.

Like it or not, there's every indication that most states will eventually become no-discharge zones. This means that you can't pump any sewage overboard, even if it is through a federally approved treatment system. No-discharge zones apply to blackwater, or sewage. Sink water, or graywater, is usually exempt. This trend has caused a great many complaints from the boating community, citing studies claiming that most pollution is caused by agricultural runoff. But while pumpouts and holding tanks are far from convenient, there is little doubt that stronger pollution regulations are improving water quality.

Trailerables are ahead of the curve in this area. Boats without an installed head, which includes most trailer sailers, are no-discharge vessels. There are some progressive ways for handling waste that would make it easy for small and large boats alike to comply with no-discharge regulations. We'll look at these in a moment.

### Installed Heads

On larger boats of 25 feet or so, you might find a permanently installed head. These are what some consider to be Public Enemy Number Two. They're hated by environmentalists and boatowners alike, especially those who've had to repair them more than once. See the procedures and regulations for MSDs (marine sanitation devices) under "USCG-Required Equipment" in Chapter 5.

If you're considering a boat with a permanently installed head and you've never used one, be sure to ask the seller for detailed instructions about using it. Never make assumptions about a head installation. One big thing to remember is that they are very easily clogged—*and there are no plumbers at sea*. It's said that something as small as a match will clog one. I'm too much of a coward to see if it's true. Fixing a clogged marine head is an extremely unpleasant experience. The *only* thing that it can take is toilet paper, and I'd recommend the special quick-dissolving kind sold by marine and RV suppliers. Another important thing to remember is to *open the seacock before operating the pump*. If you forget, and bust a hose—just *thinking* about that possibility makes me a little ill.

### The Portable Head

Much more common on small boats is the ubiquitous porta-potty. These are small, self-contained toilets that include a seat, lid, storage tank, water supply, and pump for rinsing the bowl. Most are sufficient for two adults over a long weekend. The storage tank gets dumped—carefully—into an onshore toilet. Portable heads are usually made of plastic and cost in the neighborhood of $70 to $150. At that price, it's an item that I'd much rather replace every few years than attempt any sort of repair or rebuild. My MacGregor 222 came with a porta-potty that hadn't been used in years, though the lower waste tank was about half-filled with—something liquid. It also seemed to be under pressure. I treated it like a hand grenade with the pin halfway out, and *very* carefully, *very* gently, placed it in the garbage can and bought a new one.

The best thing about portable heads is their simplicity; they have few moving parts. They have two tanks—the upper tank holds a small amount of water for rinsing the bowl, and the lower tank holds the waste. A small bellows pump squirts in a little rinse water, and a trap allows waste to drop from the bowl into the tank. The drawback is limited capacity. The lower tank typically stores $2\frac{1}{2}$ to 5 gallons. Of course, there's the pleasure of lugging around a tank full of liquid poop, and the delightful smell as you dump it in a toilet somewhere. Actually, if you use the manufacturer's recommended chemicals, it's quite a bit less nauseating than the untreated stuff.

Note that in some areas, such as Ontario, portable heads are illegal. Any boat must have a permanently installed head, with a deck fitting for pumpouts and a vent fitting. Check local laws and ordinances concerning heads before you cruise.

Portable heads aren't as bad as you might think. Yes, they are small, and they'll seem a little unsteady at first, but there are optional brackets to keep the thing in place. While some are slightly better than others, they all work pretty much as advertised.

## Alternative Head Systems

Both the permanently installed head systems and portable heads have one thing in common, and that's water. Just like our flush toilets at home, they use water to move things along through the system and to control odors (somewhat) by sealing them from the air. This works fine if you've got plenty of water and a sewage connection to carry things away, but if you don't, things just don't work as well.

An alternative way of thinking is to keep things as dry as possible and control odors by other methods. Waste can be broken down by two types of bacteria—anaerobic and aerobic. Aerobic bacteria require oxygen to grow; anaerobic bacteria do not. Anaerobic bacteria produce methane, hydrogen sulfide, and other gases that smell terrible. Aerobic bacteria produce carbon dioxide, which is odorless by itself.

Composting toilets are an alternative to the traditional permanent head installation; they use aerobic bacteria to break down waste. They require a little peat moss every once in a while to keep them going, and have a small fan to supply the air that the bacteria need to survive. Composting heads have a special bowl that separates urine from feces, which keeps

*The Air Head composting toilet separates liquids from solids.*

odors down and increases the capacity of the system. A special storage bottle holds urine until it can be dumped on shore. A composting head is expensive, at about $1,200 for a complete installation, though for a large boat it makes a lot of sense.

Smaller boats require simpler solutions. Again we can turn to our backpacker friends for help. One of the better solutions is the Wag Bag. These are biodegradable plastic bags that contain a substance called Pooh Powder. The powder locks urine into a gel, much like a baby's diaper does. It also deodorizes and begins decomposing solid waste. Wag Bags were used by the thousands in the aftermath of Hurricane Katrina in New Orleans, so they've passed the test. They are landfill-safe and legal to toss in normal garbage containers or dumpsters. One bag is reportedly good for five or six uses, and a twelve-bag supply costs about $26. They can be purchased from boat chandleries like BoatU.S. or West Marine, or ordered directly from the manufacturer, Phillips Environmental Products (www.thepett.com). The Wag Bag is an innovative and functional system with no holding tanks or dumping of liquid.

Other manufacturers make similar systems that are variations on the garbage-bag theme. One is a potty seat that fits tightly on a standard 5-gallon bucket. (Or you could get creative and build your own with a trip to a builder's supply. Line it with a heavy-duty plastic bag and toss in your own powder.) Another option (from NRS Paddlesports) is the Groover Tamer. This is a powder and spray system—the powder can treat up to 40 pounds of waste, and the spray deodorizer is good for 850 applications.

Simpler still is something called the sawdust toilet, sometimes used ashore in places where plumbing and septic systems are unavailable. It's a composting system where sawdust is used as a carbon-rich cover material that jump-starts the composting process. As long as the waste remains covered with an adequate amount of sawdust, there is supposedly little odor. The "system" is simple, and uses a 5-gallon bucket. As it is filled with waste

*The "honey pot" that came with my boat is little more than a bucket with a toilet seat. There's just enough room for it under the V-berth. With some selected dry cover material, though, it isn't nearly as bad as it looks or sounds.*

and sawdust, it's dumped in the center of an oxygen-rich compost pile. The heat from the compost pile kills pathogens, and after about a year the compost is completely inert. Although sawdust works best, other cover materials such as peat moss, rice hulls, or leaf mold (partially composted, finely chopped leaves) can be used. Waste must always be covered with a layer of clean organic material. The sawdust toilet and other forms of composting are covered in detail in *The Humanure Handbook* by Joseph Jenkins. It's free online at www.weblife.org/humanure/index.html.

Though the sawdust composting toilet was not designed for boat use—one can hardly have a compost pile on a boat—it seems that some version could be used on board, especially if you could find an inexpensive dry additive that would promote aerobic bacteria. Hydrogel powder in the form of soil additives and/or a compost activator (such as Espoma's Organic Traditions Bio-Accelerator, 4 pounds for $19) might improve such a system. Venting the head area with a solar ventilator might be required, but this would be a welcome addition no matter what form of head you use. You'd have to do some experimenting to see what will work on a boat, but this is an area that could reap some real benefits for the cruising community.

# The Trailer Sailboat Gallery

Hundreds of boats that could be called trailerable have been built over the years, so obviously it's impossible to show all the current options. If we modify our parameters to include some provision for sleeping, the list becomes more manageable. Even so, this is not a complete listing of all fiberglass trailer sailers with cabins. I've tried to include descriptions of as many boats as possible, especially current production models.

My hope is that the range of boats shown will give you an idea of your choices.

Every effort was made to ensure that the data in this section is accurate, but the statistics for each boat may vary slightly from what you see here. I listed approximate prices for new boats for comparison, but they will surely have changed by the time you read this. Used boat prices can vary greatly—consult NADA or BUC price guides for that information. (See the Bibliography.)

## BOATS CURRENTLY IN PRODUCTION

### Catalina

Catalina Yachts has been in business a long time and has built a lot of boats. It's the creator of what is arguably the king of trailerable sailboats, the Catalina 22. More than 10,000 Catalina 22s have been built over the years. (See pages 233–234 for a guide to used Catalina 22s.) Catalina Yachts has weathered quite a few industry recessions, and still builds capable boats at reasonable prices. Its current line of trailerable boats contains several from 18 to 25 feet that feature a functional sailing platform plus fairly nice accommodations belowdeck.

#### Catalina 18 Mark II

The Catalina 18 has a small cabin and is a good size for two people. At 1,500 pounds displacement, it can be pulled by most cars.

**Catalina 18 Mark II**

| | |
|---|---|
| Hull length | 18' |
| (LOA including rudder and bow rail: 20'4") | |
| LWL | 16'4" |
| Beam | 7'7" |
| Draft | 2'4" (wing keel) |
| Displacement | 1,500 lbs. |
| Ballast | 425 lbs. |
| Sail area | 151 sq. ft. |
| Mast height | 23'2" |
| Designer | Gerry Douglas |
| Contact | www.catalinayachts.com |

## Catalina 22 Sport

The Catalina 22 Sport was designed in response to owners who wanted a boat that more closely reflected the size and weight of the original Catalina 22. It's being called a family racer and is an alternative to restoring an older 22.

### Catalina 22 Sport

| | |
|---|---|
| Hull length | 21'6" (LOA: 23'10") |
| LWL | 19'4" |
| Beam | 7'8" |
| Draft | 1'8"/5'0" (cb up/down) |
| Displacement | 2,380 lbs. |
| Ballast | 550 lbs. |
| Sail area | 205 sq. ft. |
| Mast height | 25'0" |
| Designer | Gerry Douglas |

## Catalina Capri 22

The Capri 22 is basically a daysailing and racing version of the 22. The interior is similar to that of the 18, but the cockpit is longer.

### Catalina Capri 22

| | |
|---|---|
| Hull length | 22'(LOA: 24'6") |
| LWL | 20'0" |
| Beam | 8'2" |
| Draft | 2'8" (wing keel) |
| | 4'0" (fin keel) |
| Displacement | 2,250 lbs. (wing keel) |
| | 2,200 lbs. (fin keel) |
| Ballast | 700 lbs. (wing keel) |
| | 650 lbs. (fin keel) |
| Sail area | 229 sq. ft. (standard rig) |
| | 255 sq. ft. (tall rig) |
| Mast height | 31'4" (standard rig) |
| | 23'4" (tall rig) |
| Designer | Gerry Douglas |

### Catalina 22 MKII

This is a complete redesign of the famous Catalina 22. Whereas the Capri 22 is intended mainly for daysailing and racing, the C22II has an interior designed for longer stays on the water.

| | |
|---|---|
| Hull length | 22'(LOA 23'10") |
| LWL | 19'4" |
| Beam | 8'4" |
| Draft | 2'0"/5'0" (cb up/down) |
| | 3'6" (fin keel) |
| | 2'6" (wing keel) |
| Displacement | 2,290 lbs. (swing keel) |
| | 2,603 lbs. (fin keel) |
| | 2,546 lbs. (wing keel) |
| Ballast | 452 lbs. (swing keel) |
| | 765 lbs. (fin keel) |
| | 708 lbs. (wing keel) |
| Sail area | 205 sq. ft. |
| Mast height | 24'9" |
| Designer | Frank Butler/Gerry Douglas |

### Catalina 250

The Catalina 250 is a "maxi-trailerable"—while it is a trailerable, you probably wouldn't zip down to the lake to launch it for a quick afternoon's sail. It does have a very roomy cabin, however. There are two models—a fixed-wing keel and a water-ballasted centerboard model. The centerboard would be more practical for trailering, while the fixed-keel model might have better sailing performance.

### Catalina 250

| | |
|---|---|
| Hull length | 25'0" (LOA: 26'11") |
| LWL | 21'3" |
| Beam | 8'6" |
| Draft | 1'8"/5'9" (cb up, water ballast/cb down) |
| | 3'5" (wing keel) |
| Displacement | 3,250 lbs. (cb, water ballast) |
| | 4,200 lbs. (wing keel) |
| Ballast | 1,050 lbs. (wing keel), n/a (water ballast) |
| Sail area | 265 sq. ft. |
| Mast height | 33'3" |
| Designer | Gerry Douglas |

## Com-Pac Yachts/The Hutchins Company

The Hutchins Company was founded in 1957 by Les Hutchins, Sr., an inventor and entrepreneur. In the 1970s he combined a personal interest in sailing with a desire to diversify his company, and commissioned Clark Mills to "put a big sailboat in a small package." The result was the Com-Pac 16, first introduced in 1974. It was among the first small boats available with shoal-draft, fixed keels. The Com-Pac 23 and 19 were added to the line, and these boats are now considered classics. Com-Pac owners are passionate about their boats, and used models in reasonable condition are quickly snapped up. Com-Pac's current line of trailerable boats blends classic styling with contemporary hull forms, and even includes several catboat designs.

### Picnic Cat

At 14 feet overall, this little catboat is really more of a daysailer than an overnighter, but overnights could be accomplished with a boom tent and some flexibility. Clark Mills is the designer, who also designed the famous Optimist and Windmill class racers, so I'd imagine she's a quick sailer.

| Picnic Cat | |
|---|---|
| LOA | 14'0" |
| LWL | 12'5" |
| Beam | 7'3" |
| Draft | 0'6"/2'8" (cb up/down) |
| Displacement | 500 lbs. (approx) |
| Sail area | 109 sq. ft. |

| | |
|---|---|
| Mast height | 19'9" above waterline |
| (approx combined mast and gaff height) | |
| Designer | Clark Mills |
| Contact | www.com-pacyachts.com |

### Sun Cat

A pretty little catboat. There's not much in terms of a cabin, which should be expected on a 17-footer, but she'd be a more than capable weekender for two.

| Sun Cat | |
|---|---|
| LOA | 17'4" |
| LWL | 15'0" |
| Beam | 7'3" |
| Draft | 2'1"/4'6" (cb up/down) |
| Displacement | 1,500 lbs. (approx) |
| Ballast | 300 lbs. |
| Sail area | 150 sq. ft. |

| | |
|---|---|
| Mast height | 23'6" above waterline |
| (approx combined mast and gaff height) | |
| Designer | Clark Mills |
| Contact | www.com-pacyachts.com |

### Horizon Cat

A true catboat with a shallow fin keel for improved windward ability.

| Horizon Cat | |
|---|---|
| LOA | 20'0" |
| LWL | 17'9" |
| Beam | 8'4" |
| Draft | 2'2"/5'0" (cb up/down) |
| Displacement | 2,500 lbs. (approx) |
| Ballast | 600 lbs. |
| Sail area | 205 sq. ft. |
| Mast height | 29' above waterline |
| | (approx combined mast and gaff height) |
| Designer | Clark Mills |
| Contact | www.com-pacyachts.com |

### Legacy

New in 2006, this small boat is the closest thing to the original Com-Pac 16. Small and relatively affordable, it's a good choice for those wanting a new boat without the hassles of trailering a huge, heavy package. The cabin has sitting headroom and just enough space to sleep two adults. A bimini or boom tent would certainly open up more space for longer cruises.

| Legacy | |
|---|---|
| LOA | 16'6" |
| LWL | 14'4" |
| Beam | 6'0" |
| Draft | 1'4"/3'6" (cb up/down) |
| Displacement | 1,000 lbs. (approx) |
| Ballast | 600 lbs. |
| Sail area | 130 sq. ft. |
| Mast height | approx 20'3" above waterline |
| Contact | www.com-pacyachts.com |

## Eclipse

A step up in size from the Legacy, the Eclipse has more of an interior below. It's still sitting headroom, of course, but there's more room all around. It was designed to be easy to launch and trailer.

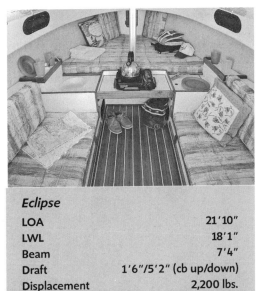

| Eclipse | |
| --- | --- |
| LOA | 21'10" |
| LWL | 18'1" |
| Beam | 7'4" |
| Draft | 1'6"/5'2" (cb up/down) |
| Displacement | 2,200 lbs. |
| Ballast | 700 lbs. |
| Sail area | 200 sq. ft. |
| Mast height | 26'0" above waterline |
| Contact | www.com-pacyachts.com |

## Com-Pac 23/3

This is a fixed-keel boat that comes with real bronze opening portlights. At 3,000 lbs, this is a maxi-trailerable, and you'd need a substantial vehicle to pull it.

| Com-Pac 23/3 | |
| --- | --- |
| LOA | 23'11" |
| LWL | 20'2" |
| Beam | 8'0" |
| Draft | 2'3" |
| Displacement | 3,000 lbs. |
| Ballast | 1,340 lbs. |
| Sail area | 250 sq. ft. |
| Mast height | 30'above waterline |
| Contact | www.com-pacyachts.com |

## Corsair Marine

Corsair Marine was established in 1984 by Australian designer and multihull pioneer Ian Farrier. He resigned from the company in 1991, but Corsair continued to build small and large multihulls with a reputation for speed.

### Corsair Sprint 750

Designed for daysailing and camp-style cruising, the new Sprint 750 can reach speeds in excess of 20 knots.

| Corsair Sprint 750 | |
|---|---|
| LOA | 24'3" |
| LWL | 23'7" |
| Beam | 17'11" (overall) |
| | 8'2" (folded) |
| Draft | 12"/5'6" (cb up/down) |
| Displacement | 1,584 lbs. |
| Sail area | 428 sq. ft. |
| Contact | www.corsairmarine.com |

### Corsair 24

The Corsair 24 has been built since 1991. With a little more cabin space and slightly heavier hull than the Sprint, this model has more amenities for cruising, at the cost of some added weight. It can still reach speeds up to 20 knots.

| Corsair 24 | |
|---|---|
| LOA | 24'2" |
| LWL | 23'7" |
| Beam | 17'11" (overall) |
| | 8'2" (folded) |
| Draft | 12"/4'8" (cb up/down) |
| Displacement | 1,690 lbs. |
| Ballast | none |
| Sail area | 364 sq. ft. (mainsail) |

## Corsair 28

Introduced in 1997, the Corsair 28 is big and fast, yet can still fold into a trailerable package that's only 8½ feet wide. This is an update of the famous F-27 trimaran.

| Corsair 28 | |
|---|---|
| LOA | 28'5" |
| LWL | 26'3" |
| Beam | 8'2.5" (folded) |
| Draft | 1'2"/4'11" (cb up/down) |
| Displacement | 2,790 lbs. |
| Ballast | none |
| Sail area | 475 sq. ft. |

## Ensign Spars

Ensign Spars is a small company in Dunedin, Florida, that builds the Ensign Classic, a reproduction of Carl Alberg's Electra Day Sailer, originally built by Pearson in 1962. It remained in production until 1983.

If you're a fan of traditional boats, the new version by Ensign Spars is a sight to behold. It's a very good-looking vessel, with plenty of varnished teak and glossy new fiberglass surfaces—a real head-turner. Ensign uses the original molds, which they purchased from Pearson when they went out of business.

The boat has a large cockpit and a small cuddy cabin with a couple of berths and not much else. The Ensign still has an active racing fleet and web presence.

## Ensign Classic

| | |
|---|---|
| LOA | 22'6" |
| LWL | 16'9" |
| Beam | 7'0" |
| Draft | 3'0" |
| Displacement | 3,000 lbs. |
| Ballast | 1,200 lbs. |
| Sail area | 235 sq. ft. |
| Mast height | 32' above waterline |
| Designer | Carl Alberg |
| Contact | www.ensignspars.com |

## Etap Marine

Etap is a Belgian builder of lightweight performance sailboats. They build two trailerable models, the 21i and the 24i. The company was bought by Dehler Sailboats in 2008, who says they intend to increase production of Etap boats.

### Etap 21i

| | |
|---|---|
| LOA | 21'6" |
| LWL | 20'6" |
| Beam | 8'2" |
| Draft | 2'4"/4'3" |
| | (shoal keel/deep keel) |
| Displacement | 2,712 lbs./2,601 lbs. |
| | (shoal keel/deep keel) |

| | |
|---|---|
| Ballast | 771 lbs./661 lbs. |
| | (shoal keel/deep keel) |
| Sail area | 256 sq. ft. |
| Mast height | 34'2" above waterline |
| Designer | Etap Yachting |
| Contact | http://www.etapmarine.com/ |

### Etap 24i

| | |
|---|---|
| LOA | 26'4" |
| LWL | 22'0" |
| Beam | 8'2.5" |
| Draft | 2'9.5"/4'11" (shoal keel/deep keel) |
| Displacement | 4,012 lbs./3,968 lbs. |
| | (shoal keel/deep keel) |

| | |
|---|---|
| Ballast | 1,145 lbs./1,101 lbs. |
| | (shoal keel/deep keel) |
| Sail area | 327 sq. ft. |
| Mast height | 38'1" above waterline |
| Designer | Etap Yachting |

## Hunter Sailboats

Hunter is another old name in the sailboat business. In the past the company built several trailerable models with sleeping accommodations; their current offerings are mostly larger boats, but they still build two trailerable boats with cabins.

### Hunter 216

| Hunter 216 | |
|---|---|
| LOA | 21'6" |
| LWL | 18'9" |
| Beam | 7'11" |
| Draft | 1'0"/3'6" (cb up/down) |
| Displacement | 1,350 lbs. |
| Ballast | 500 lbs. |
| Towing weight | 1,850 lbs. |
| Sail area | 252 sq. ft. |
| Mast height | 30'11" above waterline |
| Designer | Glenn Henderson |

**Hunter 25**

**Hunter 25**

| | |
|---|---|
| LOA | 24'6" |
| LWL | 22'1" |
| Beam | 8'5.5" |
| Draft | 2'0" |
| Displacement | 3,700 lbs. |
| Ballast | 1,309 lbs. |
| Sail area | 239 sq. ft. |
| Mast height | 31'8" (above waterline) |
| Designer | Glenn Henderson |

## J-Boats

J-Boats has built a reputation as one of the world's leading performance brands with boats between 22 and 65 feet. Its two smallest boats are trailerable but require a crane or hoist for launching. Most places hosting J-class races have a hoist to get boats in and out of the water. All trailerable models have deep-draft high-performance keels.

## J/22

The J/22 is an international class with more than 1,550 boats sailing in sixty-five fleets in eighteen countries. Twelve- to 15-year-old boats are reported to win major class races.

At 1,800 pounds, the J/22 can be towed behind an SUV. The newest J/22s are built with low-maintenance materials, such as stainless for handrails and white composite for toe rails.

(Courtesy J-Boats, Inc.)

| J/22 | |
|---|---|
| LOA | 22'6" |
| LWL | 19' |
| Beam | 8'0" |
| Draft | 3'8" |
| Displacement | 1,790 lbs. |
| Ballast | 700 lbs. |
| Sail area | 223 sq. ft. |
| Mast height | 24'6" |

## J/24

The International J/24 is built in several countries and is in an active racing class. Since the beam is over the legal limit for highway transport, you'll need a wide load permit to take these on the road.

| J/24 | |
|---|---|
| LOA | 24'0" |
| LWL | 20'0" |
| Beam | 8'11" |
| Draft | 4'0" |
| Displacement | 3,100 lbs. |
| Ballast | 950 lbs. |
| Sail area | 261 sq. ft. |
| Mast height | 36'6" |

*(Courtesy J-Boats, Inc.)*

### J/80

It's hard to believe that a boat this big is trailerable, but it is. With a 8'3" beam and weighing 3,100 pounds, it can be towed in many states behind a truck or SUV without a special permit. It's an intimidating package—the draft is 4'10", and the fixed keel means that it sits quite high on a trailer. The J/80 is ISO Offshore Certified, which means it's designed for waves up to 13 feet and winds to 41 knots. Speeds can get as high as 15 knots under spinnaker.

| J/80 | |
| --- | --- |
| LOA | 26'3" |
| LWL | 24'7" |
| Beam | 8'3" |
| Draft | 4'10" |
| Displacement | 3,100 lbs. |
| Ballast | 1,400 lbs. |
| Sail area | 338 sq. ft. |
| Mast height | 37'6" above waterline |

## MacGregor

Although MacGregor was one of the early leaders in trailerable sailboat design, the company has trimmed its offerings to one model—the MacGregor 26 PowerSailer. (The latest version of the Powersailer is the 26M, introduced in 2003, which features a rotating mast and a daggerboard. Earlier models had a centerboard.) These are designed to take up to 50 hp outboard motors, and the water-ballasted hulls are able to plane under power. This ability necessarily sacrifices some sailing performance, but for some people this is an acceptable trade-off. It's not a new idea—Lancer made a powersailer model back in the 1980s. Owners report that you have to allow 95 to 105 degrees to tack the boat, and it needs to be reefed earlier than a typical 25-footer, but then again not many 25-footers can go upward of 20 knots under power.

*MacGregor 26*

| MacGregor 26 | |
| --- | --- |
| LOA | 25'10" |
| LWL | 23' |
| Beam | 7'10" |
| Draft | 9"/5'6" (cb up/down) |
| Displacement | 2,350 lbs. (tanks empty) |
| Ballast | water ballast |
| Sail area | 281 sq. ft. |
| Mast height | 35'above waterline |
| Designer | Roger MacGregor (1995) |
| Number produced | 2,000 |

## Marshall Marine

*Sanderling*

| Sanderling | |
| --- | --- |
| LOA | 18'2" |
| LOD | 18'2" |
| LWL | 18'0" |
| Beam | 8'6" |
| Draft | 1'7"/4'4" (cb up/down) |
| Displacement | 2,200 lbs. |
| Ballast | 500 lbs. |
| Sail area | 253 sq. ft. (main) |
| Mast height | 23'4" |
| Designer | Breck Marshall (1962) |

## Montgomery Boats/Nor'Sea Yachts

This yard, started by Jerry Montgomery in the mid-1970s, built one of Lyle Hess's designs for a small, seaworthy trailerable known as the Montgomery 17. The company also built a smaller sister called the Montgomery 15. The 15 wasn't designed by Hess but was built to have similar characteristics. Though the boats performed well and were popular, Jerry sold the yard to someone who allegedly took deposits on boats that were never built, and the fate of the molds became uncertain. Fortunately, the molds and building rights were obtained by Nor'Sea Yachts, and these stout little ships are now being built by Bob Eeg in California. Jerry Montgomery is still active in the sailing community at the time of this writing, providing consulting and rigging services for small-boat owners. My own boat, *Tiny Dancer*, is a 1979 Montgomery 17, and if I ever win the lottery, I'll have Bob build me a 23.

### Montgomery 15

*Captain Rich Cottrell aboard his Montgomery 15, Really. (Mark Eichman)*

| Montgomery 15 | |
| --- | --- |
| LOA | 15'0" |
| LWL | 13'3" |
| Beam | 6'2" |
| Draft | 15"/2'6" (cb up/down) |
| Displacement | 750 lbs. |
| Ballast | 275 lbs. |
| Sail area | 122 sq. ft. |
| Mast height | 22'3" |
| Designer | Jerry Montgomery |

### Montgomery 17

| Montgomery 17 | |
| --- | --- |
| LOA | 17'2" |
| LWL | 15'10" |
| Beam | 7'4" |
| Draft | 1'9"/3'0" (cb up/down) |
| Displacement | 1,600 lbs. |
| Ballast | 600 lbs. |
| Sail area | 154 sq. ft. |
| Mast height | 21'6" |
| Designer | Lyle Hess |

*Montgomery 23*

| Montgomery 23 | |
|---|---|
| LOA | 23'0" |
| LWL | 20'10" |
| Beam | 8'0" |
| Draft | 2'5"/4'11" (cb up/down) |
| Displacement | 3,600 lbs. |
| Ballast | 1,530 lbs. |
| Sail area | 249 sq. ft. |
| Mast height | 31'9" |
| Designer | Lyle Hess |

## Performance Cruising

The Telstar 28 story goes back to the early 1970s, when Tony Smith's original Telstar 26 was launched in England. After building nearly 300 boats, he moved the factory to Maryland. A fire in 1981 destroyed the original molds, but the 26 continued to be rebuilt and redesigned over the years. In 2003, the Telstar 28 was born, a direct descendant of the earlier boats. The rigging attaches to the main hull, allowing the smaller outer hulls—called amas—to be folded quickly, even when the boat is in the water. The folding mechanism enables the boat to be kept in the water with either or both outriggers retracted. The Telstar 28 includes a patented mast raising/lowering system that lets a single person lower the mast on the water. Like the earlier boats, it's built by a small family-run business directly on the waterfront, which is becoming a very rare thing these days. More than sixty of the new Telstar 28s have been built so far.

*Telstar 28*

(Will Hershfeld, Performance Cruising Inc.)

| Telstar 28 | |
|---|---|
| LOA | 7'8" |
| LWL | 26'6" |
| Beam | 8'6" folded; 18'0" extended |
| Draft | 12"/4'3" (cb up/down) |
| Displacement | 3,000 lbs. |
| Ballast | none |
| Sail area | 524 sq. ft. (main and genoa) |
| Mast height | 35'6" |

## Precision

Precision Sailboats is one of the three oldest builders in the trailerable sailboat industry, and one of the few that are still family owned.

Precision boats, designed by naval architect Jim Taylor, have a reputation for high quality and speed.

### Precision 165

The 165 features a lead bulb keel and shoal draft, and a locker for the porta-potty.

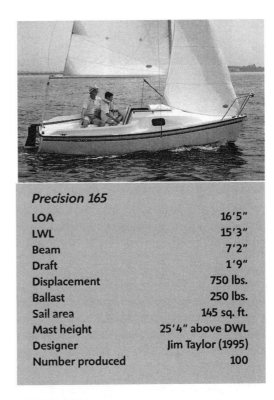

| Precision 165 | |
|---|---|
| LOA | 16'5" |
| LWL | 15'3" |
| Beam | 7'2" |
| Draft | 1'9" |
| Displacement | 750 lbs. |
| Ballast | 250 lbs. |
| Sail area | 145 sq. ft. |
| Mast height | 25'4" above DWL |
| Designer | Jim Taylor (1995) |
| Number produced | 100 |

### Precision 18

The Precision 18 has a long, shallow keel and a noncorroding fiberglass centerboard. The keel allows the board to be housed completely below the cabin sole and gets the ballast down low for stability. The fiberglass centerboard weighs 65 pounds, so fittings are smaller, it's easier to lift, and maintenance is much easier than with a heavy cast-iron keel.

| Precision 18 | |
|---|---|
| LOA | 17'5" |
| LWL | 15'5" |
| Beam | 7'5" |
| Draft | 1'6"/4'3" (cb up/down) |
| Displacement | 1,100 lbs. |
| Ballast | 350 lbs. |
| Sail area | 145 sq. ft. |
| Mast height | 27'0" above DWL |
| Designer | Jim Taylor (1985) |
| Number produced | 525 |
| Contact | www.precisionboatworks.com |

## Precision 21

| Precision 21 | |
|---|---|
| LOA | 20'9" |
| LWL | 17'6" |
| Beam | 8'3" |
| Draft | 1'9"/4'8" (cb up/down) |
| Displacement | 1,875 lbs. |
| Ballast | 600 lbs. |
| Sail area | 203 sq. ft. |
| Mast height | 30'0" above DWL |
| Designer | Jim Taylor (1987) |
| Number produced | 260 |

## Precision 23

| Precision 23 | |
|---|---|
| LOA | 23'5" |
| LWL | 20'0" |
| Beam | 8'6" |
| Draft | 1'11"/5'4" (cb up/down) |
| Displacement | 2,450 lbs. |
| Ballast | 850 lbs. |
| Sail area | 248 sq. ft. |
| Mast height | 35'4" above DWL |
| Designer | Jim Taylor (1986) |
| Number produced | 425 |

## Quorning Boats

Quorning, a Danish company that has been building boats since 1967, produces a trailerable trimaran, the Dragonfly 800. Like most tris, it's lightweight and very fast. Quorning's swing wing system allows the amas to pivot aft using a winch in the cockpit, and the amas can be folded while the boat is underway. This makes it possible to dock the boat in a regular slip, something that is difficult or even impossible for some trimarans. For trailering, the amas are placed upside down on the center hull's deck; the mast and crossbeams are carried in between the amas. Setup time is reported to be about half an hour.

### Dragonfly 800

Quorning's swing wing system allows the amas to be easily retracted while the boat is in the water, making it possible to keep the boat in a regular slip.

| LOA | 26'2" |
|---|---|
| LWL | 24'11" |
| Beam | 19'7" (maximum) |
| | 9'6" (folded) |
| | 7'10" (trailered) |

| Draft | 1'1"/4'7" (cb up/down) |
|---|---|
| Displacement | 2,315 lbs. |
| Ballast | none |
| Sail area | 377 sq. ft. (mainsail) |
| Mast height | 40'6" above waterline |

## General Boats

### Rhodes 22

The Rhodes 22 has been built for a long time without huge changes. It has a pop-top for improved headroom and is a popular race class.

| Rhodes 22 | |
| --- | --- |
| LOA | 22'0" |
| LWL | 20'0" |
| Beam | 8'0" |
| Draft | 20"/4'0"(cb up/down) |
| Displacement | 2,900 lbs. |
| Ballast | 700 lbs. |
| Sail area | 210 sq. ft. |
| Mast height | 26'0" |
| Designer | Philip L. Rhodes |

## SailSports, Inc./U.S. Yachts

SailSports, Inc., is the builder of the Ultimate 20 and the Ultimate 24. These two boats are primarily racing machines, though there is a cabin for overnighting. Designed by Jim Antrim, these boats are (according to the company's description) intended for "fast, fun, friendly, and fair sail racing competition."

### Ultimate 20

The Ultimate 20 is one of the fastest monohulls in production. Its planing hull has been known to hit speeds of 20 knots. Very lightweight, it has a big cockpit and spreads a large amount of sail thanks to its bowsprit-mounted asymmetrical spinnaker. It was *Sailing World* magazine's 1995 Boat of the Year, and naturally has a very active class racing association.

(David Kennedy)

| Ultimate 20 | |
| --- | --- |
| LOA | 20'10" |
| LWL | 18'0" |
| Beam | 8'0" |
| Draft | 9"/5'(cb up/down) |
| Displacement | 1,100 lbs. (fin keel) |
| Ballast | 450 lbs. (fin keel) |
| Sail area | 305 sq. ft. (with main and spinnaker: 657 sq. ft.) |
| Mast height | 31' above waterline |
| Designer | Antrim Design Team |

### Ultimate 24/Antrim 25

The Ultimate 24 was the winner of *Sailing World* magazine's 2004 Boat of the Year design competition. It's since been renamed and is currently sold as the Antrim 25. It features a carbon fiber mast, internal flotation tanks, and Harken hardware throughout. The boat has a bit more interior than the 20, including countertops, four berths, lockers, and a space to store a portable toilet.

| | |
|---|---|
| LOA | 24'5" |
| LWL | 21'2" |
| Beam | 8'6" |
| Draft | 2'11"/5'6" (cb up/down) |
| Displacement | 2,040 lbs. |
| Ballast | 750 lbs. |
| Sail area | 355 sq. ft. |

## Sea Pearl/Marine Concepts

Marine Concepts has built a number of boats over the years but is currently concentrating on a single model, the Sea Pearl 21 (and a trimaran version of the same hull).

### Sea Pearl 21

| | | | |
|---|---|---|---|
| LOA | 21'0" | Ballast | none (water ballast) |
| LWL | 19'0" | Sail area | 136 sq. ft. (standard |
| Beam | 5'6" | | Marconi rig) |
| Draft | 6"/2'6" (cb up/down) | Mast height | 19'6" from waterline |
| Displacement | 600 lbs. | | |

## Seaward/Hake Yachts

### Seaward 26

The Seaward 26 is a large boat, though Hake Yachts' unique keel design makes it trailerable. It is a big package to pull down the highway, but compared to earlier 26-foot sailboats, it's one of the few in its size that can be trailered from a practical standpoint. The Seaward 26's vertical keel/daggerboard system makes it a popular cruiser where the water is thin, like Florida and the Bahamas.

Hake Yachts has built several innovative designs over the years. Discontinued models include the Seaward Fox (20' LOA) and the Seaward 22, 23, and 25. They are popular boats and tend to hold their value well.

*The Seaward 26 by Hake Yachts. (Hake Yachts)*

The Seaward 26 features a very large interior for a trailerable sailboat. (Hake Yachts)

### Seaward 26

| | |
|---|---|
| LOA | 28'6" |
| LWL | 24'8" |
| Beam | 8'4" |
| Draft | 15"/6'0" (cb up/down) |
| Displacement | 3,800 lbs. |
| Ballast | 1,200 lbs. |
| Sail area | 280 sq. ft. |

## Stuart Marine

Stuart Marine is a small company in Maine that builds classic fiberglass boats. They can build three sailing designs: the Rhodes 19, the O'Day Mariner, and the JC9 sailing dinghy. Only the Mariner has a small cuddy cabin for possible overnight use. Stuart Marine is also a source for replacement parts for the Rhodes 19 and O'Day Mariner. The Mariner has an active racing fleet and class association.

### O'Day Stuart Mariner

| | | | |
|---|---|---|---|
| LOA | 19'2" | Sail area | 185 sq. ft. |
| LWL | 17'9" | Mast height | 27'10" |
| Beam | 7'0" | Designer | Philip Rhodes (1963) |
| Draft | 3'3" (keel) | Number produced | 4,193 (O'Day, Rebel |
| | 10"/4'11" (cb up/down) | | Industries, and |
| Displacement | 1,435 lbs. (keel) | | Stuart Marine) |
| | 1,305 lbs. (cb) | Contact | www.stuartmarine.net |
| Ballast | 440 lbs. (keel) | | |
| | 320 lbs. (cb) | | |

## Tremolino Boat Company

### Tremolino

The Tremolino is an interesting concept in multihull sailboats. The idea was developed by John Olin and Dick Newick, designer of the famous OSTAR trimaran *Moxie*. John started the Tremolino Boat Company in 1975. The factory builds the center hull; you add your own outer hulls and rig from an old Hobie 16 (or the factory can supply them for you). Options include a taller rig from the Supercat catamaran. John Olin passed away not too long ago; the new builder of the Tremolino is Bill Dunn, located in Port Washington, Wisconsin. You can also order plans for a home-built version.

| LOA | 23'6" | Displacement | 950 lbs. |
| LWL | 21'10" | Ballast | 1,200 lbs. |
| Beam | 16'6" (standard) | Sail area | 239 sq. ft. |
| | 18'(optional) | Mast height | 29'0" (above waterline) |
| Draft | 1'3"/4'0" (cb up/down) | Designers | Dick Newick and John Olin |

## West Wight Potter/International Marine

The West Wight Potter is a boat of legendary stature. Originally built in England, the early Potters were 15 feet long and made of plywood. One of the first Potters in the United States was sailed across the Atlantic. While today's version has been updated considerably, Potters still retain their distinctive hard chine hull form—one of the only production fiberglass boats to do so. This boat was made famous by author Larry Brown's *Sailing on a Micro-Budget*. While the price of any new sailboat isn't exactly microscopic, the Potter is one of the most affordable small cruising boats available. (I'd always wanted a 19 myself, until I discovered my Montgomery.)

*Potter 15*

| *Potter 15* | |
| --- | --- |
| LOA | 15'0" |
| LWL | 12'0" |
| Beam | 5'6" |
| Draft | 7"/3'0" (cb up/down) |
| Displacement | 475 lbs. |
| Ballast | 100 lbs. |
| Sail area | 91 sq. ft. |
| Mast height | 17'11" |
| Designer | Stanley Smith/Herb Stewart |

*Potter 19*

The Potter 19 is a very popular boat that's nearly impossible to find used. Owners seldom part with them, and when they do, prices are high. They are light, so crew weight forms part of the ballast, but compared to many boats, they are very easy to trailer and launch.

| LOA | 18'9" |
| --- | --- |
| LWL | 16'0" |
| Beam | 7'6" |
| Draft | 8"/3'7" (cb up/down) |
| Displacement | 1,090 lbs. |
| Ballast | 340 lbs. |
| Sail area | 115 sq. ft. |
| Mast height | 22'0" |
| Designer | Herb Smith |

### Sanibel 18

The Sanibel, a beautiful little trailerable sailboat, was brought back from extinction by the folks at International Marine, builders of the famous West Wight Potter. The Sanibel 18 was designed by Charles Ludwig and first built as the Skipper's Mate from 1982 to 1984; then in 1984 the molds were acquired by the Commodore Yacht Corp. and it was renamed Commodore 17. From 1985 to 1988, it was built by Captiva Yachts, first as the Sanibel 17, then renamed Sanibel 18. Somehow, a set of molds appeared in Oregon, where a startup boatbuilder had attempted to resurrect the design, without success. An individual bought the molds as a retirement project but realized that boatbuilding was a bigger job than he'd planned. Fortunately, the molds were eventually purchased by International Marine. With over 30 years' experience, IM is able to offer the first new Sanibels for sale since 1988.

The Sanibel is a pretty boat that features internal lead ballast and a centerboard that is slightly offset from the centerline, making the cabin more usable.

| Sanibel 18 | |
|---|---|
| LOA | 17'9" |
| LWL | 15'0" |
| Beam | 7'4" |
| Draft | 12"/4'0" (cb up/down) |
| Displacement | 1,300 lbs. |
| Ballast | 400 lbs. |
| Sail area | 149 sq. ft. |
| Mast height | 22'0" |
| Designer | Charles Ludwig |

## USED SAILBOATS

### Balboa

### Balboa 20

The Balboa 20 was designed by Lyle Hess. These boats are reported to be good performers, yet because of their age they are affordable—asking prices can range from $1,500 to $2,600. Nearly identical boats, like the Ensenada 20 and the RK 20, were built by other companies.

## Balboa 20

| | |
|---|---|
| LOA | 20'0" |
| LWL | 17'8" |
| Beam | 7'1" |
| Draft | 1'9"/4'0" (cb up/down) |
| Displacement | 1,700 lbs. |
| Ballast | 450 lbs. |
| Sail area | 174 sq. ft. |
| Mast height | 27'6" above waterline |
| Designer | Lyle Hess |
| Years manufactured | 1971–78 |

### Balboa 26

Lyle Hess also designed the Balboa 26. A larger version of the Balboa 20, it's reputed to be a fairly fast and reasonably seaworthy boat, though most Balboas suffer from a somewhat dated look, especially the interior.

## Balboa 26

| | |
|---|---|
| LOA | 25'7" |
| LWL | 20'10" |
| Beam | 7'11.5" |
| Draft | 1'10"/5'0" (cb up/down) |
| Displacement | 3,600 lbs. |
| Ballast | 1,200 lbs. |
| Sail area | 293 sq. ft. |
| Mast height | 33'3" |
| Designer | Lyle Hess |
| Years manufactured | 1969–78 |

## Beneteau

Beneteau is a large multinational sailboat company, with five factories in France, one in Marion, South Carolina, and two factories that specialize in commercial fishing boats. They are primarily a builder of large yachts, but they built a few trailerable models—one that's commonly available in the United States is the First 235. Over 450 boats were built in their South Carolina plant, and another 410 in France between 1986 and 1993. It was available in three different keel configurations: a deep-draft fin keel, a shoal-draft wing keel, and a centerboard version.

### Beneteau First 235

| | |
|---|---|
| LOA | 23'4" |
| LWL | 20'3" |
| Beam | 8'2" |
| Draft | 3'9.5" (fin keel) |
| | 2'5"/4'7" (cb up/down) |
| Displacement | 2,826 lbs. (fin keel) |
| | 2,936 lbs. (wing keel) |
| | 2,986 lbs. (cb) |
| Ballast | 825 lbs. (fin keel) |
| | 937 lbs. (wing keel) |
| | 750 lbs. (cb) |
| Sail area | 243 sq. ft. |
| Mast height | 33'6" above waterline |
| Designer | Groupe Finot |

## Cal

### Cal 20

This is a popular, flush-decked 20-footer with a fixed keel. Friends of mine owned one in Charleston, and they seemed to go sailing far more often than the rest of us. The fixed keel makes trailering and launching difficult, and it usually requires a hoist to launch. The cabin space is quite tiny and nothing fancy. But the Cal 20 has the stability of a much larger boat, and one even made the downwind sail to Hawaii from California.

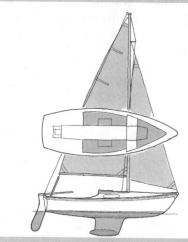

| Cal 20 | |
|---|---|
| LOA | 20'0" |
| LWL | 18'0" |
| Beam | 7'0" |
| Draft | 3'4" (fixed) |
| Displacement | 1,950 lbs. |
| Ballast | 875 lbs. |
| Sail area | 196 sq. ft. |
| Designer | Bill Lapworth |
| Years manufactured | 1961–75 |
| Number produced | 1,945 |

## Cape Dory

### Cape Dory Typhoon

The Cape Dory Typhoon, a heavy-displacement full-keel vessel, was designed by Carl Alberg back in 1967. Though quite small, it has the sailing qualities of traditional, full-keel yachts. The cabin feels tiny by today's standards, and sailing performance is markedly different from that of a lightweight boat, but it is a fine boat for overnighting and short cruising. It was manufactured in a weekender model and two daysailer versions, the daysailer having a completely open cuddy.

| | |
|---|---|
| LOA | 18'6" |
| LWL | 13'6" |
| Beam | 6'3.5" |
| Draft | 2'7" (fixed) |
| Displacement | 2,000 lbs. |
| Ballast | 900 lbs. |
| Sail area | 160 sq. ft. |
| Designer | Carl Alberg |
| Years manufactured | 1967–86 |
| Number produced | 1,982 |

### Cape Dory 22

The Cape Dory 22 is a larger version of the Typhoon.

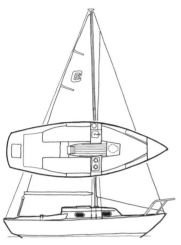

| Cape Dory 22 | |
|---|---|
| LOA | 22'4" |
| LWL | 16'3" |
| Beam | 7'4" |
| Draft | 3'0" (fixed) |
| Displacement | 3,200 lbs. |
| Ballast | 1,400 lbs. |
| Sail area | 240 sq. ft. |
| Designer | Carl Alberg |
| Years manufactured | 1981–85 |
| Number produced | 176 |

## Catalina

### Catalina 22

This boat is considered a classic, and rightly so. Thousands of these boats were built with few changes in the design. When you see a used Catalina 22 for sale, it'll most likely look like this one. Thousands continue to sail today, and there's a strong owners' association and C22 racing fleet.

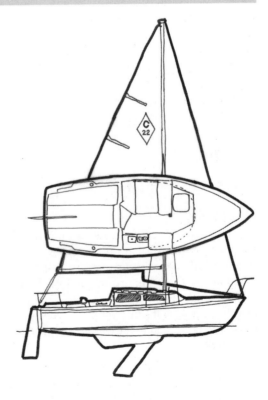

| Catalina 22 | |
|---|---|
| LOA | 21'6" |
| LWL | 19'4" |
| Beam | 7'6" |
| Draft | 2'0"/5'0" (cb up/down) |
| Displacement | 2,250 lbs. |
| Ballast | 550 lbs. |
| Sail area | 212 sq. ft. |
| Mast height | 25'0" |
| Years manufactured | 1969– |
| Number produced | Over 10,000 |

## Com-Pac

### Com-Pac 16

| Com-Pac 16 | |
| --- | --- |
| LOA | 16'11" |
| LWL | 14'0" |
| Beam | 6'0" |
| Draft | 1'6" |
| Displacement | 1,100 lbs. |
| Ballast | 450 lbs. |
| Sail area | 120 sq. ft. (main and jib) |
| Mast height | 20'6" |
| Designer | Clark Mills |
| Contact | www.com-pacowners.com |
| Years manufactured | 1974–96 |
| Number produced | Over 2,800 |

### Com-Pac 19

| Com-Pac 19 | |
| --- | --- |
| LOA | 20'1" |
| LWL | 16'4" |
| Beam | 7'0" |
| Draft | 2'0" (shoal draft) |
| Displacement | 2,000 lbs. |
| Ballast | 800 lbs. |
| Sail area | 196 sq. ft. |
| Mast height | 25 ft. above waterline |
| Designer | Bob Johnson (1979) |

## Florida Bay Boat Company

### Peep Hen 14

At a diminutive 14 feet, this is one of the smallest cabin sailboats in recent production, yet it comes with bronze opening portlights and 4'4" of "headroom" below. Some folks think the Peep is an ugly boat, but I feel just the opposite. It's tiny yet practical, which gives it a functional beauty all its own. (Also see Nimble.)

(David "shorty" Roth)

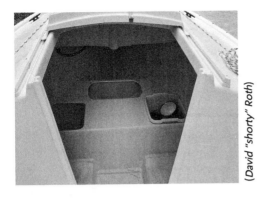

(David "shorty" Roth)

### Peep Hen 14

| | |
|---|---|
| LOA | 14'2" |
| LWL | 13'3" |
| Beam | 6'4" |
| Draft | 9"/3'0" (cb up/down) |
| Displacement | 650 lbs. |
| Ballast | 200 lbs. |
| Sail area | 115 sq. ft. |
| Mast height | 24'(above waterline, with gaff) |
| Designer | Reuben Trane |
| Contact | peephens.org |
| Years manufactured | 1981–2003 |

## Hunter Marine Corp.

Hunter Marine has produced several trailerable boats. These are just a few.

### Hunter 18.5

| | | | |
|---|---|---|---|
| LOA | 18'5" | Ballast | 520 lbs. |
| LWL | 15'6" | Sail area | 178 sq. ft. |
| Beam | 7'1" | Mast height | 27'5" |
| Draft | 2'0" | Years manufactured | 1987–93 |
| Displacement | 1,600 lbs. | | |

### Hunter 19

| | | | |
|---|---|---|---|
| LOA | 18'8" | Displacement | 1,200 lbs. |
| LWL | 14'7" | Sail area | 166 sq. ft. |
| Beam | 7'4" | Years manufactured | 1981–83 |
| Draft | 7"/4'6" (cb up/down) | | |

### Hunter 20

| | | | |
|---|---|---|---|
| LOA | 19'8" | Ballast | 400 lbs. |
| LWL | 15'6" | Sail area | 170 sq. ft |
| Beam | 7'6" | Mast height | 29'6" |
| Draft | 15"/4'0" (cb up/down) | Years manufactured | 1983–84 |
| Displacement | 1,700 lbs. | | |

### Hunter 212

| | | | |
|---|---|---|---|
| LOA | 21'0" | Ballast | 130 lbs. |
| LWL | 18'0" | Sail area | 213 sq. ft. |
| Beam | 8'2" | Mast height | 31'0" |
| Draft | 10"/5'0" (cb up/down) | Years manufactured | 1998– |
| Displacement | 1,800 lbs. | | |

### Hunter 22

| | | | |
|---|---|---|---|
| LOA | 22'3" | Ballast | 1,300 lbs. |
| LWL | 18'4" | Sail area | 220 sq. ft. |
| Beam | 7'11" | Mast height | 26'0" |
| Draft | 23"/5'0" (cb up/down) | Years manufactured | 1981–85 |
| Displacement | 3,200 lbs. | | |

### Hunter 23

| | | | |
|---|---|---|---|
| LOA | 23'3" | Ballast | 800 lbs. |
| LWL | 19'7" | Sail area | 235.5 sq. ft. |
| Beam | 8'0" | Mast height | 33' |
| Draft | 2'3" | Years manufactured | 1985–92 |
| Displacement | 2,450 lbs. | | |

## Jeanneau

The French company Jeanneau has been building fiberglass boats since 1958. Some of their boats were built in the United States under license between 1970 and 1990, but ownership reverted to Jeanneau France with the demise of many U.S. manufacturers. They've since been acquired by Beneteau, making the combined group the largest sailboat manufacturer in the world.

Of their many models, the Tonic 23 is a good example. Produced between 1985 and 1990, it shows some of the styling that these boats have become known for.

### Tonic 23

| | | | |
|---|---|---|---|
| LOA | 23'11" | Ballast | 992 lbs. (keel) |
| LWL | 22'7.5" | | 1,058 lbs. (cb) |
| Beam | 9'2.5" | Sail area | 243 sq. ft. |
| Draft | 3'6" (keel) | Mast height | 32'6" |
| | 2'4"/4'6" (cb up/down) | Designer | Philippe Harle |
| Displacement | 2,866 lbs. (keel) | Contact | jeanneau.tripod.com |
| | 2,932 lbs. (cb) | | |

## Melen Marine

### Sparrow 12/Guppy 13

I've included this boat mainly to show just how small a boat with a cabin can get. The Sparrow was designed by Herb Stewart, designer of the famous West Wight Potter. The Guppy was built by Melen Marine, which went out of business in 1977. The Guppy was identical to the Sparrow in all but the smallest of details; there was even a court case accusing Melen of making a splash mold (where an existing boat is used to make an illicit copy of another boat). This boat is so small that it could probably be towed considerable distances with nothing more than a couple of teenagers and a six-pack of Jolt.

| | |
|---|---|
| LOA | 12'0" |
| LWL | 10'11" |
| Beam | 5'8" |
| Draft | 1'8" (fixed) |
| Displacement | 350 lbs. |
| Ballast | 130 lbs. |
| Sail area | 73 sq. ft. |
| Designer | Herb Stewart |
| Years manufactured | 1969–? |

## Newport

### Newport Neptune 16

Built by various builders over the years with several different model names, such as the Newport 16, Lockley Newport 16, and Gloucester 16. There were two Newport companies, one in California and one in Florida (which later relocated to Virginia).

| Newport Neptune 16 | |
| --- | --- |
| LOA | 15'9" |
| LWL | 13'6" |
| Beam | 6'2" |
| Draft | 10"/4'0" (cb up/down) |
| Displacement | 900 lbs. |
| Ballast | 200 lbs. |
| Sail area | 137 sq. ft. |
| Mast height | 19'6" |
| Designer | C. William Lapworth |
| Years manufactured | 1969–unknown |

### Neptune 24

| Neptune 24 | | | |
| --- | --- | --- | --- |
| LOA | 24'0" | Ballast | 1,200 lbs. |
| LWL | 21'0" | Sail area | 269 sq. ft. (standard rig) |
| Beam | 7'11.75" | | 301 sq. ft. (tall rig) |
| Draft | 24"/3'6" (cb up/down); | Mast height | 28' |
| | 4'8" (fixed keel) | Designer | Bill Lapworth |
| Displacement | 3,200 lbs. | | |

## Nimble Boats

The molds for most of the Nimble line were acquired by Marine Concepts in Florida, builders of the Sea Pearl. According to Marine Concepts, the molds are in poor condition and the boats will not be built; they'll instead concentrate on the Sea Pearl 21. The last time I checked, Nimble Boats was for sale, so if you've ever daydreamed about getting into the boatbuilding business, this might be your chance.

### Nimble 20

A distinctive design with a ketch rig and canoe stern, this boat attracts attention. The shoal draft and low-aspect rig make it suitable for shoal waters.

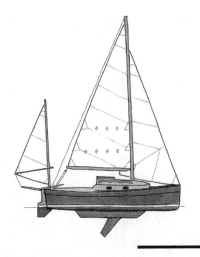

| Nimble 20 | |
|---|---|
| LOA | 20'10" |
| LWL | 19'9" |
| Beam | 7'9" |
| Draft | 11"/4'1" (cb up/down) |
| Displacement | 2,600 lbs. |
| Ballast | 600 lbs. |
| Sail area | 207 sq. ft. |
| Designer | Ted Brewer |

**Peep Hen**

| LOA | 14'2" | Displacement | 650 lbs. |
|---|---|---|---|
| LWL | 13'3" | Ballast | 200 lbs. |
| Beam | 6'4" | Sail area | 115 sq. ft. (main) |
| Draft | 9"/3'0" (cb up/down) | | |

(Also produced by Nimble Company.)

## Nordica 20/Halman 20

This is a salty, tough-as-nails North Sea design, more typical of boats built in Europe than the United States. Although the two boats are not identical—the Halman was inspired by the Nordica—the differences are so slight that they are usually considered the same boat. There's a very active website at http://www.nordicaboats.com/html/nordica-20.html.

| Nordica 20 | |
|---|---|
| LOA | 19'6" |
| LWL | 16'6" |
| Beam | 7'8" |
| Draft | 3'3" |
| Displacement | 2,520 lbs. |
| Ballast | 1,026 lbs. |
| Sail area | 188 sq. ft. |
| Mast height | 30'3" |

## O'Day

O'Day has been producing sailboats for a long time, and was an early player in the field of fiberglass. You can still find a few of the old traditional hulls, like the O'Day Tempest, but more common are designs from the 1970s and 1980s, like the O'Day 22, 23, and 240.

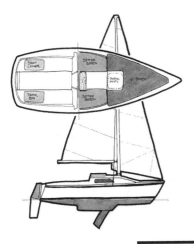

| O'Day 19 | |
|---|---|
| LOA | 19'0" |
| LWL | 16'8" |
| Beam | 7'9" |
| Draft | 12"/4'6" (cb up/down) |
| Displacement | 2,040 lbs. |
| Ballast | 300 lbs. |
| Sail area | 165 sq. ft. |
| Mast height | 26'4" |
| Designer | C. Raymond Hunt |
| Years manufactured | 1979–unknown |
| Number produced | 525 |

### O'Day 22

This boat was widely built, and many are still around. It features a weighted ballast keel that houses the centerboard, eliminating the trunk in the cabin. It's a pretty design, though some boats have a reputation for less-than-stellar sailing performance. The O'Day 22 has a strong user base and web presence, so finding specific information about a particular model year should be easy.

| | |
|---|---|
| LOA | 21'8" |
| LWL | 18'11" |
| Beam | 7'2" |
| Draft | 1'3"/4'3" (cb up/down) |
| Displacement | 2,623 lbs. |
| Ballast | 800 lbs. |
| Sail area | 198 sq. ft. |
| Mast height | 27'3" |
| Designer | C. Raymond Hunt |
| Years manufactured | 1972–81 |
| Number produced | 3,056 |

### O'Day 23

A slightly larger update of the 22. Only a foot longer, but over 1,000 pounds heavier, it needs a heavy tow vehicle. The big difference was the addition of a swing centerboard in the stub keel housing for improved upwind performance.

| | |
|---|---|
| LOA | 22'9" |
| LWL | 19'6" |
| Beam | 7'11" |
| Draft | 2'3"/5'4" (cb up/down) |
| Displacement | 3,725 lbs. |

| | |
|---|---|
| Ballast | 800 lbs. |
| Sail area | 246 sq. ft. |
| Mast height | 27'0" |
| Designer | C. Raymond Hunt |

### O'Day 25

While this boat is legally trailerable with its 8-foot beam, it requires a large tow vehicle, and rigging it takes a while. Boats like this usually are trailered from the house to the marina once a year, and many are sold without trailers. You haven't lived till you've tried to wrangle a 29-foot mast.

| | |
|---|---|
| LOA | 24'10" |
| LWL | 21' |
| Beam | 8'0" |
| Draft | 2'3"/6'0" (cb up/down) |
| Displacement | 4,807 lbs. |
| Ballast | 1,775 lbs. |

| | |
|---|---|
| Sail area | 270 sq. ft. |
| Mast height | 29'0" |
| Designer | C. Raymond Hunt |
| Years manufactured | 1975–89 |
| Number produced | 2,898 |

## Pearson

The Pearson company is another old name in the boatbuilding business. The company made history in 1959 when they introduced the Triton, a 28-footer. The economic recession of the early 1990s combined with a new luxury tax forced the company out of business. They had a reputation for building quality boats by famous designers, including Carl Alberg and William Shaw. Their trailerable-sized boats included the 16-foot Hawk, the 22-foot Ensign (still in production by Ensign Spars), the Pearson 21, and the Pearson 24.

### Pearson 22

While many of the smaller Pearsons were heavier, full-keeled boats, the Pearson 22 was lighter (than other Pearsons) and had a fin keel. It's still a heavy boat, but it is trailerable. A boat this age will probably need some work, but the price should be low and the build quality should make it worth restoring.

| Pearson 22 | |
|---|---|
| LOA | 22'3" |
| LWL | 18'5" |
| Beam | 7'7" |
| Draft | 3'5" |
| Displacement | 2,600 lbs. |
| Ballast | 1,000 lbs. |
| Sail area | 218 sq. ft. |
| Mast height | 28' above waterline |
| Years manufactured | 1968–72 |
| Designer | William Shaw |

### Pearson 23

The 23 was an updated version of the aging 22. A centerboard made for easier trailering but increases the maintenance. It's a good bit heavier than the 22.

| | |
|---|---|
| LOA | 23'0" |
| LWL | 20'0" |
| Beam | 7'11.5" |
| Draft | 2'4"/5'2" (cb up/down) |
| Displacement | 3,500 lbs. |
| Ballast | 1,300 lbs. |
| Sail area | 229 sq. ft. |
| Mast height | 30'6" above waterline |
| Years manufactured | 1979–81 |
| Number produced | 75 |
| Designer | William Shaw |

## Seaward/Hake Yachts

### Seaward Fox

The Seaward Fox was a neat little boat that featured several cutting-edge ideas, like an unstayed carbon-fiber mast, full batten catboat mainsail, and a wing keel. While no longer produced by Hake Yachts, they remain popular and are hard to find used.

| Seaward Fox | |
|---|---|
| LOA | 18'11" (17'11" without bow pulpit) |
| LWL | 16'1" |
| Beam | 8'0" |
| Draft | 21" |
| Displacement | 1,350 lbs. |
| Ballast | 345 lbs. |
| Sail area | 190 sq. ft. |
| Mast height | 32'6" |
| Designer | Nick Hake |
| Years manufactured | 1993– |

### Seaward 23

| | |
|---|---|
| LOA | 24'6" |
| LWL | 21'0" |
| Beam | 8'4" |
| Draft | 4'2"/2'1" (FB/wing keel) |
| Displacement | 2,700 lbs. |
| Ballast | 900 lbs. |
| Sail area | 240 sq. ft. |
| Mast height | 37' |
| Designer | Nick Hake |
| Years manufactured | 1983– |

## Seaward 25

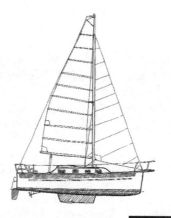

| Seaward 25 | |
| --- | --- |
| LOA | 26'9" |
| LWL | 23'0" |
| Beam | 8'3" |
| Draft | 2'1" (winged keel) |
| Displacement | 3,600 lbs. |
| Ballast | 1,200 lbs. |
| Sail area | 280 sq. ft. |
| Mast height | 33' above waterline |
| Designer | Nick Hake |
| Years manufactured | 1984–2004 |
| Number produced | 600 |

## Slipper 17

The Slipper 17 is a small fixed-keel boat originally produced by Starboard Yachts in Florida. The company was taken over by Hake Yachts in the mid-1980s. Hake has stocked a few parts for the Slipper in the past.

| Slipper 17 | |
| --- | --- |
| LOA | 16'10" |
| LWL | 14'10" |
| Beam | 8'0" |
| Draft | 19" |
| Displacement | 1,250 lbs. |
| Ballast | 425 lbs. |
| Sail area | 150 sq. ft. |
| Mast height | 25'0" |
| Designer | Nick Hake |
| Years manufactured | 1981–88 |

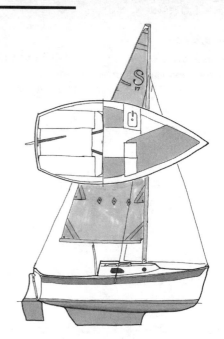

## Seidelmann

Robert Seidelmann was a sailmaker back in the 1960s, when boats using their sails won the National and World Championships in numerous classes. He focused then on boatbuilding, and Seidelmann Yachts built a number of boats from 24 to 37 feet. The last Seidelmann was built sometime in 1988.

The 245 was introduced in 1982 and was built until sometime in 1985. At one point, the company built a 24, the 245, and a 25. They're reported to be fast, able sailers. The keels are cast lead, with fiberglass centerboards, which is greatly preferred over other forms of ballast.

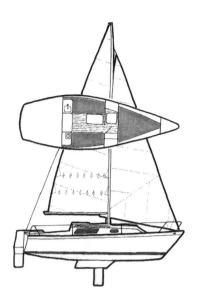

### Seidelmann 245

| | |
|---|---|
| LOA | 24'2" |
| LWL | 20'6" |
| Beam | 8'0" |
| Draft | 1'1"/4'5" (cb up/down) |
| Displacement | 3,000 lbs. |
| Ballast | 1,300 lbs. |
| Sail area | 267 sq. ft. |
| Mast height | 32'9" above waterline |
| Designer | Robert Seidelmann |
| Contact | www.seidelmann-owners.com |

## Tanzer

### Tanzer 22

The Tanzer 22 has a flush-deck design that may take some getting used to, but the practicality of flush-deck designs for trailerables gives this boat a beauty all its own. Tanzers reportedly offer the most usable space down below of any trailerable of this vintage, and are said to sail well, too.

### Tanzer 22

| | |
|---|---|
| LOA | 22'6" |
| LWL | 19'9" |
| Beam | 7'10" |
| Draft | 3'5" (fin keel) |
| | 2'0"/4'0" |
| | (cb up/down) |
| Displacement | 2,900 lbs. (fin keel) |
| | 3,100 lbs. (keel/cb) |
| Ballast | 1,250 (fixed keel) |
| | 1,500 (keel/cb) |
| Sail area | 222 sq. ft. |
| Mast height | 31'0" |
| Designer | Johann Tanzer |
| Years manufactured | 1970–86 |
| Number produced | 2,270 |

### Vagabond 17/Hobie Holder 17

This boat started out as the Vagabond 17 around 1975. In 1982, Vagabond was purchased by Coast Catamaran (a division of the Coleman Company, formerly known as Hobie Cat). She's a trim-looking little boat.

| Vagabond 17/Hobie Holder 17 | |
|---|---:|
| LOA | 17'0" |
| LWL | 15'0" |
| Beam | 7'3" |
| Draft | 10"/4'0" (cb up/down) |
| Displacement | 950 lbs. |
| Ballast | 345 lbs. |
| Sail area | 147 sq. ft. |
| Mast height | 20'0" |
| Designer | Ron Holder |

# Epilogue

One of the beauties of sailing a trailerable is that many areas become available to you that might otherwise be difficult or impossible to reach. Shoal waters and low bridges change from insurmountable obstacles to minor inconveniences. And you can go to windward at 60 miles per hour.

Just how far can you go? Take a look at Larry Brown's *Sailing America*. Larry took a West Wight Potter on a trailer sailer cruise around the entire country, sailing in places like Lake Powell in Arizona, Marina Del Rey in California, the San Juan Islands in the Pacific Northwest, and several spots in Canada before returning home to Cape Cod.

Or consider Mindy and Dave Bolduc. Mindy and Dave are probably the chief ambassadors for the kind of cruising you can do in a trailerable sailboat. They've crossed the Gulf Stream many times in their 15-foot water-ballasted sharpie, *Little Cruiser* (designed and built by Matt Layden), to cruise the Bahamas for as long as three months. You can see more about their boats and cruises on their website at www.microcruising.com/.

The best place to start is your own backyard. Spend a night or two in waters close to your home. Work out the kinks before you plan a long trip afield. Like everything, sailing becomes easier with practice. Get some charts and start looking them over; you're sure to find some adventurous spots to explore.

"A ship in its harbor is safe—but that's not what ships are built for."
—John A. Shedd, *Salt from My Attic*, 1928

If there is one thing that I hope you get from this book, it is this:

*Go.*

Go sailing. In your own boat, or at least with someone else. Get out on the water, hear the sound of open spaces and smell the air. If you can feel the breeze on your face, then you can do it. The same breeze that blows across millions of faces every day can take you to places and show you things that you can see only with a sailboat. Like anything else worth doing, it requires some effort, knowledge, and time. But do not listen to the voices that say "you can't" even if the voice comes from within.

*Mindy Bolduc and* Little Cruiser *off the Shackleford Banks, North Carolina. This little boat has crossed the Gulf Stream several times. (Matt Bolduc)*

This book is about sailing in trailerable sailboats, but it's also about getting more out of life. Taking a risk and trying something new can open your eyes to a wider world. It makes us all value our planet and time on this earth, and it's hard not to see the beauty in the sea, land, and sky. Get yourself a small boat, and learn how to sail it well. Be safe, but go. Waste not a moment.

# Sources of Supply

Note: Inclusion of companies in this section isn't intended to be any sort of endorsement or advertisement, but they're listed here for your reference. The authors and publishers of this book have no connection to these companies. There are certainly other companies that supply the marine industry; readers are encouraged to do their own research as well.

## ALTERNATIVE HEAD SYSTEMS

Air Head dry toilet, by EOS Design, LLC., P.O. Box 5, Mount Vernon, OH 43050, Phone: 740-392-3642, www.airheadtoilet.com/ Distributed by Star Distributing, www.star-distributing.com/index.html

Groover Tamer odor control powder and spray, available from NRS Paddlesports, www.nrsweb.com/, 1-877-677-4327

Organic Traditions Bio-Accelerator and Soil-Moist hydrogel powder, available from Clean Air Gardening, cleanairgardening.com/

Sun-Mar composting marine toilets, www.sun-mar.com

Todd Marine Products bucket potty seat for 3- and 5-gallon buckets, www.toddusa.com

"Wag Bags" can be purchased directly from the manufacturer, Phillips Environmental Products (1-877-520-0999, www.thepett.com).

## CANVAS AND SAILMAKING

Rochford Supply, Inc., 1-800-334-6414, www.rochfordsupply.com, an upholstery fabrics distributor that also sells marine fabrics such as Top Gun and Odyssey III. No sailcloth. They're primarily for professionals.

Sail Care, 1-800-433-7245, www.sailcare.com

The Sail Cleaners, www.sailcleaners.com

Sailrite, 1-800-348-2769, www.sailrite.com, sells boat canvas and sewing materials, as well as sail kits. Founder Jim Grant is also the author of *The Complete Canvasworker's Guide*, which has instructions for many of their canvas and accessory kits.

## CHANDLERIES

BoatU.S., www.boatus.com/

Defender Industries, www.defender.com/

West Marine, www.westmarine.com

## CRUISING GUIDES AND CHARTS

Atlantic Cruising Club, www.atlantic cruisingclub.com

Bluewater Books and Charts, www.blue waterweb.com

Charlies Charts, www.charliescharts.com

Fine Edge, www.fineedge.com

Gerrycruise, www.gerrycruise.com

Landfall Navigation, www.landfallnav.com

Maptech, www.maptech.com

Waterway Guide, www.waterwayguide.com

## DEHUMIDIFIERS

Damp-Rid Calcium chloride moisture absorber, http:www.damprid.com

HydroSorbent silica gel dehumidifiers, www.dehumidify.com

Qik Joe Ice Melt Pellets (calcium chloride), available from DIY Superstore, www.doityourself.com/icat/icemelterchemicals

## EPOXY AND FIBERGLASS

Clark Craft-Fiberglass cloth, mat, roving, and tape, www.clarkcraft.com/

Clen-L MarineDesigns, www.glen-l.com

MAS Epoxies, 1-800-398-7556, www.masepoxies.com. Supplier of epoxies for boatbuilders and boatowners.

Raka, Inc., 1-772-489-4070, www.raka.com/. Distributor of epoxy resins and fiberglass cloth. (I've ordered materials from these folks several times, and they've always provided excellent service and a great product.)

Seeman Fiberglass, Inc. (makers of "C-Flex" fiberglass planking), 6117 River Road, Harahan, LA 70122, 504-738-6035

West System, epoxy and products for boat repair. This company has been helping boatowners for decades and has a very comprehensive line of products. They're a first-class source of information, too. westsystem.com/

## OUTBOARDS AND MARINE PROPULSION

Used outboard motors, www.boatmotors.com/rebuilt_outboard_motors/

## TOOLS

Motor-Scrubber battery-powered cleaner. Reading Consumer Products, reading consumerproduct.com/MotorScrubber/index.html, available through professional janitorial supply companies

## TRAILERABLE BOAT PLANS

Benford Design Group, www.benford.us

Brewer Yacht Design, www.tedbrewer.com

George Buehler Yacht Designs, www.georgebuehler.com

Clark Craft, www.clarkcraft.com/

Sam Devlin's Mud Peep, Nancy's China, and several others, www.devlinboat.com/

Dudley Dix Yacht Design, www.dixdesign.com

Farrier Marine, www.f-boat.com

Paul Gartside Boatbuilder & Designer, www.gartsideboats.com

Glen-L Boat plans & supplies, www.glenl.com/

Ed Horstman Multihull Designs, www.edhorstmanmultihulldesigns.com

Monfort Associates geodesic small craft plans, www.gaboats.com

Newick Nautical Design, Inc., www.dicknewick.com

Norwalk Island Sharpies, www.nisboats.com

Harold H. Payson & Co. small craft, www.instantboats.com/

Bruce Roberts Yacht Design, www.bruceroberts.com/

Stevenson Projects Weekender 18-foot trailerable cabin sailboat, www.stevproj.com/

*WoodenBoat* Magazine plans service, www.woodenboatstore.com/

## TRAILERS AND ACCESSORIES

Champion Trailer supply, trailer parts and equipment, www.championtrailers.com/

Extend-A-Hitch bolt-on boat trailer hitch extension, www.xtend-a-hitchnorthwest.com/

The Trailer Parts Depot, www.trailerpartsdepot.com/

# Bibliography

## BOAT MAINTENANCE

Everett Collier, *The Boatowner's Guide to Corrosion*. International Marine, 2001, hardcover, 314 pages.

Fernec Mate, *Shipshape: The Art of Sailboat Maintenance*. Albatross Publishing, 1986, hardcover, 416 pages.

John Payne, *Understanding Boat Corrosion, Lightning Protection, and Interference*. Sheridan House, 2005, 90 pages.

Edwin Sherman, *The 12-Volt Bible for Boats*. International Marine, 2002, paperback, 208 pages.

Nigel Warren, *Metal Corrosion in Boats*. Sheridan House, Inc., 2006, 229 pages.

Charlie Wing, *Boatowner's Illustrated Electrical Handbook*, Second Edition. International Marine, 2006, paperback, 280 pages.

## CANVASWORK

Don Casey, *Canvaswork and Sail Repair*. International Marine, 1996, hardcover, 140 pages.

Jim Grant, *The Complete Canvasworker's Guide*, Second Edition. International Marine, 1992, paperback, 186 pages.

Karen Lipe, *The Big Book of Boat Canvas*. International Marine, 1988, paperback, 242 pages.

Emiliano Marino, *The Sailmaker's Apprentice*, International Marine, 1994, paperback.

## GALLEY GUIDES

Philip W. Conkling, *Green Islands, Green Sea: A Guide to Foraging on the Islands of Maine*. Down East Books, 1980.

Euell Gibbons, *The Beachcombers Handbook*. David McKay, 1967, 230 pages.

Janet Groene, *Cooking on the Go*. Sail Books, 1980, 234 pages.

Peter Howorth, *Foraging Along the California Coast*. Consortium, 1977.

Ken Neumeyer, *Sailing the Farm*. Ten Speed Press, 1981, paperback, 256 pages.

Lin Pardey, *The Care and Feeding of the Offshore Crew*. Paradise Cay Publications, 1999, 414 pages.

Linda Frederick Yaffe, *Backpack Gourmet*. Stackpole Books, 147 pages.

## OUTBOARD ENGINES

Peter Hunn, *The Old Outboard*. International Marine, 2002, paperback, 320 pages.

Jean-Luc Pallas, *Outboard Motors Maintenance and Repair Manual*. Sheridan House, 2006, 125 pages.

Edwin Sherman, *Outboard Engines*. International Marine, 2008, hardcover, 176 pages.

## RESTORATION, REPAIR, AND UPGRADING

W. D. Booth, *Upgrading and Refurbishing the Older Fiberglass Sailboat*. Cornell Maritime Press, 1988, 287 pages.

Paul and Myra Butler, *Fine Boat Finishes*. International Marine, 1987, paperback, 160 pages.

Paul and Myra Butler, *Upgrading the Small Sailboat for Cruising*. International Marine, 1988, paperback, 224 pages.

Nigel Calder, *Boatowner's Mechanical and Electrical Manual*. International Marine, 2005, hardcover, 818 pages.

Don Casey, *Sailboat Hull and Deck Repair*. International Marine, 1996, hardcover, 128 pages.

Don Casey, *Sailboat Refinishing*. International Marine, 1996, paperback, 144 pages.

Don Casey, *This Old Boat*, Second Edition. International Marine, 2009, hardcover, 576 pages.

Fernec Mate, *The Finely Fitted Yacht*. W. W. Norton & Company Limited, 2005, 606 pages.

Dan Spurr, *Spurr's Guide to Upgrading Your Cruising Sailboat*, Third Edition. International Marine, 2006, hardcover, 400 pages.

## MARINE WOODWORKING

Fred Bingham, *Boat Joinery and Cabinetmaking Simplified*. International Marine, 1993, paperback, 265 pages.

Michael Naujok, *Boat Interior Construction*. Sheridan House, 2002, paperback, 176 pages.

## MISCELLANEOUS

Larry Brown, *Sailing America: A Trailer Sailor's Guide to North America*. Seven Seas Press, 1990, paperback.

Larry Brown, *Sailing on a Micro-Budget*. Seven Seas Press, 1985, 163 pages, paperback.

Robert Burgess, *The Handbook of Trailer Sailing*. International Marine, 1992, paperback, 227 pages.

Don Casey and Lew Hackler, *Sensible Cruising: The Thoreau Approach*. International Marine, 1986, paperback, 364 pages.

Ronald Florence, *The Optimum Sailboat: Racing the Cruiser and Cruising the Racer*. Harper and Row, 1986, hardcover, 374 pages.

Annie Hill, *Voyaging on a Small Income*. Tiller Publishing, 1993, paperback, 208 pages.

J. C. Jenkins, *The Humanure Handbook: A Guide to Composting Human Manure*. Chelsea Green Publishing Co., 2006, 302 pages.

Elbert Maloney (editor), *Chapman's Piloting, Seamanship, and Small-Boat Handling*, (65th edition). Sterling Publishing Company, Inc., 2007, hardcover, 928 pages.

Tom Neale, *All in the Same Boat*. International Marine, 1997, hardcover, 376 pages.

Lin and Larry Pardey, *The Capable Cruiser*. Pardey Books, 1995, hardcover, 400 pages.

Lin and Larry Pardey, *The Cost-Conscious Cruiser*. Pardey Books, 1999, hardcover, 352 pages.

John Rousmaniere, *The Annapolis Book of Seamanship* (revised edition). Simon and Schuster, 1989, hardcover, 402 pages.

Daniel Spurr, *Your First Sailboat: How to Find and Sail the Right Boat for You*. International Marine, 2004, paperback, 288 pages.

Donald M. Street, *The Ocean Sailing Yacht*. W. W. Norton, 1973, hardcover, 703 pages.

USCG Auxiliary, *Boating Skills and Seamanship*. International Marine, 2007, paperback, 404 pages.

## SURVEYING

Thomas Ask, *Handbook of Marine Surveying*. Sheridan House, Inc., 2007, 246 pages.

Don Casey, *Inspecting the Aging Sailboat*. International Marine, 1996, paperback, 144 pages.

Andrew Douglas, *Practical Sailor's Practical Boat Buying*, 2 volumes. Belvoir Books, 1998, paperback.

# Internet Resources

The Internet is a naturally volatile and ever-changing medium. Although there's lots of good information to be found, it isn't always factually correct or well presented. Millions of websites come and go almost daily. I can guarantee that at least some of the addresses you see here will not work, but I can also guarantee that they were correct and operational at the time of this writing. This listing isn't meant to be all inclusive or complete, nor is inclusion meant to endorse the content. It's just a sampling of the information that's available on the Internet. When you encounter a nonfunctioning address, try doing a web search using the title of the site, or a subject search. You will most likely come up with something useful.

## CHARTS AND NAVIGATION

Bluewater Books and Charts, www.blue waterweb.com/

The Lighthouse Directory, www.unc.edu/ ~rowlett/lighthouse/index.htm

MapTech, online charts and navigation software, www.maptech.com/index.cfm

NOAA charts and agents, chartmaker.ncd.noaa.gov/nsd/states.html

Paradise Cay Publications, paracay.com/

Seaworthy Publications, www.seaworthy.com

## DINGHIES AND SMALL BOATS

Duckworks Magazine, www.duck worksmagazine.com/

The Flapdoodle, an 8-foot folding dinghy that stores flat, flapdoodle.250free.com/

The Home Boatbuilders Page, www. buildboats.com/

Shortypen's Pocket Cruiser's Guide, www. shortypen.com/boats/pocket/

Simplicity Boats, by David Beede, simplicityboats.com/

## GENERAL TRAILER SAILER WEBSITES

Boat Owners Association of the United States, www.boatus.com/

Sailboat database (doesn't include every fiberglass boat there is, but has lots of info not readily found in other sources), www. sailboatdata.com/

Sailrite's sail plan database, with dimensions for a large number of boats, quotesys2. sailrite.com/Search.aspx

The Trailer Sailor, a general trailer sailer website, www.trailersailor.com/

The Trailer Sailors Association, www. trailersailors.org

## MARINE INSURANCE

BoatU.S., www.boatus.com

Hagerty Marine Insurance, www.hagerty.com/marine

Marine Agency, www.marineagency.com

Marine Underwriters Agency, www. marineunderwriters.com

National Marine Underwriters, www.nmu.com

State Farm Insurance, www.statefarm.com

West Marine, www.westmarine.com

## METAL CORROSION AND PROTECTION

Anodizing Aluminum, www.focuser.com/atm/anodize/anodize.html

Building your own corrosion meter, www.oceannavigator.com/article.php?a=1062

Rust Removal Using Electrolysis, antique-engines.com/electrol.asp

## OUTBOARD MOTORS AND SAILBOAT PROPULSION

Electric Trolling Motors for Auxiliary Propulsion on Sailboats, bbs.trailersailor.com/forums/articles/index.cgi/noframes/read/23

MarineEngine.com's Outboard Motor Price Guide, www.marineengine.com/price_guide/price_guide_left.html

## OWNERS' ASSOCIATIONS, RACE CLASSES, OUT-OF-PRODUCTION BOATS

Balboa
    Balboa 20 & 26, cliffunruh.com/
    Balboa 26, groups.yahoo.com/group/balboa26-boats/
Beneteau
    Beneteau Owner's Association, www.beneteau-owners.com/
    Google Groups Beneteau Owner's Group, groups.google.com/group/Beneteau-Owners
    Beneteau 235, www.beneteau235.com/
Cal Sailboats
    Cal 21, www3.sympatico.ca/sailpair/21stuff/
Cape Dory, www.capedory.org/cdinfo.html
Catalina
    Catalina18 National Association, www.catalina18.net
    Catalina 22 National Association, www.catalina22.net
    Capri 22 National Association, www.capri22.net
J-Boats
    J-22, www.usaj22.com/
    J-24, www.j24class.org/usa/homepage.htm
    J-80, www.j80.org/
Newport Neptune 16, www.skyrover.net/sailing/en.wikipedia.org/wiki/Newport_16

Newport Neptune 24, en.wikipedia.org/wiki/Newport_16
O'Day, www.iheartodays.com
    O'Day Mariner Class Association, www.usmariner.org
Pearson
    Ensign Class Association, www.ensignclass.com/
Peep Hen, peephens.org/
Seaward Yachts, home.att.net/~seaward25/index.htm groups.yahoo.com/group/seawardsailboats/
    Seaward Fox, www.quietboating.com/www.quietboating.com/ bbs.trailersailor.com/forums/seaward/index.cgi/#7773
    Seaward 25, www.okbayou.com/
Starboard Yachts
    Slipper 17, cube.kv.k12.in.us/rdmhome/slipper/www.sailing.dittybag.net/slipper17.html
Tanzer 22, www.tanzer22.com
Vagabond/Holder 17, home.comcast.net/~vagabondsailing/

## SAFETY AND SMALL BOAT OPERATIONS

Crew Overboard Rescue Symposium Final Report, www.boatus.com/foundation/findings/COBfinalreport/

DSC radios and MMSI, www.BoatUS.com/MMSI/

Sailing Injuries, www.lifespan.org/services/travel/articles/sailing_injuries.htm

## TRAILERABLE SAILBOAT MANUFACTURERS

Catalina Yachts, www.catalinayachts.com/

Com-Pac Yachts/The Hutchins Co., www.com-pacyachts.com/index.php

Corsair Marine, www.corsairmarine.com/

Ensign Spars, www.ensignspars.com/

Hunter Sailboats, www.huntermarine.com/indexUS.html

J/Boats, www.jboats.com/

MacGregor, www.macgregorsailboats.com/

Marine Concepts, www.marine-concepts.com/

Marshall Marine, www.marshallcat.com/

Montgomery/Nor'Sea Yachts, www.norseayachts.com

Performance Cruising, www.geminicatam
    arans.com/
Precision Boat Works,
    www.precisionboatworks.com/
Quorning Boats, www.dragonfly.dk/
Rhodes 22 by General Boats,
    www.rhodes22.com/
Seaward/Hake Yachts,
    www.seawardyachts.com/
Stuart Marine, www.stuartmarine.com
US Yachts, www.ultimatesailboats.com/
Vanguard Sailboats, makers of the Sunfish,
    Zuma, Nomad, 420, Laser, and more,
    www.teamvanguard.com/2005/base/index.asp
West Wight Potter, www.westwightpotter.com/

## TOWING WEBSITES

Boat Owners Association of the United States,
    www.boatus.com/

National Highway Traffic Safety Administration,
    www.nhtsa.dot.gov/cars/problems/equipment/
    towing/towing.pdf
RV Safety and Education Foundation,
    www.rvsafety.org/
RV Travel, www.rvtravel.com/towguide.html
Sherline Products Trailer Loading and Towing
    Guide, www.sherline.com/lmbook.htm
Trailer Boats, www.trailerboats.com/
Trailer Hitches, www.trailerhitches.com/
    info/towing-glossary.cfm
Trailer Life, www.trailerlife.com/output.
    cfm?id=42175
Valley Industries Guide to Towing,
    www.valleyindustries.com/PDF/Guide_to_
    Towing.pdf

# Index

Numbers in **bold** indicate pages with illustrations